PERSONALITY AND SOCIAL INTERACTION

PERSONALITY

and

Social Interaction

ROBERT H. DALTON
Professor of Child Development and Family Relationships, Cornell University

D. C. HEATH AND COMPANY

Boston

COVER

Sculpture by Henry Moore
Courtesy of the Artist

PREFACE

This is a book about individuals in society. It is not concerned with all there is to say about either society or individuals. Rather, selected principles from psychology will be employed in the analysis of episodes from the lives of a few persons as they live in close proximity to a few other persons. The principles found most useful in this analysis have come from psychoanalysis and other dynamic psychologies, field theory and learning theory.

Man is a separate and unique individual whose actions in the main can be understood only in relation to the society in which he participates and in which he has participated throughout his history. The particular forms of individual behavior which we observe and the potentialities for behavioral expression are determined by the imposition of specific requirements and demands made by other people on the biological organism known as the human being. The central problem in the study of personality is the specific kinds of interactions between individuals which bring about the modifications in potential for action. In the last half century there have been many theories concerning the critical person-to-person experiences in the development of personality. A great deal of research has been conducted to establish the validity of these claims. As yet we cannot speak with the confidence we would like about any of them. It may well be that no particular experience is crucial in the formation of personality traits; it seems more likely that for each age and each person there are a complex of interactional forces which determine the direction of development. The case studies we have chosen represent the periods of infancy, childhood, and adolescence.

In so far as possible an analysis of personality gains in objectivity by concentrating on overt behavior and relating this to the adequate antecedent stimuli. The difficulty is that not all adequate stimuli are directly observable. Sometimes inferences about stimuli have to be made. The inferences relate primarily to motivational variables. Once inferences are permitted the door is open to error. But I would rather put up with the error while dealing with significant human problems than take the more cautious path of setting down only proven facts about human functions of limited interest.

By society I mean other people who are important in the life of the person being studied. Other people may be few or many, but generally in our culture they are few. We designate as society that person, usually the mother, who ministers to our intimate needs soon after birth, and all other persons who through direct contact impress significant aspects of themselves onto us.

The approach used in this book is the alternation of case material with theories drawn from differing psychological perspectives. Theory lends meaning to the case data, while the accounts of striving human beings lend enrichment to theory. The case histories are unique because of the peculiar experiences which each individual has had. In a larger sense, however, this uniqueness fades when viewed as variations of experiences which you and I have had, or will have, or might have had. Through the use of case material I hope we will see how the universal and particular are inextricably bound.

Two of the case histories came from the records of clinics in which I have worked. I shall not name the clinics because I would not want to lead to speculation about the identity of the persons in the case histories. The clinics were sufficiently secure in their field to allow variation in method of clinical practice. Psychotherapy is not a science, although it is struggling to become more scientific. I make no apology for the fact that I acted as therapist for several members of the two families. They taught me a great deal. At the same time I do not wish anyone to conclude mistakenly that I am tacitly recommending this procedure for all family cases or all therapists. There are occasions when such a procedure may be successfully employed.

In this book you will find more raw data in the case histories than is customary. I have deliberately included this material for two reasons: I believe that students who have had a good introduction to psychological concepts can profitably grapple with such data. My second reason—any interpretation stems from a particular conceptual scheme; if you do not agree with my interpretations, you have practically all the data I have used and may apply your own scheme for a better fit.

The book is intended for the student or general reader who has had a substantial first course in psychology. At the end of most of the chapters I have listed suggested readings for your benefit if you wish to pursue the intricacies of personality study in greater scope and depth.

I wish to thank Betty, my wife, for helping to create conditions favorable to writing. She has provided encouragement and aid throughout, even down to assisting with the tedious task of making an index. Special gratitude goes to Nancy Hart who was always ready and eager to lend a hand no matter what the task. I want also to thank my colleagues Alfred L. Baldwin for his careful reading of the manuscript and Henry N. Ricciuti for testing one of the subjects. And to my children, Alice, Anne, Robin, and Peter, who have raised more questions than I could ever hope to answer, my affectionate gratitude.

To Carol, Bill, and Peter, to the Ferrantis and the Burkes, all names chosen from thin air, I say thank you even though most of you will never read this and thus learn of my gratitude. In my search for understanding of psychodynamics you have been my principal teachers. You taught me the folly of generalization from the particular despite the fact that we are all very much alike; you also taught me the uselessness of particularization from the general when applied to individual behavior. Further you taught me the impossibility of analysis of any behavioral trend without a theoretical frame of reference and the danger of analysis with such a frame of reference. I have tried to conceal your identity from public gaze in every way I could think of. What I have said about you might be said about thousands and thousands of others like you.

CONTENTS

PERSONALITY AND SOCIAL INTERACTION

1

INTRODUCTION

Personality is a social product. What a man thinks or feels, how he talks or acts, even what he fantasies or dreams result from the kinds of experiences which he has had with other people throughout his life. A man's very conception of himself is related in important ways to the responses of others, even down to the last moment of his life. Each time a person confronts another he reacts to him, in part in terms of his interpretation of the meaning of the behavior of the other. His interpretation is based upon similar responses in similar situations in the past. If his action, emanating from his interpretation, proves to be inappropriate as judged by the responses he receives, he will normally take this into account before proceeding further. If he is not able to modify his actions in the light of unanticipated responses from others, he becomes a problem for his friends and relatives and may on occasion run the risk of losing his life.

The longer you live with another person, especially if your relationship is an intimate one, the better able are you to anticipate his responses. Likewise if you live in a homogeneous social group, you go about your daily affairs with few surprises in terms of unexpected responses from others. But now let us imagine that you find yourself in a new situation where you meet a person for the first time. How will you plan your action in relation to him? Or how will you anticipate his response to your action? You must of necessity fall back on the lumber room of memory. You must somehow create a composite image of man and attribute it to this new individual; your first acts will be in terms of the composite image. Before you can respond to him as a unique person you must have information about him, derived either from his reputation, which may have preceded him, or from direct action on his part. But neither his reputation nor an isolated act on his part will provide enough information; there must be a series of interrelated acts on both his part and yours before you can make a confident prediction concerning any subsequent actions on his part. And the more naïve you are with respect to the possible range of actions on his part, the more information you will require specifically from him. Ordinarily, in the course of social development, one learns that man is capable of almost anything. He may be kind and generous and his actions may be of the noblest altruistic sort, or he may be mean, depraved, completely unconcerned with the feelings or integrity of others. Awareness of the range of possible actions varies with the diversification of experiences which one has had. The caution with which you approach a person for the first time depends, then, upon your conception of his potentialities for action, or his personality.

The two-year-old who has lived in a benevolent society will approach almost any stranger with open arms and wide-eyed trust because he anticipates no harm or danger from association with man. His experience up to that moment has not prepared him for actions of an unfriendly character, and there is nothing in his native endowment which causes him to beware of malevolent forces before he has experienced them. In other words no substantive content has been conferred on him by nature. He has great capacity to learn. Under appropriate conditions he will learn very quickly to trust some men and not other men. An absolute prerequisite to learning, to substantive memory, is experience.

Let us return for a moment to the hypothetical meeting with a new person. Until you have had sufficient experience with him to enable you to determine the range of his potential responses, you cannot know how to act in relation to him. Further, if your knowledge of the possible range of human actions is very limited, your assessment of his behavior may be quite wide of the mark.

Each personality is unique. One important reason for this uniqueness is the social experiences which the individual has had. This book is about individuals as they interact with one another. We shall concentrate on the study of several persons who are in intimate interpersonal relationships. Some of the influences on the emergent personalities will be seen as we focus attention on the conditions found in three living, vigorous, growing families. What we learn from these individuals will illustrate and extend principles derived from general psychology. Our aim is, therefore, twofold: To explain the unique behavior of a few individuals in social interaction, and to set forth a conception of personality development and functioning which will make the interpretation of the details of any life more meaningful.

The study of personality involves: (1) description and analysis of the contemporary behavior of the person in interaction with his environment; (2) analysis of antecedents of the present behavior in terms of the relationship of the present behavior to previous person and environment interactions; and (3) prediction of future behavior in the light of projected situations. A theoretical system, to be useful, should provide a set of concepts adequate for the representation of each of the three. However, no single conceptual system in psychology seems able to encompass all the significant aspects of personality. The ones that come closest to it are field theory, learning theory, and dynamic psychology. *Selective integration of these three systems* seems to offer the most nearly adequate conceptual scheme.

Field theory offers a formal system of concepts, some of which we shall draw upon, which are convenient for a representation of the current situation. Field theory takes the situation as a whole to begin with and then differentiates the component parts; it also, and this is most important for our purpose, looks upon the behavior of the individual as a function of the field of forces which exists at the time the behavior occurs. However, field theory has failed to develop concepts adequate for the dynamic representation of the person or for the changes which regularly occur in the person.

Learning theory has developed empirical concepts and quantitative principles for describing the genesis of current behavior. It has accomplished this through the detailed study of the circumstances under which a response and a stimulus become connected. Learning theory, therefore, offers concepts to describe the acquisition and changes of many needs, attitudes and values, as well as motor and verbal behavior patterns. Learning theory is deficient, and therefore cannot be an adequate behavior theory, in that it has not developed a satisfactory system of human motivation. It tends to deal with microscopic units of behavior, and it tends to extrapolate principles from their context (particularly principles derived from animal experimentation applied to human situations).

The theories and concepts of dynamic psychology, which owes its birth to psychoanalysis, make up for some of the deficiencies in learning theory and field theory by an emphasis on human motivation, personality structure, and on molar segments of behavior as the proper units for study. Dynamic psychology emphasizes, perhaps over-emphasizes, the significance of the past history of the person for understanding current behavior. It has postulated the crucial learning situations in the life history of a person. And in addition, it offers theories which integrate a large number of phenomenologically different kinds of behavior—for example, the continuity of the normal and abnormal.

Taken together, the three—dynamic psychology, learning theory, and field theory—offer concepts which come close to taking the measure of a man's personality. We shall draw liberally from each in an attempt to understand the lives which will be analyzed and in an attempt to fit these lives into a larger, more general view of man.

Some Assumptions and Definitions

Assumptions

The following assumptions underlie what follows in this book, like the unseen shelf of rock beneath the foundation of a skyscraper.

1. Human behavior is subject to explanation.* When there is sufficient evidence, it is possible to explain a great deal of observed behavior, however incongruous the parts seen in isolation may appear. The sufficiency of the evidence is determined by a consensus of the best judges trained and experienced in the particular field of inquiry under observation. This criterion of sufficiency relative to the evidence constitutes a problem admittedly, but there seems to be no way around it. There is no ultimate criterion. Explanation, then, involves agreement. When an observed fact (or usually an agreed-upon symbolic abstraction of the fact) is coordinated into a conceptual scheme embracing other facts, it may be said to be explained. The more rigorous the conceptual scheme and the more it is coordinated with other scientific principles, the more adequate the explanation. If the item of behavior is isolable so that it may be treated as a variable among other variables, and if an experiment can be designed in line with a rigorous conceptual scheme for the purpose of replicating the behavior with certain of the variables controlled, this fact enhances the adequacy of the explanation.

2. Human behavior is functional. A basic propensity of the organism is to act in such a way as to increase or preserve its integration. What this means is that the person acts, consciously or unconsciously, in relation to internal and external stimuli in such a way as to remove those stimuli which are noxious or threatening to its well-being and to increase those stimuli which are satisfying, pleasing.

At this point some people will raise questions such as: "What about the schizophrenic? What about the suicide? Is their behavior functional? Has it preserved integration?" Such behavior is certainly not adaptive in the biological sense of promoting survival of either the race or the individual. It may sound feeble to say that it is adjustive with respect to one of the sub-systems of the personality and hence integrative. But that is the best we can do. If you have ever observed the torment which a person attempts to remove through suicide, you may agree that the act is an attempt to restore integration. But the concept of function may be pushed too far here. Self-destruction and integration certainly seem contradictory.

3. Human behavior is rooted in a biological base. Behavior, however, depends upon an interaction of biological and environmental forces. There

---

* This of course is an exaggeration. Let us admit at the outset that there are many occasions when we cannot understand human behavior, even with the best evidence. Nevertheless, we operate on the assumption that behavior is largely explainable.

is no behavior caused by a purely hereditary or a purely environmental force; there is always a convergence of the two. This is not to say that individual constitutional differences do not exist and that they do not limit the person's abilities and potentialities. It would be difficult for a man four feet tall, weighing only eighty-five pounds, to become a football tackle at Notre Dame University. Commitment in detail to specific behavioral manifestations by a particular biological inheritance, however, occurs only occasionally and in limited respects. What appears to be more important from the point of view of biological determinism is the rate of maturation of the organism. Growth is marked by rhythms of assimilation, differentiation, and integration. Changes in growth occur at different rates in different individuals. When these rates are markedly unsynchronized with the norms for his age and sex in a given culture, an individual's problem in achieving personality integration is intensified.

4. Almost all human behavior is motivated. (There appear to be unmotivated creative expressions in children and in some adults.) Behavior is also multi-determined; that is, ordinarily there are several complex motives operating in relation to any observed act. These motives may be conscious, partly conscious, or unconscious as far as the actor is concerned. Much human behavior, though by no means all, is an attempt to strive for ends explicitly formulated.

Specific motives underlying human behavior are learned. Reflexes and drives with which an infant is born are not motives, even though their expression may be necessary to his survival. Motives grow out of the experiences which the child has with other persons and with his total environment. The chief motives develop in connection with persons, and these persons are the ones who are most significant to him in early childhood. In our culture the chief persons are usually the mother and father, although they may be a maid, cook, relative, or anyone else. For a child the significance of a person depends upon the quantity and quality of the relationships which he has with that person.

Motives learned early in life influence all subsequent learning to a greater or less degree. And since motives are primarily learned within the context of family relationships, the experiences of childhood within the family are of special importance.

5. Human behavior can be understood only in relation to the field or context in which it occurs. Therefore, it is necessary to specify the properties of the stimulus complex confronting the individual actor as clearly as possible. Persons in interaction are mutually interdependent. The effect of a given force upon a personality is dependent upon his receptivity at the time. Receptivity to a force, in turn, is the result of previous commerce with that or similar forces. For example, take the nursing baby. Neither mother nor baby performs the act well until each has had experience in relation to the other. Even with experience there are two other conditions

necessary to adequate, satisfactory performance: the baby must have been without milk for a certain period of time, and the mother must have a supply of milk.

Definitions

At the present stage of development of a science of personality most of the terms used by writers on the subject have no generally-agreed-upon, accepted definitions. This deficiency is unfortunate, since it leads to confusion. It is necessary, therefore, for each author to state explicitly the meaning which he attaches to the words he uses, giving as nearly as possible the exact referent of each one. Such a task is literally impossible to accomplish in the space of a short book. We will have to take for granted that many of the terms employed have sufficiently universal connotations so that their meanings in the contexts in which used will be relatively clear. Key words, or concepts, will be defined as precisely as possible as we go along. At the moment we shall define four recurring terms: *personality, social interaction, dynamics,* and *environment.*

Personality. Historically, the term *personality* has many meanings, ranging from the popular phrase "she has personality" to the profound theological usage found in the expression "personality of God" as expounded in the doctrine of the Trinity. Personality, thus, has come to have a great variety of connotations. When we examine the word etymologically we see that our confusion is only increased; for the Latin word *persona,* from which our term personality comes, as it has been translated into various languages, may signify nobody or no one when used with a verb in the French language, or it may mean a representative of a great body, as *parson* in English. These varieties of usage only emphasize the fact that personality is a generic term which has no specific meaning, universally accepted. Even animals are referred to as "having personality"; here the connotation is characteristic individuality.

Of writers on the subject of personality, Allport (1937) has done the most adequate and comprehensive job of reviewing the historical meanings derived from the Latin *persona.* He distinguished fifty different definitions or meanings. Yet, as MacKinnon (1944) has pointed out, two opposed meanings stand out from the earliest to the latest of these definitions. On the one hand, personality is thought of as a mask, a mere shield of outward and usually superficial appearance; on the other hand, it is conceived as the inner nature, the substance of a man.

Taking several current definitions of personality, it is possible to classify them according to one or the other of these conceptions—mask or substance. Of course, it does injustice to the authors of these definitions to force them into one-word characterizations; this is not intended. Nothing could be more untrue, for example, than to say that Jung conceives of the personality as a mere external phenomenon. *Persona* as he uses the term is a defense against revealing personality; it is a social blind or shield, to be varied according to circumstances, whose purpose is to protect the person from unwanted intrusion. Personality on the other hand is the highest achievement of which one is capable and means nothing less for Jung (1939) than the best possible development of all that lies in a particular, single being. The realization of inborn individuality and distinctiveness characterizes personality. This puts Jung squarely in the center of those who emphasize the inner nature, or substance character of personality.

May defines personality as "the responses made by others to the individual as a stimulus." (Allport, 1937). Only as others see you can your personality be delineated. The attractiveness of this view for many psychologists and sociologists lies in the increased objectivity it lends to the study of personality. Trained observers watch a person in action, agree upon his "social-stimulus value" and classify him according to the results. Two serious objections to this approach, however, may be pointed out. In the first place, a man does not generally reveal his private feelings to public observers. He is obviously different when placed before a jury of experts from what he is in the company of a few intimate friends at a drinking party, or in the private company of his wife. Much fruitless research has been carried on at the "public" level of inquiry where society demands that one "wear a mask." In the second place, agreement among observers, even of public behavior, is achieved too frequently at the expense of some of their more discriminating observations.

Allport's own definition (1937) is that personality is "what a man really is." He amplifies this statement for clarity in the following manner: "Personality is the dynamic organization within the individual of those psychophysical systems that determine his unique adjustments to his environment." Obviously this is a substance definition and represents for Allport "a synthesis of contemporary psychological usage." It is sufficiently in line with the thinking of many present-day psychologists who attempt to think about personality, as to warrant closer examination. Let us look at Allport's own explanation of the terms used in the definition.

By "dynamic organization" he refers to the patterning of mental life. Some order and arrangement must be brought to the multifarious aspects of personality. This has always been a crucial problem for psychology. But organization must be thought of in a fluid, motivational, and constantly changing sense; the word "dynamic" connotes such a usage. Organization is not correlative with "health"; even in the "disorganized" psychotic we find patterning and motivation.

By "psychophysical systems" Allport refers to habits, attitudes, sentiments, and dispositions. Psychophysical implies mental and neural activity;

system refers to traits or groups of traits. Thus he pays obeisance to the body-mind problem by the use of a compound word; there is an inextricable fusion of the two.

Personality should not be confused with behavior or activity. Allport takes a stand squarely opposed to the social stimulus view of May stated above. Allport says that "personality *is* something and *does* something." Personality is within the individual and determines (i.e., "lies behind") specific acts. Personal identity arises from the fact that the systems which constitute the personality are determining tendencies more or less stable in their reactions to recurrent stimuli. The person is not a pawn, but an active agent.

Personality is conceived in functional terms. The human being "adjusts" to his environment in order to survive. The individual seeks out, is creative in relation to his world and acts spontaneously; that is, without the necessity of an external stimulus.

Frank (1938) considers personality "a process, which emerges from the impact of culture upon the growing, developing, maturing human organism." Culture he defines as the traditional beliefs and practices of a group. It is these beliefs and practices which he sees incorporated into the person, thereby giving him orientation to his world. This is hardly an adequate definition of personality. Rather it is an opinion of an aspect of the genetic process through which personality is formed. It says nothing about how this process takes place, what organization occurs in the person, or the determining influence which the organization has on the individual's behavior. The importance of the definition lies in the fact that it recognizes the implicit relationship between the cultural environment and the developing personality structure. The vast amount of data accumulated by social anthropologists during the past two decades has convinced nearly all psychologists of the intimate relationship between the beliefs, customs, and practices of a people and the content of the mind of the growing child. It is patent that the Japanese child will display beliefs and attitudes toward certain ideas and activities different from those of the American child; the American child in turn will hold to certain attitudes and beliefs which are foreign to the Tibetan child. Likewise the adults of these cultures could readily be distinguished one from the other even by an untrained observer. The skilled anthropologist could tell which culture each came from, and perhaps even the sub-culture of the three groups. Further he could tell you what kind of behavior, under specified conditions, to expect from each.

Murray (1948) defines personality as "the organization of all the integrative (regnant) processes in the brain." Recognition is here given to two important principles: Organization, and what we may call centralization. In his emphasis on organization Murray is in line with the current trend among students of personality. Localization of the personality in the brain merits elaboration here.

The brain is the seat of organization and integration. It is by no means independent of other parts of the body; rather it is immediately and directly influenced by what goes on elsewhere in the body. For example, reduction of available oxygen in the blood produces a quick effect on the brain. All of the external manifestations of personality, however, are dependent upon differentiated parts of the brain. Changes in the brain due to injury from whatever source produce changes in personality. The brain is the integrative center of the entire organism.

Murray argues that since the term *personality* is used to connote organization and functioning of the individual as a whole rather than of any subordinate part, and that since the brain is the place where afferent processes from the body terminate and efferent processes originate, where differentiations and integrations occur, the brain must be the locus of the personality. At a given moment the personality is defined by the regnant brain processes. This does not mean that Murray assigns the study of personality to the neuro-physiologist. Regnant brain processes are manifested in behavior. Many have the property of consciousness and may be verbalized; others can only be inferred through observation of movements or through analysis of fantasy or dream material. One sample of the regnant processes, however complete, is inadequate to do justice to the personality. Personality is an on-going process which is revealed over an extended period of time.

Indeed, Murray would insist that a complete study of a personality would require a history of the regnant processes in the brain from birth to death. Although such a process is scarcely possible, it cautions seriously against too easy assessment of personality on the basis of a few scraps of information collected in a short period of time and relating to one epoch of a person's life. Personality extends both backward and forward in time—it is continuous—and for an adequate conceptualization must be viewed from this perspective. The brain is the storehouse of impressions and learnings; through study of conscious and unconscious brain processes we can look backward to the crucial life experiences as they are recorded and functioning in relation to the current stimulations of the present situation. We can likewise project the personality into the future on the basis of the individual's experiences and his reactions to those experiences in the past and present.

McClelland (1951) says that "personality is a theoretical interpretation derived from all a person's behavior." Whereas this is a different order of definition from the others presented, it makes explicit something which is implicit in them all, namely that a definition is circumscribed by the conceptual framework of the author. In other words, we define personality in terms of our own theoretical horizons. May's conception of personality as "social stimulus value," for example, reflects the psychological bias of his time. In a sense McClelland denies the possibility of defining personality. Since the person is constantly changing, and since the observer's insights are variable and his theoretical position in a state of everlasting alteration, it follows that any definition of personality must be no more than a raft, a temporary hypothesis, taking us from the shore of known facts and integrated theory to the shores of further observation based on our most intelligent guesses. It makes a great difference, however, which theoretical position one assumes in his exploration of personality. Not all theoretical interpretations are equally valid.

For our purposes we shall define personality as *a construct of the dynamic organization within the individual which specifies his potentialities for action.*

Use of the word *construct* in the definition implies the provisional nature of the conceptualization. The term *dynamic organization* refers to the fact that personality is fluid, never static, although there are stable elements in it. Every day the limits of variation of response are narrowed as one's nervous system is modified through new learnings, but the personality does not become fixed and rigid. New occasions, new learning situations bring forth modified responses. No one would think of defining an individual's personality for all time on the basis of a complete examination of him at the age of five or six. Neither can we spell out his personal identity for the future at the age of thirty or fifty. To be sure, more uniformities are found in behavior with age, but there is no necessary one-to-one correlation. Marked transformations in personality sometimes occur in older people.

All this is not to say that a person is from day to day cut off from his past. There is continuity. Personality is resistant to change, and reasonable predictions of future courses of action can be made on the basis of past behavior. The impressions of each day in healthy nervous tissue carry into the next. But this is only part of the story. Man is above all a social creature. His very survival demands that he interact with others. The personalities of others and the situations created through interaction with others require constant adjustments and new learning. This new learning modifies the structure of the organism, sometimes in minor detail, sometimes in significant manner; and with each modification the personality changes. The evidences of change in personality are usually imperceptible. A traumatic experience, or series of experiences, on the other hand, can so modify structure that even the casual observer is aware of marked personality changes. Thus, whereas there is organization or patterning of the processes which make up personality throughout life, the organization is always changing.

The emphasis in this book is on the interaction between two or more personalities and the effect of one upon the other. Personality has no meaning except in a context of social forces. Therefore we will attempt to specify the dominant social forces to which the persons whom we will discuss are assumed to respond. Thus, although we concentrate from time to time on the behavior of one person, we shall always look at him in relation to the personalities of others.

Social Interaction. Social interaction refers to the reciprocal exchange between at least two persons in a concrete situation which influences the subsequent behavior of each. Here "reciprocal exchange" refers to a mutual passing back and forth—or, putting it another way, a response on the part of each to a cue emitted by the other. "Concrete situation" means that the actors confront each other in some way, by some means. "Subsequent behavior" equals the phenomenally observable effects following the exchange between persons.

The problem before us is to try to understand what takes place, what transactions occur, between two or more persons in a contemporaneous social relationship. To accomplish this we must give equal weight to each actor. The words used, with their intonations and customary implications, the movements employed, large and small muscle movements of both parties, will have to be taken into account. All this requires an intimate knowledge of the actors, and other factors in the environment in which they are interacting. Because of limited ability to perceive all that is going on and because of the multitude of variables requiring attention, we shall succeed only in part. Our best hope of success in understanding persons in real life interactions is to concentrate upon a few significant major trends in the interpersonal relationships of our subjects and try to make sense of them.

Dynamics. Dynamics refers to motivation and to the fluid, constantly changing aspects of the interacting personalities with which we shall deal. When two people come together, each brings to the transaction an organization of motives, abilities, and a self system which make up his potentialities for action. These potentialities constitute the antecedent conditions to the signals, or cues, which he transmits to the other, as well as to his response to his own cues, and the response received from the other. Therefore they must be specified in any analysis. Likewise the changes which occur in each of the actors must be noted in terms of the effects observed in their actions, as well as the mediation process which brought about the change, insofar as it can be observed or inferred.

Environment. Environment refers to the perceived psychological situation, or to all the discriminated objects in a person's world at a given moment. Environment is thus never quite the same for two people. For the young child who is not aware of objective dangers as his elders are, playing with unexploded bombs, as children did in London during World War II, is a natural, exploratory activity. Likewise there is no hesitation on the part of a child blind from birth, who has not learned the relationship between falling from a high place and pain, to climb to the top of a jungle gym and stand waving his arms around gaily. We react to an object, to our environment, as we perceive it. Thus it becomes necessary to specify whose environment we are referring to, and what the environment is like when we talk about it.

Summary and Anticipation

What a person does is socially determined and socially relevant. It is almost impossible to think of human behavior without a social referent, either as an independent or dependent variable. Thus, the study of personality becomes a quest for the significant interpersonal relationships in which one is currently involved and which one has experienced throughout life. By looking at a few frames chosen from the continuous reel of life in the case of each of our subjects, we hope to so magnify the social process that some of the subtleties of the human drama will become patent.

2

STUDY OF PERSONALITIES IN FAMILIES

A large part of this book will be given over to the presentation and analysis of data concerning interactions within three families. It is not the three families directly that interest us. Rather, our concern lies in what we can learn from them that is of general interest and may be fitted into existing knowledge and theory about interacting personalities, or may point to new directions in theory. The materials presented about the families, and the conclusions drawn concerning their interrelationships, will be employed to illustrate general principles discussed in other chapters.

Families were chosen for study, rather than interacting persons seen in another context, for the following reasons: (1) the family is the primary unit of our society, and hence a worthy object of study in itself; (2) the foundations of personality structure are laid in the early experiences in the family, a structure which will influence all subsequent experience of the individual; (3) some of the most crucial and intimate experiences of life take place between family members; and (4) in order to secure the best data for a theory of interacting personalities, it is necessary to study persons having intimate and crucial experiences *as they occur.*

Once having decided to study members of families, the question of the best way to proceed arises. There are many methods available today to the psychologist who wishes to study personality. The ones he chooses depend upon his objectives in the study and his scientific biases. The approach used in this book is largely in terms of clinical methods. "The paths of discovery are different," says Santayana, "but, if they convey true knowledge, they must ultimately converge upon the same facts, on the same ground of necessity in things."

First we shall discuss some of the methods and objectives of science in general and some of the problems encountered in personality research. Afterwards we will go into the specific methods used to collect the data which are the source materials, the backbone, of this book.

Objectives and Methods of Science

Objectives of Science

Science proceeds through the analysis of observed phenomena into elements, each element being represented by a word or symbol. These elements are then put together by a process of thought, guided by theory, in a way that will exhibit their true relations and so produce abstract formulations of the original, true events. Thus we are constantly dealing with elements and their relations. This is a shorthand aid to knowledge and understanding. Understanding for its own sake is the ultimate goal of science. By manipulating elements, first theoretically in the mind and then in the phenomenal world, we can sometimes predict their outcome and control them. These are the proximate and practical aims of science: Prediction of future events on the basis of observation of current phenomena; control of elements and their relationships toward various human ends.

Methods of Science

The scientist first observes; he then analyzes his data into elements and describes and classifies them. Such observation and taxonomy are but the first steps in the scientific process leading to the formulation of hypotheses and ultimately to the fitting of the hypotheses into an interrelated body of theory. This model of scientific procedure is seldom followed in exactly the order indicated. We may distinguish three levels of procedure which are currently found in research projects: (1) systematic explorations of broad fields or subjects, (2) the testing of isolated hypotheses, and (3) compilations of data through crucial experiment or other observations based upon hypotheses derived from systematic and integrated theory. There are differences of opinion as to which procedure is to be preferred. Psychology currently employs all of them.

In the study of personality, which is so new, and about which there is no universally accepted body of theory, it is difficult to proceed at the third level. This is the ideal toward which we work. The history of the advance of the physical sciences is replete with instances of how fruitful this procedure may be. The most publicized recent illustration is found in nuclear physics, where a systematic body of theory was worked out in advance of any attempt to construct an atomic bomb. It is in this context that specific, well-defined hypotheses have the most relevance. The first requirement of this level of research is that a theoretical frame of reference be stated in unambiguous terms. Next a set of hypothetical statements and their corollaries should be drawn up; these should be an outgrowth of, and logically consistent with, the theoretical frame of reference. The hypotheses determine the nature of the empirical observation undertaken to test the validity of the entire explicit theoretical structure.

No such ambitious program is undertaken in this book. Hypotheses will not be tested in our inquiry. Our purpose, rather, is concerned with the antecedent step—to derive and formulate hypotheses from the study of the lives we shall analyze. It is hoped that these hypotheses may serve as starting points for further explorations.

Two Problems in Personality Research

The student of personality is faced with two problems with which most other scientists do not have to concern themselves. In the first place, the psychologist himself is the chief instrument of observation; and second, he must attempt to understand and conceptualize the individual.

There are no finely calibrated mechanical instruments which will measure and record the complexities of the whole human being in action. The psychologist himself must make the observations. He uses instruments whenever they are useful—such as objective and projective tests, or sound and motion-picture recorders—but in the final analysis he has to rely upon his own perceptive abilities to make the most discriminating and critical observations. In making his observations the psychologist *selects* necessarily from the complex whole environment which confronts him. Because he is a selective operator, not a photographic plate, and because he picks out significant elements to examine at his leisure, in the process a great deal is left behind. And herein lies a danger—selection is not random. Many factors guide the observation and recording of particular items. The psychologist in his training is made aware of these biasing factors so that in his research he may take the precautions necessary to control them as much as possible.

Factors Which Influence an Observer's Selections

1. There are natural deficiencies in our sensory systems. Perceptual awareness is not acute enough to observe certain discontinuities between events, for example as in moving pictures. There is a tendency to fill in the gaps, to smooth over, to see in wholes. What we add to produce continuity where there is none in phenomenal events may be the result of observer projection rather than of logical connection.

2. Although certain elements are more stable and easily observed—for example, tics, emotional outbursts, a large nose—they may not be the most important for scientific purposes. There is a tendency to pick out the easiest thing to observe.

3. Past experience and training influence observation. The kinds of perceptual sets and habits based upon previous learning may cause us to overlook the novel and unexpected occurrence.

4. Suggestions from others as to what there is to see is an ever-present danger to accurate observation. Even the biological scientist is not im-

mune to this influence. A typical experience for a student looking through a microscope at a tissue section is to see a certain histological pattern illustrated in his textbook, only to find that he has turned to the wrong page and that his microscopic specimen has only a vague resemblance to the illustration. Almost every student imagines serious pathological disturbances in himself after he first reads a text in abnormal psychology.

5. The conceptual scheme which the psychologist has accepted guides his observations consciously or unconsciously so that he is apt to see different aspects or elements than another psychologist. Or if the same elements are seen, a different interpretation is placed upon them. It is reported that when Freud and Jung crossed the Atlantic to the first conference on psychoanalysis in the United States, they spent their time studying each other's dreams. Word has it that they could not agree upon a single interpretation.

6. Scientific fashions of the day are not without their influence also. Early psychologists like James and McDougall saw behind almost every human act some instinct or combination of instincts. In medical practice it is painfully evident that what the physician sees is frequently dependent upon the "temper of the times." A few decades ago nearly every pain in the stomach was diagnosed as appendicitis and called for an appendectomy. In child psychology every behavioral aberration at one time or another has been attributed to maternal deprivation or rejection.

7. And finally the personal and practical aims of the psychologist himself are constant deterrents to precise observation. There is a striving to prove oneself right if one has become identified, through verbal or written communication, with a particular hypothesis or conceptual framework.

All of these factors must be borne in mind as potential pitfalls and the reader should not accept the interpretations and conclusions drawn by the author without the most critical scrutiny. Only by being aware of the errors of others, and by avoiding them in planning one's own exploratory ventures, can the science of personality progress. The search for adequate, valid methods is a continuous and laborious process. Great advances have been made in technical aids in the past two decades. But we still have a long way to go in determining the best procedures to use in the investigation of the intimate and crucial aspects of persons in interaction.

The Problem of the Individual

Most scientists, including psychologists, have consistently refused to look upon the individual as a proper subject for scientific study. Because each person is unique and hence cannot be averaged with other persons to arrive at a common type along classical scientific lines, scientists generally have maintained that the individual case is not a fit subject for study. Therefore, in psychology attention has been centered on parts of persons, especially sensory functions, as these compare with the same parts of other individuals. Studying and writing about individuals in all their fullness was left to creative artists until the demands of clinical practice forced attention on the part of some psychologists to persons as persons.

Study of single variables and comparison of these variables with similar variables in a large number of persons have been the order of the day. Studies in psychophysics, psychophysiology, and learning have demonstrated the merit of this approach. The methods employed have been taken over largely from the natural sciences, with which this division of psychology is closely identified. Social and clinical psychologists and students of personality have also used the methods of natural science with varying success. Where the variable under study is one like intelligence, the problem is relatively clear-cut. If you want to know how intelligence affects behavior under specified conditions, you can control it reasonably well while varying the conditions and noting the different responses. But when it comes to variables, such as weaning, toilet training, or discipline, which are embedded in a complex of social and cultural factors the single variable approach leaves something to be desired.

Much fruitless research has been carried on in attempting to prove or disprove that one or another variable has a determinative and lasting effect on personality. It is very easy to lose track of the intricacy and subtlety of the dynamics of human behavior when one is using methods which deal with segmented and isolated bits of behavior. On the other hand, to concentrate on the personality of one individual without regard to the elements common to other persons will not produce a science of personality. A combination of the two approaches—the intensive case study and the investigation of single or multiple variables in large populations—offers advantages afforded by neither alone.

In 1894 the philosopher Windelband proposed that a distinction be made between the study of general principles and the study of the individual case. He saw no reconciliation between the two. He used the term *nomothetic* for those disciplines (chiefly in his day the exact sciences) * which attempt to derive general laws applicable to all, or to groups of individuals. This, as we have indicated above, is the process of looking at elements in one person in relation to the same elements in others. *Idiographic* refers to the study of a single or individual phenomenon; in personality research this calls for an attempt to discover the mark or signature peculiar to the individual person. It requires looking at elements in relation to other elements in the same person. Windelband insisted that idiographic as well as nomothetic methods have a right to be called scientific.

Subsequently Allport (1937, 1942) made a strong case for the inclusion

* At the present time sociology, among the social sciences, employs mainly nomothetic procedures. Psychology has been mainly nomothetic in approach also. Under the impact of psychoanalysis, however, idiographic research has found an increasingly important place in psychology.

of idiographic methods into the psychologist's research kit. The division between the two approaches is too sharp and requires, as Allport says, a "psychology divided against itself." The two methods can be employed in the same research project or the same expository writing and draw upon each other. The study of individuals, for example, may bring forth hypotheses which can be further tested through the use of nomothetic procedures. Likewise, general laws can constantly be used in an attempt to understand the organizing forces of the individual life. In the analysis of a person this is a continuous back and forth process. The aim of psychology is to increase man's understanding of man, man in all his richness and complexity. We should use the nomothetic approach whenever it is best suited to advance our knowledge of man; but we should not be stopped in our quest by the limitations of the nomothetic approach.

The psychological study of individuality is being undertaken with profound seriousness; no blind loyalty to an anachronistic ideal can prevent it. One may call it science or not science, as one chooses. Long before the method of natural science attained its commanding position with psychology paddling in its wake, there was an ancient meaning of *Scienta*. It prescribed no method; it set no limits, it signified simply knowledge. (Allport, 1937, 23)

In the search for knowledge of man we regard it as patent that the use of the nomothetic or the idiographic approach is dictated only by the appropriateness of each in relation to the kinds of questions one is attempting to answer. The problem is not solved by the exclusion of either approach. Rather the recurrent disputes in regard to the issue can be settled, as Feigl (1959) has pointed out, "by a recognition and proper allocation of the nomothetic (generalizing) and the idiographic (individualizing) components in the natural as well as the social sciences."

This book, both in conception and organization, attempts to find a proper allocation between the individual and the general. The immediate aim of the idiographic studies is to attain a maximum understanding of the individual with respect to his present personality and behavior, the contemporaneous determinants of this behavior, and the historical antecedents of his personality. The idiographic approach provides a number of important general functions. These functions are: Critical evaluation of current knowledge and theory, as it relates to the understanding of a given case; revision and extension of current theory and knowledge through the formulation of new hypotheses about the individual case for further study with larger numbers of persons; the opportunity to develop fresh ways of observing and thinking about the behavior of individuals and families; and the discovery of additional, independent and dependent variables, and the interactions of such variables which need to be considered in order to explain and predict complex behavior in living situations.

Systematic alternation of case-study data and interpretative theory, with an attempt to keep them constantly interrelated, has a healthy influence upon the kind of theory under consideration.

Specific Methods Used in Collecting Information

At this point, let me interject a personal note as to the methods I used in the three case studies that will be presented in later chapters. While the ideal method would have been to study all the members of the three families, there was no opportunity to do this. I might have studied each individual separately, but that would not have served my purpose. I wanted to pay attention to the interaction between two or more persons, a huge task. Even this proved to be impossible as far as direct observation was concerned. Only on rare occasions did I see my subjects actually confronting one another. What I did was to study them individually, but contemporaneously. I assumed certain kinds of interactions between them on the basis of what I observed in each subject. The observations of the behavior of each person were related to the behavior of every other one in an attempt to draw causal connections.

If one looks at the number of relationships that exist within even a small family, the magnitude of the task of observing all the interactional systems will be apparent. Increase this number to six or seven, and the undertaking becomes almost impossible, if one is interested in gathering information concerning more than their public behavior.

In child guidance clinics for some time now it has been the practice to study two or three members of the same family by two or three professional staff members simultaneously. Two of the three families to be analyzed in this book were seen by me in clinics. Psychological testing and interviewing were the methods employed. A somewhat unusual procedure was followed in the interviewing in that I saw all members of the family in attendance during consecutive hours. In the third family, not seen in the clinic, the methods used were interviews consisting chiefly of free association, observation in the home, participant observation on the part of the mother, and a baby biography. Now a word about each of the methods used: Interviews, tests, and observations.

Interviews

In the therapeutic work with the families seen in the clinic, unstructured interviewing was used. By unstructured I mean that I did not have a schedule with pre-drawn questions which had to be covered. The interviews were certainly structured as far as the purpose and the limits to which we could go were concerned. But during the major portion of the time the clients were free to bring up any subjects they wished and to discuss them as freely as they cared to. The interviews were carried on in one case three times a week for three months and in the other once a week for eight months. This is quite a different procedure from the single structured interview frequently employed in social science research. One outstanding difference is the development of the transference relationship which often takes place in a series of therapeutic interviews; here a strong emotional bond develops between client and therapist. This will be quite apparent in the Ferranti study. There is a place for both types of interviews in the methods kit of the psychological researcher. Each is valid for the collection of certain kinds of data. Sears (1953, 229) has stated that "a theoretical formulation of the relation between *mother's report of child-rearing practices,* as the antecedent, and *child behavior (personality),* as the consequent, can be constructed with equal validity from either. . . ." the single interview or prolonged interviews. Empirical evidence will have to determine if he is right. He goes on to say that the usefulness of either can be determined by one criterion: Whether it can produce precise and replicable antecedent-consequent laws or not. With this statement we certainly agree.

In the case of one subject, Carol Chisholm, free association was employed extensively. This method, originally developed by Freud, is difficult to use with some people. Essentially it demands that a person open his mouth and let his thoughts flow unimpeded. There are obviously many reasons, if one stops to think about it, why some people should hesitate to carry out a request to talk after this manner. Occasionally the other adult subjects were asked to free-associate to some particular idea or statement which may have come up in the course of the interview. The chief advantage of free association is that it shows the immediate preoccupations and trends of thought of the person who is able to cooperate in an uninhibited fashion. Whatever is of pressing concern to the individual is likely to come to the fore.

Tests

Many people think of the psychologist as a person somewhat more respectable than the magician but nevertheless with a bag of tricks in the form of tests to startle and to read the mind. Unfortunately we have sometimes, unwittingly I trust, fostered this impression by making outrageous claims in the name of one or another sort of testing device. A psychological test is no better than the psychologist who uses the information derived therefrom. Its purpose is to give systematic, and hopefully valid, data in a shorthand form about a given personality in relation to norms established for other similar personalities. The data obtained from tests mean nothing until they are interpreted in the light of other information, both about the person under study and about the population from which he was drawn. The psychological test, in the right hands, is an aid to understanding, nothing more. It supplements the interview. Sometimes information from tests helps in making a diagnosis, sometimes in therapy. Almost always the test provides knowledge about the person which would take much longer to obtain in any other way.

The tests which were used with the persons to be analyzed later were of both the so-called objective and projective variety. They will be listed in connection with each study.

Observations

Ultimately all science is derived from observation. The scientist uses a great variety of aids, such as the psychological tests, in making his observations, but he must decide what to look at, how to look at it, and what to do with the data obtained from such looking. Much fruitless observing takes place which could hardly be called scientific. Three conditions appear to be essential in guiding scientific observation: (1) recognition of a problem, (2) some knowledge concerning the area in which the problem exists, and (3) some intelligent guesses, or hypotheses, relating the known to the unknown. One then determines the kinds of observations to make, designed to yield the most critical data.

Cohen and Nagel (1934) quote from Herodotus an account which illustrates the process beautifully. Herodotus, in the second book of his *History*, speaks of how on a trip to Egypt the Nile aroused his attention. The Nile, he discovered, begins to rise at the beginning of the summer solstice and continues for a hundred days, then it drops and remains low all winter and until the beginning of summer again. Herodotus was curious about this observed phenomenon and recognized that the problem could be solved only by finding other facts which could be connected with the periodic rise of the Nile. But not just any kind of facts.

In determining the *kind* of data most likely to lead to a satisfactory answer, he went to the Greeks and examined their hypotheses and stated his own; he did so by a process of deduction, after becoming aware of the phenomenon, and before he attempted to make systematic observations. If he had simply started to observe the available facts, what would have prevented him from studying the differential birth rate along the banks of the Nile in summer and winter? He might have found a statistically significant correlation between the number of births in June and the beginning of the rise of the Nile. Where would such a collection of data have led him in solving his problem? Herodotus knew that he must search for an increase in the supply of water in that part of the Nile not immediately observable by the Egyptians. There must be discriminating collection of facts.

In order to be discriminating, the collector of data must have had some experience (not excluding vicarious experience) in relation to the phenomenon which he is attempting to explore. Since he cannot collect all possible data, he must concentrate on certain data. Great scientific achievements have probably never been made by one who had no knowledge or anticipation of nature. It is a truism that we must look for something if we would find it. Original insight into the problem is necessary, but from there we proceed by a process of logical deduction from previous knowledge.

Who makes observations? Ordinarily the scientist and his trained staff make the necessary observations. In the collection of certain kinds of data, however, there are situations into which no outsider may intrude. Yet it seems imperative that we know the prevailing relationships in these private situations for a complete study of personality. How can we get such knowledge? We can solicit retrospective accounts from the participants. This is the usual method, and it often gives good results. It has the weakness of all mnemonic exercises. Another way to proceed is to enlist the services of the participant himself in keeping simultaneous records of the events and experiences and feelings and thoughts which make up his day. This was done in one of the family studies to be reported. Carol Chisholm kept a biography of her baby and herself.

Suggested Readings

Allport, G. W. *The Use of Personal Documents in Psychological Science*. New York: Social Science Research Council, 1942, Bulletin 49.

Discussion of the materials needed to understand what goes on in people's minds and how valid generalizations may be made from such materials.

Lindzey, G. (Ed.) *Handbook of Social Psychology*. Cambridge: Addison-Wesley, 1954.

Volume I, Part 3, on research methods reviews in nine chapters some of the more important problems faced in social science research today.

3

SOME CONTRIBUTIONS OF FIELD THEORY, DYNAMIC PSYCHOLOGY, AND LEARNING THEORY

In Chapter 1 we said: "The problem before us is to try to understand what takes place, what transactions occur, between two or more persons in a contemporaneous interpersonal relationship. To accomplish this we must give equal weight to each actor . . ." We shall illustrate the kinds of intimate interactions which take place between a mother and her baby in the next chapter. Other, and different kinds of family interactions will be presented in subsequent chapters. In Chapter 1 we also said: "When two people come together, each brings to the transaction an organization of motives, abilities, and a self system which make up his potentialities for action. These potentialities constitute the antecedent conditions to the signals, or cues, which he transmits to the other, as well as to his response to his own cues, and the response received from the other." At this point it becomes necessary to elaborate on these statements. In the present chapter will be discussed concepts and principles derived from field theory, dynamic psychology, and learning theory.

Contributions from Field Theory

No life is a closed system. Each human being depends upon other human beings for his necessities. Each person is influenced by, and in turn influences, his environment. Through studies of the interaction of two or more persons significantly related to one another, it is becoming clear that whatever takes place in any part of the psychological environment influences corresponding changes in each participating person; and vice versa, the actions of each person influence modifications in the total psychological environment. The qualitative unity and integrality of the individual are specific, but we cannot consider the individual as a self-sufficing entity from which all the explanatory principles of its existence can be drawn.

Field theory has been developed in the main by Koffka, Köhler, Wertheimer, Goldstein, and Lewin. We shall not present a detailed account of all their findings. Suffice it to point out the central thesis of Gestalt psychology, namely, that figure-ground relation demands that the conditions of the "ground" shall participate in the formation of the "figure," and that the *structure* of the figure shall, in turn, influence the ground upon which the figure appears. From this it can be seen why emphasis is placed on the whole, as opposed to analysis into parts. It also follows that the present situation, of which the organism is a part, is the important thing to consider. The Gestaltists argue that if the occurrences of the past weighed as heavily as the Freudian psychologists would have us believe, then the figure would wield an influence disproportionate to its place in the whole.

Wholes, to be sure, are made up of parts. But the parts have no meaning except as functional aspects of the entire structure. The attributes of the parts, then, separated from the whole are of no interest. But even the Gestaltists recognize that in order to examine so complex a thing as human behavior, it must be broken into parts for analysis. What they insist on is knowing what the given part contributes to the dynamic functioning of the whole.

Angyal criticizes the Gestalt brand of field theory as being too general. He even goes so far as to say that it is a negative approach feeding on its antagonism to atomism and spending its energy in disproving the mechanistic-atomistic views. He proposes what he believes to be a more specific and positive formulation in his hypothesis of "immanence" and the trend toward autonomy, which we will review briefly. The organism, according to Angyal, can be looked upon as consisting of a number of parts or organs which have specific functions. These functions are not contained within the organ itself, but are connected with other organs. The lungs, for example, have the function of providing oxygen and eliminating certain gaseous waste products. The lungs provide oxygen not only for their own use but also for all the tissues and organs in the body. Similarly with the heart—it provides blood for all the tissues, including its own. Angyal has diagrammed this interrelationship of the parts. (See *Figure 1.*)

This "closed-circle" hypothesis assumes that the life process does not lead beyond the sum total of the functions of the parts. It is only one part of the total picture, and some very important facts which have been left out are necessary to an understanding of the simplest life. Angyal, following the same general thesis, maintains that no life—however low in the phylogenetic scale you go—is a closed system. It depends upon its environs for the sustenance of life. Each individual is influenced by and in turn influences its environment in two ways. (See *Figure 2.*)

Intake, or assimilation, refers to "the process by means of which any factor which is originally external to the organism becomes a functional part of it" (Angyal). Intake refers to the necessary nutritional elements,

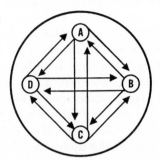

Figure 1

Organ A works for organs A, B, C, and D. The entire meaning of the function of organ A is to maintain itself and organs B, C, and D in a condition in which they can fulfill efficiently their specific functions. The function of organ B in return is to maintain in good functional condition itself and the organs A, C, and D—and so forth.[*]

but also it stands for the cultural and emotionally charged elements of which the individual partakes. In the case of nutritional elements evidence is increasing to indicate that response to perceptual cues is regulated by tissue and organ states.

Assimilation we have said is the transformation of things external into functioning parts of the living organism. Production constitutes the second break in the scheme. Life is a creative and expanding process. Reproduction provides the best example of creature-environment interaction involv-

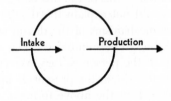

Figure 2

ing intake, expansion, and creation. Any life constantly grows at the expense of the outside world, and its creative expressions build up the outside world of which it has partaken. The use of the term "outside world" is an unhappy one, by which is meant simply the environment external to the organism's skin. In reality the distinction between *within* and *without* is false—a convenient scientific fiction—for life does not occur either within

[*] Reprinted by permission of the publishers and The Commonwealth Fund from Andras Angyal: *Foundations for a Science of Personality*. Cambridge, Mass.: Harvard University Press, copyright, 1941, by the Commonwealth Fund.

or without. It takes place within the one whole, of which both are mere aspects.

Kurt Lewin, of all field theorists, has done the most to conceptualize the person-environment interaction in terms which are useful for our purpose. Traditionally in psychology there have been two ways of answering the question, "Why does a person behave in a certain way?" Psychoanalysis and associationism point to origins and attempt to account for the presence of certain properties in the person by historical and functional relationships. Behaviorists and mechanists in general have attempted to explain behavior in terms of variations in the stimulating conditions of the contemporary scene. Lewin adheres to a position somewhat midway between these two extremes; he maintains that only existing facts can influence behavior. Behavior is a function of the total situation confronting the person. He states this proposition in the following formula: $B = f(P, E)$, where $B =$ behavior, f, function, P, personality, and E, environment. Lewin admits that in order to set up "pure cases" with which to vary conditions systematically, a special history may have to be created for the subjects in order to understand the content of the "life space" at the moment. The historical approach is acknowledged, but he chooses to start his investigations from the momentary situation in order to determine laws acting at the moment.

Actually Freud and Lewin are not so far apart in their conceptions of the total motivating forces in behavior as a surface examination would indicate. The emphasis chosen by each for concentrated study was certainly different, Lewin emphasizing the contemporary situation, Freud the past. Yet each recognized the necessity of viewing the total life space. In dream interpretation, for example, Freud insisted that the stimulus for the dream could always be found in the events of the preceding day or day and a half. But the stimulus alone could not explain the dream; such explanation involved knowledge of the mechanisms of the dream and the specific meanings to the individual of the symbols employed. The meanings were sought in the previous learnings of the person as they were recorded in the memory and hence continued to exist in the present. It may be fair to say that Freud overemphasized the P in the above formula, whereas Lewin overemphasized the E.

Many of Lewin's terms are chosen from physics. It should be pointed out that in so doing he is not trying to derive psychology from physics. The context of these concepts is determined only by coordinating them with real psychological processes. For example, forces for Lewin are in the *psychical field*, not in the physical environment. We have used a number of terms which are probably confusing to you. Let us see what they mean for Lewin and how he fits them into his conceptualization of personality.

The concept of "field" has been brought into psychology, and the social sciences, from the physical sciences where it is a commonplace. According to Einstein a field consists of a totality of coexisting facts which are conceived of as mutually interdependent. No event in nature occurs outside of some field. And every part of the field is directly influenced by every other part. Even *inherent* properties of an object are held by some field theorists to be ultimately traceable to forces impinging upon it from outside. It is the surrounding field which is construed as the effective whole; it determines the attributes and behavior of the part or parts coming within its influence.

Life Space

The psychological field has been designated by Lewin as the "life space" (LS_p). It includes both the person and his psychological environment as one constellation of interdependent factors. Thus the formula for behavior may be written: $B = f$ (P, E) $= f$ (LS_p). It now becomes necessary to represent the life space scientifically. Lewin lists five general points that should be remembered in trying to represent the psychological field:

1. Distinction between the situation as seen by the subject and by the observers. This calls for an understanding of the subject's ideals, values, fears, conscious and unconscious needs, etc., and implies subjectivity. It means that knowledge of the sociological or physical properties of a situation, important as they are, are insufficient to explain behavior.

2. The social aspect of the psychological situation is as important as the physical.

3. *Specific* items such as goals, stimuli, needs, social relations, as well as more *general* characteristics such as atmosphere (for instance, the friendly, tense, or hostile atmosphere) need to be taken into account.

4. Only facts which are a part of the present field can affect behavior. But everything existing in a given field needs to be represented.

5. The interrelation of the parts of the psychological field can be represented in mathematical terms.

For Lewin, then, life space represents all the facts influencing a person at a given moment. Life space is a function of age, momentary states (needs), personality structure, and the stimulus complex confronting the individual. The life space of the infant is very small with respect to both space and time. With increasing age and experience, differentiation of the life space occurs, memory intervenes, and temporally distant events acquire increasing significance. A reprimand or praise may long remain a present psychological fact for the person. An anticipated event may have psychological reality in advance of its occurrence. Knowledge of something, alone, may have little effect on life space, whereas a psychologically critical fact (e.g. relationship with a significant adult) may have fundamental significance on life space without a child having any clear awareness of it.

Valence

A valence is the property of an object to attract or repulse a person. Valences are the most important properties of the environment, having negative and positive strength, and correspond to the needs of the person at a given moment. Any increase in the strength of a need produces a corresponding increase in the valence of the object. As one grows hungrier, for example, the positive valence of a piece of stale bread increases until it may look very attractive. Thus valences change with changing needs. Valences are acquired in the life history of the individual through commerce with various objects. A positive valence equals what is commonly called a goal. It has strength and can be measured by the power of different incentives to attract. Lewin's use of valence is similar to the Freudian concept of cathexis. For Freud it is libido which becomes attached to objects and accounts for their cathexis. Lewin employs the construct need and the experience of the individual to account for the valence of an object.

Force

Lewin distinguishes sharply between valence and force. Force is derived from the valences in the field and is defined in terms of the properties *direction* and *strength*, which are represented by a *vector*. When a number of forces are acting at the same point at any given time, Lewin calls it the *resultant force*. Thus behavior can be explained, he says, in this way: when there is a resultant force above zero, there will occur locomotion in the direction of the force, or some change in cognitive structure will occur which is equivalent to the locomotion. Force, then, may be correlated with locomotion, and locomotion always occurs according to the direction and strength of the resultant of momentary forces. Driving forces correspond to positive or negative valences, or in behavioral terms, *approaches* and *avoidances*. Restraining forces correspond to barriers, that is interferences with, or blocks to, locomotion.

An illustration may help to clarify this idea: A child in an eating situation dislikes a particular food which is before him (his own force is in a direction away from the food), but he may accept the food in a social situation with other children or because of adult pressure. The adult or other children are induced forces bearing on the child in a direction opposite to that of his own force. If his own force is stronger than the induced force, he will reject the food; if it is weaker, he will accept the food.

The concept of force will be useful in analyzing the impact of various pressures on persons in an interactive process. Especially helpful in this connection is the notion of power field, or force field, which characterizes the relative strength or capacity of a person to influence another. For example, if the mother has more control over the child than the father, her power field for the child is stronger than his. Or again the home may be considered a power field in relation to school, church, or other institutions. The difficulty, of course, is in determining what forces in what strength are operating either within or without at any given time.

Field of Forces

Every individual lives all of the time in a field of more or less complex forces. This is simply another way of saying that a person always has some active needs striving for satisfaction in an environment of objects varying in degree and strength of attraction or repulsion. The simplest explanation of behavior would be somewhat as follows: A person perceives an object for which there is a need. The object would have a positive valence. The person would locomote toward the object, which now has become a goal, unless blocked by a barrier, or negative force. In the region of the goal there would be a discharge of the tension generated by the need. Equilibrium as far as this need is concerned would be restored. Another need would become active and therefore a new life space would take form.

For the infant, such a state of affairs generally exists. This is due to the fact that his life space is relatively undifferentiated. His needs are few, and the objects of satisfaction are limited and usually stable. The mother, or someone in the role of the mother, is on hand to manipulate the environment in such a way as to take care of the child's needs almost as they become active. Increasing experience with a variety of objects and modes of expression as the child grows older produces a differentiation of the field. Now the arousal of a need does not lead so simply to gratification through maternal manipulation. The mother comes to resist the incessant demands of the child and insists upon delay of gratification now, or again may deny it completely. This situation throws the child into a state of conflict.

Conflict

Conflict may be thought of as the opposition of field forces of approximately equal strength. Conflict increases tension which must somehow be discharged. Three basic types of conflict may be distinguished.

1. The person is caught between two positive valences. Usually this type of conflict is easily resolved, because the valences are rarely exactly equivalent; any choice factor, such as proximity, leads the person toward one goal, and the conflict is resolved. A person in love with two individuals one of whom is close by, the other in a distant city, for example, is likely to resolve the conflict by going out with the one at hand, other things being equal.

2. The person is caught between two negative valences. The fields of force in this case point away from each goal; the resultant leads the person out of the field unless he is restrained. Whenever a conflict occurs in which

there are more or less equivalent negative forces, the person will leave the field unless the situation is closed about him. Thus constraint characterizes this type of situation. A college student may dislike his studies and want to leave school and go to a more compatible situation; his parents may intervene to insist that he remain where he is.

3. The person may confront an object having both positive and negative valence simultaneously. This is called ambivalence. Satisfaction of a need in relation to the object will produce equally strong dissatisfaction through the arousal of another psychical system. A person who satisfies his sexual need in a way unacceptable to his superego, for example, will inevitably arouse guilt feelings. Resolution of this type of conflict often occurs through use of the mechanism of repression. Another way to resolve this and other types of conflict is through restructuring the field. Restructuring, or reorganizing, the field occurs when the total situation is perceived as having more positive than negative valences. For example, when an adolescent boy suddenly sees that the educational demands made on him by his parents are designed for his own personal achievement and happiness he is likely to alter his resistance to studying.

Reality and Irreality

Lewin divides the psychological environment into strata of various degrees of reality and irreality. Like all writers in dynamic psychology, he recognizes the difference between objective "facts," which a group of competent observers could agree upon as being quite independent of the subject viewing them, and "unreal planes," which include hopes, fears, dreams, and wishes intertwined with the "world of reality." The discrepancy between the real world and one's interpretation of it provides an index to what the psychopathologists call delusion. Choice of the terms *real* and *unreal* seems inappropriate inasmuch as fantasy can be more vivid and meaningful sometimes than the so-called "real" facts. The terms *objective* and *subjective* would be much better. No one certainly would deny that subjective experience is as real as objective.

Reality has but one plane, but unreality has many. The boundaries of the real are fixed, whereas the limits of the unreal are fluid. Lewin, quoting T. Dembo, says that in a plane of unreality "one can do what he pleases." This of course is an extreme statement which fails to take account of our knowledge of psychic causality.

The different levels of reality and unreality hold for adults as well as children. For the child the differentiation is less marked, and he can pass from one to the other much more easily. As he grows progressively more mature (one might say as his ego develops), the distinction between real and unreal becomes more and more clear. Here Lewin speaks in general terms, but one would have to qualify this view with the phrase "in our culture." Our knowledge of the learning of other peoples reveals that belief in the objectivity of evil spirits remains as real in some cultures as the rock which the spirits are presumed to inhabit.

Lewin says that in puberty there is a relatively slight differentiation between strata of reality and unreality. In support of this statement he points out that, sometimes for years, a life of fantasy may be led concurrently with the real life. Such an assertion requires clarification. If he means that the young adolescent is not able to distinguish between the content of his inner life and the outside world, then Lewin is obviously in error. Only the schizophrenic is so out of touch with the "facts." On the other hand, if he means that puberty is a time of heightened indulgence in fantasy due to the pressure of ungratified needs, he is correct. This is simply a restatement of the relationship between psychic life and personal needs which Freud formulated, and others have documented.

A description of the psychological environment must always take cognizance of the difference between subjective reality and objective reality. For it is undeniable that if the conditions on the plane of objective reality become too difficult and unpleasant, there is a tendency to withdraw, as it were, more and more into one of the levels of subjective reality or fantasy. In tracing the interaction between two persons it is necessary to represent the level for each person. It is quite possible—in fact, the evidence strongly supports the proposition—that the fantasy level of one person can influence the overt behavior of another who is in close association with him, just as surely as could the level of objective reality.

The Person as a Differentiated Region in the Life Space

The person is conceived as a differentiated region within the life space. He is not an entirely homogeneous unity, however. He is differentiated into central inner personal regions (corresponding to the psychical structure and motor capacities involved in action), and outer regions. "The different parts of the person differ in the degree to which they are related to each other," says Lewin. "Parts" refers to psychical systems, which Lewin never clearly defines. If one part of the person, say a wish, is fulfilled, it may change the whole person, and his subsequent behavior in all areas of his life will be altered. Election to a much-desired club, for instance, may alter one's attitude toward self, friends, and study. This indicates a dynamic interdependency between the regions or parts. The degree of dependence is determined by measuring the amount of change in one region which results from a change in another. As one would expect, a change in the central inner personal region has more far-reaching consequences than a change in the peripheral region.*

The young child has few differentiated regions, and the difference be-

* There is a close parallel here between central and peripheral regions and what other authors refer to as ego- and non-ego-involved situations. See Sherif and Cantril, 1947, for a discussion of the latter.

tween inner and outer is blurred and unclear, as we have seen in discussing Lewin's notions about reality and irreality. Differentiation of the person occurs to a large degree as a function of the situational field. That is to say, the interactions which the child has with others—particularly with his mother and other significant persons—provide the content of his differentiated self. If his world is rigid, compulsive, and tightly controlled, this is what he assimilates; if his world is flexible and free or unstructured, this he assimilates. In other words, the kinds of experiences he has determine the nature of the organization and differentiation of his psychical systems.

From field theory we have derived a number of concepts which will help us to represent the situation in which persons will perform. The person himself, however, remains to be conceptualized. In field theory he is a shadowy figure, sometimes central, sometimes peripheral, always a force in a field of forces, but somehow never quite grasped solidly and made to come alive. The person is just somehow there with a structure of needs—needs admittedly an outgrowth of his past history, a history which is almost denied, at least never inquired into—needs which influence his perception of the situation and which change with his changing experiences. But there is neither an adequate account of the formation of the needs nor of the process whereby they undergo change. For these and other concepts necessary in our analysis of interacting persons we turn to psychoanalytic and other dynamic psychological concepts and to learning theory.

Contributions from Dynamic Psychology

The year 1859 has special significance for an understanding of present-day conceptions of personality. Two publications appeared that year which were destined to change profoundly man's thinking about himself. They were Darwin's *The Origin of the Species* and Marx's *Contribution to the Critique of Political Economy*. Darwin attempted to demonstrate through empirical data that evolution of the species goes on continuously through a process of natural selection. Marx set forth the basis of his theory of economic determinism, maintaining that "human nature is constituted by the behavior and powers of concrete individuals or groups of individuals within their several physical and historical environments, changing these environments and themselves changing with those changes" (Venable, 1945). No longer could thinking man accept the theory of static condition of the animal kingdom. Nor could one any longer tolerate the prevailing notions of human development.

These two radical theoretical innovations have brought about revolutionary changes in both our biological thinking and our social planning. Add to these the work of Sigmund Freud, who originated a new and illuminating way of psychological thinking, and we see the beginnings of the formulation of three problems which have been of recurrent interest and concern to students of human growth and development. These are: First, whether development is determined by factors inside the organism or by influences impinging from the environment; second, whether there is a continuous unfolding or whether there are abrupt and sharply defined stages of development; and third, whether behavior is "caused" by single determining factors or by a multiplicity of factors.

The first of these problems has appeared in a variety of forms: heredity versus environment, maturation versus learning, constitution versus life history, and so on. Most workers in the field of human development have accepted Wilhelm Stern's *principle of convergence*, that is, the interaction of many determinants, and are now seeking to work out the proportionate influence of inner and outer factors in any particular life. One no longer tries to identify purely hereditary or purely environmental traits. The behavior of the human being is accepted, in line with Stern's principle, as the product of the interaction of both hereditary and environmental influences. And personality is assumed to be an outgrowth of this interactive process.

As the organism grows older, a fourth problem is evident: Is behavior determined more by *present circumstances* or by *earlier learnings?* The psychoanalytic school emphasizes the importance of early childhood experiences in motivating adult behavior. Allport (1937) has opposed this view with his theory of "functional autonomy," and so has Lewin (1935) who emphasized the importance of immediate environmental forces. Perhaps the simple principle of convergence has been overlooked in this controversy.

Students of personality have addressed themselves in a variety of ways to these four problems. And at present there is no universal agreement among psychologists as to either a conception of personality or as to the best methods to employ in its study. All agree, however, that knowledge of the structure of the human organism, the pressures exerted upon it, and the interaction of the two is the task confronting us. Every human being is like every other human being in certain structural components; this makes for many common needs, perceptions, and response patterns. And every human being is different from every other human being, due to individual differences in constitutional endowment and learning experiences; this makes for differing needs, perceptions, and response patterns. Moreover, every human being is like some other human beings and different from others, due to the socio-cultural milieu in which he is reared; this makes for likenesses and differences in needs, perceptions, and response patterns.

An adequate conception of the organism, the environment in which the organism lives, and the interaction between the two constitutes the problem of behavior theory. This is an overwhelming assignment. It is an assignment which cannot be completed today, or perhaps ever. We can only approach it in part, hopefully getting nearer and nearer. The theories which we shall now review, like field theory, all are concerned more or less with the three aspects of the problem. But, as we shall see, no one of them is wholly acceptable; and each deals with parts only of the whole problem. The fact is, psychology alone is inadequate to this task.

Sigmund Freud

When Sigmund Freud, after prolonged and intense introspection, published in 1900 *The Interpretation of Dreams*, dynamic psychology was born. It was the beginning, and in many ways the most creative and original, of a long series of brilliant works in which was developed the first comprehensive theory of personality. In this book Freud took a stand squarely opposed to the psychologists of his day who were interested in exploring consciousness in all its variegated aspects. Freud was not an academician; he was not even a psychologist. At this time in his life he was a practicing medical man trying to make a living for his growing family through the treatment of psychopathological patients. Already he had learned a great deal from his patients. But he learned far more from his own self-analysis, which he began in the summer of 1897. Indeed, he became convinced that a study of unconscious processes was far more fruitful in unravelling the mysteries of a dream than any amount of concentrated attention on consciousness. Study of unconscious processes became the keystone to all his activities, and the method he developed was free association.

No psychologist in history has been the target of such bitter, even vituperative, criticism and attacks, as has Freud. At the same time no psychologist has had such a profound effect upon the thinking of his colleagues, scientists in other fields, and workers in the arts and humanities as he has had. Why was he so criticized? One source of conflict was that he proposed sex to be the all-pervading, motivating force in human behavior from birth to death. In the Victorian age when any mention of sex in public was frowned upon, and in a culture where sex and sin had been linked from the age of St. Paul down to the last Calvinist doctrinaire, it is not surprising that Freud's writings produced controversy. Of course this is not the whole story. There are rational grounds on which Freud has been criticized. One source of difficulty is that he was not a systematic writer. The ideas expressed in one period conflict sharply with those forged out of new insights in another. Because frequently he made little or no effort to reconcile the contradiction, it is difficult at times to read him coherently. These, however, are minor criticisms. The two chief criticisms relate to his method and the way in which his theory is stated.

Freud did not employ the usual empirical procedures in collecting his data and testing his hypotheses. He was, as we have said, a practicing psychotherapist, and he used the material derived from his practice as the basis for his generalizations. The conditions were neither controlled nor replicated. His records were inadequate and incomplete. He never used statistical techniques. Questions of significance and reliability, as the modern social scientist uses the terms, never entered his head.

Still, the ideas he enunciated are commonplace amongst all psychologists today. His theory is widely used in clinical practice and his hypotheses have provided the basis for countless research efforts. There are four concepts basic to an understanding of Freud: instincts and their vicissitudes, unconscious motivation, anxiety and the mechanisms of ego-defense, and the structure of the personality.

Instincts and Their Vicissitudes

For Freud instincts are strivings which underlie behavior, but which are not identical with behavior. They are driving forces without, in the beginning of life, any specific objects. Much confusion has existed in the minds of American psychologists over Freud's use of the word *instinct;* let us try for a moment to clarify this issue.

Actually Freud did not use the word *instinct* in his writings; the word he employed was the German *Trieb*. It was in the translation of Freud's works into English that instinct was employed, and this was unfortunate. Instinct had come to have the connotations of not only an impulse but also an inborn pattern of behavior. This was not Freud's meaning. As early as 1915 he wrote (1957, pp. 122–123):

The aim [*Ziel*] of an instinct is in every instance satisfaction, which can only be obtained by removing the state of stimulation at the source of the instinct. But although the ultimate aim of each instinct remains unchangeable, there may yet be different paths leading to the same ultimate aim; so that an instinct may be found to have various nearer or intermediate aims, which are combined or interchanged with one another. Experience permits us also to speak of instincts which are allowed to make some advance towards instinctual satisfaction but are then inhibited or deflected. We may suppose that even processes of this kind involve a partial satisfaction.

The object [*Objekt*] of an instinct is the thing in regard to which or through which the instinct is able to achieve its aim. It is what is most variable about an instinct and is not originally connected with it, but becomes assigned to it only in consequence of being peculiarly fitted to make satisfaction possible. The object is not necessarily something extraneous: it may equally well be a part of the subject's own body. It may be changed any number of times in the course of the vicissitudes which the instinct undergoes during its existence; and highly important parts are played by this displacement of instinct.

What Freud meant to convey by use of the word *Trieb* was the quality of impulse or drive which arises within the organism and seeks expression in a variety of ways until a satisfactory mode is found—that is to say, until a mode is discovered which abolishes the condition of stimulation. Thus, for instance, the sexual instinct has no native behavior pattern, no specific goal object, and in fact attaches to a number of different objects including one's own body during the normal course of development.

Two groups of primal instincts were originally distinguished by Freud:

The self-preservative or ego-instincts and the sexual instincts. But this proposition was tentative and did not have the "weight of a necessary postulate." Later these categories were largely fused into what was called "life instinct," and a new category was introduced, the "death instinct." The life instinct was made up of libido (sexual energy) and part of the ego instincts; the death instinct was the tearing down, destructive force in the organism. Freud had not been able to subsume aggression in all its forms, either that directed toward the self (as in the case of self-torture or suicide) or that directed toward others (as in the case of war), under his earlier groups of instincts. Hence the death instinct, or *Thanatos* as it is sometimes called, was invoked. It will be remembered that Freud as medical man was well aware of the anabolic and catabolic forces at work in the organism; there is a constant process of building up and tearing down within the body's cells. Perhaps it was from this physical analogy that he drew his concepts of life and death instincts. Through various combinations and fusions of the two he attempted to explain all mental phenomena. Few, even among Freud's most orthodox disciples, have followed him in accepting an innate death instinct. A theory of aggression as an outgrowth of frustrations encountered in the course of living and interacting with other persons is much more cogent.

The concept of libido, defined as the energy of sexual instincts, is based on a physical model, a hydraulic system. Libido represents the quantity of sexual energy assumed to be relatively fixed for each individual at birth. It is libido which becomes attached during the course of development to different objects. No assumption is made concerning the primary source of libidinal energy; this is outside the scope of psychology. Whether the source is of a chemical nature or whether it corresponds with the release of mechanical forces is not known. A more exact knowledge of source is not necessary for psychological examination. Many American psychologists have ridiculed Freud for this assumption of what they call a "mysterious kind of energy." There is only one kind of biological energy of which we know: The energy transmuted from the food we eat. This energy varies and is transferred from one process to another depending upon the condition of the organism. When one is ill, the energy is diverted to physiological processes; at such times mental functions are likely to be interfered with. We know also that when we have worked hard mentally all day, we do not have a lot of energy left over for other pursuits.

One more word about the general problem of the vicissitudes of the sexual instincts from Freud (1957, pp. 125–126):

This much can be said by way of a general characterization of the sexual instincts. They are numerous, emanate from a great variety of organic sources, act in the first instance independently of one another and only achieve a more or less complete synthesis at a late stage. The aim which each of them strives for is the attainment of "organ-pleasure"; only when synthesis is achieved do they enter the service of the reproductive function and thereupon become generally recognizable as sexual instincts. At their first appearance they are attached to the instincts of self-preservation, from which they only gradually become separated; in their choice of object, too, they follow the paths that are indicated to them by the ego-instincts. A portion of them remains associated with the ego-instincts which in normal functioning easily escape notice and are revealed clearly only by the onset of illness. They are distinguished by possessing the capacity to act vicariously for one another to a wide extent and by being able to change their objects readily. In consequence of the latter properties they are capable of functions which are far removed from their original purposive actions—capable, that is, of "sublimation."

In the course of development the libido is attached to a number of objects; parts of the body as well as external objects; this process is known as *psycho-sexual development.*

Infantile Sexuality

As Freud has pointed out, he was not the first to refer to infantile sexuality. In his Clark University lectures he quoted from Sanford Bell, who specifically stated that sex love does not make its first appearance at the time of adolescence. But the development of the theory and its place in dynamic psychology are attributable to Freud. Basic to the psychoanalytic theory of sexual development, as we have seen, is the theory of libido—that in its biologically undifferentiated form, sex (or libido) is the primary source of all creative, affectional, and adaptive strivings. This source of energy is present at birth and is expressed throughout development by becoming connected with bodily functions. It is now released through one organ, now another. Subjectively there is a feeling of pleasure accompanying its expression. Thus a polymorphous striving for pleasure permeates the activities of the child.

Until Freud began to discuss infantile sexual development, he had spoken of sex and meant sex in the mature genital sense. Since this was obviously not the case with very young children, sexual now came to mean *any pleasurable sensation.*

The Oral Stage. The young infant sucks. Not only does he apparently gain satisfaction from sucking, he seems to need a certain amount of sucking (Levy, 1934). From these facts the psychoanalysts have deduced that sucking is libidinal, and that every object that goes into the mouth from the mother's nipple to an old shoe can become erotically cathected. Objections to calling these experiences "sexual" have been answered by the Freudians somewhat as follows: Stimulation of sensitive zones (of which the mouth is one) causes pleasure and a warm glow of feeling for the person who gives it. This is a prototype of adult sexuality. Therefore, childhood body-pleasure experiences are continuous with adult sexuality, and play an immensely important role in its development. The lips are very sensitive in the young child, perhaps more sensitive than other parts of the body.

The effect of the interpersonal relation and the satisfaction derived therefrom during the oral stage is presumed to be lasting in the personality structure. Thus Lorand (1944, p. 209) can say:

Constant dissatisfaction with achievements in adult life and the feeling of always being cheated may be due . . . to a brief nursing period, or having been a bottle baby in a family where the older children were nursed. The opposite of this type of character is exhibited by the individual who wants everything but who likes to exert only the slightest effort in getting it. Such a person was probably accustomed to having his way all the time in childhood, especially in the oral phase of his development, when he had only to cry out and the breast was given him for as long a period as he desired.

The act of sucking constitutes the first expression of the sexual instinct; the first object cathected by the infant is the mother's breast. Sucking not only meets nutritional requirements, it also gives pleasure through tactual stimulation; thus sucking continues in the absence of hunger need—for example, in thumb-sucking. At the time of weaning, the child usually receives his first major frustration. Now instead of compliance with his desire to nurse, he is pushed away from the breast. In our culture this usually occurs during the second half of the first year, concomitant with the eruption of the teeth, and is associated with more or less struggle between mother and child. It is common now among psychoanalytically oriented writers to divide the oral stage into two phases, corresponding to the more passive pleasure sucking period (called oral incorporation) and to the weaning and teething period (called oral sadism). This latter phase finds the child retaliating for frustrations experienced by biting and showing other evidences of displeasure.

The Anal Stage. Usually in our culture after weaning great emphasis is placed on developing sphincter control in the child. Now begins the so-called second phase of the pre-genital organization known as the anal, or, sometimes, anal-sadistic stage. There is a pleasurable sensation derived through elimination. Early in life the infant is free to evacuate at any time when the tension in bladder or colon becomes too great. This is known as the expulsive phase. During the post-weaning period he is first encouraged, then urged and sometimes beaten into withholding his urine and feces until the appropriate time and place. Now the retentive phase begins. After the sphincter muscles are mature, the child can retain or expel pretty largely at will, and the Freudians think he uses this ability as a weapon against the parents. If they frustrate him, he will defecate in revenge; if they please him, he will reward them by defecating at the right time. If he has been too rigidly trained, he may retain the feces too long and become constipated. It was this characteristic of a history of constipation in childhood associated with certain adult forms of nervousness that made Freud (1905) originally look for libidinal factors in the anal period. He later postulated (1908–1916) certain anal types which were an outgrowth of the anal retentive phase and characterized by such traits as parsimony, pedantry, and petulance. Freud believed that the anal stage of development was biologically determined by the concentration of libido in the anal region at this time.

The Genital Stage, Phallic Phase. Sometime between the second and fourth years, the genital organs are for a time a special source of pleasure to the child. Masturbation now begins and with it the battle between child and parent over sex. The outcome of this battle has far-reaching implications for adult sexuality. If great feelings of guilt are associated with sex during this period, they may carry over and interfere with adult sexual expression. In certain cultures there is no doubt that genital pleasures at this time are strongly frowned upon by parents. They shame the child, punish him, and even threaten castration in the case of boys. Later the fear insanity may also be invoked. Under this barrage of threats repression of the act of masturbation occurs.

This stage ushers in the *latency period* at around the fifth year, and it lasts until puberty. Sanford (1943) has shown that during this time there is less mention of things sexual. Freud believed this fact to be due to biological factors, but it seems quite clear now, from abundant evidence both in our own culture and in cross-cultural studies, that it is a sociological phenomenon resulting from specific repressive influences. When one of the author's daughters was eight years old, she told him of conversations which she had had with her playmates (all in the so-called latency period), which were filled with talk about sex. And yet these children's usual conversations with their parents were singularly devoid of such references, when compared to the talk of a four-year-old. Concern with sex continues during the latency period, but it is simply driven out of conversation with persons, usually adults, who will not tolerate it.

The Mature Genital Stage. The aim of sexual development is mature genital love. On this point Freud has been misinterpreted by many who have assumed that any form of heterosexual expression was a sign of maturity. Freud's emphasis was on genital *love*, which implies *mutuality of response*, rather than on mere genital expression. Writing on "Narcissism" in 1914 he had this to say (1957, p. 99):

The relations of self-regard to erotism—that is, to libidinal object-cathexes—may be expressed concisely in the following way. Two cases must be distinguished, according to whether the erotic cathexes are ego-syntonic, or, on the contrary, have suffered repression. In the former case (where the use made of the libido is ego-syntonic), love is assessed like any other activity of the ego. Loving in itself, in so far as it involves longing and deprivation, lowers self-regard; whereas being loved, having one's love returned, and possessing the loved object, raises it once more.

Erikson (1950, pp. 230–231) has formulated the psychoanalytic ideal of mature genital love cast in a social frame of reference; it should include, he says:

1. Mutuality of orgasm
2. With a loved partner
3. Of the other sex
4. With whom one is able and willing to share a mutual trust
5. And with whom one is able and willing to regulate the cycles of
   a. work
   b. procreation
   c. recreation
6. So as to secure to the offspring, too, a satisfactory development.

Unconscious Processes

From the beginning of his work Freud recognized the central importance of positing unconscious strivings underlying and giving meaning to observable behavior. The inference of unconscious processes was necessary, he said (1957, p. 99), "because the data of consciousness are exceedingly defective; both in healthy and in sick persons mental acts are often in process which can be explained only by presupposing other acts, of which consciousness yields no evidence." The acts referred to included the parapraxes, that is, slips of the tongue and pen, certain types of forgetfulness and mislaying of objects, as well as dreams, obsessions, and ideas which suddenly come to mind without voluntary effort. William James said that Freud's investigations in the whole area of unconscious processes was the most important step forward that had occurred in psychology since he had been a student of the science.

Freud was not the first to assume that unconscious processes were at work in man. Von Hartmann, Schopenhauer, and others had postulated an "unconscious mind," but Freud was the first to explain systematically unconscious processes and to assign a central place to them in personality theory. Prior to Freud, psychology was considered to be the science of conscious processes. Today this assumption is untenable. For the moment let us see how Freud came to appreciate the significance of unconscious processes.

Except for the first and last few years of his life Freud lived in Vienna. He studied medicine, and his research interests progressed as follows: Spinal cord of a simple form of fish, human medulla oblongata, diseases of the nervous system, and the so-called "nervous diseases." For financial reasons he began to practice as a specialist in the nervous diseases, his only tools being electrotherapy and hypnosis. But at heart he was an explorer. Concerning his choice of a profession he said: "Neither at that time, nor indeed in my later life, did I feel any particular predilection for the career of a physician. I was moved, rather, by a sort of curiosity, which was, however, directed more toward human concerns than toward natural objects" (Freud, 1949, p. 191). This curiosity led to an extreme interest in the case of a friend and medical colleague called Breuer.

Anna Q., as Breuer's patient came to be called, was a person of strong character. She had a critical, unsuggestible mind and a strong will. A very sympathetic person, she had a remarkable lack of interest in sex. She lived a monotonous, unstimulating life at home, and for amusement developed imaginative daydreams (which she called her "private theater"). When her illness began in 1880, she was twenty-one. The illness incubated during the fatal illness of her father, whom she adored and nursed. Her illness followed this course: (1) a hysterogenic period without continuous symptoms, July–December, 1880; (2) a bedridden period to April, 1881, when the father died; her symptoms including troubles of vision and hearing, paralysis of right arm and both legs, contracture of neck muscles, nervous cough, speech difficulties, nausea; (3) a period of normal states, although with some symptoms alternating with somnambulism up to December, 1881; (4) a period of gradual improvement to good health without symptoms in June, 1882.

Breuer first discovered that Anna felt much better when she was able to tell him all the fantasies she had had during the day in her "private theater." These fantasies were like fairy tales, and if she could not recall them, her symptoms multiplied. Next Breuer discovered that a symptom of some duration could be removed by recalling and reliving in imagination the initiating circumstances. This suggested that there was a process at work which forced conscious thoughts and feelings out of consciousness, and that these thoughts and feelings continued as active processes striving for expression, even though not available to consciousness. They found expression in symptom formation. The symptom ceased to be necessary if the thoughts and feelings were expressed in other ways. Here was the beginning of Freud's awareness of the existence and power of unconscious processes.

The normal response to a strong emotional experience is to give vent to one's feelings by verbal or physical action. A person runs or fights back, shouts, commands, or cries. This phase is followed by a mingling of the memory with other memories, and normal forgetting sets in. In the case of hysterical patients like Anna, the emotional experience is retained in memory in all its awful freshness, unconnected with other ideas and barely if at all remembered in normal conscious states. Freud and Breuer thought that all that was necessary to cure the hysterical patient was to reproduce in consciousness the original traumatic experience and abreact the affect connected with it. Thus the therapeutic problem was clear. But how to accomplish this? Hypnosis, the only technique available, proved inadequate to the task. For a time Freud attempted to use Bernheim's method of holding his hand on the patient's brow while making a suggestion to him. This technique worked only spasmodically.

Now Freud reasoned that whatever came to mind could not be irrelevant, since *all mental processes are determined.* He reasoned further that any thought which occurred to the patient must have some connection with the object of his search into the cause of illness, no matter how remote the allusion. The problem was to get the patient to talk. And so he took a bold step in medical practice—he began to listen to the patient. He encouraged his patient to talk, to say whatever came into his mind regardless of its bizarreness or apparent unrelatedness. This technique he called free association; it has remained the principal technique of psychoanalysis down to today.

Using this technique Freud discovered that his patients could not always talk freely and fluently. They were hesitant, silent, evasive, could not remember, or if they remembered, refused to talk. At times there seemed to be a terrible struggle going on within the patient. He would be depressed and mute; then suddenly a memory would pop into mind, and he would give forth with a verbal barrage accompanied by weeping. Freud thought that many memories were involuntarily kept out of consciousness; he called this hypothetical process *repression* and said that the "undeniable existence of resistance" to the recall of certain memories proved that repression was at work. He asked himself why does repression occur? His answer was that repression was a process of forgetting in order to escape mental pain. "In all those experiences," he wrote (referring to instances of repressive forgetting), "it had happened that a wish had been aroused, which was in sharp opposition to the other desires of the individual, and was not capable of being reconciled with the ethical, aesthetic, and personal pretensions of the patient's personality" (Van Teslaar, 1924, p. 36).

From this line of thought two ideas about psychodynamics gradually emerged. One was the conception of the place of anxiety in personality functioning, the other was a structuration of the personality into opposing forces. We will examine these ideas briefly now, and more extensively in later chapters.

Anxiety and the Mechanisms of Defense

On the basis of his early investigations Freud put forth the hypothesis that the libido when repressed was transformed into anxiety. He did not know how the transformation was accomplished dynamically; but he thought that further study of the phobias would provide the answer. Such study, however, rather than confirming his hypothesis, caused him to reject it. He found that the phobias were occasioned by "fear on the ego's part of the demands of the libido. Always in this situation it is the attitude of anxiety on the part of the ego which is the motive of and the incitement to repression" (Freud, 1936, pp. 50–51). Thus anxiety does not emanate from repressed libido; it is the cause of repression of libidinal impulses. Repression, then, is seen as one of the mechanisms defending the ego against overwhelming conflict.

"All symptom formation," according to Freud (1936, p. 111), is "brought about solely in order to avoid anxiety." Hence anxiety is "the fundamental phenomenon and the central problem of neurosis." As partial justification of this position Freud cites the fact that if a neurotic symptom is violently overcome, an attack of anxiety follows immediately. For example, if a person suffering from agoraphobia has always been accompanied whenever he goes out on the street, suddenly finds himself alone, an anxiety attack ensues. If a person suffering from a hand-washing compulsion is prevented from washing his hands after touching something, he suffers almost insupportable anxiety.

In the early days of the author's psychological practice a young lady of twenty-one years came to him sorely distressed; as the day of her wedding approached, she had become more and more convinced that she should not marry. She had a score of "good reasons" to support the conviction, but she said she loved the man in question and wanted to marry him. In the course of a few hours the following facts were revealed. Her mother and father were divorced; as far back as she could remember there had been bickerings, threats, counter-threats, fights, tears in her home; finally when she was a pre-adolescent, her mother had left home, and contact with her had been friendly but distant ever since; her father was alternately smothering in his show of affection and tyrannical in his demand for acquiescence to his smallest wish—she lived in a continuous state of uncertainty. She had found some peace when she left home to go to college. A premature interpretation on the author's part to the effect that she was resisting marriage and rationalizing her stand because of fear of a recurrence of the only pattern of family life which she had known, was accepted by her; and she made the decision to go ahead with the marriage. Thereupon she suffered a violent anxiety attack and could not leave her room for days.

When a person is confronted with a situation which contains threat, he may meet it by adequate defensive responses, by escape, or by positive attack responses. In such a case, there is no anxiety, or it is kept to a minimum. But if the person is helpless, and cannot make adequate responses so that the threat increases, his behavior is likely to become catastrophic, and he experiences panic. Anxiety is the experience that goes with catastrophic, disorganized behavior in response to a threat to existence. A fully developed anxiety attack is a horrible experience. Indeed, the word "panic" gives the right connotation. Anxiety is the effect one most wants to avoid. It may discolor a whole place or a whole epoch in one's life.

Not all people react in the same way in the face of threat. The usual reaction of an experienced adult is relatively ordered and is accompanied by only transient moments of anxiety. Some people of unusual ego-strength can sustain internal controls and prevent catastrophic behavior even in the face of certain death. There are records of martyrs praying for their captors while being slowly tortured to death.

Why are some people more susceptible to anxiety than others? The answer for Freud lies in the infantile experiences of the person. To begin with, the birth process is the model of all later anxiety. He speaks of the flood of excitation which the infant is subjected to at birth. The danger to the infant lies in the fact that he is helpless to defend himself in face of this onslaught of excitation. Here is the key to future anxiety—helplessness brought about by separation from the mother. There are few resources in infancy to prevent anxiety; if he is not regularly cared for, the infant experiences it often. It is not objective danger which threatens him. Rather his threats come from the inside, through the mounting tensions of unsatisfied needs, discomforts, and pains. An infant crying himself black in the face may be presumed to experience anxiety. This does not happen to all infants. Indeed the conditions of life vary somewhat from one infant to another; hence the predispositions to anxiety may be seen to vary also. But every infant is helpless, and therefore Freud seems justified in emphasizing the importance of infantile experiences in the etiology of anxiety and neurosis. This is not to deny, of course, that later circumstances produce anxiety which can be pathogenic.

The following quotation from Freud seems to sum up his opinion concerning the genesis of anxiety (1936, pp. 98–100):

I am forced to the conclusion that the earlier phobias of childhood do not permit of being directly traced to the impression made upon the child by the act of birth . . . A certain predisposition to anxiety on the part of the infant is indubitable. It is not at its maximum immediately after birth, to diminish gradually thereafter, but first makes its appearance later on with the progress of psychic development, and persists over a certain period of childhood. . . . Only a few instances of the expression of anxiety in infancy are intelligible to us; we shall have to keep to these. Thus the three situations of being left alone, being in the dark, and finding a strange person in place of the one in whom the child has confidence (the mother), are all reducible to a single situation, that of feeling the loss of the loved (longed for) person . . . Anxiety thus seems to be a reaction to the perception of the absence of the object, and there at once spring to mind the analogies that castration anxiety has also separation from a highly valued object as its content and that the most basic anxiety of all, the "primal anxiety" of birth, arises in connection with separation from the mother.

In the face of separation and the helplessness to do anything about it, anxiety is experienced. As we have said, one wishes above all to avoid this experience. Thus it follows that the person will attempt various solutions to the threatening situation, and these attempts Freud has labeled mechanisms of defense. We have seen that Freud considered repression—that is, forcing the threatening stimulus or impulse from consciousness—as one such mechanism. Also we have seen how rationalization, "good reasons," on the part of the young lady afraid to marry, constituted another attempt to avoid the threatening situation. There are other mechanisms which Freud has described and which others subsequently have examined experimentally and otherwise. These mechanisms will be discussed in later chapters.

Structure of the Personality

For analytical purposes Freud divided the personality into three parts: id, ego, superego. Because he tended to reify each of these parts, he thereby sowed the seeds for considerable misunderstanding and abuse of his concepts by later students. Early attempts to interpret Freud abound in diagrams and verbal illustrations in which parts of the personality are assigned percentages of the total and one part is set in opposition to other parts—as if they bore no relationship to one another, and almost as if they were little homunculi moving mysteriously about within the skin of the individual, each seeking to become master of the whole. There is in Freud this tendency toward reification, and his graphic language and substantive analogies certainly make it easy for one to make the interpretations indicated.

We must not forget that Freud's theories were derived from his investigations of neurotic persons. In such individuals processes at work are frequently exaggerated and brought into bold relief; indeed certain systems do operate in abscission (i.e., tend to be separated) from other systems. Thus it appears at times as if one part of the personality had the upper hand and was controlling and attempting to suppress the other parts. But we must not be misled. There is always an integrating process at work which is more or less successful, depending upon a great variety of conditions. In our brief discussion here of the three aspects of personality, let us remember then that Freud distinguished these for purposes of theoretical systematization. They constitute a whole, or if you please an interaction of theoretical systems.

The Id. The instinctual forces—the positive, creative, life-giving, sexual, all-pervading libido and the negative, destructive, hostile death-instinct (aggression)—were subsumed under the generic term *Id*. This was a regular Pandora's box of all the assaultive and sexually unsocialized urges of the personality. It recognized only one direction—outward release—in the service of a single principle—pleasure. These forces represented the natural man. Any socialized tendencies were of man's own making and from a much later vintage, ontogenetically speaking. Some writers have criticized Freud's formulation of the Id on the ground that he excluded all passive forces and social tendencies. Such critics maintain that certain gregarious and conforming tendencies—such as empathy, imitation, and identification —are innate and operate unconsciously, and therefore should also be subsumed under the Id. Murray ascribes "hallucinations, delusions, irrational beliefs as well as fantasies, intuitions, faith and creative conceptions" to the Id. "Thus," he concludes, "almost everything, good and bad, has its primitive source in the Id" (Murray, 1938, p. 136).

The Superego. The Id, in Freudian terms, obviously provides no patterns for socialized living. And yet most children become socialized. How does this happen? To answer this question Freud postulated his second division of the personality, the superego. The superego is the watchdog of the Id forces. It is the restraint which holds in check the writhing instinctual urges. It is the age-old conscience with a new name. Throughout the centuries it had been assumed that the conscience was God-given, that it was the divine guide in man. Freud denied this assumption and tried to explain its origin entirely in naturalistic terms. In *The Ego and the Id* he said that the instinctual forces are controlled through the influence of the external world by an introjection of the parents into the child. Such a process takes place as a result of the threats and punishments of the parents which create anxieties in the child and force conformity as the price of reward, or renewal of love and good will.

How this internalization of the parental dictates occurs is still not definitely known. Learning theorists would explain it largely in terms of reinforcement. The Freudians use a more mystical language, and the keystone to their explanation lies in the Oedipus Complex. Sometime around the fourth year of life, culminating in the fifth, the child is supposed to prefer strongly the parent of the opposite sex. Such a preference has a sexual basis and produces extreme jealousy of the same-sex parent, because of rivalry over the preferred object. Thus for the first time the child becomes involved in an emotional triangular relationship, realizing that love has to be shared and disliking doing so. The emotions of love and hate are involved: Love for the preferred object and hate of the rival. Because all this constitutes a very complicated emotional situation for the child, it is anxiety-provoking. If he expresses his hate toward the father, the father may turn on him and, being more powerful, actually kill him, as in fantasy he would like to do to the father. Even the mother—because she loves the father too, perhaps better than she does the child—will be angry if overt aggression is shown. The father will be angry in any event if too much love is showered on mother. Here is truly a perplexing dilemma. How is it resolved? By identification of the child with the parent of the same sex, thus aligning himself on the side of the father and removing the threat. The solution entails accepting the reality-principle of sharing love, loathsome to the young child, and abiding by parental wishes. Thus is the superego born as an anxiety-reducing mechanism.

It seems evident that this drama does take place with some children, but certainly not with all, nor perhaps with most. It must therefore be a situationally produced conflict. Some likely guesses as to why it occurs at all are: (1) that the child is completely egocentric in the beginning and for a long time holds the center of the stage—a phase which gradually wanes, and he takes his place as just another member of the family; (2) that there is a generally heightened awareness of the world and various relationships at about this time; (3) that there is possible rejection by one or both parents at this time, especially if there is a younger child coming along to hold the spotlight.

The Ego. Personality development involves not only restraint of libidinal and aggressive forces and ability for satisfactory interaction with others, but also increasing individuation and development of the ego. This aspect of Freudian psychology is perhaps its weakest link. The ego was conceived of as something of a pawn, buffeted about on the one hand by instinctual urges and on the other by a tyrannical superego. The reason for this misconception is not hard to understand when one considers the people whom Freud studied. Neurotics are renowned for the weakness of their ego structure. Thus Freud was reporting phenomena as he observed them. Nevertheless it is unfortunate that knowledge of the ego and its formation, because of this historical accident, should have lagged so far behind conceptualization of the other aspects of personality.

The ego is conceived by Freud as that part of the personality which is in direct contact with the external world. The expressions of instinctual impulses, the Id, are modified according to the reality principle, that is the demands of the current situation in which the child finds himself. Present pleasures have to be postponed in order to avoid greater displeasure, impulses have to be restrained according to cultural dictates. The ego is an abstraction of the sum total of the modifications of the Id.

Critique of Freud

Experimental and clinical evidence is slowly accumulating to indicate the strengths and weaknesses of Freud's theories. Freud clearly recognized the role of unconscious processes in the motivation of behavior. Any theory of personality today which does not take account of this discovery is untenable. Freud properly emphasized (1) that there is a strict determinism of psychic processes, conscious or unconscious, (2) that what is repressed is a wish or striving and that its dynamic quality is retained, (3) that the reason for repression is the unbearable pain and insult to self-respect which certain impulses occasion, and (4) that inner conflict results from repressed impulses which are antithetical to the moral and ethical standards of the individual.

Freud's insistence upon the importance of unconscious motivating forces was admittedly an overemphasis on his part to counteract the prevailing concern of psychologists of his day with conscious processes. That a person is motivated by rational concerns and current stimulations is evident. Less evident is the fact that happenings of a decade or a generation ago, preserved in memory, have a dynamic effect upon behavior; less evident too are the many irrational forces directing and controlling behavior. To these Freud directed his attention in order to secure for them adequate attention in the total conceptualization of personality. In this effort he succeeded. Freud's genius lay in his recognition of the significance of the hopes and fears, the doubts and strivings in the personal life of the individual.

There is no proof as to Freud's theory that libido works through innate areas of sensitivity which have a functional relationship of substitutability. It is clear that these areas do frequently become connected with sexuality in our culture. Just how the connection takes place and what is its effect on personality in general, is yet unclear. Psychoanalytic theory maintains that there is a primary instinctual response; that is, that there is a physiological pleasure derived from stimulation of the sensitive areas. This is probably correct. But such an assumption does not explain the association of sexuality with these zones, nor does it explain the lack of or weakness of the connection in many individuals.

The most feasible theory is that they become connected through complex associational relationships established through learned responses at critical periods in the life of the young child. This hypothesis is in line with that current learning theory which accounts for a learned drive. It would enable us to account for the wide variations among persons in the extent of connection between sexuality and the sensitive zones. The crucial genetic difference probably lies in the handling the young child receives from his mother and other significant persons in relation to his oral, anal, and phallic expressions. Specific acts may be suppressed and have no particular dynamic effect on subsequent behavior. Where the impulse itself is repressed, its dynamic quality is retained, and its effect on subsequent behavior is devious.

Gordon W. Allport

The psychoanalytic school, as we have seen, emphasizes the importance of early childhood experiences in motivating adult behavior. Freudian psychology with its stress on the irrational elements in human nature has focused attention on the primitive and instinctual character of much of human motivation. The fact that Freud dealt almost exclusively with psychopathological individuals—who had not been able to achieve a mature, rational approach to life and who were indeed impelled by unconscious, irrational forces—blinded him to other more positive, creative, and constructive aspects of human existence. Perhaps Freud's gravest error was to make the unwarranted generalization that all persons are subject to the compulsive urges he found in his neurotics.

Without denying the dictum that "the child is father to the man," can we not agree that the childish impulses, conflicts, and needs remain strongest in those individuals who, for whatever reason, fail to achieve true adulthood? Can we not go further and say that childish impulses alone are responsible for motivating behavior only in the immature personality? In other words, if there is an arresting of development so that the person remains immature socially and emotionally, even though he has attained physical and intellectual adulthood, he is in a sense *still* a child; he has never outgrown certain aspects of childhood. And so he is motivated by childish concerns and needs. There is another kind of person, however, who may have achieved maturity, but who under adverse circumstances reverts to "childish" ways (that is, patterns of behavior are reactivated which have long ago been abandoned, and which in the interim were not influential in directing his activities). This reversion to earlier patterns of behavior may be short-lived if the inner resources are strong enough to overcome the noxious circumstances, or if the adverse conditions can be sufficiently modified or removed. The reversion may, on the other hand, be persistent if the internal resources are weak and/or the external situation unmodifiable.

In either of these cases—where there has been an arrest in development or a reversion to earlier modes of behavior—the influence of childhood experiences and conditionings would seem to be exceedingly important. But in the case of the mature adult it seems unnecessary and not a little absurd to explain, as Freud does, every act in terms of primitive motivations. By a series of complicated and brilliant assumptions he was able to explain different character traits as "sublimations" of, or "reaction formations" against, the sexual drive. But is such a concept necessary to explain, and does it fit the facts of, mature behavior? Allport answers emphatically no! The mature interests, goals, and over-arching purposes completely overshadow the undifferentiated primitive strivings. That is not to say that these strivings have simply evaporated. They have been converted or canalized and put into the service of a hierarchical system of interests, values, and sentiments. These directive forces in life are now prepotent and motivate behavior. They may even overshadow such a basic urge as self-preservation in determining the course of life.

In rejecting the notion that every motive can be reduced to a limited number of basic innate drives shared by all, Allport (1937) states that adult motives are infinitely varied, and that they are contemporary systems, growing out of antecedent systems to be sure, but functionally independent of them. Although each motive probably originates in organic tensions, as the individual grows the tie is broken. The connection is historical, not functional. It is not the perfected talent nor the automatic habit that is autonomous and furnishes driving power, but the habit that is being formed or the talent that is being perfected. Motives are a type of striving for completion, involving unresolved tension and demanding closure. Many motives retain their functional autonomy because they never become automatic or reach closure.

As evidence for his theory of the functional autonomy of motives, Allport cites the common experience of persons who set out upon a certain endeavor for one motive and continue the activity long after the original motive has ceased to exist. For example, he speaks of the sailor who acquires a love of the sea as an incident in his struggle to earn a living. The need for food was the thing which sent him to sea initially. Now, says Allport, he is an ex-sailor and perhaps a successful broker, but still his "hunger for the sea persists unabated." The "hunger for the sea" is an autonomous motive unconnected with any more elemental motive. What Allport fails to see is that the "hunger for the sea" may have been a stronger motive from the beginning, because of experiences associated with the sea, than any nutritional motive. There are various ways of earning bread, and some far more successful than fishing. Our sailor could have chosen many other things to do. Why did he choose the sea? When we find the answer to this question, we may see that his predominant motive was not nutritional. Fortunate is the man whose basic motivational interests coincide with his means of economic livelihood.

Other, and more serious evidence which Allport arrays in defense of his theory are the circular reflex, conative perseveration, "conditioned reflexes" not requiring reinforcement, counterparts in animal behavior, rhythm, certain neurotic characteristics, the relation between ability and interest, sentiments, and the dynamic character of personal values. We cannot undertake a critical review of all these lines of evidence. A careful reading of Allport's original text in this regard will be very rewarding. It must suffice here to examine the evidence for conditioned reflexes not requiring reinforcement.

Ordinarily, Allport points out, the conditioned reflex dies out unless the secondary stimulus is occasionally reinforced by the primary stimulus. He illustrates this by Pavlov's classical experiments with dogs, in which the animal learned to salivate to the bell as a conditioned stimulus. Unless the food (unconditioned stimulus) were occasionally presented with the sound of the bell, the latter ceased to stimulate salivation. But now Allport goes on to say, "There are innumerable instances in human life where a single association, *never* reinforced, results in the establishment of a life-long dynamic system. An experience associated only once with a bereavement, an accident, or a battle, may become the center of a permanent phobia or complex, not in the least dependent on a recurrence of the original shock" (Allport, 1937, p. 199). Again if we look only at the phenotypic behavior of the individual, Allport's assumption is correct. These phenomena do occur as he describes them. Analysis of the dynamics underlying the behavior, however, frequently reveals motives not apparent on the surface, which are intermittently reinforced. It is reasonable to expect that analysis of other similar phenomena would also reveal hidden motives.

An illustration from the author's own experience will show how one event which never recurred produced behavior which lasted for over fifteen years. When I was a child of about twelve, I was reading a certain book one evening when a fire broke out in our neighborhood. We lived in a small town equipped with no fire-fighting apparatus except buckets and fourteen years before this the town had been completely demolished, save for three or four houses, by a fire. Everyone in town was afraid of fire, and especially my mother. On the evening in question I was quietly reading when I heard someone shout "Fire." The next instant my mother ran into the room, and the sight of her panic-stricken face and the horrible sound of her shriek sent spine-tingling fright through my body. I have to this day complete amnesia for the events immediately following this anxiety-provoking experience. This particular experience has never been repeated.

Sometime after the event (I cannot date it exactly, but I think it was a matter of weeks), I picked up the book which I had been reading when the fire broke out and immediately put it down again overcome with a feeling of uneasiness and dread. Several times in the years immediately following I approached this particular book, and each time I was compelled to put it down. The anxiety aroused was too great. The anxiety was reduced by rejecting the book and turning my attention to other things. I learned to avoid the book, and did so for ten or more years.

In the meantime I had studied some psychology and had learned the principles of conditioning. I do not remember thinking of the book in all these years. But now one day, when I was visiting my old home, I spied the book and approached it. I began to feel anxious. I now said to myself, "This is silly; that book has no earthly power; go ahead and pick it up." And so I did. I even read some of it. But the anxiety mounted just the same. I then began to speculate why this book had become a stimulus for anxiety-arousal in me, and I was able to uncover the original episode in memory. When this did not relieve the anxiety, I set out deliberately to recondition myself. I made a point of picking up the book and reading a portion of it whenever I entered the particular room where it was kept. In a very short time, a few weeks, the anxiety associated with the book disappeared, and I could take the book or leave it without emotion.

On the surface the original event never recurred, and my motive for avoiding the book seemed to be self-sustaining or functionally autonomous. In reality, as subsequent analysis proved, my behavior was reinforced by the reduction of anxiety each time I approached the book and rejected it. The motive, then, determining my relationship with the book throughout fifteen years was anxiety, and, be it noted, anxiety whose source was completely unrecalled by me.

Allport recognizes that behavior may proceed from unconscious motives and even from primitive motives. What he insists on, however, is that *some* behavior is divorced from such motives. Indeed, he would say that the mark of maturity is the extent to which a person's conduct is determined by functionally autonomous motives based upon adult interests having nothing to do with earlier forms of motivation. Each personality is unique, with its own individualized motives which are an outgrowth of the peculiar learning situations to which he has been subjected throughout his life. Even if two persons could be exposed to the same experiences, they would still develop different personalities, because, as Allport learned from Stern, it is the convergence of the experience and the biological structure of the organism which produce individualized traits.

For Allport the most reasonable units for the investigation of personality are traits. A trait is a directive tendency or condition of readiness for response, but not all such tendencies or conditions of readiness are traits. He distinguishes between trait and habit, and trait and attitude. The habit connotes an invariable and inflexible type of response, whereas the trait is more generalized. Attitudes and traits are frequently synonymous, but they are not identical concepts. An attitude has a well-defined object of reference, traits do not. We speak of an attitude *toward* one's mother, the state, or a political party; we speak of a trait *of* radicalism, asceticism, indulgence. A trait must be general, whereas an attitude may be either specific or general. Traits do not have a clear-cut direction; attitudes do. An attitude is either positive or negative and leads to approach or withdrawal, affirmation or negation. Both attitudes and traits are necessary, Allport thinks, in the analysis of behavior.

Henry A. Murray

For Murray behavior was a function of what goes on inside a person interacting with forces impinging upon him from outside. There was nothing new in this dictum. Others had been saying the same thing before. You recall Lewin's formula $B = f (PE)$. But unlike Lewin, Murray took the whole formula seriously. He attempted to conceptualize what goes on inside the person as well as the effective environmental forces which touch upon him.

Now this is an impossible task and Murray knew it. One must follow the course of development and functioning of an individual from life to death, including both physiological and psychological events, if one would fully understand and conceptualize his personality. So what Murray did, as a practical and theoretical compromise, was to study a few people intensively in order to discover the more important kinds of internal directive forces (which he called *needs*), and the more important stimulating conditions (which he called *press*). Study of the interaction of the two, a need-press combination, was labeled by Murray a *thema*. A thema may relate to a single episode in the life of an individual—that is, it may represent an isolated person-environment interaction—or it may relate to a succession of related interactions. The history of a man would involve knowing the route of his life's themas. The important themas in the life of a person provide the best index to his personality.

This is a simplified view of Murray's theory of personality, but nevertheless the heart of the matter. Before we elaborate on these conceptions, let us take a brief look at some of the similarities and differences between Murray's theory and Freud's. Freud provides for Murray's studies the most fruitful hypothetical framework for conceptualizing the personality in development, structure, and functioning. In the main Murray agrees with Freudian theory, although Murray has refined and extended several of Freud's conceptions. The significance of unconscious motivation, the structuration of the personality, and the importance of anxiety and the mechanisms of defense are recognized by both. It is in connection with instincts and the theory of motivation that they differ most markedly. Freud is a reductionist, in the sense that he tries to reduce all motives to libidinal and aggressive impulses. Murray finds scope in man for a variety of needs.

In the conception of personality structure the Freudian Id is the repository of primitive impulses. Completely unsocialized, it is the source of all energy and innate motives. In this Murray agrees with Freud, but he insists that it also includes impulses which are acceptable to the self and important to society. Some of these impulses are spontaneity, empathy, creativity, and all the emotions which make for socialized living.

The ego for Freud was, as we have seen, more or less a pawn. At best it served as an arbiter, inhibitor, and repressor. Although Murray recognizes these functions, he also subsumes under ego many positive organizational and directive forces of personality. The ego perceives and thinks, it plans and arranges, it controls and schedules the expression of needs. It is the central integrator of the personality. The ego may even promote the expression of id impulses in defiance of society's dictates as represented in the superego.

The superego for both Freud and Murray is born of the particular social experiences a person has had in a given culture. It acts as a guide to conduct in line with the prevailing mores of the larger group of which one is a part. The Freudian superego is tyrannical and pretty largely fixed in childhood. Murray recognizes these aspects of superego, but also maintains that it is modified by subsequent experiences in later life. The superego can grow and develop like any other part of the personality throughout life.

We return now to the principal concepts in Murray's proposals for a theory of personality: need, press, and thema.

Concept of Need. Need is a hypothetical concept. It stands for "a force or state of disequilibrium in the brain region which is manifested objectively by a trend of directional behavior and subjectively by a disquieting tension and the experience of desiring, intending, willing, or striving. The chief property of a drive is its power to orient perception, apperception, intellection, and action in such a way as to transform, if possible, a situation that is unsatisfying into one that is satisfying." * Needs may be classified into two categories: viscerogenic and psychogenic. The former are rooted in bodily events, usually recognizable physiological processes; the latter have no such origins—they cannot be localized in the body. The viscerogenic group includes: *Air, Water, Food, Sex, Lactation, Urination, Defecation, Sentience* (to seek and enjoy sensuous stimulation). Five other viscerogenic needs are specified. The first four refer to the organism's needs to protect itself by avoiding objects or conditions which are threatening, noxious, harmful, including extremes of temperature variation: *Noxavoidance, Harmavoidance, Heatavoidance, Coldavoidance.* The fifth, *Passivity,* gives recognition to the fact that people require relaxation, rest, and sleep.

Murray (1938) distinguished and defined over thirty psychogenic needs which were recurrent in his subjects. Many of these needs have been recognized by other students of personality as more or less enduring motivational units in the lives of a segment of the American culture. Many of the terms which Murray chose to designate the motivational units have been adopted by other psychologists and have wide currency in present-day psychological writings.

The principle psychogenic needs defined by Murray are: *Dominance* (control over others), *Deference* (admiration and support of and conformance to the actions of another), *Autonomy* (freedom from restraint, independence), *Aggression* (opposition, injury, punishment of another), *Abasement* (surrender, self-belittlement or injury, passive acceptance of aggression from others), *Achievement* (mastery and accomplishment, forceful exercise of abilities), *Exhibition* (public exposition of one's self), *Play* (amusement without further purpose), *Affiliation* (friendly, reciprocal relationship with another), *Rejection* (separation from and exclusion of others), *Succorance* (gratification of one's needs through the actions of another), *Nurturance* (gratification of the needs of another through one's own efforts), *Infavoidance* (withdrawal from or refusal to act in embarrassing situations), *Defendance* (protection of the self from criticism or assault of others), *Counteraction* (striving for mastery in the face of failure,

* Taken from a lecture by Professor Murray given in a course on Dynamic Psychology, Harvard University, Fall, 1942.

defeat, or dishonor), *Understanding* (attempts to comprehend the relations between ideas, variables, and the events of experience).

Characteristics of Needs. Murray discusses many characteristics of needs, of which we will mention only a few. Needs vary from individual to individual in frequency, intensity, and duration of activity. In fact, a need does not become a dominant element of the personality in the sense of directing a large part of the person's behavior unless it has somehow been obstructed in its path to satisfaction. In our culture, for example, most of the viscerogenic needs, with the exception of Sex, are regularly gratified and hence do not become strong driving forces. In the case of the psychogenic needs, once they have been established through social intercourse, they may, when frustrated, dominate the whole activity of the person for a short or long period of time. When a number of needs are fixated on a particular person, as in the case of lovers or husband and wife, frustration of them by rejection or separation sometimes leads to violent behavior on the part of the rejected one in an attempt to restore the former state.

A need may be either overt or covert. An overt, or manifest, need is one of which the person is aware and which finds more or less regular behavioral expression. Covert, or latent, needs, on the other hand, are needs of which the person is unaware. They may or may not find regular behavioral expression; but if they do the person does not know that they are being expressed. Covert needs retain their dynamic qualities. They may be objectified in play or other symbolic ways; they may be expressed through creative activity; or they may be revealed in fantasy, dreams, free associations, or the parapraxes.

Periodicity of Needs. Viscerogenic needs, Murray found, were characterized by rather regular rhythms of activity and rest. He found some evidence of periodicity among psychogenic needs, especially in the alternations of contrasting needs: sociability and solitude, talking and listening, leading and following, helping and being helped, giving and receiving, work and play. There are wide individual variations in these alternating expressions, but under certain stable conditions—where a person has developed routine habits in relation to specific persons and objects—needs may be objectified in a highly predictable, alternating fashion.

A single need cycle may be divided into: (1) a *refractory* period when it cannot be aroused; (2) an *inducible* period when it is normally inactive but subject to arousal by certain appropriate stimuli; and (3) an *active* period during which behavior is being determined by the need—the person is actively seeking expression of the need, whether he is aware of it or not. When a need is aroused, it tends to perseverate, in the sense of driving the individual, until it is satisfied. If satisfaction is only partial, perseveration continues; during this time the need has a low threshold of stimulation. It is during this time that an ordinarily inappropriate object or person may serve as a substitute for the expression of the need in the sense in which Freud used the term *substitution*. For example, one may be very friendly with the first person who comes along if one's need, *Affiliation*, for a particular person has been frustrated.

Interrelation of Needs. When a single behavioral pattern serves two or more needs Murray speaks of a fusion of needs. For example, a person may satisfy his needs for understanding and achievement at the same time through studying. If one need is activated in the service of another need, Murray says the former is subsidiary, the latter *determinant*. In the illustration of a person studying, it sometimes happens that the need, *Achievement,* is the determining need and the need, *Understanding*, subsidiary. In this case the goal lies primarily outside the knowledge being acquired in some anticipated reward; nevertheless the need, *Understanding*, operates to some extent in its own right independently. Needs may come into *conflict* with one another. When this happens, the individual is thrown into a temporary or prolonged dilemma which causes considerable misery. Murray believes that most neurotic illness may be attributed to such inner conflicts. Because one or both needs may be covert, it is very difficult for the person to take action necessary to remove the conflict.

Concept of Press. The other side of the coin of need is press. Need represents the force or directional tendency within the person; press, or stimulus, represents the directional tendency in an object (including another person) or situation. A press has both a qualitative and a quantitative aspect. The former is the *kind* of effect it has or might have on the person; the latter is its *power* for harming or benefiting the person. The individual perceives what effect another person or object might have upon him and usually adapts accordingly. Ordinarily it is not the stimulating situations themselves which affect us directly; rather it is our interpretation of them to which we respond. It is the signs and cues emanating from the situation which touch off recollections of previous similar situations which cause us to *behave* in a certain way. Usually this process goes on quite unconsciously. Murray refers to the process as *pressive apperception*. We shall see later that this plays a large part in determining the immediate behavior space which is directly responsible for initiating behavior.

The environment of a person, a social group, or an institution can be analyzed from the point of view of the press it has on a given individual. Obviously it has to be from the point of view of a specific individual, since press is only partly a matter of the potentialities of the environment; the other attributes derive from the person himself. These two aspects of press have been distinguished by Murray, who calls them alpha and beta press. The alpha press represents that which exists in the object as far as scientific inquiry can determine. The beta press is the person's own interpretation of what he perceives. Usually the two are close together, but occasionally not; when the divergence is great, we speak of delusion. If, for example, you overhear your name being mentioned by friends and assume they are plotting against you, the chances are that assumption would be delusory thinking.

Concept of Thema. Thema represents the integration of a need and press at its simplest level. It is, as Murray says, "a dynamical structure of an event." It combines the stimulus and the need of the person in explaining the behavioral outcome. When a person with an active need, *Nurturance,* confronts another with an active need, *Succorance,* it is not difficult to predict the outcome. We shall see just such a situation in the next chapter, when Carol and Peter come together under certain conditions. Of course it is not generally this simple. The complexity of need operating in both parties requires a multi-variate approach. Nevertheless, if we can know some of the major themas operating in the life of an individual, we are in a much better position to predict his behavior on a given occasion.

In the conception of thema Murray sets forth his conviction that personality is derived from and can best be explored through the interpersonal relations as found in the dyadic, or two-person, unit. To understand behavior it does not suffice to explain what is going on inside the person alone, nor what is taking place in his environment. Both must be taken into account. Two people who are interacting, and who are as fully understood as possible by the scientist, provide the best opportunity to study the influence of one on the other in the formulation of a theory of action. In this we agree wholly with Murray. This principle has in fact guided the case studies which will be presented later in this book.

Contributions from Learning Theory

A study of the learning process, recognized as critical in any full-blown theory of personality development, has occupied the attention of many outstanding psychologists. To mention but a few: William James, Edward L. Thorndike, Ivan Pavlov, John B. Watson, Edwin R. Guthrie, Clark L. Hull. The theories of some of these men, and others as well, have been set forth in considerable detail by Hilgard (1948), and reviewed, in part, in more compact form by Lambert (1954) and Hall and Lindzey (1957). Our purpose would not be served by another complete review of learning theory. Rather, as with field theory and dynamic psychology, a selection of those principles which are especially pertinent to an understanding of the interaction of personalities will have to suffice.

Repetition and Reward

For many years the role of repetition played a prominent part in learning theory. William James (1890) made it the most important and almost the only factor. His well-known theory of habit included learning through repetition. His was a brain-path theory of learning, likened to water cutting a channel. The structure of the brain was plastic; that is, it was weak enough to yield to an influence, but not weak enough to yield all at once. Therefore repetition was necessary, and frequency became for him the *sine qua non* of learning.

It is only natural, since man's thoughts are influenced by his teachers, that Thorndike should have accepted the importance of repetition when he came to formulate his now famous "laws" of learning. He performed some of his first experiments in learning in the basement of the James home, using some of James's old books with which to build mazes. But Thorndike did not stop with the concept of repetition; he also took into account the importance of reward and punishment. The latter he called the "law of effect." It is divided into two parts: the principle of reward and the principle of punishment. The principle of reward states that, other things being equal, the individual tends to repeat and learn quickly those responses which are accompanied or followed by a satisfying state of affairs. The principle of punishment, which is its counterpart, states that, other things being equal, the individual tends *not* to repeat or learn quickly those reactions which are accompanied or followed by an annoying state of affairs.

The "laws of repetition" were likewise formulated in two parts: use and disuse. The principle of use stated that the strength of a modifiable connection between a situation and a response is *increased* upon exercise, other things being equal. And its converse, the principle of disuse, stated that the strength of a modifiable connection between a situation and a response is *decreased* when not exercised, other things being equal. This "connection" theory of learning followed closely James's brain-path theory.

These theories have been scrutinized and subjected to test and retest for a half-century. The evidence is impressive that only the principle of reward can be experimentally supported. Thorndike (1931, p. 14) himself has denied, on the basis of his experiments, that repetition *per se* is effective in modifying behavior. "If a certain state of affairs acts upon a man 10,000 times, he will, so far as any intrinsic action of the 10,000 repetitions is concerned, respond in the same way to the last thousand as to the first. The repetition of a situation may change a man as little as the repetition of a message over a wire may change the wire. In and of itself, it may teach him as little as the message teaches the switchboard. In particular, the more frequent connections are not selected by their greater frequency." One could hardly make a more conclusive statement than that; yet, as Mowrer (1947) has pointed out, in his later writing Thorndike (1943) tended to revive his earlier faith in the principle of repetition.

It is not necessary here to marshal the evidence which has undermined belief in the principle of repetition. Suffice it to point out that the work of Pavlov and his followers on experimental extinction would seem to provide objective refutation of the principle of use. They have shown how a response which is established and then unrewarded, on repeated elicitations becomes progressively weaker rather than stronger. Likewise experiments on retroactive inhibition have shown that it is not mere disuse, but rather additional learning, that is chiefly responsible for forgetting. And even when "forgotten," if the proper cue is given, an item may be recalled. Free association, properly employed, may "uncover" such memories. Also it is a common experience for one who has "forgotten" an experience of early childhood to recall it vividly upon returning, after many years, to the scene of his boyhood days.

In everyday life one may observe how punishment is employed to stop undesirable behavior, or to "break" a habit. A child is spanked for some action, and he discontinues it. At first glance punishment would seem to be the effective agent in extinguishing the habit. If we look a little deeper into the matter, something like this seems to be the case: The painful stimulus serves to interrupt the action, but unless some alternative method of satisfying the drive force is introduced, or unless some stronger drive is elicited, the original behavior will persist after a short interval of time. The child who is spanked for eating with his fingers is rewarded for picking up his fork, and thus a new behavior pattern is reinforced.

It is interesting to note that men who are punished for breaking laws, by and large do not give up the behavior patterns which led them to be punished in the first instance. This is a very complicated problem, but one factor which stands out is that the criminals are not generally rewarded for adopting new modes of behavior. Instead, society brands them as ex-convicts after they have been punished, and continues to hold out little reward to them. So we may conclude that the principle of punishment, whereas it is descriptively valid, is not enough to explain behavioral changes, or learning. The evidence favors the conclusion that learning requires reward.

Reinforcement

The law of reward, then, seems to be the only one of Thorndike's original "laws" which has been shown to be valid. Trial-and-error learning, in which the law of reward operates, is the simplest kind of learning. A hungry child looking for the place where his mother has hidden the cookies is an illustration of this kind of learning. The formula for trial-and-error learning has been written in several ways. Shaffer (1936) says there are four factors: (1) *motive*, some discomfort, drive, intense stimulation; (2) *thwarting*, something which prevents easy reduction of the motive; (3) *varied response* (this is where the trial and error comes in); (4) *solution*—if learning occurs, one of the varied responses must be successful. Success is thought of here as reduction of the motivation.

Miller and Dollard (1941) likewise have four factors, but they drop thwarting and introduce one new factor necessary to learning. Their four are drive, cue, response, and reward. The drive is still the motivating factor which causes response, and reward is the reinforcing agent. The cue determines "when a person will respond, where he will respond, and which response he will make."

Mowrer and Kluckhohn (1944, p. 79) do not find the barrier of Shaffer or the cue of Miller and Dollard necessary in their formula for the most elementary type of learning. They write it thus: Motivation → variable behavior → reduction of motivation. Motivation is defined as "any state of affairs which puts an organism into action"; and variable behavior they believe "may take the form of gross overt activity, or sensory exploration (looking about, listening, smelling, etc.) or symbolic exploration (thinking, fantasying, dreaming, talking, calculating, etc.)." Reward is whatever reduces the motive. In the process something happens, presumably within the nervous system, which subsequently modifies behavior. That which causes the strengthening of the connection between motive and successful response has been called *reinforcement*. Mowrer and Kluckhohn (1944, p. 80) say: "It is now well established that of those variable responses . . . which precede a rewarding state of affairs, that response which occurs closest in time to the reward is most strongly reinforced." Not only the successful response becomes connected with the drive, but also the responses which preceded the successful one; those most temporally distant become progressively less reinforced. This is called the *gradient of reinforcement*.

Hilgard and Marquis (1940) list several kinds of gradients of reinforcement. The importance of the concept for a theory of interaction is readily apparent. In those societies where reward follows immediately upon the desired responses, you would expect that socially approved behavior would be much more readily learned than in societies where this is not the case.

A subsidiary principle of reinforcement important in interpersonal relations is that of *mutual reinforcement*. Davis and Dollard (1940) have shown how a lower-class Negro receives little inducement from his middle-class teachers and thus persists in his lower-class-rewarded ways. The middle-class pupil, on the other hand, makes the correct responses and thus rewards (pleases) the teacher for her efforts, who in turn praises (and gives good marks to) the pupil, thus reinforcing his behavior.

Conditioning

The physiologist, Pavlov, while studying digestion in dogs, accidentally discovered that salivation sometimes occurred in the absence of food in the mouth. From his experiments came the first understanding of the process of conditioning. Pavlov reported his findings in a book titled *Conditioned Reflexes*. What he had discovered was that a previously inappropriate stimulus, called the conditioned stimulus, could after repeated pairing with a food stimulus produce the response, salivation, which normally only food was able to produce. To Pavlov we are indebted for a number of important principles of learning, in addition to conditioning, that shed light on interaction theory. We shall mention three: *generalization, discrimination,* and *extinction.*

Generalization

In experimenting with his discovery of the conditioned stimulus, Pavlov found that if one stimulus is like another, except for a difference in a single dimension, either may be used, once one of them has been conditioned, to elicit the response. This process is called stimulus generalization. An example from everyday life: A child who has learned to call a particular man "daddy" may call all men daddy—to the sometimes considerable embarrassment of his mother—until he has learned to discriminate among men.

In addition to stimulus generalization there is its counterpart, response generalization. Responses which are similar may be evoked by the same stimulus. As an illustration, Bekhterev found that a dog who had been conditioned to lift one foot would lift another when the original one was secured. These two kinds of generalization may be graphically represented as follows:

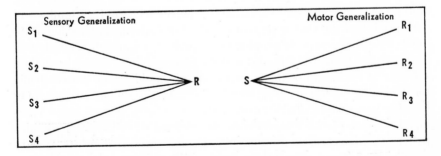

Discrimination and Extinction

Discrimination means cutting out some of the stimuli which will lead to the correct response, or cutting out some of the responses which will follow the given stimulus. It can be brought about by not rewarding (extinguishing) the responses which one does not desire the subject to make. For example, at a certain stage in his early development, a child who calls all men "daddy" learns to discriminate between men by the different kinds of responses he receives from them. In a society where all men acted the same way toward all small children, the child would continue to confuse "daddy" with other men for a longer period of time. Cutting out the response "daddy" to all men and reserving it for one man is what is called the process of extinction.

Skinner (1953, p. 70) has written about the phenomenon of extinction thus:

Behavior during extinction is the result of the conditioning which has preceded it, and in this sense the extinction curve gives an additional measure of the effect of reinforcement. If only a few responses have been reinforced, extinction occurs quickly. A long history of reinforcement is followed by protracted responding. The resistance to extinction cannot be predicted from the probability of response observed at any given moment. We must know the history of reinforcement . . . There is no simple relation between the number of responses reinforced and the number which appear in extinction . . . the resistance to extinction generated by *intermittent* reinforcement may be much greater than if the same number of reinforcements are given for consecutive responses. Thus if we only occasionally reinforce a child for good behavior, the behavior survives after we discontinue reinforcement much longer than if we had reinforced every instance up to the same total number of reinforcements.

Contiguity

Thus far we have been discussing learning from the point of view of reinforcement theory. But not all learning theorists subscribe to this concept as the underlying, or certainly the sole, principle of learning. Probably the outstanding opponent to reinforcement theory is Guthrie. For Guthrie the only necessary condition for the connection of a stimulus and response is that they occur simultaneously. For example, in teaching arithmetic the teacher says, "Two plus two equals ——," and the child is told to say "four." Since the stimulus and the response have ocurred together, subsequent elicitation of the response "four" should follow automatically the stimulus, "two plus two equals ——." Guthrie's views concerning learning have been called contiguity theory, a form of associative learning. The principle of association he has defined as follows: "A stimulus pattern that is acting at the time of a response will, if it recurs, tend to produce that response" (Guthrie, 1952, p. 23).

We do not need to enter the controversy as to whether contiguity or reinforcement is the most basic, or indeed the only, principle of learning. Others have discussed it at considerable length (Mowrer, 1950; Skinner,

1938; Schlosberg, 1937). It seems that at present both concepts are necessary to explain the phenomena encountered in the study of personality development and interaction. The need for reinforcement theory is patent. But there appear to be experiences in life which occur only once. The response to some of these experiences is never again reinforced, as far as we can tell, and yet it may continue in the repertory of the individual's responses undiminished in strength for years. This is true of what is sometimes called the neurotic reflex. An example would be a tic developed after an especially horrifying experience. Although the experience itself may never be repeated, the involuntary tic persists.

Concepts of Personality Development, Structure and Functioning—a Brief Review

This chapter has set forth the major concepts to be employed throughout the book. Some of them play a larger part than others, and some will be elaborated at greater length as we go along; but all appear necessary at present to our understanding of interacting personalities. Certain concepts are used in common by all of the theorists discussed. There are some mild, some violent disagreements. Each has something new to offer.

At this point let us pick out salient concepts from various sources. In so doing we shall accomplish two things: We shall reveal our own theoretical preference concerning a framework within which to think about personality, and we shall forecast the remainder of the book. Three questions underlie our brief summary and stage-setting effort: How does the personality develop? How does it change? What gives it stability?

Development of Personality

When a baby is born, he has a very rudimentary personality consisting of an energy system and viscerogenic needs which have no specific objective referents. He has no motives, no ego, no conception of self, no consciousness. His personality consists chiefly of his characteristic way of expressing himself; and indeed this is unique from the moment of birth and even before birth. Some babies cry lustily, while others rarely whimper; some thrash about actively, while others lie supinely unless vigorously stimulated; some suck on anything which comes in contact with the lips, while others have to be coaxed and prodded to take enough milk to stay alive.

So too do the mothers of these babies differ markedly. Some give their whole and complete attention to the care and nurture of the baby; they cuddle them, suckle them joyously, examine their bodies, brush their hair gently, and even kiss their toes. Other mothers attend their babies only as duty demands, carrying out scrupulously, albeit perfunctorily and sometimes with distaste, the necessary chores in connection with keeping the baby fed, clean, warm, and dry. Still other mothers are so preoccupied with their own concerns that the baby scarcely exists for them; in extreme cases mother and baby have to be separated for the protection of both.

Thus the stage is set for a long series of interactions between two people, the outcome of which has far-reaching, lasting consequences—certainly for the baby, most likely for the mother. Here is the beginning of the learning which will influence the whole future course of the infant's development. How he is handled and loved, how he is nursed and weaned, how and in what manner his mother reacts to his bodily evacuations and the training of sphincter controls, how he is encouraged to stand and walk—these and many other interactions are the seed-beds from which his personality grows.

Later, as the young child moves from mother to father to other persons young and old, as he moves from a more to a less protective social situation, as he is challenged rather than accepted, other interactions call forth new responses. New situations demand modification of older patterns of response and development of new ones.

As we trace the course of development in any life, there are three aspects of the process of which we should be aware: (1) the interaction of the organism with his environment; this means paying equal attention to both persons in a dyadic relationship; (2) critical learning situations such as those which Freud has emphasized, plus others like learning to walk, leaving home for the first time, going to school, making friends, etc.; (3) the manner in which learning takes place, whether as a result of deliberate efforts at reinforcement by someone else, whether by the accidental congruence of events, or by some other process which produces restructuring, and new orientation.

Personality Structure

In thinking about the stability of personality it is convenient to talk in terms of structural components. To do so is all right if we remember that they are fictional. We can speak of an Id, Ego, Superego, of needs, of anxiety, or of mechanisms, if we remember that we are not quite sure what we have named; but, more important, if we remember that we *are* quite sure these names have no substantive existence, cannot be seen, touched, or weighed. They are hypothetical intervening processes. It is assumed that when a person is confronted with a specific task, or when he encounters a particular event—an invitation to speak in public or an implied insult—his responses to these different circumstances will be partly conditioned by the processes named above, which have been learned by him on previous occasions. Three implications arise from this statement: The names given to so-called personality structure stand for

processes, the processes are relatively enduring, and they have an ontogenetic history.

1. *Personality structure as process.* We must rid ourselves of the habit
and natural tendency to think concretely when it comes to conceptualizing personality structure. There are no actual substances which stand
apart inside the body to be labeled Id, Ego, etc. What there are, are dispositions, motives, tendencies to act in certain ways under certain conditions, and expectations concerning the world around us.

2. *Stability.* The experiences a person has are recorded in nervous tissue and remain relatively unchanged until new experiences modify or extinguish the original recording. Some experiences, especially those with
a strong emotional accompaniment, are more resistant to change than
others. We do not understand entirely why this is so. Ordinarily the more a
response tendency is reinforced, the more stable and predictable it is.
Therefore, homogeneity of experience tends to produce greater stability
in personality.

3. *Ontogenetic determination.* The processes of personality are engendered during the life history of the individual. In order to understand
the origins of these processes one must know this history. Structure can
be assessed at any time during the life of a person and prediction of behavior based on the assessment without knowledge of history. For knowledge of how the structure was derived, however, it is essential that the
history of interpersonal processes be known. There is no implication intended that a person is strictly a product of his own life span. Such a
conception would not be faithful to the facts. It takes generations of experiences handed down from grandparents to parents to sons to create
the conditions of interaction between any parent and child. It is literally
true that you have been influenced in your development by experiences
that occurred to your ancestors long before you were born. But the effects
of these experiences were transmitted to you by concrete acts or omissions
on the part of those who attended you most intimately during the ordinary and critical times of your own life. So when we say that personality
is ontogenetically determined, we mean simply that the processes operative in you today were fashioned by specific, concrete events in your life.
That the quality and character of these events were partly influenced by
historical events is recognized.

The Contemporary Situation

No one lives in the past. Whatever you do is in response to something
in the present scene. To be sure, the present scene evokes processes which
have grown out of previous experiences. But it is not enough to study the
past alone in order to understand behavior. The contemporary situation
too contributes to action in a determinative way. Objects and persons
have a structure and force of their own, and no matter how we may per-

ceive them, they resist being used in certain ways. You may perceive a stone as a piece of cheese, but the stone is not turned to cheese thereby. You may perceive a sadistic murderer as a kindly, loving old man; but if you provoke him in a certain way, he will still beat you to death. The only way to modify or extinguish old patterns of response is through experience in the present.

We agree with Allport that motives may be the result of contemporary interests and values. This does not mean that they are unrelated to the whole motivational system of the individual or that they have no historical antecedents. It does mean, however, that we do not *have* to look to infantile strivings and their tortuous course as the source of all adult motives. Nor does it mean that all motives derive from conscious interests and values. Not infrequently interests and values spring from unconscious motives and serve as a convenient shield, or rationalization, for them. We recognize both types of motivating forces.

Suggested Readings

Allport, G. W. *Personality: A Psychological Interpretation.* New York: Holt, 1937.
A comprehensive review of definitions, methods and problems in personality. Development of a trait theory and the concept of functional autonomy of motives.

Angyal, A. *Foundations for a Science of Personality.* New York: The Commonwealth Fund, 1941.
A new look at field theory with emphasis on increasing autonomy and homonomy as general growth trends throughout life.

Freud, S. *The Interpretation of Dreams.* London: The Hogarth Press, 1953.

—— *New Introductory Lectures on Psychoanalysis.* New York: Norton, 1933.

—— *An Outline of Psychoanalysis.* New York: Norton, 1949.
The first of these books by Freud, *The Interpretation of Dreams,* published in 1900, is probably the most original and creative of all his writings. In a sense it foreshadowed all that was to come from his mind and pen.
The second and third titles by Freud provide historical perspective to his thinking and give his more or less final views on many important problems, notably the concepts of ego, superego, anxiety, and psychosexual development.

Hall, C. S. and Lindzey, G. *Theories of Personality.* New York: Wiley, 1957.
An excellent review of the more important theories of personality in contemporary psychology.

Hilgard, E. R. *Theories of Learning.* New York: Appleton-Century-Crofts, 1948.
A survey of the different theoretical positions taken by psychologists who study the problems of learning.

Lewin, K. *Dynamic Theory of Personality.* New York: McGraw-Hill, 1935.

—— "Behavior and Development as a Function of the Total Situation."
Chapter 16 in Carmichael, L. (Ed.), *Manual of Child Psychology.* New York: Wiley, 1946.

These two writings represent Lewin's thinking about the major forces operating in the development and functioning of personality.

Murray, H. A. *Explorations in Personality*. New York and London: Oxford University Press, 1938.
A landmark in dynamic psychology. Penetrating inquiry into the lives of fifty college men and a bold attempt to make sense out of the findings. Warning: Don't let the strange language frighten you.

Skinner, B. F. *Science and Human Behavior*. New York: Macmillan, 1953.
Behavior theory is explained and applied to a variety of human problems.

4

A CASE STUDY OF MOTHER–BABY INTERACTION

In this chapter you will see the beginnings of personality. You will see some of the social forces which help to create from the raw materials of a nonconscious human organism a unique, partially self-directed person. Some of the principles and concepts discussed in the preceding chapters will be concretely exemplified.

In order to get the most out of this case study, it is well to keep in mind certain objectives. On this page below these objectives will be put in the form of questions. As you read the case, make notes which will help you to answer these questions. When you have finished reading the case write a paragraph or two in answer to each of the questions. Consult your notes and the case material as much as you need in order to give a succinct, documented, and well-considered reply. Then after you have written your answers, read Carol's comments (pages 119–123) and the author's summary and interpretation (pages 123–140). Look for agreements and disagreements between your answers and the author's. In class discussion you will have an opportunity to compare your interpretations with those of your classmates. Remember that interpretations of an episode in the life of an individual may vary considerably. Concensus does not necessarily make for correctness, so do not give up your interpretation too readily. Rather look for supporting evidence for your hypotheses. Do not hesitate to speculate and make guesses. Only remember that your guesses must be tied to data and rational theory. You may not find either adequate data or compelling theory sufficient to unravel the complex human personalities presented in this book. Well enough, but do not cease to inquire in a hard-headed fashion until you have gone as far as you can go toward finding the answer.

Questions

1. How do you account for Carol's easy-going, serene manner?
2. What are the chief sources of conflict in Carol's life?

3. By what mechanisms of defense did Carol attempt to resolve the conflicts?

4. Why could Carol not admit freely to herself that she wanted a boy baby?

5. What methods were used by Carol's and Bill's parents to control their children?

6. Carol looked forward to her own children having some of the experiences which she had had as a child. How do you explain this desire? Is it unusual or typical?

7. Can you pick out several instances to show how mother-child interactions had consequences for both participants? Note: Keep in mind that mothers interact with their children in two ways: (1) conscious acts on the mother's part intended to bring about certain responses on the part of the child, (2) acts on the part of mother which may be conscious or unconscious but which are not intended by her to produce the responses obtained.

8. What hypotheses have you concerning Peter's illnesses?

9. What are the historical antecedents to Carol's reactions when she was in the presence of her parents-in-law?

10. What are your predictions about the content of Carol's thought as evidenced by the number of times she herself, Bill, and the baby enter her free associations? What are your reasons for your predictions? Note: Divide the time into eleven periods: three before the baby was born, eight after. Indicate how you think the content of Carol's free associations will vary at each monthly interval.

11. What predictions would you make concerning Peter's activity rate, intelligence, and general psychological health at the age of four-and-a-half years?

12. What are your predictions for the future concerning: Carol's and Bill's marriage? Number of children they will have? Relationships with both sets of in-laws? Bill's success in business?

Introduction

In the spring of 1948 Carol Chisholm was twenty, a junior in college, married and pregnant. Bill, her husband, was twenty-one and also had one more year before he would finish his college course in mechanical engineering. Carol's baby was due to be born around the end of May, and she was already worried about how she would be able to take care of the baby, manage a house, and carry a full load of school work during the coming year. She wanted to graduate with her class, not because of any intrinsic interest in education—she was a major in child development—but out of a sense of duty to her parents. She came to the author and proposed that she take a special reading course the following year so that she could be at home more frequently. Various possibilities which would at once permit her to spend more hours with her baby and accomplish an educational objective were discussed. Because of the author's interest in studying the beginnings of a mother-child relationship he proposed that the object of her study be herself and her child when it was born, and that reading be of secondary concern.

After several conferences Carol and the author agreed upon the following aims for the study:

1. To determine the major mental preoccupations of the mother before the birth of the baby and during the subsequent year.

2. To trace the course of growth and development of the child for one year.

3. To observe the developing patterns of mother-child interaction for one year.

Methods

The problem of what methods to use in the study of personality development has been discussed in an earlier chapter. It remains here only to state the explicit procedures used in this inquiry.

Three methods were employed: A baby biography, or diary, kept by the mother (occasionally by the father); observations of mother, baby, and father; recorded free associations of the mother.

Baby Biography. Carol kept daily records of the baby's and her own behavior, with a liberal sprinkling of information about her husband. Any special events occurring in the family were always recorded. Mimeographed forms were supplied the mother, one for each day, with spaces for recording behavior concerning the following: sleep, feeding, elimination, bath and dressing, motor development, social-emotional development, mother's feelings, thoughts and behavior, special events. In addition there was a space for recording observations of behavior of all members of the family which did not fit into any of the above categories. A guide consisting of the kinds of behavior to observe in connection with each category was supplied Carol.

Observations. Most of the observations of the family were made by the author. These consisted of regular talks with Carol, plus visits to the hospital during her confinement, and periodic visits in the home. In addition, the aid of two assistants in making observations was secured; one was a nurse in the hospital, the other a colleague. The nurse supplied information about the mother and baby from the moment of birth until they left the hospital. One week after Carol and her baby were discharged, a special observer went into the home for four days. During this time she made twelve systematic observations of baby, mother, and father.

Free Association. Eighteen hours of free association by Carol were electrically recorded. Eight of these hours were in weekly sessions preceding the birth of the child. The other ten followed the birth at one-month intervals. Carol lay on a couch in the author's office while he sat behind her and out of sight. A microphone was placed above and to the right of her head in full view. Before the first recorded session the technique of free association was discussed and agreed upon.

Carol proved to be a remarkably good subject. She learned the technique quickly and easily; she was cooperative throughout. She talked about most things without inhibition. She hesitated to talk about certain little privacies between herself and husband. For example, it bothered her when she spoke of Bill putting his hand on her abdomen to feel the baby kick. After one session she said that she had thought of but suppressed the private name which she and Bill had for the baby. The name was "Buffle." It had been derived in this way: when she first felt movement of the foetus, it felt like a bubble breaking, but it was muffled.

Part One: Before the Baby

Carol's Family

Carol grew up in Regent Heights, a suburb of a large middle-western city. Bill's family also lived there, but there was no commerce between the two. "My family lives in a very different part of Regent Heights than Bill's family does," Carol said, "but ah . . .* we both went to Regent High. That's where I met Bill."

Carol's father was a successful, well-liked high school teacher.

> We called my father last night because it was his birthday and he was telling us that somehow he'd let out the week before that he was going to be 49 years old on Monday and he, and the morning class, the first morning class, the kids brought him a cake. He said it was half as big as his desk and he cut it into thirty little pieces or so and everyone sat around eating cake and licking his fingers most of the class period. And then during his lunch hour he said another class was outside singing happy birthday till he had to go tell them to pipe down 'cause class was going on. They were not to be outdone, though, and the classes he had in the afternoon had collected all the pieces of spice cake from the cafeteria and done 'em up in aluminum foil and presented them to him with a fork sticking out. And of course he was tickled by it, but he's the last person in the world that would have let it out intentionally . . . He feels very strongly about the . . . about children not giving presents to teachers.

Ralph Johnson never made much money, but he was a contented man. He enjoyed teaching and liked young people. In the spring and summer

---
* Dots . . . indicate a pause in the flow of speech during free association; number of dots indicates approximate length of pause.

his leisure hours were devoted to gardening. When he could not be out-side, he was puttering in his woodwork shop. He had bought a small place in Canada on a lake, and each summer after school was out, he and his wife and the children went up for two months. He was an even-tempered man, not given to excesses. Carol remembers few times when he lost his temper. He was very fond of his family, and they in turn thought he was wonderful.

My whole family is going to descend on us after the baby comes. We need their help so badly and Daddy's going to help Bill build on the porch. It's just something I wouldn't be able to do even if I had all my strength . . . so it's going to be quite a madhouse. My brother and sister, and my mother and father coming the twelfth of June, or so . . . stay for three or four days in our unfinished house . . . and then they're all going up to Canada.

Carol's mother also worked. She was a special teacher in the elemen-tary schools, doing remedial work in reading and arithmetic. Carol re-members many nights when she had to get dinner for the family because her mother was late getting home. Almost always she had to start the dinner in anticipation of her mother's six o'clock arrival. This chore was accepted by Carol as a natural thing to do since she was the oldest child; she never felt any particular resentment about it.

Mrs. Johnson was a very ambitious woman, ambitious for herself and her family. Although she was very able in her professional work, she never achieved the status which she craved, and consequently looked upon herself as a failure. She wanted for her children, therefore, some-times more than they were able to deliver. She tended to direct their ac-tivities, and even their desires, in such a subtle way that there was seldom cause for open rebellion on their part. They were all genuinely fond of her. If she tended to nag them, she was forgiven because she was almost always tired. As soon as she got home from school, there began a round of household chores. Not only was the final preparation of the dinner awaiting her, but the dishes were to be done, the house cleaned, the chil-dren's studies to be supervised, and their musical education encouraged. Not a few times Mrs. Johnson felt like holding her head in her hands and stopping up her ears to avoid the din and confusion.

Carol had always been very fond of her mother. After the baby was born, her family came for a visit. Later, Carol said:

The only person I felt comfortable leaving the baby with was Bill . . . or with my mother when she was here . . . and uh, . . . by the end of July or when we go up to the lake it'll be really a vacation because mother will love hav-ing the baby to take care of and I'll be able to leave him without worrying about him . . . and do some things on our own . . . There'll be a lot of people up there probably on that weekend that we haven't seen in an awful long time . . . a lot of my old friends that I grew up with.

Carol recognized clearly that her mother controlled the affairs of the family.

I think parents can make up their minds about things they'll not even admit to themselves . . . because if you were to suggest to my folks that they had definitely . . . were forcing either Sue or Jim into a college that perhaps wouldn't be best for them, they honestly couldn't see that they were doing anything like that. And yet some of the unspoken assumptions that Jim will go to Yale and Sue to Vassar. And they sort of think of going there themselves because they want to . . . Of course my folks let me make my decision. I was going to Vassar, too . . . but that's because I sort of stood up and said I'm going to Cornell. Jim'll do that, too. But Sue won't, I'm afraid. Besides she thinks it's what she wants to do herself, anyway. I don't think Vassar's the place it used to be—Mother went to Vassar, and she's convinced it's the best school in the world . . . And I think it's changed from what I've heard. It's going to be an awful hard situation for Sue to go into . . . because she's a little bit quiet . . . And she doesn't have . . . she won't have the clothes and the social position and everything else that seems to be . . . well, it seems like most of the girls there come from wealthy homes, and if she's working on scholarship, she's going to have an awful rough time of it . . . Even in high school she's in a rather awkward situation socially. She has such a good time in the summer, sort of a belle of the ball situation, and then she comes back to high school and . . . well, just a few teen-agers have the power over her and the others . . . and they're making Sue's social life rather miserable.

All in all, the Johnsons could be characterized as a happy, successful middle-class, white, Protestant family. There was nothing distinguished about them. Like millions of their fellow countrymen they lived quiet, unheralded lives, experiencing their little triumphs and setbacks, their joys and sorrows, without coming into the focus of public gaze. They owned, except for a small mortgage, their little gaily painted frame house situated on the edge of the finest residential district of their city. They were proud to belong to the Regent Heights district. Carol and her younger sister, Sue, occupied a bedroom together. But it was more than a bedroom. It was a playroom, a study place, a practice room, and a place to gather for bull sessions during high school days.

The Johnsons were liberal in their political and social views. Of course they thought Harry Truman went too far, but the working man had been oppressed too long and needed a break. They had a few Jewish friends and they had, without thinking anything about it, had Negro students in their home. In matters of sex Carol put it this way: "In our family it never occurred to us that uh . . . anyone was overly shy or modest about his body." Questions about sex were dealt with in a straightforward manner as they arose.

The Johnsons had a good time together as a family. Here are some comments which Carol made about one year when, after school, they were packing to go to Canada.

At the last minute there was another suitcase that had to go in the car, too
. . . so we took out all the duffle bags and everything else and proceeded to
re-pack and it took, well mother finished repacking (laughs) the morning we
left . . . and the house was in a complete uproar all that time . . . And
then I was wondering, it seems that if you have two children that are close
together they always have adolescent wranglings, because my brother and
sister, Jim and Sue, can get going on each other, and I think they're just to the
point where they don't want to be told what to do, and yet each feels he can
tell the other what to do . . . and after awhile they can get on your
nerves . . . And I was wondering whether that was just Sue and Jim or
whether all families have the same sort of thing . . . Funny my brother and
I always got along better than Sue and I have . . . We're much more alike
and I think that the four years between my sister and myself is a . . . well,
it's always seemed to me an unfortunately large gap between one child and
the next. Jimmy was enough younger so it didn't seem . . . I don't know, it
just seemed to be less conflict . . . Because Sue and I certainly have fought
in our day . . . I remember my mother saying that when we grew up we
would be good friends.

On another occasion Carol spoke of her summers in Canada.

. . . and my cousin Phyllis has just been, just like a sister to me as far as
closeness, because we grew up together every summer. They have a cottage
right on the, on an island right next door practically, just through the woods
a bit. . . . And Phil and I spent every single summer of our lives up there
until I started working in the summer . . . But, uh, she's married and I
haven't met her husband. I guess they won't be there when we go, they're up
there now . . . and I was wondering whether Petie and our children would
ever know Phil's children, or have any kind of relationship the way Phil and
I did . . . was hoping that . . . we'd have a chance to be up at the lake and
the lake wouldn't be much different . . . not that, well we won't be able to
be up there very much for quite a few years, but after that we might be able
to . . . It's a very unusual place and . . . the people and everything unusual . . . activities, and there's a . . . just a delightful little island . . .
people live on the island and they, it's like a community . . . and there are
square dances on the weekends and sail boat races and the young people just
have the most marvelous time doing all sorts of things. They go off on trips
all day, up the creek where the falls are and the river. Sometimes we came
back all banged up and everything from the rocks . . . our feet were cut and
everything but otherwise all right . . . Dave and I broke our toes in the
rapids about the last time we went up . . . and now he has a law degree this
June from Harvard . . . It's the sort of thing I would like very much for
Petie and . . . our other children to enjoy . . . And the people will probably be the same people, because they're greedy about their land. They . . .
the houses aren't close together . . . it's a wilderness and every now and then
there's a cottage in the woods, on an island or some place. But people don't
want cabins built up all over the place, and they won't sell their land to people, other people . . . Still it's a complete cross-section of different kinds of

people from . . . very wealthy, too . . . not very poor, but . . . I know in our gang we had . . . well, Grace's father's a colonel in the army, my father and Phil's father are school teachers . . . John's father worked in the Quaker Oats factory in Peterville, Lynne's father was the, well, some big shot in the Royal Air Force . . . And Mary's father was a doctor . . . Just, just all complete, different types of people . . . and yet no one ever thought that they were better than anyone else . . .

Bill's Family

We're going to Florida for spring vacation, which is something we were hoping that we would be able to do. The whole thing was resting on the decision of Bill's parents, and they decided that they would like to see us enough so that they could afford to pay our way down to Florida. It's going to be very nice for both of us, because we've been working pretty hard on, not only on school work, but on building our house. We'll have a complete change of scenery and responsibility and everything else and can come back kind of rested.

These were the first words Carol uttered to the author about Bill's family.

Mr. and Mrs. William Standish Chisholm, Sr., spent six or seven months each year in Florida. They went down in the fall almost as soon as the first frost, because of Mrs. Chisholm's health, and they did not come back until the baseball season was well into its second month in the spring.

The Chisholms lived in the old part of Regent Heights in a large stone house which they had built and had lived in for thirty-five years. Bill was the youngest of six children, the only boy, and the recognized favorite of the family. Even the girls doted on him, and did not seem to have been overly jealous.

Mr. Chisholm was a mechanical engineer. For many years he had been head of his own firm, which manufactured small tools and special parts for other concerns. He had many trusted employees who operated the business, but when the old man came around, he was the unquestioned boss. It was understood that Bill would some day take over the business. Although Mr. Chisholm was very proud of Bill, he had difficulty realizing that he was now a man. He still thought of him as, and treated him like, a young boy.

We really get along very well . . . ah . . . with Bill's parents, but . . . they're both of them getting old, his father is as nervous as he can be and, for one thing, well, Bill was driving the car, for instance, and every time we came to a corner, every time Bill went over twenty miles an hour, every time he turned, every time there was a light, or anything like that he got told about it from his father—"You better get over now—you better turn here—you better slow down." But it's just because he's getting old and he's nervous anyway. Bill's much more easy-going than I am, and it's, ah . . . it's aggravating . . . We were glad to leave.

Another time Carol told about Bill's relationship with his father in these words.

Bill is working with another boy on an idea of his that he really is very enthusiastic about. It's for some kind of aluminum building that can be, ah, prefabricated. It can be put up by just ordinary men with ordinary tools. It can be used for all sorts of things, especially in cold climates like Alaska where you can't work outside. And it's fun because it's his own idea and actually something that might be possible . . . something practical and inexpensive and not just theoretical. And he was working on it that last night before we went to Florida. He took it down to Florida and showed his father, and . . . ah . . . his dad kind of sat on a few of Bill's ideas and Bill was a little bit discouraged about it. Then I think we both realized that what his father tends to do is say "No, that's not right" to anything that is ah . . . is not quite what he himself would think of at first. It's going to be something of a problem he and his dad working in the same office . . . I often wish that his parents just had decided absolutely nothing instead of going to such pains to make sure that Bill would be in his father's firm. When two people are as far apart in age and everything as Bill and his dad are, there are . . . they have very little common ground, even if they are both the same kind of engineer . . . and his father is seventy at least, and it's, ah . . . going to be hard for him . . . If it's what he wants to do . . . and sometimes I wonder if he's even positive that's what he wants to do.

Mrs. Chisholm, Sr., was the dominant member of the family. Coming from a very wealthy family, she had an independent income in excess of her husband's, and she never let him forget it. Pieces of furniture, silver, or a painting were referred to by members of the family with the words: "This is something Mother's money bought." But her money was not her real source of power. Whenever she wanted something which she could not seem to get through persuasion, she became ill. Here is one episode which Carol recounted.

I was thinking about going home before November because we promised that we would have Peter baptized when both sets of grandparents could be present and . . . we plan to go home and have it done before Bill's parents go to Florida and uh . . . then Bill's mother had another heart attack. She wanted to have the christening at home and we wanted to go to church, and ah, now she's not going to be able to, and so we're going to have it done at her house. It's just one of those things which you'd rather not, at least I'd rather not . . . but what can you do? I'm sort of disappointed about the whole business.

From the beginning Carol found herself in great conflict over Bill's parents. She wanted to like them for Bill's sake, and she did not want to estrange them because of their money.

When I stand back and look at myself I know that rationally I'm very fond of Bill's parents and I have every reason to be and that they're fond of me . . .

and yet every now and then I get fed up with the whole situation . . . And I don't like to see Bill slip into this business of all the children around mother . . . Sunday night we came in and Bill had to go in and kiss her good night, and I had to, too. It's, uh, just so artificial . . . And yet the whole thing is what Bill's grown up with and everything else and mother has always been the center of the family and I . . . I feel sorry for his father, now and then, because as Bill's mother puts it, Bill's father supplies the bread for the family and she supplies the jam. And uh . . . yet to kiss the jam's much more fun than the bread.

Courtship and Marriage

Carol and Bill both went to Regent Heights High School. He was one year ahead of her. It was then that they met and began to date. For each it was the first serious courtship. After two months they were talking about marriage, even though Carol still had a year and a half to go in high school. Bill was at the Johnsons' house almost every day. The whole Johnson family liked Bill, and for his part he found it a most congenial place to be. He had never known a family like the Johnsons, where each one spoke his mind freely, eliciting nothing more than a sharp verbal counterattack. Carol went to Bill's house rarely. His parents were away in Florida; Bill's older sister was in charge of the house, and Carol did not find her very congenial. It was not until the end of the school year, Bill's senior year, that Carol met Mr. and Mrs. Chisholm. The meeting was not very pleasant. Carol will speak of that in her own words in a moment. Before they met, Carol had already decided that she would not go to Vassar to college as previously planned; she would follow Bill to Cornell. She was in love with him, and she had no intention of giving him up.

. . . Well, we got off to a very bad beginning in my relationship with Bill's parents. And it's . . . ah . . . it's remarkable how, how good it is now. I'm genuinely fond of them, but I do feel they have a great many idiosyncracies. And when . . . my grandmother is younger or at least the same age, I guess, as Bill's father . . . it ah . . . makes it an even more difficult job I think to deal with people that are as set in their ways as Bill's parents are. . . . . I was thinking that you . . . you tend to see your side of the family all in the right light or the best light and see, see the other side perhaps in not such a good light. I really think that we have a much easier, natural relationship with my folks. I mean they let us do whatever we please, and when we visit them it's, ah, we make a genuine effort to do our share of things like dishes and everything else and help with things, so that we don't act like the honored guests in the house, but that ah, it's more or less that we tell, we discuss what we're planning to do and ah, beforehand, so that we make plans to do things together and on our own. But there's not the feeling of having to please them with everything every time we do anything, or not having any time that is really our own, to do what we want to do. . . . And like in Florida there's

an awful lot of things that you could do if ah . . . you had the time and
money and . . . even without too much money, it's, when a place is new . . .
it's . . . there are lots of attractions. . . . . But they made it as, as
you know . . . quite an adjustment . . . for them . . . the idea of Bill's
getting married . . . as soon as he did . . . and ah, to be honest . . . to
honestly say that I am really fond of them . . . I mean the fact that I *can*
be honest and say that after . . . . . . and everything and that I can feel as
at home as Bill does . . . with them . . . or almost, I think almost as much
as he does, is . . . something to be thankful for . . . not something that
. . . something that . . . . I was sure never could happen
. . . . and they were very against me . . . .
in the beginning . . . . . . I mean the idea that Bill would get married so
soon was the biggest thing, but also he had been dating a . . . the daughter
of one of Mrs. Chisholm's very good friends and it was sort of . . . oh, one
of those things that mothers twitter and smile over. But they, ah, thought that
he was not old enough or mature enough to be married. I really don't think
they ever thought of him as being anything more than a thirteen- or fourteen-
year-old, because they've been so out of touch with him for so long . . .
'cause they were in Florida and he was in school, and then summers he worked
on the boats that were there . . . oh, coal boats or something that went up
and down the lakes, so he wasn't home then. And it meant the only time he
actually even lived with his parents was the fall and spring, and, ah . . . it
. . . but they, they were against me too, personally, in lots of ways. They in
the first place, when I first knew Bill his parents were in Florida and his sister
was living with him. He and his sister and a maid were living in the big
house, and his sister is, I guess eight or ten years older than he is, and she
thought that she ought to be able to boss him . . . and he had had enough
sister-bossing all his life to rebel against her right in the beginning, I guess.
And she wrote terrible tales of what I was—how I was corrupting him and everything else down to his parents and ah . . . it was a long time before I
even met them because when they came back Mrs. Chisholm had a heart attack. And she wasn't home and she was sick and everything else and ah . . .
it wasn't until just before Bill went away to Cornell that I even met them.
And ah . . . I don't think I was quite what they had in mind for Bill to be
going steady with . . . and ah . . . then . . . the more serious he got, the
more they disliked me.

Carol followed Bill to Cornell the following year. By the end of her
freshman year they had decided to be married. Bill wrote of the decision
to his parents. By return mail he received a reply which was alternately
demanding and entreating. But Bill was steadfast in his decision. Then,
during the following summer when Carol visited Bill's home—it was the
second time she had ever seen his parents—the storm really broke. Mr.
Chisholm told Carol that the marriage was impossible and that she would
have to break it off since Bill was so stubborn. She replied that she loved
Bill and wanted to marry him.

"Don't talk to me about love," screamed Mr. Chisholm. "What do you know about love, you, you little tramp. You're not good enough for Bill, and I won't stand for it. I'll kill you first. I have a gun upstairs, and I'll get it and kill you if you don't stop this nonsense."

Carol was terrified, but she held her ground and said nothing. Bill tried to hush his father up. The old man became more and more violent. Trembling with passion, his eyes flashing hatred, he seized Carol by the throat and started choking her. Bill tore his father's hands from Carol and pushed him down on a sofa.

The next summer, after Carol's sophomore year, they were married. Bill had always thought it would be fun to build a house, so they decided to build one while going to school. They came back to Ithaca early; and by the time school started, the roof was up, and they moved in with the tools and lumber. Carol became an expert helper. "Everything I knew about building I learned from Bill. I don't know very much. But I don't think I ever thought about the design of a building before I met Bill."

By the time cold weather came the sheathing was on, the windows were in, and the furnace installed. There were no interior walls and only rough flooring. But they loved it. And they loved each other. They were having a wonderful time. Each day was an adventure. They went to school and rushed home to work on the house. They were proud of every little accomplishment. They even entertained friends amongst the piles of building materials. This continued up until the time Carol went to the hospital to have her baby.

. . . the next thing we know it'll be May . . . so there isn't very much time. We have a whole baby's room to make . . . and we have to get some of it done right away because the further along I get pregnant, the less I'll be able to do in the way of physical work . . . so we'll have to get the ceiling up right away. We were really worrying about that yesterday, because we were putting up those great big sheets of wallboard, and they're really too heavy for me to work with now and Bill doesn't want me to, but ah . . . it'd be kind of hard to ask anyone, any of your friends if they'd like to come and help, because it's drudgery and it really isn't interesting, and there's nothing glamorous about it. It's not fun like painting or wall-papering, that you can, you start with something that looks like nothing, and you end up and it looks pretty.

This was the beginning of the eighth month of Carol's pregnancy.

Life was glorious! The thought of the baby coming and the house being unfinished did not worry Carol. But when she contemplated the possibility of some of Bill's family visiting them after the baby's birth, she was perturbed.

If one of Bill's family got the idea that they'd like to come and help me after the baby came—well, my folks can come and if they find us in a horrible mess, it won't affect them, but none of Bill's family have ever been in a . . . place like ours . . . and I'm afraid I wouldn't be able to just let everything go, which we're going to have to do this spring . . . So I'm just hoping none of his sisters think that they would like to come and help me when the baby comes . . . which would be a very nice thought, but . . . it would be very hard to say no thank you to them. But we'll manage a lot better just the two of us, even though it'll be an awful lot of work for Bill. We can manage a lot better than having to appear that we went along smoothly when sometimes we don't . . . . . there're a lot of things about living in an unfinished house that sometimes can get in an awful mess.

College Experience

Carol went to college with high hopes and bubbling enthusiasm. She had made a good record in high school. Though not a brilliant student, she was quite able to pursue a college course with profit and enjoyment. Carol thought that she wanted to become a writer, particularly of articles and stories about children. So she enrolled in home economics, with a concentration in child development.

It had been understood in her family from the time Carol was old enough to think about school that she would go to college. As we have seen, the original plan for her was Vassar, in line with her mother's choice. But when Carol insisted on going to Cornell to be with Bill, that was an acceptable substitute. The Johnsons financed Carol's education out of their meager savings and current income. Even after she was married, they continued to pay her tuition fees and sent her $150 a month for living expenses. As we shall see, this was a source of considerable conflict for Carol.

College did not prove to be what Carol had anticipated. Before the end of her first semester she began to be disillusioned. By the close of her sophomore year she was discouraged, disheartened. She never regained her enthusiasm for studying and learning. She finished college for three reasons: her parents wanted her to, it was the conventional thing to do, and she wanted to complete a task she had set out upon. But let Carol speak for herself.

I guess I'm trying not to think about my paper . . . I've had such a period of writing papers . . . I can't forget last spring, in which I had to write something and it didn't matter whether I said anything really or not as long as I wrote it in proper grammar and paragraphs and everything else, that, uh, when I come to write a paper, when I feel I have something to say, it's, uh, it's the usual experience and I have to get over a barrier that I feel against writing anything, because of this English course I took . . . I never used to have any trouble writing anything at all . . . I used to enjoy it . . . and now I'm . . . since I took that course in writing . . . and every paragraph had to turn and look back on itself and yet give new directions to the next paragraph, every sentence had to do I don't know what—we had to write a theme a week —Maybe I couldn't think along those lines, but I certainly didn't. I didn't want to. But it convinced me that I couldn't write . . . and everything . . . I flunked! And ever since then, everything I came to write came out so mechanical for the first little while until I really get going and really get interested in what I'm saying. And I tear up everything that—with more paragraphs turning on each other . . . Before I took that course I thought maybe I'd like to write some professionally about children and about . . .

In addition to pursuing a regular course in college, Carol and Bill built a house, as we have pointed out. These activities, plus the entertainment of friends and occasional parties at Bill's fraternity made for a very busy life. Little wonder that Carol was tired a good deal of the time, and that her school work suffered from her sheer exhaustion as well as her lack of interest. Carol's study habits had always been erratic, and the conditions of her present life were not conducive to regularity. Assignments were put off until the last minute, and papers were usually turned in late. Here is Carol's description of their pattern of life.

We lead a very, uh, flexible life. If we decide we're going to go, oh, out for a drive on a Sunday morning . . . and get off past Binghamton someplace, we eat lunch out, have hamburgers, and maybe we don't even came back until after we've seen a movie or something like that, an, uh, uh, get back sometime in the morning. Because we can do this and let things drop, we don't live in a state of tension . . . because we've got an awful lot of things that we have to do, and we go through periods of terrific work and then we take off, and, uh, . . just forget about things.

Part Two: A New Life Begins

In your first pregnancy you enjoy, or are fascinated even, by many things that probably will be old stuff in the second pregnancy . . . And that made me think (laughs) of, of the first time I felt that baby move! I was very sure that's what it was. Bill was fast asleep, and I jumped straight up! He couldn't feel it, because it wasn't moving that much . . . It felt just like a bubble bursting!

Every sensitive, self-conscious mother experiences the mystery and wonder of creation. There were times when Carol was speechless in the face of what was taking place within her. At other times she was bubbling with excitement; her words fairly tumbled out in orderless, chaotic fashion. Fortunately some of these occasions took place in front of the microphone. Some of her thoughts will be reported verbatim. Carol was not a poet nor even, as we have seen, a very good writer. Her expressions were sometimes rough, sometimes half-formed. But there was a candor in her voice and manner and a simplicity in her words which bear an unquestioned validity. We shall review her anticipation of birth in five parts: conception, movement of foetus, name and sex of baby, physical condition, psychological manifestations.

The Beginning

I've decided all our children will come so I won't have most of my pregnancy during the hot weather . . . This is a very easy thing to decide and (laugh) another thing to prove that you can do.

Did you plan this one?

No, not really. If you want to know the actual truth, it's just—I don't really know it wasn't planned, and yet it wasn't unplanned . . . Well, I really don't know because . . . We'd been using birth control and, and we stopped . . . and it was right about when we were starting again because of after I had talked with my mother and she was worried that we would have a baby and she actually had asked us . . . well, I think I wanted very much to be pregnant, but I didn't want, we didn't want to plan a baby because of a certain amount of responsibility for finishing school . . . Well, I was tickled . . . You see it's just that . . . (sigh) . . . well, we just weren't using contraceptives carefully and religiously . . . and, and I know that, that I . . . that I often wondered at times whether I could become pregnant . . . and we both of us, both of us want babies . . . I was very pleased. In fact, the second time I went to the doctor, I wasn't even two months pregnant because he wanted me to come back to make sure if that's what it was. And, ah, . . . knowing very little about the ins and outs of, oh, how fast you change and everything else and when you start wearing maternity clothes and so on, and . . . I simply wasn't holding my stomach in because I wanted to look pregnant. . . . I was very anxious to wear maternity clothes, to look pregnant.

On acceptance and rejection.

I wonder if doctors tell patients things just to make them feel better? I think they do because my sister-in-law, when she was pregnant, wouldn't even admit it to herself until she was five months pregnant. And she told me in all seriousness that, that I would reject the baby terribly. This is what her doctor told her, that all mothers do . . . I think that her doctor told her that just because she had, was rejecting—feeling a rejection about her coming baby. He, uh, wanted her to feel that this wasn't something that she should feel terribly guilty and badly about . . . So I didn't say anything. But I think that's probably why he told her . . . Well, I don't think we're rejecting this baby in the least. It's very curious. I keep thinking I wish I had a zipper so I could see what's going on.

Strange, moving sensations.

I'd just love to know what this baby's doing right now. Sometimes it's this sort of steady, oh, pulse-beat sort of thing . . . And I wonder what in the world that is . . . I mean not just moving around . . . right where it is—it's always been on the right side, on the right side, and, uh, sometimes it pushes out in a funny way. I can just tell that's his rump . . . I think of a note that my grandmother's friend wrote her and that she sent on to us. She's a wealthy old maid, and her reply to the news that I was going to have a baby was that, quote, "I am so glad that Carol is going to have a wee little stranger come and live with her." (laughs) Bill said if she could only know how much this baby influenced our lives last night. . . . I think how in the world could anything that was already as much a part of our family as the baby is have anything remotely connected with, with the . . . of a stranger . . . because it's definitely come to live with Bill as much as it's come to live with me already. Poor Rose, she doesn't know very much about anything . . .

I think a lot more about the baby now than I did before. [This was two months before the birth.] But that's uh, only natural because it keeps reminding me that it's there . . . When I was sitting in class on Wednesday (laughs), I was sitting there and every so often my whole tummy would move from one side to the other . . . and I kept sitting there watching it. I was fascinated, and I kept forgetting what people were talking about . . . I was thinking about Sally's calling me up the other day—she's the girl who's going to have a baby the same time I am. She was telling me that in one class her baby moved completely from one side to the other, and that there were two boys that sit on either side of her, that watched this . . . Then I was thinking I told Bill last night, and we were laughing, that we were having twins because one was in one position and one was in the other, and we didn't see how one baby could be moving in the same place, so far apart.

Last night I was up and down and everything else, and uh, I was reading in one of my books, and they were talking about, well, I was looking up what they had to say about pre-natal activity . . . and this one woman reported tremendous activity all of thirty minutes long. I think she's nuts if she thinks that tremendous, because really from about oh, say nine o'clock until after eleven this baby was going at it constantly . . . You wonder how it can get up so high! . . . hmm! The baby was moving just then, and I was thinking that as far as I am concerned, we have about the most active baby in the world. And I was thinking that actually I have no comparison, I have no way of knowing whether this is an active baby. And I was thinking of all the studies based on mothers' reports of movement before birth correlated with later activity—how much they cry, whether they had colic, and so on—it always seemed to me that they were pretty poor studies, because how does the mother know what criterion to use for activity?

Will it be a boy?

. . . There's absolutely no one who thinks the baby's going to be a girl. Bill and I don't have any thoughts in the matter. I mean we don't care. My grandmother sent us a layette at Christmas time—for me and for the boy, boy underlined three times. Bill's parents think it would be nice if we had a boy. My parents are sure it's going to be a boy, but they say they don't care . . . The only thing that makes me think it's going to be one sex or the other is that everybody's so sure it's going to be a boy, it'll probably be a girl . . . And I don't really think I care in the least . . .

. . . It's complicated . . . of course Bill's parents are rooting for a boy because Bill's the only Chisholm boy and if we don't have a boy, why that part
of the Chisholm line will be dropped. So, whereas it doesn't make any difference to us which (sigh) kind of baby this is . . . I'd like to have a few of
each sex eventually, but I don't, I don't care what this one is . . . it, ah, sort
of makes a big difference on that side of the family.

The last time the author saw Carol before the baby was born, the day
before she went to the hospital, she was very anxious. She had just
learned that the baby would have to be removed by Caesarian section.
Her associations during this hour will be reported shortly. After the hour
was over and the recorder was turned off, she sat up rubbing her eyes
and said she was afraid everything was going wrong now. Then she
added: "You know how I feel about the sex of the baby. I don't care!
But recently I have come to feel that I can't stand it if Sally and John
have a boy and we don't. I know it's silly, but there it is. There is a value
on boys, you know, in our group and I can't help it."

Nine days after Peter was born Carol told the author during a home
visit that she really had preferred a boy all along, but that she was fully
prepared to accept either a boy or a girl readily and lovingly.

What's in a name?

. . . If we have a girl, we're going to name her Jennifer, and then we're going to call her Jensie, because I like that so well. I think it's such a pretty
nickname. We're still in a dilemma about boys' names . . . because the name
we like best Bill's sister, April, has already used and since this family is such
a big, close family and little Christopher is only two years old, it wouldn't be
good to have another Christopher . . . and the second choice is Peter, and
since we've decided that we'd like Peter, everybody that's been born has been
named Peter . . . So we're sort of at a loss. Because we don't want to have
a William III, Bill being William, Jr., because we think every child has a right
to its own name completely . . . And, of course, the feeling on the part of
the Chisholms is that Bill wants very much for this to be William Standish III
if it's a boy, and that it's merely because I am insensitive to what he wants so
much that I insist on calling him something else. . . . . . I'm afraid they're
going to be pretty surprised if it is a boy, because it isn't going to be William
Standish III.

Physical Condition

Carol was a strong, healthy woman who had no special problems during her pregnancy. Even the anticipated dietary idiosyncrasies did not
materialize—"People keep asking Bill if I don't wake up in the middle of
the night and make him go out and get something strange to eat. (laughs)
He always answers that I have too much trouble trying to wake him up
in the morning, let alone trying to wake him in the middle of the night."
She had grown accustomed to controlling her body and making it respond

to her wishes. She was, therefore, unprepared for a certain slowing down, an unusual tiredness, and aching legs.

That's one thing I've learned about pregnancy, you can't decide you're going to do such and such and the heck with how you feel, because once you get really pooped out, you don't bounce back again; you have to take it easy. Up to this time whenever everything seemed to be piling up on me, I'd just stay up all night and finish up whatever I had to get finished. And I can't do that now . . . I think I've definitely slowed down.

When they went to Florida for spring vacation, the doctor had told Carol that she could go swimming as long as she did not overdo it. She was eagerly looking forward to the prospect of riding the surf on a rubber raft. Upon her return Carol put it this way: "I had just been dying to ride on one of those things, oh, for the longest time. We finally did rent one, and if you don't think it's hard to belly slam when you have as large a protuberance as I have, you'd be surprised. I wore myself out. It was easier after awhile just not to try."

She was experiencing her first real discomfort. In addition to tiring easily, her feet began to swell. On the plane going down to Jacksonville she was afraid to take her shoes off for fear she might not get them on again. So she suffered with her feet. But she was not discouraged. Later she even joked about it: "I thought to myself that my feet were stretching just like my tummy. And you know it's sort of a miracle that anybody can stretch as much as I am and still go on stretching and then get back after not too long to a more or less normal size."

During the last two weeks before the baby was born Carol was uncomfortable a good deal of the time. The weather was unseasonably hot and humid, and she was trying to get her school work done, so it would not be hanging over her head. On top of everything else her legs began to bother her. Through it all, however, she made few complaints; and the joy in her heart grew and grew. When she and Bill had been having breakfast on Sunday morning, a week before going to the hospital, they had looked around, and the stark, gray wallboard had depressed them. They thought of how beautiful their little house would look if it were papered. They decided to put the wallpaper on right then.

And so we started putting it on, and it took a lot longer than we expected. I was on my knees and up and down, up and down. Oh, I was so tired last night! My legs were aching, twitching, and I had crampy pains. We didn't get to sleep until four-thirty. . . . . I was thinking about, after we've had such a hard night of it, hard for both of us, because if I get up to try to let Bill sleep, he gets up with me, and, uh, when I'm in bed I can't lie still, because my legs ache and then they sort of jerk. Even when I try to lie still for Bill's sake, it's almost a reflex action; I don't have any control over it. I get so tired! And I keep thinking if I could just sleep . . . . . but it just keeps me awake.

And therefore keeps him awake. Yet this morning, when we were getting ready to come up to school, uh, Bill said something about, uh, it being fun, being pregnant, in spite of nights like last night . . . and that we really have had a lot of fun the whole time through, except for a night here and there. And those have been few and far between . . . Something I made up my mind about, because, oh, this man who was living with us before we moved, his wife had just had a baby; and all the tales of woe about how his wife suffered and everything else through all nine months. We both saw how clearly he suffered, too. I made up my mind not to take advantage of my so-called delicate condition like I think his wife did. Nights like last night are something that Bill wants to share with me. We share the fun and excitement of the baby coming. And, uh, it's something that makes me feel awfully good . . . inside . . . and, uh, I don't know it's sort of a private tenderness between the two of us. It makes me, I don't know, it's just ours, ours.

Psychological Manifestations

This is an arbitrary heading. The physical and psychological are so intertwined that it is often impossible to say where one leaves off and the other begins. We have just seen ample evidence of the tender emotions and sentiments in Carol. What remains is to show how she handled her anxieties, and, insofar as possible, what occasioned them. The first overt statement indicating anxiety occurred five weeks before parturition.

We were going over a bumpy road and I was, we were teasing about the fact that after all I didn't know what labor pains felt like and maybe the baby would start coming and I wouldn't know it. The next time we have a baby, we'll know everything. But, ah, well, the only thing that, that I think worries me most is that, ah, the baby will start coming sometime when I'm in class or something. That doesn't really worry me, but ah, as far as the pain, I expect it will be . . . I think I compare it to when I had my appendicitis attack . . . that was painful . . . and I expect having a baby will be quite painful. Yet it's, ah, it's something that's certainly worth it. I don't expect the actual birth to be as painful as perhaps the last part of labor because I know Dr. —— doesn't believe in natural childbirth as such, and he won't commit himself and I don't think he should, I mean promise that I'll have any one type of anesthetic. But what I think I'd like is ah, the local and then gas that you can give yourself, because I'd like to watch, and he said he's willing to rig up a mirror so that I could watch. I think that if you can be interested and see what's happening and everything else that's going on, that the time will go quicker. And then you can have the gas whenever you want it . . . the only . . . sort of little bugaboo I have to get over I think is the idea that ah . . . if I decided that it's too painful, and ah, want the gas that I'm not being a complete coward or a queer or anything else to . . . take it . . . and ah, in other words, decide in the middle of the stream that I don't want to watch or something like that.

One week before parturition Carol said: "I will be very glad when the baby's here and I can count all the fingers and toes and everything else and make sure it's all right. Bill says it's just me when I get tired and I start figuring out all sorts of things to worry about . . . a good thing he's understanding . . . it's a very nice thing 'cause whenever I do worry about something, I can talk it over with Bill and after talking it over—just talking about being worried, and then it doesn't seem like there is anything to worry about after all . . ."

The next time Carol came for her regular hour of free association—the day before she went to the hospital, as it turned out—her usual buoyancy and vivacity were missing. She walked with a weight. Her face showed strain and fatigue, and her eyes were slightly red. As soon as the door was closed, before she lay on the couch, she said that her doctor had announced to her yesterday that the baby would have to be taken by Caesarian section. X-rays had revealed that the baby was in a breach position. The risk of a normal delivery was too great to take. Here is Carol speaking as she began to get settled on the couch:

Oh . . . . get myself all arranged . . . (sigh) . . . I don't think I have any thoughts . . . except right now that my leg itches . . . I think something bit me . . . (sigh) . . . I feel all washed out and I don't know exactly why because I don't, I don't think I feel . . . Oh, I don't know, that upset about this whole business . . . I think the thing I worry most about is that the baby's going to be all right. . . . . Then I was thinking, ah, the few people I have told, ah, not that I don't want people to know, ah I . . . don't feel like rushing up to everyone and telling them all my news and, ah, the reaction that aggravates me the most is that 'Oh, isn't that wonderful because it will be so much easier than having to go through labor! and . . . that's not the way I feel about it in the least . . . that ah . . . whereas I wouldn't want it any other way now because of the circumstances, it certainly isn't any way I'd choose to have it . . . (sigh) . . . but, ah . . . I think a lot of little things keep cropping up . . . in my head about it and that's, oh, for instance, like I was going to watch the baby being born and, not only can I not watch this one, but, since all the rest of them will have to be Caesarian, I won't be able to watch any of them . . . and then it, ah . . . it made me know we can't have all the children we might want to have and both of us have always planned on having a . . . a big family . . . and the idea that . . . isn't this wonderful?—because I don't have to go through labor is very aggravating. . . .
. . . .
    Then I just, I'm just, I'm on edge, I'm jumpy . . . and I don't know exactly why . . . and I was last night too . . . . . . 'cause I was going to get some work done, and I just couldn't. . . . . . As long as I was doing—something, something else yesterday, and really not thinking too much about it, I, I was all right and then, and then I'd stop right when I was clearing up the dishes last night and I got all . . . sort of upset without any one specific thing upsetting me . . . . but it's, it's, ah . . . It was an awful good feeling to see, when I, ah, after I saw the doctor, I went up and got Bill out of class and ah . . . we just drove around and I could sort of let down, because it was, it was a blow and it is a disappointment, and I didn't want to cry or anything else in

front of the doctor or in the middle of the hallway, but I could let go and then we could talk it over and, and everything else as soon as I—we were together . . . Last night I was sort of all—on edge! Went out to have supper and . . . went to the movies instead of doing school work, 'cause when I tried to, to work, I was just . . . . a mounting feeling of, of . . . on edge or something. . . . . . What worries me most is just that, because things have been so easy and everything else before this that I'm just afraid that everything isn't all right with the baby . . . and it's . . . sort of a . . . a silly fear, and yet I'll be awful glad when I, when it's over with and I can . . . check and make sure that everything's all right. . . . . But we were, when I was talking to Bill last night . . . talking about anything I wanted to (sigh) sort of . . . talk about all the little worries et cetera that . . . that uh . . . kept cropping up . . . we cried . . . makes things so much better. . . . . And I was just thinking that I didn't know how anybody could go through any kind of disappointment that made . . . quite as big a difference and not have . . . your husband to . . . share it with . . . Like girls whose husbands are overseas or something when they have their babies. . . . . Even, even, even now I just sort of ah . . . get a, a . . . panicky sort of feeling! I don't know what it is really from, because I don't think it's ah . . . that I, I'm scared about any one particular thing . . . ah . . . it's just a feeling, sort of, that, that when I think about it, when we talk about it et cetera, then ah, it's . . . sort of something to take matter-of-factly, and yet when I . . . without Bill, I think I lose a little bit of the security that I feel when I'm with him, and then it's sort of panicky feeling that's building up in me. . . . . . That's why I wish that I could . . . (sigh) go home on Wednesday night and then come back on Thursday morning, 'cause having to stay in the hospital all day Wednesday and, well, from eight o'clock or so in the morning until . . . well till after I go home after the baby's come . . . 'cause I think I'd be a much calmer and relaxed person on Thursday morning after being home on Wednesday night than I will be after being by myself on Wednesday night. . . . . And it isn't just that ah, he ah, he helps me forget about it, because it isn't. I don't know, Bill seems to know when I just talk about something and when . . . I just need to not say too much and perhaps just cry a little bit, and when I need to do something that takes my mind off . . . and, and . . . like going out and having supper out last night. . . . . And I was thinking when we came home ah . . . last night from the movies . . . that it was . . . ah, an awfully wonderful feeling to be so happy and calm and everything else when it was a blow to both of us and I really think I was, I don't think I was pushing anything out of my mind at all and, and . . . this morning everything was fine and now, just since eight o'clock this morning . . . I feel shakier and shakier. I was thinking that, ah, one of the girls was telling me this morning about the, the, ah the girl I told you about expecting her baby the day after we were expecting ours, had the baby on Saturday . . . Funny thing about the hospital, too. I went down last Friday to look around to see, and ah . . . although I have a, really feel every confidence in the world in the doctor, Tompkins County is a very poor hospital from everything I've ever seen. I've seen three hospitals, actually, I mean, well to know what they're like inside, et cetera, and two of them are big city hospitals; the other one which I was in for a week a couple summers ago is a brand new hospital in Canada. It's about as modern and as beautiful and everything else as a hospital can be and ah, Tompkins County is a very poor comparison, and it's just its sort of exterior look and I know it is and I can see when I think about it logically that they have what counts in the way of equipment and the things to do a good job with, but the, ah, the rooms and the ward and just the atmosphere is, is one that, ah . . . well it still, it gives me less confidence than the, ah, because it makes such a poor comparison with every other hospital I've ever known. The wards are very, very large, and they have the ghastly pink curtains that pull around each bed to make it separate . . . and, ah . . . I had been holding out for the idea that I was going to be in a ward because it was cheaper, and, ah, Bill wanted me to be in a, a private or semi-private room, just because I think he has the idea that you get better care than in a ward. And I had won out and, ah, but then the combination of seeing it which as I say . . . and, ah, then having an operation instead of having it the way we wanted to have it. He still wants me to be in a semi-private room, so . . . the all three just . . . They are slightly better than the wards in that they don't have those terrible pink curtains and that's such a silly thing to be, ah, to make any difference because it's not the pink curtains or lack of pink curtains or shiny beds or fancy equipment that makes the difference. It's what they have for the medical care that you're going to get, and yet the emotional impact that it had on me to see that ward must . . . It must have at least twenty beds in it and, ah, I thought the wards in the Infirm were big, and they had ten when I was in when I had measles . . . and, and another thing about it was the fact that . . . (sigh) you have a feeling that if you want anything or anything like that in the middle of the night, that you're, ah, going to be waking up at least fifteen out of the twenty other people in the room which isn't fair. . . . . Wishing I could calm myself down, I'm so shaky. . . . . Makes me so mad when I think of all I was going to get done this week end! I really was going to do it.

Mother and Child

Peter was a full-term baby delivered by Caesarian section without incident. He weighed 8 lbs., 6 oz.

When the author visited Carol in the hospital three days after the birth, Bill and a friend were present. Everyone was smiling. There was some good-natured joking about how ugly the baby was at first. His face was red and puffy. Bill said: "His feet are just like mine." Carol was a little worried because Peter had vomited twice during feedings. She thought perhaps her milk was too rich, or that it came too fast. She remarked that the baby sometimes fell asleep while nursing.

Carol went home at the end of seven days. Two days later the author visited her at home. She said she felt somewhat cheated not having had the baby normally, for she had looked forward to the experience. She repeated her irritation over people saying that having a baby by Caesarian section was the easy way to do it. She denied that it had been easy. She expressed guilt over unwrapping the baby at the hospital when he was brought to her for nursing. She wanted Bill to see him entirely undressed. The nurses had warned her that the baby might get contaminated by germs that the father brought in.

It was a hot, humid day. Carol, who looked tired and worn, said she was upset because of so many visitors. Earlier in the afternoon she had just gotten undressed to take a sponge bath when one of the neighbors came in. Since there were no interior doors yet hung in the house, there was no privacy, and she had had to dress hurriedly and entertain.

On the next day she looked rested and said she felt much better. The baby was sleeping peacefully. It was a beautiful, clear, warm day.

On the following day, eleven days after the birth, she was very cheerful and gay. She said her strength was coming back. The day before, she and Bill had taken Peter for a ride. Carol referred to the baby as "Petie" or "Petie-boy." The baby was on a self-demand feeding schedule. That morning he had awakened at 4:00 A.M. and was fed on one breast. At about 5:00 he was ready to go back to bed, but just at that moment he had a "huge bubble" and seemed to be hungry again. So Carol fed him on the other breast. Then his diapers had to be changed again. It was light outside before he got to bed.

When the author arrived, the house was in a very unkempt condition. There were dishes in the kitchen sink and on the counters, empty cans here and there, papers and books scattered over the living room. Beds were not made. Bill was in his study, which adjoined their bedroom and doubled as a nursery. The author's assistant, who was making systematic observations of mother and baby, was with Carol. Shortly, the baby woke up. The author absented himself so that Carol could nurse the baby; the assistant remained and later reported that when Carol exposed her breasts, the milk was running freely from both nipples. The baby rooted around to find the nipple, when put in position; but instead of the nipple he found his thumb and sucked it. Carol said, "I can be as patient as you are impatient." She slowly took his thumb from his mouth and pulled him toward her breast, but did not insert the nipple in his mouth. The baby continued to root around and finally found the nipple. He sucked well for several minutes, stopped awhile and then started sucking again. Carol seemed to be totally preoccupied with the baby. She talked about nothing else.

Peter's Development During the First Two Weeks

On the fourth day of Peter's life the nurse in the hospital nursery reported that Baby Chisholm rarely cried in the nursery, but that when he did, his cry was normal and healthy. She further said that he slept all the time and had to be awakened at feeding times. He was, she said, the least active of all the normal babies in the nursery at that time. The nurse had been with Peter eight hours a day since his birth.

When Peter was eight days old, the author's assistant went into the home for the purpose of making observations and conducting simple sensory tests with the baby. During the next four days she made twelve systematic observations of Peter, observations which were scattered throughout the time. For this purpose she used the Brownfield-Smart Infant Observational Chart (Brownfield, 1956). Six auditory tests were given. In addition, casual observations were made of parental behavior.

Activity Pattern. The scores on the Brownfield-Smart Infant Observational Charts, each of which covered a three-minute period, ranged from 2 to 142 with a possible range of 0–180. Peter's mean Spontaneous Activity Score was 64, while the mean of the sample of normal, newborn infants previously studied during their first week of life was 80, with a standard deviation of 19. Peter's mean was almost one standard deviation below the sample mean. His mean Spontaneous Activity Score would place Peter with the least active third of the sample, who had scores ranging from 72 to 34 with a mean of 61. Whereas in many ways Peter was found to react and behave similarly to this least active group, in no way did he resemble the most active upper third of the sample.

Sleeping-Waking Behavior. Of the twelve times observed, Peter was awake during six observations, asleep during four observations, and in a borderline condition during two.

The borderline condition, which is a state between sleeping and waking, is defined as follows:

1. Infant seemed drowsy, but not actually sound asleep.
2. Difficult for the observer to record the sleeping-waking state of infant with any degree of assurance.
3. Infant awake during some of the period and asleep during the remainder of time.

Some infants are quite active in their sleep, moving the segments of the body and face, and at times even vocalizing in a fretful manner without awakening. But Peter slept very soundly when he was observed, with very few body or facial movements and no fretting behavior. The following tabulation shows the sleeping-waking condition of Peter expressed in percentage of total time observed.

Awake	50%
Asleep	33⅓%
Borderline	16⅔%

Compare these percentages with the following from the Brownfield study.

Thirty-three Most Active Infants		Thirty-three Least Active Infants	
Awake	56%	Awake	28%
Asleep	40%	Asleep	69%
Borderline	4%	Borderline	3%

Crying–Fretting Behavior. Two kinds of vocal behavior observable in newborn infants may be distinguished; these are crying and fretting. Neonates frequently vocalize in a whimpering, fretful manner that is dissimilar to crying. Fretting differs from crying in that it is not as loud nor as continuous. Also the baby does not expend as much energy nor show as much bodily activity when fretting as he does when crying.

During seven of the observational periods Peter showed no vocal behavior; of these times he was awake twice, in a borderline condition once, and asleep four times. These seven periods with no vocal sounds represent 58 per cent of the total observational periods. This is slightly lower than was found in the research alluded to, which showed no vocal behavior in 62 per cent of the total 1354 observations made on the 100 infants.

Only two infants in Brownfield's sample of 100 had scores as low or lower than Peter's score for Crying Behavior. These were both very quiet infants, one of whom never cried during fifteen observations; the other cried only once. In all the time the observer was in the Chisholm home during the four-day period, she never heard Peter cry really hard.

Sensory Tests. Peter was given two sensory tests. One, called the Auditory test, consists of stimulating the infant with a loud sound. During this test the infant lies in his crib near a metal-topped table on which is placed the testing apparatus. This is a small wooden box inside of which is suspended a brass cylinder weighing 500 grams. When the experimenter presses a small catch on the top of the box, the weight descends four inches, striking the wooden floor of the box and the metal table top with a loud thudding sound. The response of the infant to the sound is recorded, as well as his activity for the next thirty seconds. The second test, the Auditory-Vibratory test, uses the same testing apparatus, but this time the experimental conditions are different. The infant is placed on the table near the box, so that he is stimulated by the sound and also by tactile vibration which reach his skin from the table top. The first situation tests the infant's auditory sense organs and his responses to loud sounds. The second tests, in addition to the auditory sense organs, those sense organs in and near the skin that respond to tactile stimulation.

Each of these two sensory tests was given three times, at approximately the same time on successive days during this infant's second week of life.

Peter failed to give a startle response to the auditory stimulus on any of the three times it was presented. In the first series he was sleeping and gave no response to the loud sound of the 500-gram weight hitting the table. In the second series his eyes were closed when the stimulus was given, and he only tightened his eyelids; no other movements were observed. In the third series Peter had his eyes open when stimulated by the sound; he blinked and made slight movements of his extremities. In each of the three auditory tests he moved his body segments slightly for the thirty seconds following the response, with no vocal sounds.

Peter's behavior score on the Auditory test placed him in the lowest quartile of the group studied by Brownfield.

The failure to startle when the auditory stimulus is presented and the low level of activity during the thirty seconds following stimulation that was observed in Peter, are characteristic of quiet infants. The auditory test differentiates statistically infants who have previously been rated active or quiet on the Brownfield-Smart Infant Observational Chart.

Peter responded with a startle each time the auditory plus vibratory stimulation was given. The first time he was tested he gave a slight startle, followed by five seconds of mass behavior, moving all segments of his body so fast that they could not be counted, then twenty-five seconds of fretting behavior. This was the most activity exhibited by Peter at any time during the testing situations.

The second time the vibratory stimuli were presented, Peter gave a regular startle, but he was not very active following the response. For twenty seconds he moved the segments of his body slowly enough to be counted; then he was quiet for two seconds; then he moved body segments again for eight seconds. On the third test he repeated his performance of the second test.

Peter's Vibratory Behavior Score on his first test is slightly higher than the mean for the Brownfield sample of 100 infants also based on the first vibratory test given, indicating that his reflexes function satisfactorily.

Mother-Infant-Father Relationships. Carol devoted herself whole-heartedly to the care of Peter during the four days of observation. Her own comfort, rest, or desires were secondary to her attempts to understand and meet his needs. Beginning to think of him as a little individual, she spoke of him more frequently as "Peter" or "Petie" and less often as simply "the baby."

Carol and Bill seemed very happy together, and talked of little else than the baby. If one of them noticed the slightest change in the baby, he or she was quick to call it to the other's attention. Bill talked about

Peter almost as much as Carol did. He watched the baby intently and helped with his care.

When Peter was observed nursing, he showed a good strong sucking reflex. He actively participated in the nursing process by a rooting response until he himself located the nipple. He did not fall asleep during nursing. He had already established good eating and sleeping habits before the end of his second week of life.

Abstract of Mother's Records

Although the categories used for recording the mother's observations in this study were somewhat different from those used in comparable studies, comparison has been attempted with the work of three others, the most similar being *The Biography of a Baby* by Millicent W. Shinn. The other two are nomothetic studies, *The First Two Years* by Mary M. Shirley and *Infant and Child in the Culture of Today* by Arnold Gesell and Frances Ilg. Where there are comparable categories the findings of these authors will be indicated. The abstract from the Mother's records follows:

During the first month several motor activities were noticeable. Petie "rooted" with his mouth when held in a nursing position, the "rooting" best described as a searching movement of the head, with mouth open. Petie slept in a bassinet, and he repeatedly worked himself to the end of it in the second week. Much of this progress was related to crying, for his whole body was a mass of activity when he cried. His face took on expression, too, for he would turn down his mouth, squint his eyes shut, stiffen his whole body, and break into indignant howls, accompanied by furious activity.

Just before he was four weeks old, he lifted his chest off the dressing table. At four weeks he could maintain this position for forty seconds. (Shirley's median of nine weeks was based on sixty seconds.) He could also suck his fist (Shinn records her baby *trying* this at ten weeks) and he could secure his thumb, usually his left one. A happenstance made us think he could turn over at four weeks. His father was lying beside him on the bed and Petie raised up on his arms, arched his back, pushed with his feet, and threw his weight down hill, so to speak, and rolled over. He did it again, but could not do it on a flat surface. During the afternoon of the same day, I put him down on the floor on a piece of foam rubber, tilted it somewhat, and he repeated his morning behavior. The next day he did not repeat the behavior.

At four weeks he "played" by vigorous movements of arms and legs. Often the legs would be brought up and shot out together.

At five weeks he could follow the bright red rings of the cradle gym with his eyes when he moved them. He seemed to enjoy staring at the rings, and also enjoyed staring at the window.

At eight weeks kicking was still part of happy activity. He was beginning to bring his knees up beside him in a "pre-crawl" position. We put him in the play pen where he could look at the cradle gym. He would kick and coo, especially if I moved the rings. He tried to hit the rings, at times, it seemed. He would raise his fist jerkily as if trying to control it. He would pull hard on the cradle gym rings if we put them in his fists. By ten weeks he had enough control to reach up and hit the cradle gym rings. Then he would watch them move, and when they stopped he would jerkily, slowly, reach up and bat one of them again. It was surprising that it took so much effort. Often his whole body was involved—his legs would move up, as if sympathetically. The banging of the rings was a means of self-entertainment, and he was content to play alone in the pen for short periods. His fist, in itself, was something to watch at this point, and he seemed to watch his left fist the most.

A week later (eleven weeks) we found him lifting the bumper of his car bed up and down, watching the gay figures on it. He also arched his back when we went to pick him up. (Shirley's median, fifteen weeks.) During feeding he would strain forward, almost sitting up by himself, with his mouth open for the next bite.

At twelve weeks he enjoyed being held up in a sitting position. One would need only to hold his hands and he supported the rest. He could also sit propped up. (Shirley's median for sitting supported on lap is eighteen weeks, and Gesell mentions it at sixteen weeks; but Shinn records her baby enjoying a "sitting position" at six weeks. By twelve weeks Shinn's baby used her tongue to reach out and feel others' cheek and face.) Petie reached up with his hands to touch my face with a sort of raking motion. He was gaining more and more control over his hands. He would carefully watch as he brought his fists together.

When he was thirteen weeks old, Petie grasped the dangling cradle gym rings. He used his right hand for this. He also enjoyed playing with the rattle, holding it and banging his face against it. A week later he had enough control to grasp the cradle gym rings and knock them together or hit them against the center bar. (He was doing all this at a stage when Shinn records that her baby "grasped at a rattle once, sat propped in high chair, tried to pull self from lying to sitting, picked up objects from high chair tray and without looking put in mouth." At four months or sixteen weeks Gesell lists the following accomplishments: Able to grasp, Kicks, Turns head, Sucks thumb, Clasps hands, Vocalizes, Loves to be in sitting position, Engages in finger play. Each of these activities Peter had already accomplished.)

He was beginning even larger muscular activity. While supine, he would arch his back, twist, and push with his feet as if trying to roll over. He would move from one end of the dressing table to the other by lifting his rear end and pushing with his legs. (Shirley gives twenty-five weeks for knee push and swim.) By seventeen weeks he could hitch himself around the crib by raising up on his haunches and pushing with his toes. He would finger his fingers and would grab anything within reach and put it in his mouth. He loved to chew on objects like his rubber Plakie Bear.

(At seventeen weeks Shinn's baby did not put things from her hand to her mouth. She had reached out to grasp things, and she had rolled over. The latter Peter did not do until the fifth month.)

At five months Petie rolled over from his stomach to his back. We bought him a car seat and he seemed to love sitting in it. During meals, he would grab the spoon and try to feed himself. He was able to direct the bowl of the spoon to his mouth. He liked to bounce up and down when someone held him standing up.

(Shinn records her baby sitting alone for one-half minute at five months. Peter was behind her in this. There is no comparison in hand control. Records for the sixth month also showed things that Peter did not do. Shinn records deliberate throwing of toys on the floor which Peter didn't do until two months later. She also noted imitation. Shirley's medians give thirteen weeks for stepping while being held standing. Peter did not step but stood stiff and straight until six months. At that time, he could almost climb.)

His crawling progress at six months now involved pushing with his hands so hard that he went backwards. (Shinn, 9 months; Shirley, 45 weeks.) A week later he would get up on his hands and knees and rock. Within two days he could get anywhere he wanted to in his playpen. He employed a half-hitch, half-creep. His activity increased markedly. He rolled from one side to another; he could arch his back to reach things lying by his head; he was always chewing something. The hard rubber bear was his favorite. He tried to hold his drinking cup and at one time he raised an empty glass to his lips as if to drink. Dressing him was like trying to put clothes on an octopus. At twenty-seven weeks he turned over from back to stomach. (This corresponded to Shinn's baby.) He could play while sitting up, and he really made use of his toys.

At twenty-eight weeks Peter sat up by himself. He was on his stomach, got up on his hands and feet, and dropped back into a sitting position. (Shinn's baby did this at thirty-four weeks. Gesell says that at twenty-eight weeks an infant enjoys the supine.) Peter wanted to sit, to creep, to do anything that meant moving. His creeping was much more refined. He used his whole forearm and pushed with his legs. (Shirley's median 44.5.) His father called it an "infiltration crawl." He banged on the table or whatever was near, and made a game of it with his aunt. This was the first imitative play Peter engaged in. (Shinn's baby had been taught to wave bye-bye at seven months.)

At thirty-two weeks Petie pulled himself up to a standing position. (Shirley's median 47.0.) He soon learned to balance well and to let himself down. At thirty-three weeks he crawled perfectly on hands and knees; he just got up and crawled. He had a perfect pincer and had learned by himself first to spin his mechanical top by holding it upside down and then by pumping it. He dropped things one by one from his high chair tray, and had complete mastery of grasp and release. He engaged in the following gross motor activity: standing, sitting, crawling, banging things, pulling things, lifting things. He was on the go all the time.

Thirty-Five Weeks. He leaned over while standing to pick up a dropped toy—by holding on to play pen with one hand, bending knees, and picking up toy with other hand. He tried to throw things, but could not always release the object at the time of thrust, though sometimes he succeeded.

Thirty-Six Weeks. Petie and Carol played a game. She put her hands over her face and said, "Where's Mommy?" He laughed and pulled her hands off. They both laughed. When she stopped, he put her hands back to her face.

Thirty-Seven to Forty Weeks. Records poor—Petie waved at reflections in mirror; continued vigorous activity; crawled from one end of room to other.

Forty to Forty-Four Weeks. He bounced on the couch; listened to records; babbled "da, da, da"; turned pages in a magazine with his mother's help; pulled himself up to the couch, grabbed a magazine, and tore out pages. He dropped objects from his high chair. If they were returned to him, he dropped them again.

Forty-Five Weeks. He babbled "ah, gah, de, ga." He pulled himself up to the dishwasher and took silver from the basket a piece at a time.

Forty-Six Weeks. He stood up without support.

Family Interaction

The interactions which take place within a family are so numerous and intimate, so intricately interwoven, that one almost despairs of being able to capture and portray them with any degree of confidence. Yet the importance of being able to understand the process of exchange and mediation, so crucial in personality development, urges us on. Here we shall set down some of the interacts which seem to be important in the understanding of personality in early formation. Carol's daily records of what she perceived going on in their lives will be placed in a column parallel to her periodic free associations. Each will supplement and give meaning to the other.

From Carol's Daily Records

June 22. Smiled at me after feeding. This was a less fleeting and stronger smile than other two times he has smiled.

From Carol's Free Association

June 22 . . . I was thinking about the picnic we went on yesterday . . . and the baby'd just eaten and he was sound asleep . . . and when we got there he decided he wanted to eat . . . so, we had a pacifier and he chewed on that, but he doesn't like it . . . But if he didn't suck on that he'd suck on his thumb and, and he sucks on his left thumb so much that it's almost, it's going to be raw if he keeps on sucking on it. . . . And I was thinking about going to Bill's home . . . and just hoping

From Carol's Daily Records

From Carol's Free Association

that the baby would be good . . . because his parents are going to think that we spoil that baby . . . because they, well, his mother has never even heard of self-demand . . . she suggested on the phone the other day that when the baby was hungry I should give him sugar and water . . . and I didn't say anything, either yes or no, but as far as I can see if he's hungry he needs to eat . . . and it doesn't mean sugar and water . . . but it's going to be less easy to do something like that when we're at their house . . . so I just hope everything runs on schedule . . . which is probably day-dreaming 'cause I'll be nervous about it, and if I'm nervous that will probably upset the whole applecart.

June 25. Fussy this afternoon. Would stop fussing if I jiggled some rings over his head.

June 26. Smiled at Bill this A.M. Wears me out to nurse him when he is fussy and on and off the nipple.

June 29. Left for Bill's home.

July 1. Baby seemed very puzzled at everything.

July 2. Fussed at April's house (Bill's sister) during meal.

July 3. Fussy all afternoon.

July 4. Many visits to relatives. Long crying spell this afternoon. Feedings irregular.

July 5. Fussy. Vomited at night.

July 6. Long trip home. Exhausted. Petie fussy. Vomited.

July 7. Petie upset all day. Vomited. Called doctor. I was cross all morning. Both Bill and I out of sorts.

July 9. Petie all right again. Smiled and smiled when I talked to him in a high voice.

From Carol's Daily Records

July 14. The heat seems to bother him. He cried a lot today.

July 16. We left for Canada today. I was very tired. Petie fussed until Buffalo. Rest of trip easy.

July 17. Petie very good. Mom looked after him while Bill and I went to a dance.

July 18. Lazy day. Sailing. Petie good all day.

July 19. Early this morning after Petie's 6:00 o'clock feeding, Bill and I kept him in bed between us. He smiled and "talked" and almost laughed. For about an hour we had a grand time, laughing, talking and singing. Got off around 10:00. Very easy trip. Baby slept beautifully. Home before midnight.

From Carol's Free Association

July 21 . . . When we went to Bill's house . . . Well, he started toward the end of the week to be fussy and sort of, well, for instance on Saturday night we went to sister April's for dinner and I had to hold him on my lap across my knees the whole time. And Friday night we went to Ann Arbor to dinner, he was fussy for quite a period then, too. And so it was toward the end of the week he started getting upset . . . And then on Sunday I was sort of knocked flat by an allergy, because the Chisholms' house is in, has quite a number of large trees, and when it's damp, then there's a little spore that I'm allergic to that flies around . . . and I was really miserable on Sunday. And this may have made him a little more upset, too . . . And later Bill was hit full force by it, too. He was so miserable he flopped right down on the porch on a couch, with his eyes all swollen, practically swollen shut, and the bridge of his nose was all swollen up and he was

From Carol's Daily Records

From Carol's Free Association

coughing and everything else. That's when Peter was really upset the most, and we did everything we could to quiet him down, but we couldn't. . . . We went up to Canada to see my folks. Petie slept most of the way, uh, that is after Buffalo, or not really slept, but was quiet and happy . . . and uh, the sailboats were all fixed up, so we got out in the sailboats . . . and the nice thing about it is that there's such a raft of baby sitters that there's always someone to watch him, and, uh, I could go off and leave him every now and then . . . without any qualms or worrying about him, because they were more or less fighting over who was going to watch him . . . and uh, we went to the square dance with a friend of mine I haven't seen in years and years . . . We had a wonderful time there. . . . Then we had a lot more sailing on Sunday and came home Monday. The trip back was just perfect, went beautifully. . . . . .

July 25. Bill's folks called and said they were coming to see us next week end, which means we have to cancel our plans to go to the lake for the big Regatta.

July 26. Today was hectic. We poured concrete for the steps and Bill needed my help. Petie screamed and screamed.

July 30. Hot, lazy day. Petie was fine all day.

July 31. Bill's folks arrived about 3:00 P.M. Hectic getting dinner, but all right I guess. Petie slept well. He has eczema.

August 1. Petie didn't sleep well today. He was grunty off and on. Didn't eat well. Hard feedings. I was very upset over his poor even-

From Carol's Daily Records

ing nursing. I was depressed and tired after a long day. Bill's parents were with us all day; they left about 11:00 P.M.

August 2. Petie constipated. He seemed much happier today.

August 3. Thought we'd never get off for trip to Canada. Good trip. We're very tired after it. Petie cried real hard tonight.

August 4. Broke the tiller of the sailboat and had to row home in pouring rain.

August 5. Petie screamed when screen door banged shut.

August 6. Bill lost his glasses in the water. Spent all day looking for them. Found them tonight. Later went to dance together.

August 7. Pete arches his back when you pick him up. Bill helped Dad all day. Discouraged because Bill and I haven't been off as much as I'd like.

August 8. Bill and I were sort of cross at each other today, I went to church and he took care of Petie.

August 9. Long, but easy trip home. Got off around 1:30 P.M. Didn't get to sleep until 3:00 A.M.

August 14. Bill has gone on a trip for ten days.

From Carol's Free Association

August 18 . . . And that reminded me of a dream I had . . . yeah, it was yesterday afternoon when I was sleeping with Petie and I dreamt that Bill's sister and brother-in-law had come to Ithaca to visit . . . and decided that they were going to raise cows here or something like that, it was all mixed up in with a lot of other things and I was . . . oh, indignant and very hurt and everything else that they could decide

From Carol's Daily Records

From Carol's Free Association

to live in Ithaca and stay here and find something that they wanted to do here and everything else and we couldn't. . . . . . We're both very fond of this place. . . . . . I wonder sometimes if Bill didn't have the opportunity to go in with his father and do that type of work just what he would decide to do. It's funny how people are sure they haven't decided for their children what they're going to do, and yet I think Bill's parents did too much deciding for him . . . and in a very strong way . . . and yet his mother is . . . well, she thinks Bill inherited the engineering interest . . . and that she's never pushed him and that it was his own decision. . . .

. . . . I was just thinking of, of uh, oh, how terribly, terribly important it is that all these plans that his mother has for him are to her, and uh, she's terrified that he's not going to go in with his dad . . . the thing as far as I'm concerned is that Bill will be able to mold the business into the field that he wants to go into . . . and that's the thing that thrills him is the fact that he's going to be within ten years or less pretty near his own boss and certainly have a controlling voice . . . And yet it's all tied up with loyalties and things, emotional feelings certainly from his mother . . . And I was thinking, well, it's a corporation and his mother has so many shares, and his father has the same amount, or something like that, it's divided up . . . and the shares that are his mother's are to be Bill's . . . they're willed to him, so they'll be Bill's when she dies. And it's very . . . . . maybe it's because they've got so much to will to people and

From Carol's Daily Records

From Carol's Free Association

my family doesn't, but . . . I get awfully sick of all the talk about what's going to be whose and what's coming to who and how this is going to be divided and that's going to be divided, when we die . . . because it just seems so unimportant . . . There's only one thing I've ever wanted that Mrs. Chisholm has and I have sort of a very emotional feeling about this . . . it's a silver coffee set. I don't particularly care for it. But one day she was talking about how this was willed not to, to be shared by all of us combined, and I was thinking of . . . all of a sudden I had a fierce desire for it . . . oh, have it to pass on to our children . . .

August 24. Petie played happily. He's such a happy, cheerful baby.

August 25. Bill back. Petie cried and cried when Bill mooed at him like a cow. Seemed not to recognize him. I had to quiet him down.

August 31. What a day! It rained hard, stone retaining wall fell in. I worried about money. My folks arrived around 5:00. Everyone loved Petie and picked him up. He woke up during dinner and I nursed him.

September 1. For Petie the time went rather well. He seemed happy. Mom urged me to stop nursing because she thought it would be too much for me while going to school. I just hated the idea, yet was almost convinced. Hectic time for me, yet fun. I *love* to have them here but I feel pushed and I worry about money and our easygoing life becomes rushed.

September 3. Petie upset when I left him with my sister today. Came home to an upset little boy who

From Carol's Daily Records

calmed down and stopped crying as soon as he was in my arms.

September 5. Bill's mother not well. He's worried about her.

September 6. Folks left today. I cleaned house after they had gone. I've got a little cold.

September 8. Petie's day and mine very upset and irregular. I slept off and on. Felt very tired. Neither of us had good meals. Got nothing done. I've got quite a cold.

September 9. I am not going to stop nursing now! I don't want to and the doctor doesn't see why I should.

September 10. Worked hard and felt fine. Petie fine. Loved his bath today. Has a new noise he loves to make—sort of a guttural "ah." Nursed well and steadily.

September 21. Started school today. Left Petie with Mrs. Lee, a sweet old lady. She said he was perfect all day. I didn't notice any difference in him at all when I came home. Feel a bit jealous of her time with Petie and the fact that he will get to love her, too.

October 1. Left Petie with Bill while I went to store. Bill says Petie got mad because he didn't pick him up immediately and screamed and screamed. I was upset because I didn't want Bill to be upset.

From Carol's Free Association

October 5 . . . And then I was thinking about going home, which we have to do before November, because we promised that we would have Petie baptized when both sets of grandparents could be present . . . Bill's mother had another heart attack, so I guess now we're going to have it at his house . . . but I . . . . . would rather that it could

From Carol's Daily Records

From Carol's Free Association

be done some place else . . . Sort
of disappointed about the whole
business, sort of provoked because
we had been sort of waiting to see
how she'd be before we made any
plans and then we were going to
write the minister and ask him if
we could have it done on the weekend that we would be home, and if
she couldn't go to the church that
. . . we were going to sort of ask
her if she would mind and offer and
everything else. And they called on
Sunday and she'd already talked to
him about it and we haven't even
said anything to him about it. And
I don't know—it's just all decided.
I was so mad I could have spit nails,
because I don't think it was any
business of theirs to say anything
about it whatsoever! Bill thinks I'm
being childish! So I guess I am . . .
But still I don't think it's any of their
business! . . . I think I wanted the
chance to show the baby off to the
congregation. . . . And since Bill's
mother couldn't go to the church I
think it was up to her or at least up
to us to offer to have it done at
home. It certainly wasn't up to her
to do anything about it! . . . I get
so mad when I think that . . . oh,
just wait and then do it sometime
later. Yet it's not something worth
getting all pettish about. . . . . .
I've been thinking a lot about Bill's
mother and I'm not being very fair
about it, but I was awful disappointed . . . It was something I was
looking forward to. I've been planning it more than Bill has. Actually
all summer long. We were going to
have a sort of dessert party, mother
and I, at my folks' house. Then Bill's
mother got sick! And I more or less
am blaming her, and that's not her

From Carol's Daily Records

October 13. I was very provoked with Petie this afternoon. When I picked him up, I did so roughly, which made him cry louder. I felt a bit chagrined and took time to comfort him.

October 21. Petie is very independent at times. There are times when I just love him so much and want to cuddle him and he'll have none of it. (This doesn't really bother me. I don't want a mama's boy.)

October 25. My birthday. Bill took me out for lovely dinner and celebration.

October 29. Took a plane home. My folks met us at airport. Petie cried when Mom took him in her arms. He was so good all day.

October 30. Stayed at Bill's folks' house. Nice birthday dinner for Mom and me at my house. Petie stayed with Mom in P.M. while I went shopping. He was fine.

October 31. Baptism. Petie was good. A bit hectic before baptism. Later he seemed confused when all the (28) people were there talking and milling around. I sneezed my head off this morning! Felt dead.

November 1. Petie has a cold. Good plane trip home. I feel tired and discouraged over amount of school work I have to do.

November 2. Have a horrid cold. Petie has a cold. Stuffed up nose and coughing.

From Carol's Free Association

fault at all—she had this heart attack . . .

November 2 . . . I usually start sneezing when I'm at Bill's house . . . it could be just the feather pillows . . . but then Bill's father was coughing, too, so I thought maybe something set us both off. Maybe

From Carol's Daily Records	From Carol's Free Association
	besides the feathers . . . It was very hectic in the beginning on the baby because everything had to be just so when we were . . . Bill's mother was dashing around so that everyone was sure she was going to have another attack . . . Bill's parents were as sweet and nice as they possibly could be to us and to me, and . . . on the surface, and even deeper than that, everything is just perfect, and yet sometimes they make me so. . . . . And it's, uh, its little things, because they're very generous and . . . we feel very natural and at home that I can . . . well, I wouldn't tell her what I thought under the circumstances (of course I'd tell my own mother) . . . yet I don't, I wouldn't even want Bill to know if I were aggravated I guess, because . . . it seems unreasonable to him. But sometimes it just seems to me to be an awful matriarchal situation . . . But the things she has to give away . . . and yet, when some of the jam is something that comes our way, I don't mind accepting it. So it's not fair in some ways to criticize her. . . . . I wonder. I don't know enough about it really, but I just have the feeling that, although I can tell myself now it is all fine and dandy, whether I really in some ways accept that it is . . . and . . . without getting hurt . . . aggravated. . . . . . I didn't see much difference in Petie. He was upset a little bit every now and then . . . maybe that he's too little to be bothered very much by all the confusion but, he certainly . . . I think he realized, or was aware of the change in the environment . . . and he was very diplomatic and smiling at the right places . . .

From Carol's Daily Records

November 3. Petie has worst cold he's ever had. Coughed quite a lot tonight. I studied until 3:00 A.M.

November 4. Petie's cold better. Wow! Two exams today. Pooped. Bill discouraged because wall is falling down again.

November 8. Normal day for everybody. Petie's cold gone.

November 16. Petie fussy today. He's teething and he had a shot.

November 20. Six months old today! Smiled, talked, and laughed with Bill tonight. Played with his teddy bear.

November 25. My family arrived tonight for Thanksgiving.

November 26. Had our Thanksgiving today. Petie rolled over from back to stomach. Everybody loves him.

November 27. Petie has been a little doll. He's let everybody hold him and take care of him. This visit has been wonderful.

November 28. Petie gets up on hands and knees and tries to crawl. Folks left today.

November 30. Practically crawls all over dressing table.

December 7. If Petie doesn't like something, he is much more vigorous and loud in his protest than before.

December 17. Bill and I stayed up 'til 5:00 A.M. doing Christmas cards. Exhausted.

From Carol's Free Association

December 17 . . . Did you know we were going to Florida for Christmas? . . . They're paying about $30.00 a day to have us down there. . . . . . I've got Christmas presents to make. And we still haven't figured out anything for Bill's mother . . . This Christmas Bill and I decided that regardless of

From Carol's Daily Records	From Carol's Free Association

From Carol's Free Association

anything we're going to buy each other something, because we never have before. And I'm going to get him an electric drill . . . I'm not supposed to spend that much money, but I'm going to anyway—because he wants it. . . . . . A truck came down the hill and ran into our car, in the back of it, and we're constantly having flat tires anyway—so we have to get a new car. We just got a mortgage on the house and we're going to have to use some of it, the mortgage money on a car if we can . . . that's another thing we have to do before we go to Florida: straighten out all our finances and pay our bills, because otherwise we won't be in the University, because we owe them $155.00 . . .

December 18. Stayed up 'til 5:00 A.M. again. Pooped!

December 19. Peter was very good all day.

December 20. Plane trip to Florida from New York. Petie was fine. Very happy and friendly on the plane. Bill's parents met us.

December 21. Petie cried a great deal tonight. Had a hard time getting him to sleep. I began sneezing today.

December 22. Petie puts his arms out to be picked up. Sneezed my head off this morning. Wears me out.

December 23. Peter sucks his thumb more than usual. Stayed with Bill's folks while I did some shopping. Fussy throughout the day.

December 24. Petie has a slight temperature. Pretty fussy. He's teething. Very demanding. I get impatient and cross with him.

From Carol's Daily Records

From Carol's Free Association

December 25. I am worried about Peter. He's so fussy and cranky—not himself at all. I'm sure whatever's bothering him is more than teeth.

December 26. Saw doctor this morning. He says Peter has sore throat slight earache. Up three times during night with him. I was so tired and sort of cross.

December 27. Petie more cuddly than usual. Seems to need very much to be with Bill and me. His cough is worse.

December 28. Peter broke out with German measles today. Cough is still bad. He fights medicine. What next? I'm disgusted.

December 29. Left Peter with Bill's mother today while we took a boat ride.

December 30. Flew back to my home today. All of us have colds and feel miserable.

December 31. Left Petie with Mom while Bill and I went out to buy a car. Got a new station wagon! Miserable cold.

January 1. Pretty good day for Petie. Didn't do much today. Gave mother a home permanent.

January 2. Drove home in new car. Petie very good. So good to be home!

January 3. Petie acts very insecure. He sucks his thumb, won't play by himself. Doesn't want to go to sleep and finally when he does he wakes screaming. Wants to be held all the time. Not his cheerful self.

January 11. Petie has not been the same with Mrs. Lee since we got back. He doesn't seem to want to

From Carol's Daily Records

be left alone with her. Otherwise he's his old sweet self again.

January 13. Peter played happily today. Back to normal with Mrs. Lee.

January 14. Very good day today!

January 18. Still has a little croupy cough from Christmas.

January 22. Strangers here today. Petie didn't mind them at all. Bit me today nursing! I think it's time to stop!

January 24. Stopped nursing. Petie cried hard this morning. Has a little cold.

January 26. So far no ill effects noticed from stopping nursing.

January 28. Petie was cross at Bill when he wouldn't let him play with electric cords. He kept going back to them. Bill finally spanked his hands and said "uh! uh! uh!" Later when he went back, Bill said, "uh! uh! uh!" and he stopped. This was his first real punishment.

January 31. Shows signs of affection on his part. Snuggles his face into my neck. Pats us, too.

February 2. He plays "Peek a boo" with me now.

February 3. Plays by himself very well. Also loves to twirl around in my arms.

February 4. Amused himself most of the day. Got very little attention from us all day.

From Carol's Free Association

February 4 . . . then about, oh, the second day we were in West Palm Beach he started to be awful cranky . . . and Bill and I got a cold, and I was sneezing the whole time I was there anyway . . . and I kept thinking to myself, if this is mental I'd better cut it out because it's all

From Carol's Daily Records

From Carol's Free Association

foolishness . . . but I don't think it was . . . so we all just felt pretty miserable . . . Christmas was just terrible . . . poor old Petie would wake up about every night between 2:30 and 4:30 and cough and cough and cough . . . he wasn't really sick except for the coughing, he didn't have a fever, and during the day he felt pretty good . . . when we came back and while we were in Florida, well, he uh, he had a terrible time at night going to sleep and, uh, he wouldn't take a nap and he wouldn't eat . . . and when we came home, when he'd wake up from his nap he would wake up just screaming! And he acted like a very insecure little baby and I think all this . . . we were staying in a room, and we were living, and eating and everything in Bill's parents' apartment and he had a nap there and he slept in a different crib at night . . . And we noticed that he settled down in his bed easily the first day we were home, then he'd wake up . . . just, just screaming —a high, piercing sort of scream! And he sucked his thumb a lot more than he ever did before; and he demanded a tremendous amount of attention . . . But he's all over any of that by now . . . The trip was hard on Petie . . . It was hard on all of us in a lot of ways . . . But he was very friendly with everybody. He's never, so far, gone through a shy stage, except in his reaction to other babies. I think it's important for him to see other babies, because he sees only grownups in the major course of his day.

February 6. Peter woke up from his nap while Betty and Judy were here. He is usually cranky after his

From Carol's Daily Records

From Carol's Free Association

afternoon nap. Judy (same age as Peter) screamed at Petie and he cried. Then she did it again, and every time she screamed, he cried.

February 9. My two boys are asleep in their beds—and how I love them!

February 16. When he's over-tired and excited, his behavior takes on a certain pattern. He laughs and yet is quick to cry at the drop of a hat. Grabs things quickly and jerkily, cries when you take them away. Quite often he will bite me (not attack, just seems to be working off tension). He's tenser in his body. He was this way tonight.

February 20. Perfectly friendly with all sorts of strangers. Stares at first, then smiles and waves. I wish Mary, who's pregnant, weren't so set on having a boy.

February 21. Was furious when I took him out of bath. Cried and hit me and tried to squirm away.

February 25. Loves to crawl from one end of room to other laughing and laughing, looking around to see if I am chasing him.

February 26. I was so mad at Bill this afternoon! If he hadn't started that saw Petie might have slept another half an hour.

February 27. Great fun squealing together. He yells and then I squeal. Then we both laugh.

February 28 . . . I don't think I have anything to say. . . . . Guess I have to talk about what I'm thinking about, because I'm thinking about it, but I don't feel like talking about it . . . . the only trouble is that I just hate money, completely. . . . . It's a long complicated story . . . . . . (sighs) I just got a letter

From Carol's Daily Records

From Carol's Free Association

from my sister (sighs) . . . I just, I don't know where to begin. . . . . But I get so mad, and also I feel so guilty, because, well, my grandmother is very sick and has got to be put in a nursing home, and it's going to cost $35 to $40 a week . . . and . . . well . . . every time anything like this comes up in my family, then there's a general . . . I don't know . . . upsetness, or whatever, because . . . the budget is always so close that every penny is counted, and all the bills don't get paid even so, and so there's no room for any $35 to $40 a week, even once a month. And the brothers and sisters are supposedly going to . . . uh, split it up, each one taking a week a month. . . . . . And it makes me feel guilty because I'm taking money from my parents . . . I just *hate* it when they, everybody gets so upset about money . . . and Sue, I don't know whether Sue's writing just for herself or my whole family, and then mother gets practically psychosomatic sick about it . . . Sue thinks that my aunt and uncle should pay more, because they have so much more money, and . . . . . . everybody is so concerned about how other members of the family spend their own money, when it's none of their business how they spend their money. . . . I don't think that much emphasis should be put on money, and on the other hand I get all worked up and moody about money all the time . . . I have to devise a whole new system of economy . . . My folks have to pay $40 a month more too . . . and if they weren't paying us $150 a month then they'd

From Carol's Daily Records   **From Carol's Free Association**

have $40 a month plus quite a few more. And I think maybe I could economize more and we wouldn't need to spend so much money or something, and I just, I don't know . . . it's, it's a crazy situation, this whole financial business, because my parents want to give me money. I know that they want to give it to me. And they don't give it to me with any strings attached to it at all. And yet I feel guilty about taking it. And if I didn't take it, I couldn't go to school and it would be one of the biggest disappointments to my mother and father. It would be a disappointment to me, too, but it would disappoint them more than it would me if I didn't get my degree. . . . And then on the other hand the other letter that I got today was a very lovely letter from Bill's mother. She's just bought everybody in the family electric frying pans. They're worth, oh, I don't know, $40 apiece or something like that . . . We live on, I feel like I live on, two levels of, standards of economy. And they're so different . . . but . . . the whole . . . I don't know, my whole outlook on money is peculiar, because I, I just, am sort of in the middle of these two completely different levels . . . and even though neither side of the family gives us money with strings, it's . . . you don't have the feeling basically, that we can do whatever we want to. I'll be so glad when we're making our own money. But it upsets, it just upsets me when . . . my family is so pinched . . . when we are accepting money from them . . . and yet it's a dilemma, because there's no other way. . . . . It makes

From Carol's Daily Records

From Carol's Free Association

me so angry when my mother's family gets this sort of . . . well, we're the poor ones and everyone else is recklessly spending their money, and they shouldn't because . . . they should give more to their grandmother, or something else . . . And they're free with the advice. . . . . . I just keep feeling I should do something, or should be able to do something, but I don't know what . . . and then I get the feeling that Bill and I are living better than my parents and the rest of the family . . . and yet logically, when I think about it, it isn't really true . . . But it's, it's another time when I start feeling guilty about it. . . . . I'm thinking about mother's working and the . . . sort of breaks that have come along . . . that have been, practically everyone has gone against her . . . and this is another thing which when I get all upset about this sort of thing I think it's my fault, because if she were, she wouldn't be working if she wasn't trying to send us through college. . . . .

March 1. Petie standing on couch bouncing up and down to music, whispering da, da, da. Bill bounces, too. Petie stops and watches Bill, then he starts again, whispering as if keeping time.

March 6. Record player going. Petie crawls near the record player and sits down and listens.

March 9. Sits watching me in playpen. Picks up small piece of paper and puts in mouth. Plays with tongue. Jumps up and stands "talking" to me. Laughs when I sneeze.

March 20. Standing up without support more and more. He was playing beside Judy this morning. Still cries if she screams at him.

The record-keeping stopped at the end of March. Carol had too many things to do during the remaining two months before she and Bill packed up to leave Ithaca. The house had to be completed and sold, papers had to be written, examinations taken. Carol came in for one final hour after she and Bill had graduated. In the interim they had visited their parents for a long weekend. Carol and Peter both remained well. She remarked, "It was the first time I have been in the Chisholm house since our unpleasantness before we were married that I did not sneeze my head off." After Mr. Chisholm had tried to choke her, she said she swore she would never go back into his house again. Her mother had urged her not to be hasty, to remember that Bill loved his parents and would not want to be separated from them. Carol was sure that she came first with Bill and that he would leave his parents if necessary. Still she did not want to hurt him, so she stiffled her pride and went back, acting as if nothing had happened. She never told Bill how she felt until just before this last trip. He was understanding and loving. She felt much better to have shared her feelings with him.

Carol's thoughts turned to leaving Ithaca, and to the future.

I'm scared of other doctors . . . when you have confidence in one doctor and you know the rest of your babies should be Caesarian . . . well, I'm faced with the problem of wanting very much not to wait any longer, so the babies will be close together . . . and being frightened by a lot of unknowns . . . Well, when I was pregnant with Petie, I had the feeling all the time that I was physically fit. I was . . . healthy and everything else, and if worse came to worst, I could practically have the baby all by myself . . . and . . . now, I don't have any of that feeling. I have a feeling that . . . if I get a doctor that bungles, then we won't be able to have any more kids, and that if . . . something happens that it would rupture or . . . I don't know, and I don't have . . . maybe I would, but I tell myself maybe I wouldn't have any of these fears if I could have my babies here . . . Because I don't know anything about Caesarian operations. It's just a big word. And I don't want anything to happen. We want a big family. And I don't want anything to happen so we can't . . . So before I leave I'm going to ask the doctor to sit down and tell me all about just what it is and how complicated it is . . . I don't know how to choose doctors . . .

Part Three: Carol Reflects after One Year

At the end of the year, Carol was asked to go over all the records, including the transcribed free associations, and write her impressions, evaluations, and comments. Here are excerpts from what she wrote:

As background to my discussion of the relationship between Petie and me, I think a sketch of our pattern of living would enable a better understanding of us both. I am very happily married. It is the love and security that Bill gives me that makes me the basically happy, sure person that I am. We lead a very busy life. We tackled a job too big for ourselves by deciding to build a house and do all the work ourselves. This meant that we have had a great deal of extra work, besides our school work and household chores, during our college years. The pressures have been considerable, and we have not always managed the many demands on our time as well as we might have. Despite this we are usually happy, calm people. We depend on one another for support. We have established a firm basis for understanding. We can and do talk out our differences and, consequently, they are few and far between. Bill and I have worked hard together and accomplished the building of a small, comfortable house, in spite of predictions that the job was impossible for us. It was to this house that we brought our small and already much-loved son.

We both wanted a boy. This is the one prenatal attitude neither of us could admit we had. As far as we were concerned, we were sensible; we knew its sex was decided, and we didn't care either way. We were dying of curiosity, though. I'm not saying for a moment that we would have rejected a little girl, but we both wanted a boy.

The only time I was worried about the baby prenatally was when I learned that I would have to have a Caesarian section. Petie was in a breech position and my doctor felt he would be risking brain injury if he let him come normally. I worried that his head, which had been pushing up against my ribs, was already injured. As I look back now, I think I was less worried by specifics than I was troubled by a general uneasiness. Things had gone so well up to this point, and now it seemed they were not going as well. I went to the operating room slightly apprehensive about the welfare of my child, confident that my doctor was as capable as any in the world, and very excited because the baby we had wanted for so long was almost here.

The next thing I remember I was being lifted to my bed. I dimly heard someone say, "She had a boy." But I couldn't seem to remember, and I'd ask over and over again, "What did I have? Is he all right?" The nurse brought a small bundle in to me and let me feel a small foot. When I tried to remember my baby, all I could remember was the soft, little foot I had held. Bill was there, he had seen the baby, the baby was all right. Bill had told our families. I didn't think much about the baby. I hurt, I wanted to hold Bill's hand, and to sleep. When I woke I remembered a small, velvet-like foot and went back to sleep.

Hours later another nurse brought Petie in for me to see. He wasn't beautiful. I thought he had curly hair. He looked so angry as he slept, and I remember hoping that that wasn't his natural expression.

As the days went by Petie became more and more a reality to me. I took off his wrapping blanket and sneaked a look at him. Everyone said he was a big baby (8 lbs. 6 ozs.) but he was absolutely tiny to me. He wasn't really ours until we brought him home. We were so proud, so excited, and I was so weak. Bill had never even held Petie before. He took over, diapering Petie on the new changing table that was ready for us when we came home. We were really parents now . . .

Over a year has passed since we brought Petie home. Our relationship with him has changed, as he has changed. We grow to love our baby more each day; we are no longer unsure of ourselves with him. Our attitudes toward him reflect what we expect of him. He is a personality in his own right. We expect him to be a baby. We feel he needs the benefits of a bottle still, as he needed the benefits of nursing before. I am in no hurry to wean him to a cup, but he drinks from a cup during meals. I feel that the bottle he gets before his morning nap and before he goes to bed for the night provides a good time for a very active boy to calm down and prepare for sleep. It is a quiet time when I can cuddle him and tell him how much I love him. Peter is not toilet trained, either. I have felt that this is another place where we are in no need to hurry. We plan to start training soon for bowel control, because I will soon be home with him every morning, and he has established a regular bowel movement time. He will be more comfortable if he does not have soiled pants.

We believe in fitting our environment to Petie's needs. Life provides so many necessary restrictions on a small boy for his safety that we feel home should be a pretty free place. Almost everything within Peter's reach around the house is something he can have. He may look at the magazines on the magazine table and no one is surprised if a magazine gets torn. Magazines which matter to us are put up out of reach. There is a low drawer in the kitchen with different interesting kitchen utensils he may play with, and there is another drawer in our bedroom. This is not to say that Peter has no restrictions. There are certain *definite, enforced,* and *constant* "no's" in his life already. He may not play with the electric cords and outlets; he may not pull off his father's glasses and play with them; he may not climb into the fireplace; and he may not stand at the refrigerator door when I open it and throw things from the bottom shelf onto the floor. I'm sure he feels that these, especially the latter, are real restrictions to his freedom.

We believe in giving Peter as many opportunities to try things and experience things as is possible. We try to set up situations where he can climb up and down. We let him play in the yard, in the gravel, and in the sand. He gets very dirty, but dirt washes off, and he is gaining valuable experiences. I try to take him where he can "play" with other children his age. He does not get enough of this experience because of the terrific demands on our time and because there are no other babies in our neighborhood.

Peter finger feeds himself table foods at most of his meals. Except when I simply haven't the time or patience, he has a spoon to use when I feed him cereal, or vegetables, or other foods from a dish. He only succeeds in getting a few spoonfuls in his mouth, but he is interested in trying.

Before I close this discussion of my attitudes toward Petie, I should mention one attitude which is so basic I almost skipped over it. That is Bill's importance in Petie's life and vice versa. Saturday mornings when I was in school, Bill took care of Petie. Right from the very first day he has taken a great deal of responsibility. Sometimes when Petie is upset, he turns from me to his father, and again vice versa. Since the comforting is provided by both of us, I do not feel jealous when he turns to Daddy.

We are a family of three. We enjoy eating together, playing together, going places together. Petie, I think, knows he is a part of his mother's and father's love for each other and for him.

It was a shock for me to read over the free associations of a year ago. It could, with only slight revision, be what I might say now, or the term before they were recorded. I was tired out, swamped with back work, almost panicky at the thought of the end of the term so near. I had never before recognized this recurring pattern for what it is. Each year something practically catastrophic was keeping me from getting done what I should. But it was only when I read the free associations that I realized there had been some catastrophe in my life at the close of every school year.

Petie is just learning to walk. He can walk ten or twelve steps before falling. This is the latest of the motor developments to appear. The mental processes are hard to detect and record. His first smile of recognition of a human face came at four weeks and seemed to be a big step. As he grew older, he would watch things—the branches overhead or the bright red rings of the cradle gym. Small, gurgly noises other than fussing or crying came next—as first steps in the long road to speech. Being able to play with his cradle gym rings involved mental processes as well as motor. Sensing new places, such as the car bed, and new noises, such as cello playing, at three months shows the beginnings of environment perception. When he was five months old, he would sit, watching us eat, opening his mouth when we opened ours. Each of these, and other, processes grow. Today Petie knows his Daddy and Mommy and his "Grammy." He says "Da Da" to mean Daddy. He can, and does, make just about every sound. He holds long "conversations" with people. His curiosity knows no bounds. He wants to see, to try, to taste, to feel everything he comes in contact with. He engages in imitative dramatic play. The best example of this is his use of the toy telephone. He takes the receiver off, he dials, he talks with the receiver to his ear, and he hangs up. He bounces up and down to music, and has done so since eight months. What a year ago was a bundle, sleeping and eating, is now an engaging little boy.

Petie's patterns of emotional expression have followed a parallel to his mental development. He has reached a point where he expresses his affection. He comes up to you, puts his head down on your knees or shoulder and pats you, saying "aahh." When you prevent him from doing something he is intent on doing, he is very likely to sit down hard and scream and protest. He has always shown his protest against things he doesn't like. When he was only a couple of months old, we thought it too soon to attribute these outbursts to temper, but they most closely resemble that now.

It seems like I always wanted a baby. I adored my doll and played dolls until after I was in junior high school. Then my doll went to my sister, but she was still my "baby." Of course my feelings about a child of my own grew as I fell in love and married. A child would now be *our* baby!—part of the man I loved and myself. When we knew I was pregnant, a child became more real, and more wanted.

During the first part of Petie's life our relationship was essentially give-and-take. I gave and he took. The nursing situation was indeed the most reciprocal of all, but even without doing anything, Petie gave us a great deal of joy.

As Petie grew, our relationship grew also. We three would spend an extra hour on a Sunday morning all in bed "talking" and laughing together. Petie belonged.

Now Petie is a little boy. We know more what to expect from each other.

We have special times during each day we take off from busy activity when I hold him, cuddle him, and give him a bottle. I think that our relationship is best seen in the fact that he is a happy son of a happy mother.

Another comment on the relationship between Petie and me is the seemingly positive correlation found between a disturbing emotional situation for me, and Petie's subsequent behavior. Our first trip to Bill's home was made when he was just under two months old. Petie was sick for one week after we got home. When Bill's parents were here in August, he was fussy during the visit, but not overly so. He contracted a cold after our trip to their house in October and so did I. Christmas time he came down with German measles and we all had colds. He was especially insecure in Florida, where he had come down with the measles, and took a long while to calm down. After our last trip this May, however, he was fine. I am not sure this is enough evidence to provide a meaningful correlation. At other times when I have been under a great deal of stress, Petie has shown no adverse effects.

Part Four: Interpretive Summary

You will recall that this study of Carol and Peter was guided by the following objectives:

1. to determine the major mental preoccupations of the mother before the birth of the baby and during the subsequent year,

2. to trace the course of growth and development of the child for one year, and

3. to observe the developing patterns of mother-child interaction.

It was not without theoretical preconceptions that precisely these objectives were chosen. What these preconceptions were have already been discussed. Suffice it here to point out that personality is conceived as emerging from a definite series of interpersonal situations throughout life and as striving for satisfactions through interpersonal situations. Personality in the absence of other persons, present or imagined, is meaningless. Thus the basic unit of study is the interaction of two or more persons. One of the most significant interpersonal situations is the family, and within the family, especially in the early years, the mother-child interaction.

One can look at a given, immediate situation and analyze the responses of each actor in terms of the observed stimulations impinging upon him. Frequently this type of analysis of human behavior is entirely adequate, especially for molar motoric activity. If one boy throws a ball to a second, who puts out his gloved hand to receive it, there is no mystery here if the two boys *and* the observer have grown up in the American culture. If one of the boys, however, has just arrived on the scene from a non-baseball-playing culture and the ball is thrown at him, he may duck quickly, or he may catch the ball in self-defense and hurl it back at the head of his presumed opponent.

This latter behavior may occur on occasion between two acculturated American boys; but in this case we say the behavior requires explanation. In the first instance we tacitly assumed they were playing ball. In the second, this assumption does not hold, and we are forced to infer another reason or motive. In order to infer the motive we must generalize from previous similar situations or we must inquire into the immediate antecedents of the act. Did boy A say something to offend boy B? Or did boy A break an agreed-upon rule in such a way as to arouse the ire of boy B? When the answers to these and other similar questions are discovered, we would be able to say that we had an explanation of the observed interaction. We would be even more convinced if we could repeat the sequence, interjecting the isolated antecedent variable at will and observing the aforementioned response as a consequence. Not often can this be done in the everyday world. It requires patience and fortuity to come upon such repetitions. But they do occur, and we shall search for them in our personal documents.

We shall, then, look for antecedents, not to all the behavior we have observed, but rather antecedents to the major trends which have been exposed. We lay no claim to a complete understanding of Carol or Peter, and certainly not to the other persons who have appeared in supporting roles on our stage.

Carol's Preoccupations While Free Associating

The transcriptions of Carol's free associations were analyzed to see how frequently she spoke of herself, Bill, and the baby, and what changes occurred over the course of a year. The analysis consisted of a simple counting of the number of times each was mentioned. A point was given for each reference to the person. One year later the documents were scored again to determine rater reliability. The correlation coefficient was .93. Since Carol was more loquacious on some occasions than others, and since sometimes the recording period varied as much as ten minutes, a correction was made in the raw scores. A word count for each session was made and the mean determined. A correction was made in terms of deviations from the mean for each period. The chart on page 125 is a graph representing the corrected, equated scores.

A few comments about the content of Carol's thoughts might make the chart more meaningful. The first and highest peak, which occurs at the third month, represents what was taking place the day before Carol went to the hospital, and the day after she had learned that the baby would be delivered by Caesarian section. You will recall that she was extremely anxious. She was concerned about her own safety and the baby's welfare. She mentioned Bill frequently as a source of great comfort to her. Dread of the unknown procedure which she faced was her chief preoccupation. At only two other times did Carol's thoughts center upon

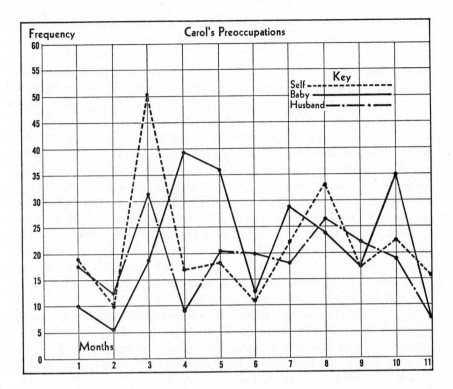

Frequency — Carol's Preoccupations

Key
Self ----------
Baby ——————
Husband —·——·—

Months

herself more than on Bill or the baby—months 8 and 11. Month 8 was the session during which she related their trip to Bill's parents' house on the occasion of Peter's baptism. Month 11 revealed her conflict and guilt over the double economic systems between which she was caught.

Immediately after the baby's birth there was a shift in Carol's preoccupations. This shift to concern with and for the baby is seen not only in the free associations, but also in every observational record available. Months 4 and 5 depict the situation quite clearly. She seemed to talk of nothing but the baby—how he ate, how cute he was, how much he weighed, how he responded to her, et cetera.

Then at month 6, when Peter was three months old, there was a drop in her discussion of him and his affairs. The next month showed a marked rise, however, occasioned by anticipation of his baptism. During months 8 and 9 there was again reduced attention, only to have it shoot up to a peak once more at month 10, when Peter was eight and a half months old. This rise in preoccupation with Peter came at the time of his most severe and prolonged illness during and following the trip to Florida to visit Bill's parents at Christmas time.

In addition to Carol's preoccupation with herself, Bill and Peter, there are two conflicts which are recurrent themes, and one minor irritation.

The conflicts concern Bill's parents and money; the minor irritation has to do with her school work.

Present, past, future. "I am very happily married. It is the love and security that Bill gives me that makes me the basically happy, sure person I am." Thus did Carol characterize herself, and thus did she feel about herself. In the author's contacts with her she was nearly always cheerful and optimistic, never depressed—hostile, yes, anxious, yes, but not depressed. She was too outgoing and expressive to be depressed. She had an easy, free relationship with Bill, whom she deeply loved. They had developed a mutual dependence, a healthy dependence, and neither let the other down. Carol had no fears that Bill could not be counted on for support, even if it should mean rejecting others with whom he had deep affectional bonds. In her moments of anxiety, it was to Bill she turned for comfort, and he was always there. When she had a new experience, or accomplished something special, or anticipated some new pleasure, it was to Bill that she turned to share it. She was delighted to be pregnant with Bill's child. She wanted to please him.

Yes, Carol was a basically happy, secure person. She had her anxieties, to be sure, but they were non-neurotic anxieties, and she dealt with them for the most part in a healthy, straightforward manner. Her chief anxieties centered around the birth of the baby and visits to her in-laws. Her anxiety over the birth was minimal until she learned that she could not have a normal delivery. That knowledge, in the face of ignorance of what would be involved in a Caesarian operation and the threat it posed to her safety, produced a strong anxious reaction. But certainly it was not an abnormal reaction. In no way did she attempt to evade or avoid what was necessary.

How do we account for Carol's easy-going, serene personality? Except for the two conflicts which we will discuss in a moment, and the irritations occasioned by pressing academic assignments, Carol would have been supremely happy. I think we must look in two places, perhaps three, for an answer to our question, an answer, admittedly partial. In the first place, she was psychologically and physically healthy. She did not view the world with a jaundiced eye. People's actions were taken at face value; she spent little or no time reading deep and dark motives into the behavior of friends and associates. She viewed the world fairly objectively and herself with a rationally appraising and not too critical eye. Carol had grown up in a family where she never questioned her complete acceptance and belongingness. She was loved and, in turn, she loved. The atmosphere in the home, because the parents practiced the democratic ideal in family relationships, was one of give and take. Love was taken for granted; because there were many expressions of affection, arguments, disagreements, and occasional harsh words could be engaged in and tolerated without arousing undue anxiety. If one stepped out of line, whether in the performance of household chores or in verbal debate, others were quick to point out the lapse, and one was brought quickly back to the sharp point of reality. Carol held a place of special status as the first child; although she was jealous of her sister, and never liked her as well as she did her brother, she did not feel that the sister posed any real threat to her position. Carol and her family had a good time together; they worked hard in the winter and played hard in the summer on their island in Canada. There were no insurmountable problems.

The Johnson family were respected members of the middle-class community in which they lived. Carol participated in and accepted this respect without thinking about it. She was a good student in high school; she made top grades without exerting herself very much. She had many friends. By the time she was sixteen she had already met and fallen in love with Bill. Her parents approved and encouraged her relationship with Bill.

Thus we see that for Carol while she was growing up life posed no problems with which she could not successfully cope. What she had to offer was accepted; she was not asked for more than she could give. Not until she reached college did she begin to question her ability to master anything she turned her hand to. But her level of aspiration was never very high, and by the time she began to question her intellectual and creative abilities, she was married and had a child on the way. These more than compensated for any deficiencies which she may have begun to feel in herself.

The second place we look to explain Carol's serene personality is in the current situation. Here we see that Carol's mutually satisfying relationship with her husband and baby made no demands on her that she could not meet, and this was the most important aspect of her life. Had she valued academic achievement more, had she been compulsively neat, had she felt a threat to her security in Bill's plans to return to his father's business, had she felt cheated out of youthful freedom by an unexpectedly early motherhood—then we would have had a different story, and a different Carol. She not only accepted her current situation, but she participated in the making of it. Carol had a definite sense of power in her everyday affairs. What she said and did made a difference in her world. It was she and Bill who decided to build the house. They were not forced by external circumstances. They wanted to build the house and build it they did, in the face of numbers of warnings as to the lack of wisdom of the venture. It turned out well. They had a sense of real accomplishment and real sharing.

Before we turn to the conflicts in Carol's contemporary life, let us look to a third possible source of her serenity—to her future aspirations. As Carol looked ahead, she saw nothing but a bright future. Everything she wanted she expected to be able to achieve. The only possible doubt arose in connection with her ability to have as many children as she wanted in view of the complications of delivery.

Conflicts. Carol wanted very much to like Bill's parents. She wanted to because she loved Bill and he loved his parents; she wanted to because families were important to her and children naturally love their parents; she wanted to because her child was their grandchild; and she wanted to because they were in a position to do many things for her and her own family. Instead she hated them because they had rejected her. They had said to her in a violently overt fashion, "You are not good enough for us." This judgment stung deeply. It was the first time Carol had had occasion seriously to question her own worth. She hated them because they were dictatorial and inconsiderate of the wishes and feelings of other people. And she hated them because they had something she wanted, and she felt dependent on them—she "liked the jam" too much.

She was in conflict! She wanted to like them, but she hated them, and she had to act as if she loved them. Under these conditions a considerable strain is placed upon one's self-respect. She had to force herself where she would not go. It is at moments like this that mechanisms of defense come into play. In Carol's case we see two such mechanisms: rationalization and retreat in illness. She tried heroically to justify her actions, even excusing her mother-in-law's dictational invalidism. But this defense alone was inadequate and a retreat to illness was resorted to. We do not know why this particular mechanism developed in Carol. Presently we shall see how Peter was caught up in this conflict of his mother's.

The other source of conflict for Carol was money. This is not unconnected with the conflict over Bill's parents. If they had not had so much money, which Carol coveted, it might have been easier for her to defy them, tell them exactly what she thought of them, or even reject them outright.

Money had always been a problem in Carol's family. Although there had never been very much, they always seemed to have enough for a good life. But there was no reserve for emergencies. They spent their income as fast as they received it. It bothered Carol that her mother had to work in order for the family to maintain the standard of living they enjoyed—including her college education. She felt guilty when she compared the money which she and Bill spent on luxuries—the trip to Florida and a new car—with the hardships her parents endured for lack of money. She would have liked to stop taking money from her parents and turn to Bill and his parents for her complete support, but her pride would not permit it. Already she had sorely compromised her self-respect, as we have seen. She could not become completely dependent on the Chisholms economically even if it meant continued bondage for her own parents.

The conflict over money became acute when Sue wrote about the impending crisis occasioned by the necessity of placing the grandmother in a nursing home. Carol, in great distress, never was able to solve this conflict satisfactorily. She attempted to protect herself first by lashing out at Sue and her other relatives, projecting her own concern over money onto them. This was easy to do because in reality they were concerned. To be successful, however, this mechanism had to be accompanied by another, denial; Carol had to deny that the question of money was of great moment to her. This she tried to do, but she could not convince herself, and so the conflict continued.

The minor irritation referred to above was in connection with Carol's school work. At first it was quite a blow to her to realize that her academic efforts did not win the acclaim to which she had grown accustomed in high school. She was puzzled and hurt. She reacted by blaming the courses and making fun of the instructors. They were inadequate, not she. How long she would have been able to maintain this defense if she had not had other overreaching interests and values is uncertain. It is quite clear that many students faced with a similar dilemma break under the strain and leave college; or, if they have sufficient capability and high aspirations, buckle down and produce satisfactory work. Carol did not place a college education high in her hierarchy of values. She wanted a degree to please her parents, so she did just enough to get by. Her real interests lay in pleasing Bill and subsequently her baby. In both of these pursuits she was eminently successful.

Growth and Development of Peter

Peter grew at a normal pace. In the differentiation of certain functions there were, to be sure, variations in the rate of growth from the normative portraits we have of other infants. In some areas he was slower, in others faster in maturation, but always within normal limits.

When Peter was still less than two weeks of age we had accumulated a considerable amount of data concerning his behavior. Much of this information indicated that he should be classified as a quiet, inactive infant. The nurse in the hospital reported that he was the quietest of the normal infants. Our own observations and tests placed him in the quiet category. On the basis of these findings, and in the light of the work others have done on energy expenditure (particularly Margaret Fries' publications), we predicted that Peter would continue to be an inactive, quiet baby. We did not expect that he would be forceful in making demands on those who attended him, or that he would be vigorous in expressing his displeasure. We were wrong on all accounts. And we must try to understand what evidence we overlooked, and what evidence we over-weighted in making our predictions.

In the first place Peter did not fall asleep while nursing, as many quiet babies do. His mother insisted that he "work" for his food. She did not allow him to lie passively while she forced the nipple into his mouth. She would bring him into position, hold him securely and make the nipple available, but in order to obtain milk he had to "root around" until he made contact with the nipple. And if he lost it, he had to find it again. Thus right from the day of birth Peter was put on his mettle to reach out and actively participate with the surrounding world. The power of this reinforcement of his activity was overlooked.

Another factor which was not taken into full account was the fact that Peter was a Caesarian baby. It appears likely that from the point of view of the infant this is a somewhat less traumatic entrance into the outside world than is the usual pulling, tugging, and squeezing that accompanies passage through the birth canal, with or without the aid of forceps. The reaction to the Caesarian experience would be less severe and the activity of the infant during the first few days after birth accordingly reduced.

We compared Peter with infants in Brownfield's population (Brownfield, 1956), but there were three inadequately weighed differences between Peter's situation and that of these other infants: (a) observations on Peter were made at home, while those in Brownfield's study were made at the hospital. Aldrich, Sung, and Knop * have shown that infants cry more while in the hospital, where they are cared for by nurses, than they do after they go home and are cared for by their own mothers. (b) Peter was on a self-demand feeding schedule, while Brownfield's infants were on a strict, four-hour schedule. Whenever Peter showed signs of hunger, his mother was very prompt to pick him up and offer him the opportunity to nurse. He was never permitted to become very uncomfortable from hunger pangs. When he was observed, therefore, he was not in a state of tension which is observed in very hungry infants. (c) Peter was breast-fed; Brownfield's infants were bottle-fed. In the hospital situation the infants were given a fixed number of ounces of milk and no more until the next feeding time, regardless of any evidences of hunger which the infant might reveal. Peter's mother, on the other hand, had an adequate supply of milk and allowed him to take as much as he wished at each feeding. If Carol thought he was hungry an hour after eating, she would put him on the other breast. She always took her cue from Peter as to when he wanted to nurse and how long he wanted to nurse.

These conditions undoubtedly influenced the reactions which we later observed in Peter. We tended to overestimate at first the constitutional factors at the expense of what was going on in the immediate situation.

Peter grew into an active, alert baby, interested both in people and

---

* Aldrich, C. A., Sung, C., and Knop, C., "The Crying of Newly Born Infants, I: Community Phase." *Journal of Pediatrics*, 1945, *26*, 313–326; "The Crying of Newly Born Infants, II: The Individual Phase." *Journal of Pediatrics*, August, 1945, 89–96.

immobile objects. He became a very responsive little boy, probably as a result of the stimulation provided him by his parents.

Mother-Child Interaction

From an undifferentiated mass, and a slow-moving one at that—one in which the startle response could not always be elicited—Peter, at the age of twelve months, had turned into an alert, responsive, and actively seeking little boy. In the beginning he had no ready-made patterns of response more complicated than the blind "rooting around" which he did with his mouth and head when he was hungry and brought in contact with warm flesh. At twelve months he could make his wishes and his dislikes known in a variety of ways: walking, pushing, grabbing, hitting, biting, talking, singing, crying, whining, smiling, hugging, and even kissing. His wishes and dislikes and the multitude of patterns of behavior used in their service had been learned in a relatively short period of time. He would never again learn so much in so short a time. And the learning which had taken place, which had transformed that relatively undifferentiated mass into a highly functional, mobile little boy, had created a distinctive personality. Where at first there were no psychological systems, now there were many. With the development of each psychological system, his potential for response was reduced. That is to say, as he learned to respond in a given way to his satisfaction under given conditions, the likelihood of his responding in a dissimilar manner was reduced. Thus he was developing need-dispositions, almost automatic patterns of response to specific stimuli, some of which would be altered by subsequent experience, some of which would remain relatively unchanged and perhaps unused throughout his life.

What are some of these patterns? And can we show how they came into existence? We will concentrate only on those patterns which developed in relation to the mother, unquestionably the most significant person in his life up to this point, although admittedly not the only important one. Much learning occurred in relation to other people: Bill, for example, and Mrs. Lee, but we do not have the evidence to trace this learning. Much learning took place in relation to the inanimate world, as Peter tried to manipulate and bend objects to his use, and as he experienced over and over again the fact of gravity. Again, we do not have the evidence to trace the steps through which he went in such learning. Our evidence pertains to the mother-child interaction. Even here, the evidence is sometimes scanty, and we shall have to fill in the gaps as best we can.

Learning the tools of communication. Neonates do not have any ready-made communication systems. But, you say, they cry, and that is certainly a means of communication. Does it not bring mother running? Sometimes, yes; sometimes, no. If yes, the cry quickly becomes a pattern used by the neonate in relation to certain internal stresses. And from the point of view of the outside world, it is a very effective means of control. If no one responds to his crying—after a while he will cease; no pattern of communication is developed. At this early age it takes very little reinforcement to establish a pattern of response. Therefore learning occurs very rapidly—so rapidly, in fact, that many parents are convinced that the "cute little tricks" their babies use must have been a part of their original equipment.

If a mother, or whoever takes care of the baby, does not respond to the child's undifferentiated motoric expressions, he does not learn specific responses. The ability to communicate involves emitting a cue which is perceived and responded to in such a way that the sender receives a confirming report back. For example, let us take our crying baby. He may cry all day, but if no one picks him up, if no one cuddles him, if no one feeds him or changes his diapers in response to the cry, that cry is not a communication. If, on the other hand, one of these actions occurs while the baby is crying, it becomes a confirming report to the baby, or, if you please, a reinforcement of the cry. On a future occasion of similar internal stress, the cry is more likely to occur. If the response comes promptly, we may say that a pattern of communication has been established.

We know that these patterns of communication are not ready-made at birth because in some children they do not develop. There are autistic children who are unable to make their wishes known to anyone and who seem to dwell in a world apart from others. That they are potentially capable of communicating is demonstrated occasionally, but rarely and with great therapeutic difficulty, when one of them is gradually retrained so that he functions in a near-normal fashion. It appears that the autistic condition develops due to a failure to establish a responsive, give-and-take relationship with another person. The failure may be the result of inattention on the part of the one responsible for the baby, or it may be due to some defect in the perceptive organs of the baby, thus limiting his capacity to receive confirming reports. Whatever the cause—and a great deal more research is needed to establish it with confidence—the baby ceases to send cues with any expectation of a confirming response from outside himself. It seems as if he develops a system of cue-response within his own skin; in other words, he emits a cue which he then responds to himself. This circular process effectively excludes intrusion from the outside world. One of the most difficult tasks which any psychologist faces is to try to penetrate that private world of the autistic child.

Peter was far from being autistic. We have already indicated that he developed many effective systems of communication. How did this take place? As we have seen, Carol was very pleased when she found out she was pregnant. She followed the course of development of the foetus with intense curiosity and interest in each stage. She was in a very receptive frame of mind when the baby was born. When he proved to be a boy, she was overjoyed and wholeheartedly accepting of him. From the first she was attuned to Peter and instantly responsive to his several expressions.

Peter's first contact with the world in which communication was established was through his mouth. He "rooted around" with his mouth and head. When his lips came in contact with the nipple of his mother's breast, he closed over it and a sucking reflex followed. Shortly he was sucking vigorously. The next time he was put to the breast, having been without food for three hours, he "rooted" again until the nipple was located. By the time he was twelve days old, a pattern had developed so that when he was put to the breast, he immediately took the nipple into his mouth, without preliminary "rooting," and began to suck smoothly and strongly. In the process of developing this habit pattern the mother played an important role. It was she who responded to his cry and brought him into position so that his lips could engage the nipple. It was she who, aware that a rapidly sucking baby takes in air as well as milk, turned him over her shoulder and gently patted his back until a series of bubbles escaped from his stomach. It was she who put him back to the breast, realizing that the released air left space for more milk. In all this she was responding to cues which she received from him. He, in turn, was responding to cues arising from within himself and presented from the outside world. If either had been unresponsive, this pattern would not have been established so readily, so easily—perhaps not at all.

Not only in regard to nursing did responsive patterns develop between mother and child. As Carol said: "Petie slept in a bassinet, and he repeatedly worked himself to the end of it in the second week. Much of this progress was related to crying, for his whole body was a mass of activity when he cried. His face took on expression, too, for he would turn down his mouth, squint his eyes shut, stiffen his whole body, and break into indignant howls, accompanied by furious activity." In the beginning these bodily expressions were a part of undifferentiated activity. They took on meaning, differentiated function, as Carol responded to them. Gradually the cry became a signal which Peter could use to signify that something was wrong. He and Carol both learned the signal. Whereas at first he used it undiscriminatingly, and Carol responded in similar manner, gradually she learned that the cry was a generalized response to all sorts of internal and external stimuli impinging upon Peter; she further learned that the quality of the cry varied with the kind of stimulus which evoked it. Thus she began to alter her response to the cry as she became more discriminating in her perception of its significance. Those cries to which she readily responded by attending to Peter became established in his growing repertory of behavior patterns. Those cries to which she failed to respond shortly ceased to be emitted, or if they were emitted, they were abortive.

By the age of four-and-a-half weeks, Peter's attention could be arrested if Carol jiggled some wooden rings over his head. At eight weeks he would kick and coo if she moved the rings; occasionally he would strike out at the rings as if he were trying to hit them. If the rings were put into his hands, he would grasp them and pull hard. By ten weeks he was able to control his hands sufficiently to reach up and strike the rings. He would watch them move, and when they stopped he would slowly, jerkily reach up to hit them again. Thus he was learning to manipulate inanimate objects—objects which had been put within his reach by Carol, who realized the importance of providing adequate stimulation for her young baby.

Sometimes the response which Peter evoked from Carol was different from his usual reception. "I was provoked with Petie this afternoon. When I picked him up I did so roughly, which made him cry louder." He was beginning to learn that the same object was not always the same. Later he would be able to make such fine discriminations that he could appropriately interpret the slightest frown that crossed his mother's face.

At thirty-six weeks Peter and Carol had developed such excellent reciprocal responses that they were able to play a game of peekaboo. Carol would put her hands over her face and say, "Where's Mommy?" Peter would laugh and pull her hands from her face. Then they would both laugh. When Carol stopped putting her hands to her face, Peter would reach up, take her hands in his and place them over her eyes. Could anything be clearer as to meaning? Is there any doubt that they were communicating?

Thus far we have given examples of interrelatedness between Peter and Carol in which Carol, at least, was responding to Peter in an intentional or purposeful manner. She had certain goals in mind for Peter, and when he made the correct response to her stimulation she reinforced it by a variety of counter-responses—giving him milk, smiling, cuddling him. Many, many learnings of a young child occur after this fashion. But not all.

Sometimes a baby, and for that matter an older child, will respond to a cue given by a mother in a way that she did not intend he should. Or let us put it this way: although mothers are not always aware of the cues which they send forth to their children, the children nevertheless receive and respond to them. Thus a great deal of unintentional learning takes place. The same principles of learning apply in both cases; the only difference is that on the one hand the reinforcement is intentional, whereas on the other it is not. One instance of such unintentional learning on the part of Peter, and some of its historical roots, will close for the time being our discussion of this mother-child interaction.

In Carol's summation she said there was a "seemingly positive correlation found between a disturbing emotional situation for me, and Petie's subsequent behavior." She went on to say that whenever she and Peter came into a face to face relationship with Bill's parents, she was emotionally disturbed and Peter became ill. This statement merits further investigation.

The chart on page 136 shows the number and location of interactions between Carol and Peter and both sets of grandparents. It also gives briefly Peter's reactions to each situation. Examination of the chart will show that invariably when Carol and Peter were in the presence of the paternal grandparents, whether in their own home, the grandparents' home, or visiting them in Florida, Peter reacted violently to something. His reactions took the form of crying, fussing, spitting, demanding attention, vomiting, and contracting a cold or a cough. On one occasion he broke out with eczema. Contrariwise, when visiting or being visited by maternal grandparents no such behavior was elicited. On the last recorded visit to both sets of grandparents, Peter's behavior was normal; that is, he presented no special problems. Shortly before this last visit Carol had confessed to Bill the intensity of her dislike of his parents. She had held off expressing her hatred for two-and-a-half years because she did not wish to hurt him. Bill, however, was completely understanding and sympathetic. They discussed at length her feelings and the reasons she felt as she did. The hostility of his sister when they had first met, the refusal of his parents to meet her for months, the outbursts and threats of the father, the tyranny of the mother—all were poured out, at first hesitantly, then, with encouragement, vehemently. Bill neither criticized nor defended his parents. He understood completely how Carol felt; he let her talk and talk. When she had spent herself with her outpourings he took her into his arms. She wept softly.

The record shows that whenever Carol was in the presence of Bill's parents she was extremely anxious, distressed, physically uncomfortable, and usually became ill. The record also shows that at the same time Peter's behavior changed. From a smiling, active, inquisitively exploring baby, he became fussy, demanding, clinging, crying, physically ill. This relationship was invariable. Peter's reaction can hardly be accounted for by a simple change of locus, by fatigue after long travel, by contact with many people. These same conditions obtained when they visited Carol's parents, only then Peter remained fairly constant. The obvious variable antecedent to Peter's change in behavior was the change in Carol herself, which she recognized when she reviewed the records she had kept and the transcribed free associations before their last recorded trip.

If it is true that Peter's reaction was to a perceived change in Carol,

Peter's Reactions to Contacts with Grandparents

Paternal Grandparents		Maternal Grandparents	
At grandparents' home	At own home	At grandparents' home	At own home
June 29–July 6 Spitty, fussy at meals. Whined and cried five hours at a stretch. Sleep irregular. Vomited.		**July 16–19** (Canada) Very good. Easy take care of. Left with baby-sitters.	
	July 31–August 1 Eczema. Grunty, fussy. Did not eat well. Very hard feedings.	**August 3–9** (Canada) Reacted normally. Screamed once when screen door banged. No problems.	**August 3–September 6** Cried when left with mother's sister. Calmed immediately when mother returned. Carol got a cold, but not Peter.
October 29–Nov. 1 Seemed confused. Developed a cold.			
December 20–30 (Florida) Cried a great deal. Sucked thumb and fussed more than usual. Wanted to be picked up all the time. Got a terrific cold and German measles.		**December 31–Jan. 2** Left with grandmother. Got along fine. Petie still has cold contracted days ago, otherwise well and happy. **May 5–7** Easy trip. No problems with Peter.	

what was the mechanism whereby the perception took place? To invoke the mysterious concept of "empathy" here would add nothing. That a baby, under favorable conditions, grows to be sensitive to cues, even unconscious cues, emitted by his mother is amply demonstrated. Known principles of learning appear to be adequate to explain this developed relationship. But what precisely are the cues sent forth by the mother which the baby perceives? We cannot say exactly. Research in this area is long overdue. In the case of Peter and Carol we can only point out some of the changes which Carol recognized occurring in herself. That Peter reacted to the changes violently is patent. To exactly which of the changes in their relationship he reacted, the combination of changes necessary and the magnitude of change required to produce such reaction we cannot specify.

Ordinarily Carol was a relaxed, easy-going person, who was mostly patient with Peter. If he took a long time to nurse, she did not mind, because she enjoyed it. She held him firmly and tenderly. She cuddled him and talked softly and sweetly. She sang to him, because her heart was free. She danced with him in her arms. If he was fussy or showed signs of discomfort, she was especially tender and loving. She would spend any amount of time attending to his needs, even in the middle of the night. Now let us get a picture of the way she felt and acted when she was visiting the Chisholms . . . "And then on Sunday I was sort of knocked flat by an allergy . . . and I was really miserable . . ." "I usually start sneezing when I am at Bill's house" . . . "Sneezed my head off this morning. It wears me out . . ." Petie is "very demanding. I get impatient and cross with him." "Up three times during the night with him. I was so tired and sort of cross." . . . Petie's "cough is still bad. He fights medicine. What next? I'm disgusted."

We do not know how these changes in Carol were transmitted through her motoric system to Peter. More evidence is needed on this crucial point. But the picture we have of Carol when she is at home and when she is visiting Bill's parents is vastly different. It is not unreasonable to assume that her anxiety, her tiredness, her impatience showed in a strained voice, in a quicker handling of Peter, in preoccupation with other matters than the little cues which Peter emitted and to which she was usually so prompt in reacting. It is not even unreasonable to assume that as he became more cranky and demanding she became rough in her treatment of him. If these speculations be true, Peter found himself in a changed world, a world in which his patterns of interactions failed to produce the usual responses. In a word, his communication system had broken down. And he reacted violently.

Historical perspective. Carol had grown up in a family where she was loved and respected. She had learned to anticipate these positive responses from people, and to give them in turn. She and her family had many good times together. Although they had also differences of opinion and quarrels, these were usually in line with the realities of the contemporary situation. Thus Carol developed a sharp sense of the appropriateness of one's reactions; she had no neurotic response systems. She was able to express her hostility immediately, and be done with it, without a long period of brooding or self-incrimination as a consequence. Equally she could express her love openly, warmly, physically.

It is important to know all this when we come to examine the contemporary situation and make predictions about the future. There are times when the forces of the present scene are so arrayed that an individual's reactions are atypical—out of character, as the novelist would put it. Such an occasion might be following marriage, when a person is subject to excessive and, usually, tender affection. Another occasion might be following the birth of a child, when what one has to offer, in the case of a mother, is greatly in demand. These are situations designed to bring forth responses which temporarily overshadow the more typical modes of response. If one observes only the immediate situation, without knowledge of the history of reinforcements, one's predictions may go sadly awry.

With Carol we know better. Her reactions at any given moment were in line with her typical, life-long responses—save only her response to her parents-in-law. Thus we can predict with confidence, barring some unforeseen accident of great magnitude, that Carol will remain a healthy, happy person and that her relationship with Peter and any subsequent children will be, in the main, on a positive note.

One other significant background factor—Carol grew up in a middle-class, white, Protestant, American family. The social and cultural learning which this setting prompted left its mark on Carol. Her treatment of her son, especially with regard to socialization, her relationships with her husband, in terms of mutual expectations, and in fact her whole view of the world—all were conditioned by the matrix of forces in which she developed.

Contemporary situation. For the moment let us treat Carol as the E in the formula: $B = f(PE)$. Let P stand for Peter. Now let us look at the ensuing behavior of this PE interaction. We have seen that Carol's orientation of action toward most people, and particularly toward Peter, is positive. One episode will suffice. Peter is newly born. For some hours he has been without nutriment. It may be assumed that the viscerogenic need hunger is producing certain bodily tensions. He begins to squirm, move his arms and legs about and show other gross physical movements, including crying. Carol responds to these cues by taking him into her arms. Peter begins to "root around" with his mouth and head. Carol assists him to his yet unknown goal by placing the nipple to his lips. Contact is followed by taking the nipple into the mouth and the beginning of the sucking reflex. In a little while he is sucking vigorously. Three hours later, unless Peter awakened sooner, the process was repeated. The record shows that within twelve days Peter had developed a behavioral pattern, need-disposition if you please, in relation to Carol. After this, when he was put to the breast, if he had been for some hours without food, he immediately took the nipple without preliminary "rooting" and began to suck smoothly and strongly.

Both Peter and Carol responded well in their respective roles. If either had faltered for whatever reason—clumsiness, constitutional inferiority, inattention, or revulsion—the behavior pattern would not have developed, and, instead of a healthy, growing baby, we would have had a sickly, languishing child. Here we see the perfect mutual reinforcement process. Carol gave milk, warmth, and support to Peter. In return she received physical gratification in the emptying of her distended breasts and psychological satisfaction in the response of her accepting child. The breast for Peter became a positively valent object, highly prized, before he could even focus his eyes upon it.

Now indeed did Peter's life space begin to be differentiated. The first differentiated object was the breast. The sequence in which other objects became differentiated we cannot be certain. But surely quite early he differentiated his mother's voice, her step, and other noises she made, as well as physical pressures associated with the preparation for and the act of feeding. Soon she began to form a kind of pattern, variously perceived, any part of which produced the response of alertness and cessation of gross movement and crying.

At this time it was not Carol herself who was discriminated. For any other object similarly constituted and making nearly equivalent sounds and movements was, by generalization, equally cathected. Had Carol disappeared from the scene forever at this point in Peter's life, and had another person as well equipped and as efficient taken her place, the difference to Peter would have been almost nil. Not so a year or eighteen months later. At that time a disruption in the relationship for even a few weeks would produce a violent reaction in Peter. For by that time Carol would have become the sun around which Peter spun his orbit. She would be the center, and all other differentiations and discriminations would be made in reference to her. We have seen that even before Peter was twelve months old, Carol was such a strong power field in his environment that any change in her responsiveness to him produced an immediate reaction, sometimes outlasting the initiating stimulus.

Peter learned to expect from Carol certain responses and gratifications. He developed psychogenic need-dispositions out of this interaction. Regular intercourse with Carol, through which these need-dispositions were satisfied, became essential to his well-being, to his equilibrium. Viscerogenic needs played little part in his motivation, because these were regularly taken care of before they became pressing. He never knew real hunger or prolonged physical pain; ordinarily his needs were met in routine fashion. Occasionally this was not so, and on these occasions Peter voiced his displeasure at frustration by a variety of means, aggressive outbursts and illness being the foremost ones.

The situation which brought about the frustrating circumstances for Peter was the interaction of Carol and her parents-in-law. In their presence, real or fancied, she was in genuine and severe conflict. This conflict created a tension which could not be resolved except by leaving the field through illness or physical removal. Carol became angry and impatient with herself, as well as with others who approached her. In place of her warm, receptive, gentle manner of handling Peter, there was a crisp voice and quick, rough movements as she attended his needs. Peter's expectations were not met. He was bewildered, baffled, frustrated, and his reactions followed upon his situation. Equilibrium was not restored until Carol had left the field of the parents-in-law and returned to her customary way of interacting with Peter.

Part Five: Follow-up Study

When Peter was four-and-a-half years old, Carol and Bill brought him back to the author's office so that he could be examined.

Peter was an alert, active, responsive little boy. He came to the examining room without hesitation and remained as long as forty-five minutes without tiring or complaining. Testing revealed an I.Q. of 156 without pushing him to the limit. In the play room his behavior was creative and spontaneous. The following excerpts from his conversation will illustrate his superiority. He made an "Empire State Building" out of blocks. Then he said: "It doesn't fall down even if it catches on fire because it's made of steel and iron and metal, and they won't burn."

He picked up a toy telephone and carried on an imaginary conversation. He was asked if he would like to talk to a playmate at home. He replied that he "couldn't talk on this phone, 'cause the wires would have to go all the way to Regent Heights." He was then asked for the differences between a real 'phone and a toy 'phone. He said: "A real 'phone wants you to try to talk. It has a plug. It carries electricity to any city." What is electricity, he was asked. "Electricity runs many things: telephones, stoves, fireplaces (not always, sometimes by matches), lights, even the tape recorder," he said, pointing to the one which was recording the session. Where does electricity come from? "Special offices that make it," he replied.

Carol and Bill both read and approved the case report as written. They asked that one or two little things that might identify them be changed, just in case someone who knew them might read this book. Two days after reading the material Carol spontaneously made the following comments: "While I was reading the report I kept saying to myself, 'I know all that' and had a tendency to skip over the part about Mr. Chisholm trying to choke me. I pushed it out of my mind. After a while my nose began to fill up and I started sneezing. So I took an anti-histamine and didn't think any more about it. Then last night we went to Cortland to visit some friends. We talked about the study and I told them about the rough time I had with Bill's father before we were married. I started sneezing my head off. On the way home from Cortland I talked with Bill about sneezing at Cynthia and Joe's and wondered if it could have anything to do with his Dad's trying to choke me. Well, you won't believe it, but I started sneezing right then all over again."

It might be added that Carol did not have a cold at the time. She had not just gotten over one, nor did she develop a cold subsequently. She talked about going to the Chisholm house and said she did not get terribly upset when she went there. Once in a completely different context she started sneezing when a friend was telling a group of which she was part about somebody getting choked. Several times Mrs. Chisholm has apologized to Carol about the premarital incident. Carol said she was always pleased when this happened. At the same time she always experienced a little guilt over feeling so superior and being glad over someone else's discomfort.

Portions of an interview that took place in the author's office follow:

INTERVIEWER: How would you account for the fact that you have been happily married for as long as you have been?

CAROL: Sure—I love him.

INTERVIEWER: All right, any other reasons?

CAROL: Well, come on help me! (Indicating Bill)

INTERVIEWER: You see, this is something that very seldom gets into a record. It's easier to say why something goes wrong than why something goes right.

BILL: Well, when we started going together, we were young enough and not too set in our ways in anything; the marriage was compatible and complementary in every respect.

CAROL: And what we became interested in because there weren't any set interests either. We more or less set a pattern. I just *love* flying (facetiously). That's part of it. If he's going to be determined he likes flying, then I don't have to think it's the most marvelous thing in the world. But I go too.

INTERVIEWER: But you do go flying?

CAROL: Yes, I go flying, I still marvel when I think I'm going to throw up.

INTERVIEWER: Are you scared of flying?

CAROL: Yes, a little bit.

INTERVIEWER: But even despite this you wouldn't try to stop him from flying?

BILL: No, I was just trying to make her exert pressures on me to stop flying.

CAROL: Yes, he thinks I ought to say to him, "You can't go flying." He's a grown man and we talk about this and, logically, if I thought that it was in the same category as riding a rocket to the moon, I think I would feel much more strongly that it was terribly dangerous and I wouldn't want him to do it. But although I don't accept flying emotionally as such—it makes me sick to my stomach—but riding on a plane makes me sick to my stomach and I don't like roller coasters and he likes roller coasters but I think intellectually or something I can accept that flying isn't a terribly dangerous thing. Bill flew all over the place when he got his pilot's license. He knew when I began turning green that it was time to come down because I was getting sick to my stomach.

BILL: The trouble was we were flying right before lunch. There were a couple of poor times . . . By and large I think one of the most significant reasons that we are as happy as we are is because before we were married and just after we were married, we made quite an effort to talk things out—minor feelings—minor disturbances, rather than pooh-pooh at nothing or go sulk about it, and it took quite a little effort to be able to say what you feel even though you feel nasty and to say the nasty things and know you are not going to mean them and everything else. It is better to say them and get things cleared up immediately. So I think we can *communicate* much more closely than 99% of all the people we know.

CAROL: One of the things he demanded . . . I sometimes found because, I think well I'm angry and I'm going to say things I don't mean or I'll lash out and so forth and in other words I'll say, "It's nothing"; and there is nothing like saying, "It's nothing" that will make him feel like wanting to take my head and beat it against the wall.

BILL: The amount of talking that we have to do now is a little bit less because we know what the other person is feeling and thinking by and large, and I think what the result has been that we know each other much more completely and the other's make-up than most people do.

CAROL: As it was before, if something was bothering—I think more with me than with him—I would close up on it. I am more likely not to say I feel sad or I feel such and such and tell him why and go to him with it rather than . . .

BILL: . . . . case where we have a minor disturbance and it was either the decision to let it simmer or actually making enough disturbance to get the air cleared and sometimes it was the case of almost precipitating, deliberately, in order to get the air cleared.

CAROL: Wasn't it when I said nothing . . .

BILL: Yes, in other words, it would be small but not nothing and it was the matter of getting things up to a point where she . . . gave in.

(laughter)

CAROL: I don't think this is wearing the pants. I think it is something else, but I do feel that we feel very comfortable in our roles. I am happy being a woman, and I don't like people that aren't, and we are comfortable, and I don't want to wear the pants.

INTERVIEWER: Now, are there any major areas of disagreement that you have not been able to solve yet?

CAROL: You mean to decide whether Peter should go to an optometrist or an oculist?

BILL: It is not a question whether he should go to an optometrist or an oculist. It's just a question whether he should go to my eye man or hers.

CAROL: Because he is a medical doctor. You mean are there any big things we disagree on?

BILL: Yeah.

CAROL: What—whether we should adopt a baby?

BILL: No, there is no disagreement there.

CAROL: There is too.

BILL: Oh, we have some of our worse fusses over politics. Probably because we neither know enough about what we are saying. . . . .

INTERVIEWER: Your family are pretty staunch Republicans, Bill?

CAROL: Staunch, oh!

BILL: Conservative Republicans.

CAROL: There isn't anything with a large "D" Democrat that is not like being with the Devil.

INTERVIEWER: How do you solve this?

CAROL: We eliminated everything past what? Past 1948?

BILL: We stopped discussing FDR. And pretty much came to the conclusion that . . . as far as organized politics . . .

CAROL: Well, it's just that there is good and bad and that our job is to evaluate properly . . .

BILL: . . . both political philosophies and we found that our own political philosophies were very similar.

CAROL: As long as we don't try to label it to one party.

INTERVIEWER: Would you mind if I asked how you voted in the last election?

BILL: Split.

CAROL: Very split.

INTERVIEWER: You mean you split between yourselves?

CAROL: No.

INTERVIEWER: Did you vote alike?

CAROL: Not entirely, no. Some people I like he didn't vote for, and then some things I didn't want to . . .

INTERVIEWER: Well, that's all I need to know. I don't care what particular candidates.

BILL: I voted for a couple of Republican candidates that I didn't really particularly like, to preserve some sort of balance. And I accepted some things I didn't agree with, because I agreed less with the alternative.

CAROL: But we did a lot of hashing out together. We got all sorts of literature. We got League of Women Voters and we got the Americans for Democratic Action endorsements and the Republican endorsements and the Newspaper endorsements and we stayed up until 3:00 o'clock one night reading and hashing and . . . . . so that a lot of it we hashed out.

INTERVIEWER: Are there any other areas which you consider big areas which you have not come to agreement on?

BILL: I think Carol is a little bit more ready to start adopting a child.

CAROL: I don't want to adopt one, I just want to think about it. Think about how you think about it.

BILL: Well, we have been thinking about it.

CAROL: But I don't think you think it is a good idea.

BILL: Well, I don't think it's a good idea until we get to the place where we can pay our bills a little more easily. I mean it is one thing to try to have a child of your own, because when you do you will manage and be very happy about it; but there is a little bit more of an opportunity to select whether you are going to adopt and when you are going to adopt, and . . . it is just a drag on both of us when we have to spend so much of our time figuring which bills we are going to just pay this month and which bills we will just put off.

CAROL: But I am not sure that you would ever really want to adopt a child, ever.

BILL: Well I'm not sure about that—not positive but want to think about it, that's for sure. The chances that you won't have other children are so negligible. It's not the case of adopting children as the only alternative to having no family. It's just the matter of adopting a child to fill the gap between Petie and your next child.

CAROL: He feels that if we are going to have another child we *will* have another child.

BILL: No, it's just a matter of time until we do.

CAROL: And the other thing that my doubts from this are due to, I want to adopt a child just so I can relieve myself of this feeling of anxiety that I have. I don't want to have an only child. I don't think it's good for Peter or for us or for anything else and I also don't want to have a seventeen-year-old and a one-year-old.

BILL: Well, do you want to have one with a five- or six-year split because of your own experience?

CAROL: Well, I have gotten over that somewhat, but Sue and I were almost five years apart, and to me this was the one thing I didn't want. I wanted a child before this five-year split, because I thought ours were so unfortunate, but heavens, I think I have gotten over that pretty well.

BILL: If your anxiety to adopt a child is based a certain amount on removing this particular time distribution, I don't think that this is a sound enough basis to adopt a child.

CAROL: Well, I agree with you. But I don't know just how I feel, but I also have this feeling because it's awful hard to try to have a baby and to do the temperature business and I went down to have my tubes blown out and it's terribly painful and although you forget the pain, when I first lay there after it was over and you are just panting, you can't breathe really and you are completely exhausted, and I have done this twice now; and the first time I got up from the table and passed right out and I thought I couldn't go through this again—not for anything. Well, I'd go back right today if it would do any good, but you can't forget it, for every morning you have to get up and take your temperature and report it, and you watch what the graph is doing. So you build up and you build up, and if you go over the normal length of time which I have done every now and then, you still have a period —it's like a steam roller rolled right over you and I feel the need for some counter plan where it would be all right even if it never comes to anything— it's worth a try, but if it never comes to anything after such and such a length of time, we will still be able to have a family or we will try to have a family in another way, because I don't feel sure that this will ever produce anything.

BILL: And there's the basic difference.

CAROL: And he feels sure. . . .

BILL: I feel quite sure and she feels very unsure.

INTERVIEWER: Is there anything else at the present time that looms as a problem to either of you?

BILL: We both feel uneasy about my situation of work. Maybe Carol even more so than I, because I am probably an optimist.

CAROL: What am I, a pessimist?

BILL: No, maybe I am much more than even I should be. I have the feeling that things are, by and large, going to be right. I can't look back at any of them —any area in my life, some of them which have been quite bad—without feeling that I have gained more because they happened than I would have had they not happened; and I think basically, I have the outlook that maybe our not having a baby when we didn't would be much better for all concerned, and probably the same philosophy carries over toward things at work, that, by and large, it probably will work out fine; but there is an awful lot of uncertainty about it and there is a lot of uncertainty about how we handle things. Uneasiness about them—the things. How much money we have to work with. I am one of the lowest paid men in my class, although I think I do as well as anybody and have the capabilities of doing much better than I did . . . . right near the bottom as far as money is concerned.

CAROL: Oh, we have gone kind of out on a limb. We have bought an expensive house that we borrowed a lot of money for.

BILL: That's right and the bank—any conservative bank wouldn't even talk to us about money. They wanted somebody who was making $10,000 a year to be able to buy a house that was going to cost $25,000 or $30,000, and we knew where we wanted our house to be because of the school system and the importance of the proper environment for Petie and for us and future children, and we felt that we were willing to spend more money on a house—a larger proportion of our money on a house—because our future was bright. We had a good sound financial basis—we knew that if we ran into financial difficulties, we would never be really out—my folks—our whole family is close enough so that if any of us ever got really in a bad plight, we all know that it would be taken care of with a minimum amount of uneasiness, but when we did get there, we found that people in the banking business just weren't interested in talking with anybody except people who didn't need to borrow money. Then when we did find a house and things we wanted to do with it and be really happy with it—it isn't that our mortgage payment has been a quarter to a fifth of our total income and. . . .

CAROL: When we talked about it, when we were first in Detroit, we anticipated that he would be starting at this salary and that soon that he would have a substantial raise.

BILL: It was a matter of six months or a year that there would be a $50 a month raise so that it would just remove the terrific bind; and with the way things have slowed down since then, there is just no raise in sight.

CAROL: No, in fact they were talking about less money.

BILL: Not only is there no raise in sight, but we have the knowledge that it is going to be a period of four or six months after things pick up before there will be any money for raises, because of a lag when business comes in and when payments come in, so now it's the situation of not managing on a tight budget for a very limited time, but having to manage on a tight budget with no immediate relief in sight.

INTERVIEWER: Then you probably feel—uneasy about it.

CAROL: I don't feel as uneasy about the money as I don't feel that he is getting the satisfaction from the work that I would like him to have, and I don't know whether he is ever going to.

INTERVIEWER: In this situation.

CAROL: Uhhuh. But I think that it is far the wisest thing to stick it out and see —for if it works, it probably is the best thing in the world.

INTERVIEWER: There are two or three more questions. When you go to Bill's house now, how do you feel?

CAROL: Quite comfortable.

INTERVIEWER: Do you feel more comfortable the more often you go?

CAROL: In fact, on the contrary, of the times when we seem to be going very often I think I am less comfortable.

BILL: I was just wondering whether or not her discomfort comes from the fact that my folks are pretty old, and just Petie's normal activities, even though Petie is pretty much favored with them—begins to wear on them.

CAROL: Oh, I think that this is probably true. This is very true.

BILL: After we have been over there a couple of times in a row, it is a little bit harder for them to take Petie's activities very long—running around, general uneasiness.

CAROL: Ummmmm.

BILL: Also, a little bit of distress he gets placed under because they are expecting him to be—

CAROL: a little gentleman.

BILL: Contained, whereas he can be contained for a little while.

CAROL: It is a house that has a lot of lovely things that mustn't be touched and can't be bumped into, and this sort of thing, and I worry about this.

BILL: And we're a little concerned about the necessary restraint on Petie.

INTERVIEWER: Does Petie act differently when he is there than when he is at your home?

CAROL: Not very much. He is very comfortable with his family, although he is different with the two sets of grandparents. He does different things.

INTERVIEWER: What kinds of things?

CAROL: Well a . . I don't know, he talks differently. My mom gets a kick out of exploring things with him and he talks, and talks, and talks to her and she knows how to talk to him, I think a little bit better, whereas Bill's mother will say, "Grandma doesn't love you very much does she?" And although this isn't being quite fair to her, because it sounds worse than it is, but he doesn't know how to talk to her.

INTERVIEWER: She is teasing him, you mean.

CAROL: Well, she—this is her way.

BILL: She is not teasing.

CAROL: No, she is just saying how much she loves him.

BILL: Asking for a negative reply to the question—fishing for compliments.

CAROL: Yes, that's right, and he doesn't know what to make of it; whereas at my house he follows my father around like a puppy dog and goes down and gets apples . . .

BILL: . . . and has a delightful time with them, largely because they participate with him and are able to communicate with him and interest him in the things that he is capable to be interested in.

CAROL: Well, we found that when he would go into Bill's house as a cowboy the first thing, the whole thing he would want to do was to kill his grandmother with guns. This was very funny at first and she would laugh and so forth, and it became evident that this was wearing. It was terrible every time we went. He just doesn't know what to say to her, so I would give him clues before we went in on what to say. They have a chord organ—and she likes to play the chord organ—and he can go and push the—he can read 1, 2, and 3—and he can go and push the chords, and so now he goes in and delights her by asking to play the chord organ, and he enjoys doing it with her and he has found this communication that he didn't have before.

5

THE INTERACTION PROCESS

When you see a person moving about in the social world, you note that, as he proceeds from one person to another, his manner of behavior varies considerably. For example, take a college student and picture him in a "bull session," on a date with his favorite girl, or before the faculty disciplinary committee. You can readily see that his actions in the three situations will have little in common. How are we to explain the differences? What variables are necessary to understand the different transactions which occur?

You may reply that any one can see that different responses were obviously demanded in the three situations. While this is true it is also a fact that people regularly respond quite differently in each of these situations—sometimes to their own detriment. We must conceptualize people's relationship in such a way that what each party *brings* to the situation, as well as what each *does* in the situation (that is, in response to cues from the other) become clear antecedents to the resulting consummatory action. This attempt to formulate a theory of interaction will provide a framework for the remainder of the book. In the present chapter only the outline will be developed.

Components of the Interaction Process

1. The unit of consideration properly should be the total psychological field. Most often this involves several persons in context—for example, a club or a family. The psychological fields would comprise knowledge of significant relationships within and outside the groups, plus all the cultural, socioeconomic, and physical forces impinging upon them at a given time. Since this is obviously more of a task than we can encompass, we shall choose, for the sake of convenience, the simpler relationship between two people, the dyad, as the unit of consideration.

2. Anything which arouses action in the individual is a stimulus. The stimulus may emanate from the external world or from within the skin of the individual; it may be a grasshopper, a slap in the face, or a sunset; or it may be an inner drive, a sleeping foot, or a headache. When two persons are in interaction, each reacts to the stimulus of the other—not only because of the actions each performs but also because of what each expects the other to do. Expectancies vary with the internal state of each actor and the history of his previous commerce with the other or similar others.

3. The response on the part of each participant has two parts. One is the response to the initial action, or cue, of the other. The second is the response to the effect perceived in the other as a result of the stimulus which the original actor emitted. Let us illustrate these two types of responses with two people called Alpha and Beta. First, Alpha responds to a stimulus given by Beta. Secondly, Alpha responds to the response which Beta gives to the stimulus which Alpha originally provided. The second type of response provides the best example of mutual interaction, where each is sensitive to the slightest change in the other. Communication may be said to have been achieved when two persons in a reciprocal relationship learn to respond to cues emanating from each other in a manner recognized as significant by each. There is no implication that the motives underlying the stimulus provided by either party to the dyad need be conscious. They may be conscious to both, to neither, or to one of the two. It is necessary to assume only that the motive be conveyed by the stimulus cue and that the latter be perceived by the recipient as a basis for behavior.

Dyadic Relationships

Each person responds in terms of his interpretation of the demands of the momentary situation. This interpretation we will call "immediate behavior space," following Tolman and others. It is the same as Lewin's "life-space." Immediate behavior space is a resultant of contemporaneous internal states in conjunction with the confronting stimulus compound. This statement will be elaborated presently. In any given situation, if a person's interpretation of the external stimulus is in general agreement with the interpretations of others, and if internally he is in a state of relative equilibrium, his behavior will be socially acceptable. On the other hand, if his interpretation is at variance with others—due either to previous peculiar commerce with the stimulus, or equivalent, or to a disequilibrated internal state—his behavior is likely to be peculiar, if not bizarre.

The author once knew a student who refused to go on the campus after dark because when she did any shadowy figure was perceived by her as a big black bear. Discrepancies in perception of this sort have long been recognized as indices of illusion and delusion. Behavior resulting from distorted perceptions in human relations can sometimes lead to tragic consequences, as when the love-starved old maid falls for the attention of the suave confidence man. Ordinarily perceptions are brought into consensual agreement by the responses of the other party to a dyad, and behavior space is corrected accordingly; in such a case, mutual consummatory action is anticipated. However, if one person is deceiving another, as with the confidence man, mutuality is not the goal sought; rather, it is one-sided consummatory action, in this case probably theft of the other's money.

In the previous chapter, Carol and Peter provided us with an illustration of a happily functioning dyadic relationship. When Peter was hungry and nursed well and when Carol was rested and had plenty of milk, each gave the adequate response to the other. The relationship ceased to function well when either ceased to give the appropriate response, as when Carol was emotionally disturbed or Peter was "spitty and fussy."

The dyadic relationship may be diagrammed as follows:

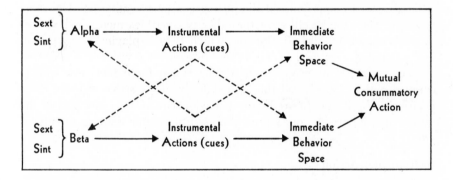

The broken lines indicate perceptions on the part of each to the cues emitted by the other. These perceptions lead to alterations in the instrumental acts and the immediate behavior space, hence to modifications in both the timing and mode of the consummatory response in order to achieve mutuality of gratification. The solid lines simply indicate directional tendencies. We will discuss the stimulating conditions, the instrumental acts, and the immediate behavior space in turn.

Stimulating Conditions

As the diagram indicates, the stimulus may be external (Sext) or internal (Sint). Internal stimuli refer to the conditions of drives, need-dispositions, and other regnant physical and psychological states and systems of the personality, especially the self-system. These internal stimuli will be discussed more fully in later chapters. External stimuli refer to the other person of the dyad and to the other properties of the field in which the interaction takes place.

Let us assume that Alpha is an unmarried, unattached, healthy man of twenty-one and that Beta is an attractive woman of approximately the same age. Alpha has been excluded from the company of women for several months because of a special assignment which has demanded his attention. Beta, an old acquaintance, comes into his presence ravishingly dressed in an evening gown and begins an animated conversation. With this much information can one make a prediction as to what Alpha's response will be, other than that as a socialized person he will not act the part of a boor? No. At least two other facts relative to the external stimulating conditions are necessary before one could make any reasonable prediction.

First, the setting: Alpha will respond differently depending upon whether their meeting takes place in a large gathering—a party if you please—or in a small, intimate group or in his own private rooms. It is a well-known fact, as George Simmel (1950) has pointed out, that in our culture a woman may be scantily dressed and carry on a flirtatious game without fear of compromise if the setting is a party gathering. The same behavior, however, in either of the other two settings mentioned assures no such immunity. Second, the role which Beta is playing is important. Is she married to a good friend, is she a prospective wife, or is she from another social status group than Alpha? When these facts are known, coupled with knowledge of the immediate behavior space of each, there need be no hesitation in predicting behavior. However, if any part of the information is missing, one's prediction is little better than an intelligent guess.

Instrumental Action

Communication, the key to interaction, occurs as a result of the concrete acts of one party to the dyad which are perceived by the other as cues to his own action. Communication is effected by three mediating agencies: Namely, verbalization, goal-directed action (which may or may not include verbalization), and non-verbal expressive acts.

Verbalization, the most commonly used form of communication, requires no elaboration here except to point out that words derive their meaning in part from the context in which they are uttered. You may recall the expression used by Owen Wister in *The Virginian,* "When you call me that, smile!" Thus we see that even in articulate speech the cue property is derived to a large extent from the concomitant expressive act.

Goal-directed action involves direct observation of what the other person is doing or trying to do. No inference or analogy is required. The actions of the other are perceived in terms of the further acts that are required functionally to round out the sequence and give it closure. For example, in such a simple thing as clearing the table after a meal the goal is immediately perceived.

Non-verbal expressive acts are mediated by neuro-muscular, especially facial, expression, gesticulation, and posture. They may be consciously employed, as when one opens his arms to greet a loved one, or they may be the result of unconscious motivation, as when one involuntarily laughs on hearing of the misfortune of some unloved acquaintance. It is still not entirely clear how meanings are communicated through expressive acts, although associationist and Gestalt theories help to account for the phenomenon. According to the associationists, interpretation is based upon the recurrent contiguity in experience of two factors—the expressive act and emotion. If on a subsequent occasion the act is expressed without the usually accompanying emotion, the latter is inferred. A four-year-old boy illustrated this when he asked his mother one day, "Why are you mad with me?" The mother replied, lying, "I'm not mad with you." Whereupon the boy said, "Then why do you walk mad?"

Gestalt theory holds that expressive behavior reveals its meaning directly in perception. This theory is based upon the principle of isomorphism, according to which processes taking place in different media are nevertheless similar in structural organization. This means that the forces which determine overt physical behavior are structurally similar to the simultaneous mental correlates. If this be so, it becomes more understandable why psychological meaning can be observed directly from a person's appearance and conduct. Thus we find a perceptive Caesar saying, "Yon Cassius hath a lean and hungry look."

The Gestalt hypothesis is ingenious and may correctly explain how communication occurs among certain lower animals. At the human level, however, a more acceptable hypothesis is that visually perceptible body shifts, variations of which are repetitively observed, are learned. An immediate partial justification for this hypothesis is found in the fact that out of the total range of possible movements, social and cultural groups tend to choose a discriminated range for social interaction. Thus we find, for example, that in the middle classes of American society circum-eye movements combined with hand motions are the prime situation-definers. Birdwhistell (1955) has shown that in the upper classes people gesticulate least, while the lower classes often use gestures and physical action more than words. Families develop special non-verbal communication systems.

People in other cultural groups, particularly the so-called Latin countries such as France, Spain, and Italy, use many more gestures and body movements while talking. Some groups use gesture in culturally meaningful ways, such as in the dances of Bali and Hawaii, in which a story is told by bodily movements.

Observing non-verbal communication is a difficult task. First, non-verbal communication is often fleeting in nature. To add a further complication, the cue is sometimes very slight. A third difficulty is that imagination often deceives us into believing a non-verbal communication has occurred simply because we are anticipating something. Possibly the greatest problem, however, is due to the overwhelming quantity of raw material presented in any interaction situation. All humans, to a greater or lesser extent, react to each other's facial expression, bodily movements, and vocal expressions. Thus, there are so many fleeting gestures and movements involved in any social situation, and these reacted to with so little conscious analysis, that even the conscientious observer may have difficulty in gathering his data.

With these qualifications in mind, it is permissible to speculate about non-verbal communication in the human being, beginning with its emergence in the neonate. Gesture is a basic aspect of our personality, possibly originating in our magic gesture strategy in infancy, when movement and crying brought the world to our feet. An infant only a few weeks old can assert himself in various ways by crying. The baby early gives non-verbal expression to its feelings of love and hate, affection and defiance, by sucking, biting, licking, vomiting, and later by holding in or voiding its bladder or bowel contents. Every bodily function can be a means of emotional communication.

In the family preverbal expression is essential until the infant acquires words. The differing sights, sounds, and tactile stimulations come to define behavior before words are understood. Studies of the comprehension of gesture have shown that at six months the infant is able to respond to specific movements, and at eight months reacts to differences in intonation. Within the context of the family, much of the earliest communication from adult to baby consists of facial expression with some sound accompaniment at times—moods, ideas, and commands are thus transmitted. The parent frowns and utters sharp, staccato sounds; or the mother smiles or gurgles, and food or comfort follows.

The learning of conventional gestures, including facial expressions, is manifested by the infant well before his first birthday. For example, the infant learns the rudiments of verbal pantomime. Before learning to speak, he acquires the tonal pattern of speech and its mannerisms. The child understands gestures before words, and uses them long before language proper, though often accompanying them with vocalizations. As might be expected, gestures are used most effectively upon the young; the younger the audience, the easier it is to move it by gesture, and the more profound and lasting the effects.

When children, especially twins, develop an unusually effective gesture language, their development of true speech may be retarded for some time. We shall see an instance of this in the next chapter. While the infant uses whole-body language, the elders of the child intervene so that these general movements and postures gradually pass into symbolic ones, and thence into words. The hungry infant seeks the bottle with its whole body, but the movement becomes abbreviated and directed through the solicitous cooperation of the mother. Conventional "part" gestures, usually the earliest part of an action, are in childhood substituted for the entire actions; and then these, which were originally only accompanied by vocalizations, may recede as vocal language develops.

In the main, all forms of non-verbal communication tend to diminish as children grow into adulthood, and acquire more skill at verbal and written communication. For example, childhood play is a form of non-verbal expression which undergoes this transformation as the youngster grows into adolescence. Thus, the expressive non-verbal behavior of the child becomes regularized by pressure during his socialization; narrow limits are set and effective norms imposed before he is incorporated into the group.

Although non-verbal communication is no longer primary, it never disappears completely. When we have difficulty in expressing ourselves verbally, we may bring our whole bodies into action. To think without movement is difficult, and the adult often argues with his whole body. Man is continually weaving non-verbal communication into his daily interactions with others. For example, in all love-making much importance is placed upon non-verbal communication. Partners respond to non-verbal gestures, postures, and body movements; each learns to detect the moods and feelings of the other through muscular tensions.

Non-verbal communication can indeed alter the meaning of the spoken word: a smile, a sneer, or a wink after an earnest remark alters its meaning. One may praise an act verbally and simultaneously reject it with one's body. Gesture conveys its meaning before the cultivated word is uttered, lending credence to the saying, "actions speak louder than words." Interaction on the non-verbal level is marked by spontaneous and direct response to gesture and actions.

Immediate Behavior Space

Both parties to a dyad respond as they do, partly because of the cues which they receive from the other—all the cues, not just the ones which the other consciously intended to employ. As an example, take the case of a perceptive child who does the exact opposite of his parent's request without a rebuke. The child has simply learned that the parent does not always mean what he says. He has learned to attend to minimal cues accompanying verbalizations to enable him to discriminate between the occasions when the parent's direct statement should be taken at face value and when it need not be so observed.

Herein lies an important clue to understanding the dyadic relationship. All the cues, gross and minimal, emitted by both parties have to be rapidly assessed before an appropriate response can occur. And such an assessment does not have to be in the focus of consciousness to be functional. Another illustration of the parent-child interaction occurs when mothers, or sometimes fathers, leave their young children at school for the first time. One parent will deposit his child in the waiting room, pat him on the head, pass a word with the teacher, and be off without a backward glance. Another will bring his child in, help him get his wraps off, suggest a particular game or activity he might engage in, and depart only when the child is happily playing; the departure is not abrupt, but neither is it equivocal. A third parent may go through all the motions of the second leave-taking but in addition ask the child, "Are you going to be all right now, dear? Mommy has to go." Then she moves hesitantly off, but halfway down the corridor, still in sight of the child, she turns and looks back to make sure all is well. At this point she remains frozen while her child rushes toward her, sobbing and begging her not to go.

Some mothers, when it is pointed out to them that their hesitancy and ambivalence are responsible for the child's reaction, can muster sufficient strength in a short while to leave their children with a firm tread and without the fatal backward glance. Others, unable to bring themselves to do so, remain tied to the school for as long as six months, ashamed of themselves, a nuisance to the teachers, a deterrent to the child's growth. During all this time neither mother nor child is able to let the other go. Studies of the dependency relationship have thrown light on the dynamics involved in such a mother-child interaction.

These examples of different kinds of interaction between parents and children suffice to point up the necessity of knowing more about the personalities of the parties to any interaction before we can understand the outcome. In the diagram on page 151, the "Immediate Behavior Space" must now be considered.

Immediate behavior space is a resultant of the stimulating conditions, including one's own instrumental acts as well as those of the other person in the dyad, plus the personalities which both bring to the situation. We have examined what we mean by instrumental action. Now let us look at the part which personality plays in dyadic relationships. We have defined personality as the dynamic organization within the individual which specifies his potentialities for action. To understand the personality fully, we would have to trace the entire history of the organism and all of its experiences. Since this is literally impossible, we must be content with choosing those aspects of personality which are deemed most important as antecedents to immediate behavior space and to behavior. These are abilities, need-dispositions, and the self-system, including the psychodynamic mechanisms.

Abilities. Abilities refers to all the inherent and learned traits and capacities of the individual. Such things as size, neuro-muscular coordination, energy output, strength, I.Q., and special handicaps or talents markedly influence an individual's stimulus value to another, and hence the kind of reception he will get. In turn, the kind of reception will partly determine his counter response. The child who goes to school bubbling with energy, full of ideas which he can readily verbalize, and anxious to climb a jungle gym will be treated quite differently from one who is sluggish in movement, slow in speech, and timid where any danger is involved.

But we must not overemphasize the role of abilities. Certainly we do not know exactly how these variables of ability are influenced by and related to the other variables of personality at a young age. Hence we can say very little about them. We do know that, at the extremes, abilities make a tremendous difference. The badly crippled, spastic child or the feeble-minded call forth responses different from that of the well-coordinated or bright child. But whereas one child with a major physical handicap is received with ambivalence, if not open hostility, into a given family, and eventually develops a serious psychopathological condition; another similarly constituted from birth may be received into a family with loving and open arms, from which care he develops a pleasing and healthy personality. We suggested earlier that one reason why some children become autistic is that they do not respond initially to the overtures of their parents in such a way as to establish a mutually satisfying interactive relationship. But this remains hypothetical. Most children fall within the normal range as far as abilities go. For these children it is very unclear just how these abilities influence their interactions with the significant persons in their environment.

Full discussion of the development and functional interrelationship of need-dispositions, the self system and the psychodynamic mechanisms will be deferred until later chapters. Each is sufficiently complicated and significant in the structure of personality to warrant fairly extended treatment. For the present, we will be satisfied to state simply what these terms refer to, how they influence the behavior space, and hence help to determine the character of dyadic relationships.

Need-dispositions. Need-disposition implies that objects in a field have been positively or negatively cathected through learning and that they have been cognitively discriminated from other objects. Need-disposition, then, refers to the internal condition of the organism which makes a particular object what it is for the individual. In Chapter Four, when Peter Chisholm cried out for his mother and was unconsoled by the approach of any other person, he had developed a need-disposition for his mother which made her special in all the world.

At the present stage of development of the science of physiology, we cannot specify what the nature of the internal condition is which is the ground of the need-disposition. It seems most likely, as Murray has argued, that its seat is in the central nervous system. Despite our failure to pinpoint it in the physical organism, we can demonstrate how a need-disposition operates to orient and impel the organism. We can also show how, in the main, it functions in accord with the laws of learning. Every object in the behavior space has a corresponding need-disposition in the organism derived by commerce with the object or by generalization from other objects experienced. Thus, if an object has in no way been experienced it has no meaning, no significance, for the individual and is no part of his behavior space until commerce with it has occurred.

Let us illustrate this by watching a baby who is being weaned from an exclusive diet of milk to solid foods. His need-disposition toward milk is well established. When a certain internal condition exists, after a lapse of time without food, and a bottle or cup of milk is presented, the baby automatically orients toward the milk and begins to drink it. If the same internal condition obtains but instead of milk pabulum is presented, it will be ignored or, if forced upon him, rejected. It will continue to be rejected until sufficient commerce with it has been had to establish its hunger-abating properties. Henceforth, however, it will be discriminated as a food object, and the child will have a need-disposition toward it. This is prototypical of the learning of all need-dispositions throughout life. Of course, as one grows older and is able to utilize symbolic thinking, he need not have direct commerce with an object to develop a need-disposition in relation to it.

The Self System. As a child grows older, if all goes well in his psychological development, one object is differentiated from all others and stands in a central relationship to them. This object he comes to call "I" and its extension "me" or "mine." It is to this we refer when we use the construct *self system.* It includes all that one regards as peculiarly his own. Two aspects of the self system will be distinguished for purposes of discussion, although it is not certain that this distinction is more than a heuristic device—namely ego and superego.

The ego refers to those functions of the personality which are identified by terms like self-esteem, self-identity, self-extension, perception, rational thinking, planning and executing, knowing, and time-binding. The superego is the residue of cultural learning. It is a subsystem of the self system which includes both interdictions and ideals. The parents and other culture bearers in their efforts to socialize the child employ punishments and threats of punishments in connection with undesired behavior on the part of the child. Through a process of conditioning the child comes to associate anxiety with certain behavior or even the idea of the behavior; thus anxiety acts as a restraint to action of a certain kind. In addition to punishing, parents also reward their children for what they consider appropriate behavior and hold out promises of rewards for future accomplishments. This rewarded behavior and the hope of rewards for future accomplishments become standards of conduct and ideals, respectively, of the growing individual. They are sometimes retained long after their usefulness has ceased to exist.

Anxiety, as we have just said, is evoked in anticipation of punishment in connection with behavior of certain kinds. If it is intense, anxiety is a painful experience, an experience which one seeks to avoid, often at considerable cost to one's own well-being and social position. One of the functions of the self system is to allay anxiety. This purpose it accomplishes through what have been called the psychodynamic mechanisms. These mechanisms, such as repression and rationalization, serve to ward off anxiety while permitting the individual to continue to act after a fashion.

Personality and Perception

The immediate behavior space of the individual determines the action which he will perform at any given moment. The processes of immediate behavior space are so interrelated that it is impossible, except under most unnatural conditions, to observe any one of them in isolation. When we isolate them for scientific or didactic purposes, we are aware that we do injustice to their functional interrelationship. The rest of this chapter will be devoted to a brief consideration of some of the results of efforts to study perception in a social context. The effect of motivation, as well as the influence of other processes, on immediate behavior space will be discussed in subsequent chapters in greater detail.

In the case study in Chapter Four we have seen that Carol Chisholm acted differently toward her parents-in-law than she acted toward any other persons at any other time. It did not matter whether she was with them or away from them, since recollection produced strong emotion. Furthermore, the differences in her behavior were temporally, and probably causally, related to marked changes in the behavior of her baby. In the case of the baby, Peter, the most economic explanation of his changed behavior is that it was a direct response to a perception of change in Carol. We do not know exactly what he perceived or how he perceived— that is, through what senses. We do not know why he gave the responses he did, although we assume that he was utilizing his available repertory of responses to remove a threatening, unusual situation. What Peter perceived in Carol could have been perceived by any alert observer. Can the same be said concerning Carol's reactions? Did she perceive something in her parents-in-law which signified danger to her and which led to her primitive, adjustive responses?

The answer to this question depends upon how you conceive of perception. If perception is thought of as an autochthonous process in which the properties of the stimulus determine exclusively what is received by the viewer, then you get one answer. If perception, on the other hand, is viewed as a resultant of both personality factors and stimulus properties, you get a different answer. There is a vast amount of controversy in psychology today over these two conceptions. We cannot begin to review here all the evidence concerning perception; nor is this necessary, since F. H. Allport (1955) has recently done an excellent job in this connection. All that we shall attempt is to state a point of view with some supporting evidence.

Perception is both an individual and a universal process. Accurate perception with regard to certain objects and configurations, primarily nonsocial, has been demonstrated. However, each individual is sensitized to perceive in his own way certain objects and configurations, especially social ones. This sensitization to perceive in a certain way results from experiences of the individual organism. Carol Chisholm was perfectly aware of the fact that her parents-in-law did nothing in her presence when she visited them with Peter which could entirely account for her reaction. If she had been asked, along with other observers, to describe all the physiognomic properties of the senior Chisholms, undoubtedly there would have been good agreement. Interpretations of what they had seen, however, would be different. Perception, as we are using it, includes both sensory input and interpretation. In order to account for Carol's peculiar response we must assume that her previous commerce with these people had influenced her present perception of them, even though their current behavior was in no way (as observed by others) the same as their earlier behavior which had threatened her. It is evident that perception is here mixed up with memory, anxiety, hostility, and perhaps other processes. Perception usually operates in this way in social situations which are emotionally charged.

Social Perception

Perception is a biologically adaptive process. In order to remain alive, one must perceive objects correctly. A flying stone coming at one's head, a sudden chasm opening up in front along the path one is walking, a rattlesnake coiled to spring—all require quick and accurate perception, and action.

Historically, perception has been studied in a psychophysical frame of reference. It has been assumed that perception is determined by the laws of stimulus relations, or adaptation-level, or constancy, or by organizational processes that dealt with simple configurational aspects. Laws determining perceptual dimensions and thresholds have been sought without regard to such "central" processes as memory, motivation, association, interpretation. In recent years social, clinical, and personality psychologists have questioned whether perception is indeed so "pure" and unrelated, so uninfluenced by other processes and systems operating within the individual. It is now maintained by many that perception is not so closely stimulus-bound as was formerly believed. The personality of the individual adds something to the process under certain conditions which alters the percept. Just exactly how this effect on perception takes place or what are the limits within which it occurs, are not at present known; a great deal more research is required to answer these questions. We may be sure, however, that motivation and other central processes produce changes in perception. We may also be sure that despite the effect of central processes, perception of the physical world, of people, and of events that occur physically is highly accurate in the normal person. In short, regardless of how powerful a drive or need may be, a tree is usually seen as a tree.

One of the clearest results of the effect of the social situation on perception is found in an experiment by Asch (1952). Eight or nine subjects were presented with the perceptual task of selecting from three lines differing in length the one that matched a standard line in length. Twelve such comparisons were made. The subjects were seated in a semicircle, and each announced his judgment aloud in turn. In one form of the experiment all of the subjects except one, the naïve subject, were confederates of the experimenter. They were instructed to give uniformly false answers at pre-established points, thus placing pressure on the single naïve subject. The perceptual conditions were simple and clear. The differences in the lengths of lines to be discriminated ranged from one-quarter to one and three-quarters inches. The unequal comparison lines were obviously longer or shorter than the standard. The critical (naïve) subject was usually placed next to last in the circle of those responding. The experiment thus became one in which the full impact of the majority opinion of the group was registered before the judgment of the critical subject was called for. How would he respond to and account for this strange situation? In order to understand more clearly the effect of the social situation on the critical subject, he was engaged in discussion following the experimental sessions. Talk centered on how to account for disagreements, who was correct, and how much confidence the naïve subject had in his judgments.

Two-thirds of the responses of the critical subjects were correct and independent of the judgments expressed by the majority. The remaining one-third made errors identical with those of the majority. Extreme individual differences were noted in response to the majority pressure. Of the thirty-one critical subjects, six remained completely unaffected; in other words, their judgments were always correct. At the other extreme were two subjects whose judgments agreed with the majority without exception.

Regardless of response, none of the subjects was indifferent to the judgments of the majority or regarded them as irrelevant. All of the subjects reported confusion and bewilderment by the disagreement. Most frequently in their search of an explanation, they located the reason for the discrepancy within themselves. They thought they were at fault and blamed their vision. Some even feared that something was basically wrong with their judgment and did not wish to expose themselves. They attempted to concentrate their full attention on the problem in order to increase the clearness of their perceptions and judgments. Every subject experienced moments when he doubted the evidence of his own senses and wished to be in agreement with the group.

The reasons given by the subjects for their responses are interesting. Of the two thirds who reported correctly throughout, some did so with considerable confidence, while others felt obliged to report what they saw even though they feared it might be incorrect. Of the one third who reported incorrectly, one subject actually saw the lines as the majority reported them to be; in other words, he had a misperception. Most of those who reported incorrectly did so because they were convinced that they were wrong and the majority right. A smaller number were dominated by the desire to appear like everyone else. They perceived correctly and felt their judgments were accurate, but were relatively unconcerned about the correctness of their responses.

Following

The question now arises as to what are the personality correlates of those subjects who "follow" the group and of those who remain independent of the majority opinion. For preliminary answers we turn to Crutchfield and Hugo. Using modification of the Asch technique, they obtained essentially the same results. Crutchfield (1955), working with an adult population, found the following differences between the "follower" and the "independent." The follower has less ego strength, less ability to accept responsibility, less self-insight, less spontaneity and productive originality; he is more prejudiced, places greater emphasis on external and socially approved values, and has more authoritarian attitudes. The extreme followers described their parents in highly idealized terms; the independents offered a more balanced picture. The followers described more restrictive child-rearing practices on the part of their parents. The followers tended to come from stable homes, whereas the independents more often indicated that their homes had been broken for various reasons.

Hugo (1956), building on the work of Asch, Berenda (1950), and

Crutchfield, investigated the frequency of following and independent behavior in random samples of fourteen- and seventeen-year-old boys and girls from public high schools, and the relationship between such behavior and the variables of age, sex, ordinal position, and parental attitudes and practices. Hugo states his conclusions in the form of hypotheses, because he recognizes that more research is needed to substantiate his findings. "Following," as he uses the term, refers to the number of changes a subject made in a correct answer given on a prior control test to agree with a false, experimentally induced, "group" answer.

1. In boys, following tends to decrease and independence to increase with age. This trend begins at least as early as age seven and normally continues at a steady rate up to about nineteen or twenty years of age.

2. Following in girls between the ages of seven and twelve or thirteen years tends to decrease steadily and at about the same rate as in boys. After age twelve or thirteen, following in girls continues to decrease, but at a slower rate than in boys.

This second hypothesis is based on results which showed that there was a tendency for the fourteen-year-old girls to follow more than the fourteen-year-old boys and the seventeen-year-old girls more than the seventeen-year-old boys. The implication was that after age thirteen or fourteen, girls and boys differ in the rate with which they achieve independence.

3. Sex differences in following result from the differential treatment accorded to boys and girls in our culture; girls are sheltered and restricted, while boys are allowed relatively more freedom and independence.

This third hypothesis, which has far-reaching implications, is difficult to test. Hugo's study demonstrated fairly conclusively that there are sex differences in following, at least during the adolescent period. It is not likely that these differences are directly attributable to biological causes, although it might be argued that they are indirectly related to biological differences. It seems much more probable that the sex differences in following are due to differences in the treatment of boys and girls which are more or less culture-wide.

4. Extreme following in both boys and girls results from restrictive, harsh, authoritarian, parental discipline.

This hypothesis, if true, could account for both sex and individual differences in following. It is founded on the idea that capitulation to group pressure is related to the manner in which the individual perceives himself in relation to others. Independence is considered to be a matter of having self-confidence, self-respect, and faith in one's own judgment when that judgment is contrary to the judgment of others. Implied here is a notion that a high degree of independence in judgment is normal and will occur if development is not inhibited. It is further proposed that harsh, restrictive, heteronomous parental control interferes with the development in the child of that confidence in his own judgment which is necessary for independence.

There is some evidence from Hugo's study to support this hypothesis. The results showed a tendency for the parents of extremely suggestible children to be more authoritarian and restrictive in their attitudes toward child-rearing than parents of extremely independent children. The results were not significant statistically, but the trend could not be denied.

5. Following in children is related to birth order; first-born children tend to be more suggestible than subsequent siblings in the same family.

This hypothesis has received some indirect support, but needs further investigation. Lasko (1954) has shown that parents tend to be relatively restrictive with first-born children and to relax somewhat their control of later children.

6. Independence is positively correlated with socio-economic status and school grades.

There were scant data in Hugo's study to support this hypothesis, but the definite impression was gained during the course of the investigation that the parents of the independent children were as a group superior in socio-economic status to the parents of the extremely suggestible children as a group. It also appeared that the independents tended to be better students than the followers. This is in line with Crutchfield's findings that his independent subjects showed more "intellectual effectiveness" than his dependent subjects.

7. Children who follow tend to come from broken homes and unstable home environments; independent children more frequently live with both parents in stable homes.

Hugo's evidence is directly opposed to that of Crutchfield, in respect to the home backgrounds of the followers and independents. Crutchfield reported that the high followers in his sample came almost without exception from stable homes; the independents much more frequently reported broken homes and unstable home environments. In Hugo's study, five of the eight subjects who followed most frequently came from homes broken by divorce, separation, or the death of a parent. Among the parents of the other extreme followers who were contacted, one father was deceased, another was confined to a nursing home, and there was one case of divorce. In contrast, all but one of the sixteen most independent subjects were living with both parents; and in the one exception the mother had very recently died in an automobile accident.

Perceiving the Other as Stimulus

We have stressed the fact that action depends in part on perception of the demands of the social situation. Few people enjoy the autonomy of social isolation; when their responses differ from the group they are uncomfortable, and sometimes much distressed. Some people deny their own judgment and sometimes their senses in order to agree with the group. In the experiments just cited, the stimulus emanating from the group was quite clear. In everyday situations the stimulus is frequently equally clear. A person may find himself a minority of one in a club vote, a political debate, or on a moral consideration. To stand one's ground in line with one's best judgment creates a chasm in relation to others; to bridge this chasm and close ranks with others is to deny one's judgment, and sometimes one's principles. When the situation is clearly defined, it is not so difficult to take a position and hold it firmly, even in face of isolation. However, when the issue is ambiguous, it becomes increasingly difficult to stand alone.

When one is in a dyadic situation, the meaning of the stimulus may or may not be clear. Yet this is the relationship in which we find ourselves many times every day. Face to face with another person, without any possibility of validating our judgment against the judgments of other persons, we are required to act; and sometimes these actions have lifelong implications. While at times our own needs are so powerful that we act in accord with them, scarcely being aware of the intention emanating from the other, ordinarily this is not the case. Usually we accommodate to the moods, desires, intentions of the person with whom we are interacting. We may do this on a trial-and-error basis or on the basis of an immediate perception of the other's intentions, which may or may not mutually interlock with our own. In trial and error it is as if we set up simple experiments to test hypotheses about what the other intends. Depending upon response we alter the hypothesis and try again. Many times, however, we are called upon to act without the possibility of testing an hypothesis. Here we have to rely upon immediate perception.

How good are people in perceiving the intentions of others? The question is more readily raised than answered. Undoubtedly there are wide individual differences. There is the well-known social boor who is impervious to the most obvious cues, as well as the socially sensitive individual who can tell you what you are feeling almost before you are aware of it yourself.

Bruner and Tagiuri (1954), who analyzed studies on the perception of people, tentatively offer the following conclusions on the judgment of personality characteristics from external signs: the more similar two people are, the more accurate one is in judging the personality characteristics of the other; the trait being judged must somehow be manifest in behavioral cues, otherwise accuracy becomes very poor; judgment of others is improved under certain laboratory conditions if one is intelligent, socially adjusted, and detached; intuition and a global approach seem to improve judgment; errors in judgment are related to halo effect and logical error, as well as to a tendency to project one's own characteristics onto the person being judged. These statements, which pertain to how well people are able to perceive and judge others, show us that science can as yet tell us very little about this subject.

Still, man goes on performing in a remarkably efficient way. Critical decisions based on the intentions and desires of others are made regularly, as they have been down through history before the scientist became interested in the problem. One of the reasons why scientific study has contributed so little to understanding the perception of people is that attention has been focused in the laboratory on such variables as size, color, shape, and so on, without proper regard to the relationship between these properties and the wishes, motives, goals, and other intervening variables of the person. We know full well that the same movement of the arm or tilt of the head can mean two different things depending upon the context in which each occurs. We do not judge an individual by such isolated acts; nor by any summation of isolated acts. It is as they are seen in a pattern, influenced by what is going on inside the individual, that we are able to judge him and respond appropriately.

What is the process involved in perception? Much of what has been learned about the laws governing the perception of objects can be applied to person perception. Laws pertaining to constancy, embeddedness, and stimulus configurations which you probably studied in general psychology, tell us a great deal about the "how" of perception. We need to study these same laws in a social setting. Only then will we be able with confidence to say how intentions are mediated; how one knows that another is loving or hostile, grasping or generous. Only then will we be able to say how much of Carol Chisholm's perception of her father-in-law was based on cues emanating from him, and how much a projection of her own motives. There is no simple coordination between the senior Chisholm as a stimulus compound and the behavioral response of Carol. This is a complex business, requiring not only knowledge of stimulus patterns but also knowledge of such intervening variables as hopes, fears, expectations. Somehow the external stimuli and the intervening variables form an interlocking pattern which is the immediate behavior space. What one perceives in the social situation cannot be extricated from the interlocking pattern. Perception thus faces two ways, toward the stimulus and toward the personality of the perceiver. Any given social perception is an accommodation to the two parts.

The importance of the personality in perception will become clearer in the next case study. There you will see how twin boys project their own inner struggles and conflicts onto the immobile and relatively nonsuggestive materials in the psychologist's "play room." You will also see how their use of the materials changes, suggesting different perceptions, as their relationship with their mother is altered.

Suggested Readings

Allport, F. H. *Theories of Perception and the Concept of Structure.* New York: Wiley, 1955.
A review and critical analysis of theories of perception, with an introduction to what the author calls a dynamic-structural theory of behavior.

Bruner, J. S. and Tagiuri, R. "The Perception of People." in Lindzey, G. (Ed.), *Handbook of Social Psychology.* Cambridge: Addison-Wesley, 1954, Vol. II, 634–654.
Excellent review of studies concerned with judgment of emotions and personality characteristics, as well as how impressions of other personalities are formed.

Heider, Fritz. *The Psychology of Interpersonal Relations.* New York: Wiley, 1958.
A synthesis of common sense, or naïve, psychology with some findings from scientific psychology.

A CASE STUDY OF A FAMILY IN TRANSITION

In our discussion of the Chisholm family in Chapter 4, we saw how intimately interrelated are the lives of family members. The baby, who is positively oriented toward his mother and dependent upon her for the satisfaction of practically all his needs, responds to changes in her behavior almost instantaneously. Any change in the mother which is perceived as a threat to his safety and security produces in the baby a violent reaction. The baby, of course, is dependent on the mother; without her regular ministrations he would die. Little wonder that he is attuned to modifications in her responses to him.

Now let us consider the reactions of an older child whose security is threatened. This child can move about freely. He can voluntarily avoid many of the dangers in his environment. He knows where food is stored and can seek it out when he is hungry. His world has become differentiated so that it includes many people, not just one. Will he still respond as violently to cues from the mother (and from other people also if he has developed an interdependent relationship with them) as young Peter Chisholm did? The answer is, yes. Of course, with the older child the response will be more complicated and subtle. Instead of the immediate and explosive reaction of a baby, if he feels insecure he may develop a headache or some other somatic complaint. He may destroy his property, or other people's property, as an expression of his aggressive impulses. He may become overly demanding of attention, or he may become withdrawn. In the present chapter you will see at the center of the stage two older boys and their mother, and you will see some of the forces to which they respond.

Katherine Burke, age 26, with her two boys, came to the clinic for help. The boys, seven-year-old identical twins, were having difficulties in the first grade of school, which they were repeating for the second year. They were especially inept at learning to read. After the social history, psychiatric examination, and psychological tests were completed, a conference was held in which it was decided that the boys should have individual tutoring in remedial reading, in addition to play therapy sessions. The reading tutors were to work with the boys three times a week; the author was to see them once a week. Simultaneously the mother was to be seen three hours each week. The father would not cooperate in regular conferences, although later he did come in once on his own initiative, after the treatment of his wife and boys led to events which threatened to upset his routine habits. The Burkes had a third child, a girl, four and a half years old.

Questions Concerning the Case

Keep the following questions in mind as you read the case history. Make notes as you go along. Before you read the author's interpretive summary, write a paragraph or two in answer to each question.

1. How would you characterize Mrs. Burke's behavior when she first came to the clinic?

2. In Mrs. Burke's life history, what are some of the principal antecedent conditions to the development of the behavior patterns you have just described?

3. What contemporary forces contributed to Mrs. Burke's behavior?

4. Why was Mrs. Burke able to solve some of her critical problems in such a short time?

5. Identify two important conflicts in Mrs. Burke's life and indicate what mechanisms she used in attempting to resolve them.

6. How do you account for the aggressiveness and destructiveness of the twins?

7. What were the important antecedents to the reduction of aggressiveness on the part of the twins?

8. How do you suppose Mrs. Burke, in her daily contact with the boys, revealed to them her feelings of dissatisfaction and rejection?

9. What mechanisms of defense did the boys employ?

10. Try interpreting the TAT stories before you read the remainder of the case material.

Diagnostic Testing

Some kind of diagnosis always precedes efforts at psychiatric treatment. Usually in clinics interviews, conducted by the psychiatrist and social worker, are supplemented by a battery of psychological tests as part of the diagnostic procedure. The raw data of these tests are rarely given in actual case presentations; rather, interpretations of the data are given.

However, the TAT (Thematic Apperception Test) stories of both mother and boys will be presented here in their entirety. In addition to the TAT, the boys were given an intelligence test, a reading aptitude test, and an auditory test. The results of these tests will be given later.

One of the pictures from the Thematic Apperception Test that was given to Mrs. Burke. See page 173 (*Number* 11).*

The TAT is a projective test in which a person makes up stories in response to a series of pictures which are shown to him briefly. In the process of making up a story, the person reveals a great deal about his own motives, anxieties, and characteristic ways of dealing with conflict situations. As you read the stories, try to imagine what these motives, anxieties, and behavior mechanisms are in the lives of these three people. Also try to see if you can find any connection, or interrelatedness, among the three sets of stories. Some people are very good at interpreting a TAT without having had any previous experience with it. However, skillful use of the TAT requires years of experience and practice—and even then psychologists make mistakes.

* Reprinted by permission of the publishers from Henry A. Murray: *Thematic Apperception Test*. Cambridge Mass.: Harvard University Press, Copyright, 1943, by The President and Fellows of Harvard College.

Thematic Apperception Tests

*Mrs. Burke's TAT Stories**

1. A young boy contemplating a violin which rests on a table in front of him.

(Laughs)** If I weren't in a psychological place, I could do better. The possible prodigy! He can't see all the infinite possibilities of the violin as he looks at it. He's too young and yet he must be sensing . . .*** he must have the feeling. He may have heard music. Perhaps . . . he actually heard a great master play the violin. He doesn't look as though he were aware of its possibilities. He looks as though he needs a lot of help if he were ever to do anything with the violin. He also looks as though possibly it had been forced on him and he never did hear the lovely music . . . I think the outcome will probably be a prodigy . . . , lovely music while he's young.

2. A middle-aged woman is standing on the threshold of a half-opened door looking into a room.

This is an old lady and she's about to go to bed . . . And as she closes the door she's looking back toward the fire . . . and remembering the years past when she shared the room and the fire with her husband who is dead (with emphasis) . . . The things that they shared in the room must have been quite lovely. She has nice human, sympathetic eyes and she loves flowers. She does rather well with them too, and music . . . She's . . . living a life mostly a memory . . . I think she's kind of hoping she'll die too before long.

3. A gaunt man with clenched hands is standing among gravestones.

Oh, Lynn Ward, eh? I've always wanted to see him work. . . . That's a picture obviously distorted by overemphasis. The man is literally wallowing in death. He's absorbed it until it's a complete part of him. He came there to mourn, and I don't think he's mourning anyone in particular. He likes the atmosphere . . . He would rather dwell on the sordid than live any other way. I think his apparent anguish is unrelated to anything personal. I think the outcome is that he will probably go mad—really mad.

4. The silhouette of a man (or woman) against a bright window. The rest of the picture is totally black.

What went before—was either sordid or the end of an era for the man. I think he's done a job. It was a hard job. He finished it and for a while he was exhausted, but then he realized that it was done and although perhaps an ordeal, he did it well. And now he's trying to free himself, his mind and his spirit from the strain. He's even begun to plan the future. After he's relaxed and seen ahead a little, I think he'll get excited. He'll look for another job. He has the gift of . . . restrengthening himself. He will go on and his life will be a series of well-done jobs, and through his technique he will acquire a great soul.

* The stimulus pictures are from H. A. Murray's published series, *Thematic Apperception Test*, Harvard University Press, 1943, plus several additional pictures.
** Words or phrases in parentheses indicate behavior on the part of the subject, or comments made by the therapist.
*** Dots indicate pauses in speech.

5. *A young woman's head against a man's shoulder.*

Femininity . . . she has been pulling some girlish tricks. She's been trying to get something. She's not altogether sure it's the right thing (laughs). He loves her. He understands her femininity. He's patient with it, and amused by it. I think that makes her feel, after she's gotten all wild, ashamed. I think ultimately if he keeps loving her that way, she'll find it's unnecessary to play the female game. She will absorb from him some of the honor and integrity of a man and be a better woman for it.

6. *A road skirting a deep chasm between high cliffs. On the road in the distance are obscure figures. Protruding from the rocky wall on one side is the long head and neck of a dragon.*

Man is a very little thing, pushing himself against the elements, pushing himself against the earth, pushing himself against things with no brains and not much strength. These men have built something out of the earth. They had a purpose in view; in some way they figured they were conquering the confusion of things as they found them. It looks like a Herculean job they did —but it's really very small, inadequate, There are greater forces at work against them than they realize. I think they would have made better use of their brains than brawn. Certainly their little wall and barricade are no protection now. They'll have to use their brains. For the moment their brains may save them . . . They'll never learn their lesson.

7. *A dimly defined enlargement of a thumb showing part of the nail. There is a dark spot on the skin.*

This is a picture of a finger. It's been cut. It's bleeding. It's a doctor's finger. He was operating. It was a tense operation. The room was very hot and everyone was working very fast. He didn't notice that he cut himself. When he did see, he didn't tell anyone. When he took his glove off he threw it off so no one would see. Because of the tension in the room he knew that it would be too difficult to get any calm reaction for the fact that it was too late for him to save himself. He did what he could, but he never told anyone. He feared he had maybe two weeks before the poison would get him. In that two weeks he realized for the first time the great significance of a doctor's work. He wrote it out and he left it to be printed after he died. Ah! He wrote with more inspiration, more understanding to all medical students that followed. And it was all the more powerful because he never told. He gave everything he had, even his life, and he asked nothing . . . and he received real understanding and gave that too.

8. *Two nude standing figures of a young man and woman. The woman rests her head on the man's shoulder. Beside them stands a draped woman with a baby in her arms.*

The man and girl have loved . . . They had a child. . . . . . (sigh) . . . They weren't . . . as interested in the child as they were in each other —in themselves . . . (sigh). They were somewhat ashamed but grateful when her mother elected herself to take care of the child . . . If the four of them stay together in the same relationship, this love will ultimately be worn down. What they thought it would prove, it won't. The mother, because she possesses the child, will possess them. They will have no freedom. Mother . . . has . . . only scorn for their . . . love . . . She doesn't think they are practical enough. She's also jealous because she never had such a thing when she was young. By using the child she sets herself to destroy it. If the man were a little stronger, he would perceive what's happening, but he's weak. He only wants to indulge himself. He doesn't want to do anything but let things happen, and when the mother does finally destroy them, he can blame only her.

9. *Two chairs beside a tea table.*

The elegance of antiques. That's a ball and claw wing chair. Why, it's a perfect set—they're all ball and claw—Chippendale. The story is the daughter of rich parents. All her life she wanted to get married. She wanted to have things of her own. She wanted to express herself in her immaculate taste. She was a perfectionist. She had all the money she wanted so that she could afford to be a perfectionist. She didn't have much imagination of her own. She knew what ought to be, what went together, what matched. But actually all she could express was her knowledge, none of herself . . . She knew the tradition of tea. . . . She knew the tradition of antiques. She copied all techniques —everything was just lovely, but it had no feel, no warmth—it was a reasonable facsimile . . . She lived with things and her money and her acquisitive desire for perfection all her life. She imposed it on her family. And she left them all without warmth, without the slightest vestige of human understanding . . . . . . (laughs—sighs—lights cigarette).

I didn't like that one—that's sterile. Imagine putting oriental rugs under antiques, but you have to keep up tradition.

10. *An outline drawing of the head of an old bearded man—with another old man apparently sitting cross-legged on his shoulders. In the background is the outline of a splintered tree.*

The man who drew this picture was bound to be different. He couldn't draw anyway. He improvised a technique, to startle, original. I think he might have been trying to express a farmer and the farmer's eternal battle against the elements. The farmer gets very much upset about the elements and yet he's absolutely determined that with his strength and hoe he will not be beaten and he will grow his crops. I think subconsciously the farmer is aware that God is on his side and not on the side of the weather. That gives him the strength and the fortitude to replant his crops after a frost, to cut down the apple tree that the lightning struck and use it for kindling wood. Year after year he plants his farm. Year after year the same things happen, and yet in spite of the wind and frost and snow and rain and the drought, he's fed and he's happy. The momentary frustrations only make him more determined not to be defeated by the weather. The outcome is that he goes back to the original fertility of the earth—the eternal fertility (laughs).

Second Sitting

11. *The portrait of a young woman. A weird old woman with a shawl over her head is grimacing in the background.*

The lady in the foreground is about thirty-five years old. She didn't mature very fast. She's just now beginning to face problems which she should have faced ten years ago. She lived alone and didn't go too deeply into anything. And now she's beginning to realize that she missed her values. At the present moment everything seems very confused. She not only doesn't know what she thinks but she doesn't know what to do about it. The old woman isn't really there at all; she's a symbol. She has lived long. She has found her values. She's pretty sure of what she thinks. She lived without being afraid to face things squarely. Because of the younger woman's lack of practice in thinking, the only solution for the present dilemma is to simply accept the wisdom of age.

12. A bridge over water. A female figure leans over the railing. In the background are tall buildings and small figures of men.

The men . . . are filling a storage barn . . . It's quite a lucrative business. They work at it night and day. They fill it up and then they sell it, and then they fill it up again. That's all they care about. From a little shed they've built it up over the years until it's a widespread system. And they've made a lot of money and they intend to make a lot more. The girl is the wife of the owner. She married him when it was only a shack. She shared his ambitions in the beginning, but she began to feel neglected when things really got going. She did everything she could to keep the balance between the home and the business. But more and more the work took the husband's time. When he came back to her, he could only think of the business, talk it. He was always too tired to do anything but go to bed. She wanted to have a child to fill up her time and to give them a common interest. He said, "No, wait until we are really set." Now she's reached the point where she's given up. She feels she's lost him to the business. She thinks by jumping off the bridge and drowning in front of the men that she can tell him once and for all what he did. And then it will all be maybe too late for him to have her. He may realize that business isn't everything. That's just what she does.

13. A young boy is seated at a table with an open book before him. Behind him stand two little girls.

That is a family at home. Mother and daughter and son. As a family they are interested in life. They're curious and interested in knowledge. They read and talk together. They have ambitions for each other. Right now in the midst of the general homework time, they're listening to the radio. Someone on the other side of the world is speaking in their language—family's language—about his life, his way of living. Because of the fact that they have a chance to get such infinite supplimations—is there such a word?—they're the—available—the already available sources; they will know more of the reality, more of the real picture of the times in which they live than most families. The combination of their curiosity and interest and the availability of information will make them exceptionally full people.

14. A young man leaning toward a young woman who has her head turned away from him with an expression of refusal.

They have been lovers. After a great deal of wooing she finally consented to go up into a hotel room with him. They had cocktails and a lovely lunch served in the room. And then they slept together. He thought that was just fine. He was very happy about it; he could see a long time of such nice experiences ahead. She, on the other hand, was ashamed. It wasn't anything she had hoped for. Instead of being beautiful it was sordid. She felt cold, clammy inside. Rather than seeing anything in the future, she wanted to get out of there as fast as possible and never see him again. The moment of the picture is her attempt to leave. She hasn't expressed herself very well. She doesn't really care whether she does or not. He is abashed, a little sore, and a little amazed. He doesn't understand at all. He's trying to convince her that she's just a little upset. The more he tries, the more determined she becomes. Finally she does go. She never does see him again.

15. *A young woman is standing with downcast head, her face covered with her hand. Her left arm is stretched forward against a wooden door.*

That is a woman who is married. She married a drunk. Gee, we're sordid this morning, aren't we? And she loved him very much and she thought that with her love she could so fill his life that he'd stop drinking. They bought a farm and they worked on it together, and she worked alongside of him. She kept him amused when they weren't working, and it looked as though everything was going to work out nicely . . . Sometimes he seemed to get restless, bored, but she never lost her faith. She'd think of new things to do, extra exciting things, keep him busy. After a couple years it seemed as though his restlessness was getting worse. One night he got drunk and told her that he hated the life, that it was sterile and he was bored and that he wasn't going to stay. He didn't want to be a farmer. He wouldn't be stuck in the sticks. He was going to go and enjoy life. She could come if she wanted to, but he didn't really care. With that he left (said with great emphasis).

16. *The face and figure of a bearded man reflected in a mirror.*

That gentleman was born a dandy. He turned into a cosmopolitan. He went into business and married a rich wife—a rich woman—and he wore flashy neckties and got into all the ubiquitous men's clubs. And he drank scotch and sodas and took extensive trips to Europe and made love to young women. He always surrounded himself with nice things, just the right style, just the right quality, just the right color. He collected first editions which he never read. He made up fancy cocktails to give friends. He played bridge. He had a horse which he rode on occasions. He made a charming impression wherever he went. He was excellent if superficial company. His life was charming, but it neither proved anything nor added anything.

17. *A woman has her hands squeezed around the throat of another woman whom she appears to be pushing backwards across the banister of a stairway.*

That was a schoolteacher. She lived in a boardinghouse. She had a very dull, mousy life until one day she met a man. He caught her when she fell in the subway and took her home. He used to come and see her, took her to movies. Once he bought her a gardenia. That changed her. She got a new hairdo and she began to use some lipstick and she got to be a much better teacher, and from being just kind of dull and sorry for herself, she became quite gay and was very happy. One night when he came to see her they got to talking and he stayed later than the boardinghouse rules permitted . . . As he said goodbye, he kissed her (emphasis) and her happiness was tremendous (with real feeling). As she was listening for the front door to close, she heard the landlady talking with the man. The landlady made some very insinuating remarks about what he had been doing until so late, and finished by nastily saying that she wouldn't allow him in the house again, and if he came, she'd report him to the police as a molester. He left and the teacher came downstairs, and she looked at the landlady and as she realized what had happened to the life that was so wonderful, all the old frustration came up and blinded her, and she choked the landlady to death. Which only made the ending of the happiness worse.

18. A young servant girl looking backward through a door.

Have I a one-track mind? Now what else could she be doing? That's a young maid making eyes at her mistress' gentleman caller. She tries it once or twice. He thinks it's all right, pretty nice. He asks her when her day off is. But the mistress overhears, and she fires the nifty little maid. But the little maid gets another job and continues to make eyes at her mistress' gentleman callers.

That's all; I didn't like that one.

19. A young man is standing with downcast head buried in his arm. Behind him is the figure of a woman lying in bed.

(Sigh) That's a picture of a typical American midnight scene. It doesn't make any difference whether they're married or not, . . . it all begins with what they call love. They believe that love is a justification for indulging whatever desires they have. They get drunk and they tell each other a lot of nonsense. They say their love is beautiful, that there's no other love like it in the world, that God will condone their consummation. They haven't got the brains to control their animal . . . ; they've dulled their sensibilities with liquor so they don't even recognize their own distortion of beauty. They consummate but they have no understanding beyond the animal. They hardly realize what they do. Pride keeps them from admitting the game and when they wake up in the morning—their messy bodies and their hangovers—they insist . . . upon continuing the game. They go on and on, maybe just with each other, maybe with lots of people, until they're too old and unattractive to play the game, never realizing, never admitting. Gee! that would bring tears to the eyes of your grandmother.

20. An aged man with a white beard seated at a table with his head bowed and his hand over his eyes.

I love old men. That's a fine old man. He's lived a fine life—a good full life. He's appreciated—everything. He's picked and chosen until he's absorbed the truth of the finest things. He's very wise, very tolerant, very understanding, and yet he's strong and sure of his truths. Right now he's wondering if there can't be some way to give the youth he sees around him the benefit of all the experience that has given him his simple philosophy and the certainty that he finds from living with it. What he's trying to figure out is how to break the independence and the stubbornness that youth shows to any philosophy that he hasn't been able to live himself. Without knowing it, he has helped many youths. Eventually they will be stronger sooner, because of what he said to them.

Interpretation of the Thematic Apperception Test

The Thematic Apperception Test cannot be scored and interpreted as simply as can many psychological tests. There are no standard scores or procedures. Psychologists use different methods of analysis and interpretation. Also different things are looked for in the TAT. The clinician wants to know what are the general and specific personality characteristics and trends of behavior. The researcher wants to know how specific variables are affected by the introduction of different instructions or other antecedent conditions.

The purpose of giving the TAT to Mrs. Burke was clinical. We wanted to know what her motives and feelings were, how she approached her world intellectually, emotionally, and behaviorally. We wanted to know what the dynamics of the family situations were, about her sex adjustment and what kinds of defenses she had built up. All this information was desired so the therapist would be able to take advantage of it in planning his work with Mrs. Burke. The same was true for the twins.

Below is the actual interpretation made on the basis of Mrs. Burke's stories, before any therapeutic interviews were held with her. You will want to compare your own interpretation with that given here. Be reminded that there is no single interpretation of any TAT, and that it takes years of training and experience before high agreement in interpretation is reached between two interpreters.

A brief interpretation will also follow each of the boys' stories.

Interpretation of Mrs. Burke's Stories

1. *Intellectual Approach.* Her logic is emotional, not traditional. She *feels* the reality of a situation, without being able to think it through coherently. Ideation is carried on through symbols, emotional abstractions, which are personally very meaningful. She has a deep religious sense, but probably not a conventional expression of it.

2. *Creativity and Imagination.* She has an artist's sensibilities, and is not without talent. People, experiences, the work of man—in short, the whole of life—are perceived through a sensitive, aesthetic veil which automatically screens out the ugly, the disproportionate, the crude, the prosaic.

She passively submits to her own unconscious images and strivings. Much time is spent in reverie and day-dreaming. She has a strong need to be succored. Despite this, however, she has a realization of what ego strength and counteraction in the face of obstacles might be or do for her. She is very proud, ashamed of her weakness, and has a boundless admiration for one who makes the effort to overcome his weakness. She is a fighter, and will not be stopped by recurrent setbacks.

3. *Behavioral Approach.* There is a tendency toward repudiation of the American culture, which she considers coarse, superficial, and un-aesthetic. She has a deep sense of her own values and a strong need to express them. Her world provides little opportunity for such expression.

The typical American male is likewise repudiated. He is disgusting. He is interested only in self-indulgence—drinking, trivialities, lustful sex-uality without any of the aesthetic, feeling elements.

Old women she sees as wise and nourishing. Wise old men are strongly positively cathected. They are idealized and unapproachable, thus out of the contemporary scene. Her need for succorance is especially directed toward older men.

4. *Family Dynamics.* Her marriage has been a failure. The husband is a coarse, once-born, weak, unintellectual man, lacking any artistic appre-ciation. He is a drunkard. Sexual relations with him are disgusting to her; and she is probably frigid. She has had a few other sexual experiences which were equally sordid to her.

She has rejected her children for a variety of reasons. Some of the dy-namic elements underlying the rejection are:

1. Contempt and hate of the husband. This is transferred to the chil-dren who are symbols of a loathsome union.

2. Creative type. Her creative energy is directed into some form of art, and she is impatient and annoyed with the prosaic duties and obliga-tions incumbent upon a mother.

3. Identification with man. She is a feminine type, with her sensitivity and aesthetic interests, but with a masculine attachment.

4. There is perhaps an underlying father fixation which she is im-pelled to sublimate through her artistic expression.

The mother is seen as conventional, artificial, cold and heartless, and is thus repudiated. Antiques are collected by her merely as prestige sym-bols, class symbols, with no appreciation of their intrinsic value. There is conflict, misunderstanding, and open bitterness between them.

5. *Inner adjustment and defense mechanisms.* The main sources of con-flict in Mrs. Burke are:

1. Passivity—counteraction. She is a proud woman and does not give up easily. Counteraction is very high. However, there is a strong tendency to submit, to be passive, and through this passivity gain her purpose.

2. Weakness and confusion of mind—strength and rationality. She is aware that she is confused and knows she needs help. Her confusion arises over her dilemma as to her proper role. Femininity she considers as

weak and lacking the essential qualities of strength she desires. Masculinity (especially that of older men) is synonymous with integrity. She wants to be strong in order to be rational and solve her problems.

3. Dependence—independence. She leans heavily on others for support and accepts it as a child. Simultaneously she loathes being dependent and asserts her independence in numerous ways. In her desire to free herself from the protective aegis of her mother, rebellion has marked her path. As a result she has probably become involved in many situations which were bewildering.

6. *Emotional reactivity.* She is an imaginative, subjective person, given to romantic flights of thought and action. Her actions are frequently stimulated by fantasies and aspirations which are not grounded in reality, but rather in a yearning for a half-conscious ideal.

7. *Sexual adjustment.* She is aware that sex is a vital force, rejuvenating and recreating. Sexual urges stir her creativeness, and, therefore, she has probably fallen into affairs, led on, without resistance, by an impelling force, but always revolted and disgusted afterwards—cursing herself for her own weakness. She does not have the necessary control to wait until she gets what she really wants. Her creativeness has also made her a victim of the illusion of being able to reform man.

8. *Summary and suggestions for psychotherapy.* The subject has been unable to make a satisfactory adjustment with her husband; further attempts along this line will probably be futile. If she has not already divorced him, she probably will.

She has rejected her children. She may never be able to accept them and provide them with the maternal love which they need. On the other hand, if she can find adequate expression of her need-dispositions through some kind of creative work, her whole feeling toward them may be changed.

Her outstanding characteristic is artistic sensibility. She views the world symbolically in terms of her own largely unconscious values. If she has specific talents she should be encouraged to continue and concentrate on whatever she is doing in this direction. If she has no medium of artistic expression, the suggestion that she attempt to discover one may be offered profitably.

The TAT with the Twins

Because of the extreme distractibility of the twins and because there was some question as to the effectiveness of a visual stimulus alone to stimulate stories in children so young, the Thematic Apperception Test was given to the boys while they were playing with clay figures. This procedure caused the stories to be somewhat more disconnected than they might otherwise have been. Clay was used because the boys were accustomed to playing with it and liked it, and because it can readily be moulded into any shape which the occasion demands. The figures used here were the same ones used later in the play therapy sessions.

Samuel's TAT Stories

1. A young boy contemplating a violin which rests on a table in front of him.

He's trying to make a boat—a violin. (Pounds the figure of mother with hammer.) Even the back is being socked in (referring to figure); now I'm going to do this side. ("What's the little boy thinking?") * He's thinking how to play the violin. Now see how flat she is. Now I'll sock her legs. (referring to Mother) He's learning piano lessons. (What is he going to do?) (Pounds mother's foot.) See how thin that is? He's going to go outdoors and take violin and play for his father. (Takes mother's head off and pounds it flat.)

2. An elderly woman standing on the threshold of a half-opened door looking into a room.

That lady is looking in the door. Is it a lady or a man? I don't know. She's looking to see if a little dog is in there—to find her little doggy. Oh where, oh where is my doggy? Tomorrow is the dog's birthday. I want him. ("Where is the dog?") He's under the couch, that's where he is. He squeezed under there. He was a baby puppy and she got him for her birthday. Her father gave it to her.

3. A gaunt man with clenched hands standing among gravestones.

This gentleman is praying to be good . . . ("What is he saying?") He's saying not to crawl over everything and count all the money, and not to fight any more . . . ("Is he saying anything else?") Oh please, oh please, don't be bad to me and I'll be good, amen. (All this time he has been hammering the figure of the Mother.) That's the end of you, lady. A gas bomb dropped on her for two hours. Does it look like the end of her? Now, goodbye. (With that, he throws her in the basket. Takes up father and begins pounding him.)

4. The silhouette of a man's figure against a bright window. The rest of the picture is totally dark.

The man is closing the window to go to sleep and not to wake him up and make him freeze because it's cold as night. Guess what I'm trying to do? I'm trying to hammer this old thing (Father's head). (Pounds Father's head violently into the body.) ("What about the man closing the window?") He goes to bed and to sleep. Before he says thy name, thy kingdom come, thy will be done, amen. Then he says I am going to sleep, goodbye. But he's dead. (Pounds father some more.) That's the end of him; he's worse than Mother is. (Throws him in basket.) ("How did the man die?") He dies when he gets in bed. He was very old, so he died. (Pounds the figure of Joe, which represents himself.) I'm dead.

* Questions in parentheses were asked by the examiner.

5. A young woman's head against a man's shoulder.

This man is thinking about the war—how this gas bomb business is going to stop. (Pounds Billy, the figure representing his twin brother.) Not very good for the clay, is it? Now I'll flatten it out thin. Now where is my body going to go. I'll go to bed now. Hallowed be thy name, thy kingdom come, thy will be done, Amen. How will I be a good boy, Amen. That's all, good night.

6. A road skirting a deep chasm between high cliffs. On the road in the distance are dim shapes. Protruding from the rocky wall on one side is the long head and neck of a dragon.

A bridge . . . ("Can you tell a story about it?") I don't understand it so I'm not going to do it. (Gets up and walks off to window.)

7. A dimly defined enlargement of a thumb showing part of the nail. There is a dark spot on the skin.

I see black and a swordfish. What is that thing? I don't know what to think. (Pounds clay violently with hammer.) (That is a thumb, see.) A big nail, a big spike. (Takes clay out of mouth.) See my teeth marks in the clay? He was hammering on a telephone and it slipped. (Chews clay with vigor.) That's a fingernail and it bled like the dickens, and off went the fingernail, 'cause it made a hole into the fingernail. ("And then what happened?") He cried and cried, and said, mama, mama, I want a fingernail in the hospital. Mama said no, no no, you can have the doctor come here. He cries, mummy, I don't want my finger cut off. And she says you can go to the hospital and have your finger cut off. All right (with tremulous voice). Come on with me, mummy said. And he went to the hospital and cried and they cut it off.

8. Two nude standing figures of a young man and woman. The woman rests her head on the man's shoulder. Beside them stands a draped woman with a baby in her arms.

That's a statue and the lady's being killed. She's dying. Goodbye, goodbye. You know Lord Jesus is very nice. See Lord Jesus (pointing to the lower figure in the background). They're going to ask that lady if they can have her clothes. They're going to rip that lady's clothes off because they want some clothes and they're going to run away and put them on. And then they're going to buy some food and eat it. (Takes a wad of clay and puts it in his mouth.) Can I skip that one? ("Tell me a little more, you're doing fine.") That lady's hugging that man because she likes him. ("Are they saying anything?") She's saying nothing. He's saying, will you please go over to that thing and go to sleep. (Pounds clay again.) They're going to sleep and get a blanket over them and wake up and die and get out of here. All right?

Interpretation of Samuel's Stories

1. Samuel is very aggressive toward the mother. He is probably also resistive and negativistic in his relationship with her. She has neglected or completely rejected him and he is attempting to gain her affection through various attention-getting mechanisms.

2. He is also aggressive toward the father. The father does not allow

him the freedom he desires to crawl over things and play where he wants to. He imposes physical restraints and probably is the one who punishes him. At least Samuel considers him worse than the mother. It may be that Samuel interprets restraints and punishments and neglect as rejection. It is likely that the father actually has rejected him.

3. Some aggression is also shown toward Donald, his twin brother. This is either a transference of aggression felt toward his mother and father or the result of frustration and deprivation caused by Donald.

4. His picture of the family situation is very confused. There is evidence of a great deal of emotional insupport and rejection. He is totally unable to understand the conflicts warring within him, and in his attempt to deal with them we see various trends:

a. Desire to avoid difficulties and run away from a noxious environment.

b. He takes precautionary measures to escape from dangerous situations. He may lie, or he may try to do whatever he thinks would please mother and father when he feels threatened.

c. There is a suggestion that he tries to solve his dilemma by giving up and not struggling in difficult situations.

5. He displays a strong desire to have someone wait on him and do things for him.

6. There is considerable oral aggression, which suggests that he was deprived of the breast very early or had an inadequate supply of milk to satisfy his needs when he was an infant. This oral aggression represents an accumulation of tension which he attempts to discharge by biting and eating objects.

7. There is a marked castration fear. Either he has been threatened with castration for masturbation or he has been circumcised and interpreted it as castration; or both have occurred.

8. He has completely repressed his curiosity over the anatomy of the opposite sex to such an extent that he is very uncomfortable when faced with nude figures. He has to dress them immediately.

9. The stories as a whole indicate that Samuel is more aggressive generally than Donald. He is probably the more assertive of the two and dominates situations in which they are both involved.

Donald's TAT Stories

1. A young boy contemplating a violin which rests on a table in front of him.

He is going to work for a half-hour, and he will not disturb . . . He is going to play a violin . . . He's looking for someone to play with him, to play the piano so they can have a band. Then they plan, and he goes home. All the children come and they have a party . . . And they don't fight. They . . . in the night. They are playing ghosts. The ghost jumps up. . . . He calls, "Father! Father!" He jumps into the sky. Nobody knew who the ghost was.

2. *An elderly woman standing on the threshold of a half-opened door looking into a room.*

She's looking at this room. It's all lighted. She feels sad. She doesn't know what's in there. "Are you a wicked lady?" he asked. She said, "No, I'm not." He came over and smacked her face. She didn't like it and called the cops. They said, "Are you in trouble?" She said, "Yes, he is bad . . ." ("Who was the man?") His name is Jack. He was in her house when she woke up. He was stealing things. He was a robber. She couldn't find any of her clothes. He took them all. The cops didn't like the robber. They hit him over the head with an axe. He didn't like the axe on his head. He screamed and screamed. Tomorrow he'll die. Tomorrow he died. He put everything in the car. The policeman smashed the car in and took the clothes. So he took everything out of the car and gave it to the lady, and stabbed the robber to pieces.

3. *A gaunt man with clenched hands standing among gravestones.*

She's saying her prayers. She's not good. She's bad. She's saying bad prayers to God. . . . The Devil's swearing at God. He teaches everybody to swear. He swears, and God says nice words. He swears, and swears, and swears. He's praying 'cause he doesn't want God to say all those nice words. He's going to do something wicked. He's going to smash the Lord's bricks and tell everybody to do bad things. He kept telling 'em, and God kept speaking and speaking. He told 'em to do bad things, and God said, "No, no." (Follows about a minute and a half of incoherent mumbling in which the characters God and Devil urge "Do it," "No, you better not," etc.) God told 'em to do good, but they forgot and forgot. ("Then what happened?") Nothing. I want to go look out the window . . .

4. *The silhouette of a man's figure against a bright window. The rest of the picture is totally dark.*

The man is going to fly away. He's not going to jump. He's up in the night. He doesn't want to be disturbed. . . . If you disturb him he puts you farther and farther down. . . . ("What's he looking for?") He's looking out the window with his strong muscles 'cause he's going to fly away. He doesn't like this home. "Do you like this home?" said the Devil. "Don't pay any attention to the Devil," God said. "Don't pay any attention to the Devil." The man forgot about the Devil, and prayed to God. . . . The Devil started to sing. He told everybody to sing. . . . God told nobody to mind the Devil. . . . (Again, incoherent mutterings about "God said," and "The Devil said," all concerning singing or not singing.) The Devil didn't sing because he had in mind to kill everybody. Then when everybody dies, they come 'live again . . . ("Did the man die?") He came 'live again, I told you! ("Then what happened?") Let's look at the next picture.

5. *A young woman's head against a man's shoulder.*

I'll make this one awful. An awful one. Two boys go to school to learn how to be bad boys. God taught them how to be good. They never thought how to be bad. They thought how to be good. Not bad . . . good. They'd be bad . . . they are starting to be bad. The more they learn to be bad, the gooder they get. They are trying to be bad, but they can't. God won't let them. Because when they're bad, they get more money, and they really don't.

6. *A road skirting a deep chasm between high cliffs. On the road in the distance are dim shapes. Protruding from the rocky wall on one side is the long head and neck of a dragon.*

What is that? ("A dragon.") What do dragons do? You tell me what they do. He is looking at the fly. It is . . . You know it isn't. I know it is. About all the junk . . . do dragons look like that? They do not. What do dragons do? All the animals . . . the fly is dead. The dragon is not dead. He is not happy. He does not like anybody right now. He does not want to be happy. He says, "Don't bother me until I am happy 'cause I'll get madder and madder. If I get mad enough I'll . . ." The fly says, "I am not dead." "You are too dead." "No, I am not dead." It is not a dragon. It is a duck. The duck said, "No, no, no; where are you going? Aren't you going to like it . . . don't you go, don't you go away from me." That's the only fly there is in the world. "All right, you may eat me." The duck said, "You may eat me." The fly came up and said, "No, I may not." You may eat me. I don't want to eat anybody. I don't want to eat you. They don't want to eat you; you don't want to eat them. Are you bad or good? No, I am good. "You are bad," said the fly. He is bad and the ducks are good and the fly is bad. The fly told the duck he was bad. Awful . . . it was an awful story.

7. *A dimly defined enlargement of a thumb showing part of the nail. There is a dark spot on the skin.*

It's a stream of light. . . . (Continuous playing with clay. Examiner explains that it is a thumb.) That's blood (pointing to drop). Oh, something happened—something . . . What do you want to know for? ("What happened?") Nothing happened. I don't want to tell, that's why.

8. *Two nude standing figures of a young man and woman. The woman rests her head on the man's shoulder. Beside them stands a draped woman with a baby in her arms.*

Ugh! Well, they didn't have any clothes on. They went to town. This lady gave them some money, and they bought clothes. I don't dare tell very long ones because I don't like to. The mother was very happy. They never had any more trouble in their life. ("What about the baby?") Oh, the baby's dead.

Interpretation of Donald's Stories

1. Donald's aggression is much more directed toward the father than toward the mother. However, he does not seem to be as direct in identifying the father as does Samuel. Father-surrogates are the target of his displeasure. This may mean that he is either more afraid to express aggression toward the father because of experiences in which he was punished, or it may mean that he feels a closer bond of unity with the father than does Samuel and is loath to jeopardize that relationship by overt attack.

2. Aggression toward the mother if quantitatively less is equally intense and more direct. He does not hesitate to call her by name and to electrocute her. In whatever way the mother has frustrated him at least she seems to have permitted a freer expression of the hostility aroused. He may actually hit or kick her. More likely he calls her names and in other ways verbally releases his aggression.

3. Like Samuel, Donald expresses some aggression toward his twin brother. He is both more violent and more vocal in this expression, however, than Samuel. This suggests that he may be the more dominant of the two and control his brother by talking him into whatever he wants him to do. It is possible that he is stronger and uses physical force to gain his ends.

4. Considerable aggression is shown toward Jane, the younger sibling, whom he also calls "baby" in one story. Every time he refers to her she is either dead or he is going to kill her. One would expect to find intense sibling rivalry and perhaps outbreaks of anger and overt attacks on the sister.

5. There is a great deal of concern over good and bad, God and the devil. Likewise there is confusion over the meaning of death. People are killed and are revived at will. This ambivalence shows the struggle he is waging to do what he thinks is right and at the same time the impulse he has to be "bad." The father seems to represent the bad man, but there is a desire also to have him be good. The father is very capricious in dealing with him, sometimes playing with him and being very kind, another time being very impatient and cross and excluding the child from his world. The use of the words "God" and "the Devil" indicates that he has been associated with someone, either the parents or a friend or maid, who has talked about such concepts in a completely confusing manner.

6. He presents a picture of many arguments between the mother and father, and paints the father as being exceptionally passive.

7. Like Samuel he dislikes nude figures and dresses them.

8. He also displayed the oral aggression which suggests an early deprivation as in the case of Samuel.

9. There is a fear of castration, but it is considerably more repressed, or less intense, than it is in Samuel.

Results of the Stanford-Binet Test

Both boys came with the examiner to the testing room willingly, although Samuel was a little timid. They entered actively into the tasks set for them, but Samuel was not so self-confident as Donald. He was more inclined to distrust his own ability and look to the examiner for help. That is not to imply that Donald was high in reliance on his own ability, but simply that he had somewhat more self-confidence. Both boys were easily distracted by extraneous stimuli, and apparently by their own impulses as well. It was very difficult to hold their attention. Both wrote and drew with their left hands. Their scores were:

Donald: C.A. 7–7   M.A. 7–4   I.Q. 96
Samuel: C.A. 7–7   M.A. 6–10   I.Q. 90

Results of Reading Aptitude Test

The Primary Form of the Monroe Reading Aptitude Tests was used. Again both boys came willingly with the examiner. Donald was very talkative and somewhat boastful. Even though it was a chilly day, he declared that he was not cold. He said that he wouldn't even be cold if he did not have any clothes on. When Donald did not know an answer, he reflected briefly and tried again; Samuel just gave up in dismay, complaining "I'm tired. I wish I could stop." Donald was less dependent upon adult reassurance in the test situation, and his interests were somewhat less fragmentary than Samuel's. Samuel sat in a lethargic manner during most of the test. Donald was up and down from his chair. He wanted to know how the stop watch worked. He spied some squirrels out the window and plied the examiner with questions. "Why don't they see each other?" "Why do they bury their nuts?" "How do they crack them?" "Can they fly?" Both boys sucked their thumbs and bit their nails.

Summary of Scores

	Donald	Samuel
	Percentiles	
Visual	23	22
Auditory	28	28
Motor	63	59
Articulation	81	74
Language	40	35

The examiner spelled a number of words and asked each boy to identify them. The results follow:

Responses

	Donald	Samuel
cat	cat	cat
boy	barn	Bob
dog	dog	dog
rat	rat	rat
sat	sat	sat
fat	fat	fat
hat	hat	hot
ball	barn	Bob
sit	sat	sat

Neither boy was able to read "dog" or "cat" when seen in print.

The auditory tests revealed that both boys were within the normal range for hearing in each ear.

Background Information

Katherine Martin Burke, age 26, is the only child of Professor and Mrs. John Martin. The Martins are stable, highly respected, influential members of the upper-middle-class society into which they were born. They have always been economically and socially secure. They have neither feared a decline from their status in the community, nor have they aspired to upward mobility; they are satisfied with the prestige and position which are theirs.

Professor Martin is a scientist of great talent and considerable accomplishment. Early in his undergraduate days at a large Eastern university he showed promise of the brilliant career which was to follow. He was graduated with honors and elected to Phi Beta Kappa. His father, a successful physician, had encouraged him to study medicine, but his interest in theoretical and abstract problems directed him into the academic life. After receiving the Ph.D. degree, he returned to his Alma Mater as an instructor. He has received many acclamations from his professional colleagues, and on two occasions has been invited to deliver lectures in Paris and London. However, his daughter characterized him as being a "farmer at heart," and said that he was "physically old before his time." He suffered with duodenal ulcers intermittently throughout his adult life until ten years ago when he became active in a religious group renowned for its insistence on faith and "guidance" from God as the solution to all ills. He has an excessive amount of red hair covering his body and has to be shaved periodically during the summer in order to keep cool.

Mrs. Martin, like her husband, has been troubled with duodenal ulcers much of her life. Unlike him, however, her faith has provided no permanent cure, and she has had three recurrences during stressful periods over the past ten years. She is a very vivacious and energetic person, with what her daughter calls a "creative urge and no outlet." At fifty she is still physically attractive; she was considered a beautiful girl in her youth. At present she devotes her energies to women's club work, gardening, and to active participation and leadership in religious activities. Quoting her daughter again, "She loves to take old clothes or broken-down people and fix them up." Her father was a lieutenant general in the United States Army.

Katherine was born in Philadephia. Birth was normal after an uneventful eight hours of labor. From the beginning she was her father's "golden-haired girl." She attended nursery school at four and kindergarten at five, and got along well. From the age of six to thirteen she attended a Country Day School from which she was expelled for "general noncompliance with the rules." The culmination of this noncompliance came when she threw a geranium pot out of the window in a rage. Of this school she remarked, "It was a fiasco, bah! They said do what you want to, and when I did, they just couldn't take it."

For one year thereafter she attended a suburban public school. She was asked not to return a second year because she was considered a "disturbing influence." For the next two years she was placed in a boarding school. The life there was enjoyable, and she was disappointed toward the end of her second year when she was expelled. Her sixteenth and seventeenth years were spent in a fashionable girls' finishing school. There she got along very well, was graduated with honors, and was the recipient of several prizes for outstanding achievement.

Upon leaving school she went home to live, and in October of that year she was introduced into society with what she regarded as "a swell party." Then began a series of incidents which culminated a few months later in her being forced to marry a man she did not love. In one of the early interviews she tried to recall the date of her wedding, but was unable to. Said she, "It was all such an awful thing that I figure I don't want to remember it."

Shortly after the "coming-out" party she went out with a boy, became intoxicated, was taken to a hotel room, and there she experienced her first sexual intercourse. She was disgusted with herself afterwards and was depressed for three weeks. She had wanted to remain a virgin until marriage. Finally the depression lifted, and she thought to herself, "Oh, what the hell, I can't get it back, so I might as well have a good time." Nevertheless, she continued to hate the boy.

On another occasion when she went out with him, he anticipated a repetition of the previous experience and made the customary overtures. She led him on until "the crucial moment" and then she kicked him in the stomach and got up and walked home. Her antipathy for this boy was not generalized, however, and within the next four or five months she had sexual relations with several boys. She was not in love with any of them. She was impelled to release a great urge which she felt, but without any particular feeling for her partners.

When she became pregnant, she was disturbed and upset; not so much because of the anticipated disapprobation, but because she felt that it augured the end of her freedom. She attempted abortion in various ways without success. She did not know how to reveal her secret to her parents. They had tried to get her to join the religious group to which they belonged; she had always resisted. Now it occurred to her that it would be easier if she became a member of the group and confessed her "sin" among the devotees. This she did in the fourth month of her pregnancy.

It was a bombshell! But it was nutriment to the voracious reforming appetite of the religious groupers. They avidly took the problem unto themselves, and decided that she would have to marry the boy. She did not object—she even convinced herself that she was in love with him. She wanted to be married in a little chapel which she had occasionally attended, but the collective Puritanical conscience of the old ladies would brook no such insult. Although they could vicariously enjoy her sin, they were not prepared for such a flagrant defiance of the superego. So in the seventh month of her pregnancy the ceremony was performed in one of the rooms of the Women's Club; and the couple were bundled off to New York for a honeymoon at the headquarters of the religious group. In due course she gave birth to twin boys. With some sense of humor in the situation, she opined that God had paid her doubly for her sins.

She had married one Jesse Burke, the pampered youngest son of a successful banker. At twenty-nine he is an inveterate drinker with no sense of the adult responsibilities which are his. In an interview he said that he had always "just drifted" and taken the easiest course. He does not like to exert himself and has willingly accepted both financial and emotional support from his own parents and from his parents-in-law. He drinks, he says, in order to dull his mind so that he will not have to think about things. His education consisted of two years at a preparatory school after completing the ninth grade in public school. He is a bond salesman and likes his job.

Developmental History of the Twins

The twins were born June 8, 1948. The condition of the mother during pregnancy was good, despite her several attempts at abortion. Labor was induced and lasted forty minutes. Samuel was born ten minutes before Donald, and both births were normal. There was a single placenta. They were breast fed until three and a half months, when they were weaned to the bottle. According to the mother, there were never any feeding difficulties; they always had enormous appetites and were feeding themselves regularly by twenty-six months.

Both were trained to "pots" from three weeks with suppositories and transferred to the toilet seat with ease before six months. Their bowel movements have always been regular. Occasionally between the ages of one and two there were "mistakes" in bed, and they smeared feces over bed and walls.

The mother reported that once she told Samuel that if he played with his penis, he was liable to pull it off. This happened when she saw him masturbating one day when he was about five years old.

Their more recent history reveals that they both have occasional temper tantrums, especially when the father uses force in effecting discipline. Donald's tantrums are more violent and occur more frequently.

Both boys have always destroyed their toys almost immediately upon receipt of them. They tear papers and magazines and cut other things into scraps. They are afraid of fires and talk a good deal about fire engines and what would happen if the house caught on fire. Samuel is afraid of speed of any kind, whether in a boat, an automobile, or on a train. They do not have nightmares or walk or talk in their sleep; their reported dreams, which are very similar, are related to stories of the Donald Duck

Developmental Items Reported by Mother

	Donald	Samuel
Birth weight	7 lb. 1 oz.	6 lb. 11 oz.
Weaned	3½ months	Same
First creeping	14 months	Same
First steps	19 months; walked very cautiously for several months	Same
Handedness	Left tendency as a baby; has persisted until the present	Same
Tonsil and adenoid operation and circumcision	3 years	Same
Speech	First words after thirty months. Speech was and has remained somewhat muffled and babyish	Same
Bladder training	Never completely trained; enuresis has continued through the present. Occurs about once a week at night and occasionally he wets his pants at play.	Never completely trained; enuresis has continued through the present. Occurs two or three times a week and not infrequently he wets his pants while at play.
Bowel training	Trained to "pot" from three weeks with suppositories	Same
Thumb-sucking	Mother reports only occasional thumb-sucking	Same (Tutor reports daily thumb-sucking)
Masturbation	No masturbation in recent years. Manipulated genitals occasionally from one to three years. (Observed manipulating genitals once in two months period by tutor)	Same (Observed manipulating genitals several times during two months period by tutor)

variety. Sometimes they dream of the Russians. In the latter case there are always airplanes and bombs and people being killed, with themselves as heroes.

Completion of the Family Picture

Besides the mother and father, described above, the twins have in their immediate family a sister, Jane, two and a half years younger. The mother's favorite, she is characterized by her as "willful," "friendly," and "extremely curious about everything." She tries to keep up with the boys in whatever they do. Toward Samuel she is very aggressive. Her golden curls make it easy for the mother to identify with her; she is energetic and enthusiastic about life, just as the mother used to be as a girl and would like to be now. Mrs. Burke commented about her, "I suppose it's only natural for a mother to like her daughter better." Both twins vent their hostility on her at the slightest provocation. They blame her for things which they have done and beat her up whenever the opportunity arises. The mother said, "For a long time I didn't dare leave them alone, or they would surely have killed her."

Despite the general rejection of the twins, both parents have consistently shown less affection and regard for Samuel than for Donald. The mother reports that the father "picks on Samuel all the time and makes him feel inferior." He calls the boy "cry-baby" and continually compares him with Donald. The mother's own impression of the twins at birth was as follows: "Sammy was born first. He was all jaundiced, pinched up, and elfish-looking. Ugh! a ghastly mess. I had to nurse them on account of him. But Donnie was rosy and plump—a really pretty baby."

Larger Family Contacts. The maternal grandmother is very fond of all the children. She takes them on picnics and has them visit her, and they enjoy being with her. The maternal grandfather is preoccupied but friendly with the children. The paternal grandfather is dead. The paternal grandmother speaks to the twins in beautiful Quaker parables which they do not understand. She compares the twins one with the other at Samuel's expense. They do not like her. There is a Negro maid who tells the boys fabulous stories about Jesus, and they are fascinated by her tales.

There is no shared family interest, although occasionally they take walks together. The twins are negative and resistant toward their father.

Neighborhood Environment. The Burkes live in a suburban village on the seashore, close to the harbor and fishing piers. The twins roam the town. Especially they enjoy watching the activities on the wharves where the fishermen are at work. Their home is half of an old colonial house which has been made into a duplex. The yard is spacious with plenty of places to play, in addition to space for flower and vegetable gardens. In the other half of the house live a deaf spinster and her hypochondriacal boarder. The twins love them and are in and out of their quarters daily. Donald and Samuel share a room where, on rainy or cold days, they play. If the weather permits, however, they play around the docks or on the beach. They cannot swim but are courageous in the water, splashing around.

Donald is accepted everywhere in town, by everyone. Samuel is not so popular. He makes friends slowly, is often called a "cry-baby" by other children, and he cheats in fights. Donald takes the leadership role in all their joint activities.

School History. The twins went to nursery school and are at present repeating the first grade. When they started in the first grade they liked school. They made friends and got along well. During the middle of the year they began to lose their enthusiasm. At the beginning of the next year, when told they were repeating the first grade, they hated everything about school. At this time also they were separated and placed in different rooms at school. Although neither of them liked this separation, Samuel was especially upset by it. He asked continually for Donald, paid no attention to the teacher, and whined a great deal. His teacher was very irritated with him. Donald, on the other hand, was "teacher's pet," even though he did not like school. Reading was singled out as a special target for their disfavor, and when they came to the clinic, they were unable to read anything except their own first names.

The school made the following report to the clinic:

Donald's temperament is the opposite of Samuel's. Whereas Samuel is too deferential to Donald, the latter is rudely domineering over Samuel. Donald does not, however, seem to be entirely secure himself. He is a thumb-sucker, and feels it necessary to repeat often how good he is. He seems to be more mature socially than Samuel; he is very friendly in his manner, and his teacher likes him. Neither boy concentrates on his work, but Donald shows signs of arriving at the self-critical stage, with some drive toward accomplishment.

A mistake on the part of the remedial-reading tutor during the first week the boys were at the clinic showed how inferior Samuel felt to Donald and how he retreated in the face of implied invidious comparison. The tutor reported:

He had been working along happily and cooperating nicely. He was then shown a picture which we talked about. I asked him to close his eyes and tell me how many things he could remember. He named fewer than I felt he was capable of, judging from previous experience. So I urged him to try again without results. I said casually, "we wouldn't like to have Donald know that you couldn't think up any more." Samuel then stopped trying altogether, laid his head on the desk, sucked his thumb, and said his head hurt. He repulsed all my suggestions as to new games we might play, pushed things on the floor, said he didn't like me, and that he wanted to go home.

Therapeutic Relationships

During the time the Burke family came to the clinic, twenty-four interviews were held with Mrs. Burke and eight play sessions with each boy. The interviews were not recorded electrically. After each hour with Mrs. Burke extensive notes of the conversation were written down, quoting her exact words as often as possible. The main themes of each hour were not difficult to capture. The exact order in which things were discussed and the precise words employed proved more of a problem. The words which the twins used to accompany their play actions were written while they were talking.

The clinical data will be presented in chronological order—first the mother's interviews and then the boys' play sessions—so that you may see the reactions of each as they were seen in the clinic, and so that you may infer from the data the kinds and quality of interactions which took place elsewhere—at home primarily. Since the mother was seen three times a week and the boys only once, there will be three of her hours, followed by one play period for each boy, except during the middle period when several hours will be bunched together. Some of the information derived from the mother has already been presented. What follows here is an abstract of the notes, designed to show the kind of person Mrs. Burke was through the interactions she described with some of the more important people in her life; and similarly what the boys were like through their imaginary interactions.

Mother's Interviews

First Interview. Mrs. Burke was brought into the therapist's office and introduced by the Director of the Clinic. After he left, the following ensued.

T.° Did Dr. —— tell you something of the purpose of this meeting?

C. Yes, he said you wanted to talk with me in order to get a better picture of the twins' situation.

T. That's right. You see special problems at school, such as the reading difficulty the twins are having, are not unrelated to the family situation, and especially the emotional atmosphere of the home. It is reported that one of the problems connected with their inability to read is distractibility. Now that in part at least has an emotional basis. If you would like to spend some time discussing the total family picture, it would enable us to deal more intelligently with the problems which the boys present.

C. Oh, I'd like to cooperate in any way I can.

° T stands for therapist; C stands for client.

Second Interview. A brief family history was taken. The remainder of the hour was spent by the subject in relating the difficulties she had had in school and the sexual episodes and involvements which had led up to her marriage at the age of eighteen. She spoke of having a good time with Jesse (her husband), but said that she had never been in love with him. Just prior to her marriage she had been going with a boy who was a student of philosophy at —— University. He had wanted to marry her, and she had been very fond of him. They had read poetry, talked philosophy, and gone to concerts together. She described it as an ideal relationship. She admired him a great deal.

Third Interview.
C. Well, what do you want me to talk about today?
T. Anything you would like to discuss. Whatever you think is important.
C. I guess I resent everybody. Oh, my mother, the children, Jesse, everybody. My mother is so bossy and possessive. She can't leave me alone. She's always butting in and making a fuss over us. She's not happy unless she's patching somebody up. If she can't find somebody outside the family, she has to work on us. She always wants us to keep up appearances, no matter what else. She's practically supported us since we were married. You know that "You have to live in the accustomed manner" bunk. She has always told us what to do and what not to do. When Jesse and I were married, he had a job which paid sixty dollars a week. Well, we couldn't live on that, and his folks and mine gave us an allowance to live on. They set us up in a big house with all the trimmings. It was absurd. We both drank a lot, and Jesse wasn't interested in anything. He just wanted to drink. We had parties all the time, and the people often stayed all night. It was all so messy. I fell in love with Guy Swasey, one of the men who used to come to the house, and we had an affair which lasted two years. He was married and got a divorce, even though I didn't want him to, and wanted me to marry him. But I couldn't see it. His ideas of living and mine were so different. He thought it was fun to just travel around and live in a trailer. Jesse knew we were that way about each other and that seemed to make him drink worse. I felt responsible for him because he was always weak and leaned on me. Once I insisted that we take a house in the country and live on our own income, so we got a place and gradually paid off our debts. Now I invited people to the house who would take only three highballs instead of ten. And when mother sent me checks, I returned them. But it didn't last. Gradually we got in debt again, and I had to go and ask mother for more money. I've never enjoyed sexual intercourse with Jesse. In the beginning I used to have relations with him because I thought a man needs it, and if I didn't, he'd drink more. He has never been interested in my side of the thing. Once when I became aroused and touched him, he jumped out of the bed like he had been shot. He was disgusted and told me that it wasn't nice. He wouldn't come back and go through with the act. He's so squeamish. The next time we did have intercourse, he made sure nothing like that would happen by pinning me down so that

he almost smothered me. Marriage is nothing like I had anticipated. The only time he wants intercourse is when he is in a drunken stupor. He never makes any advances when he is sober. He's so inconsiderate and rough. He lies on me heavily and kicks me. I don't mean he's sadistic, but he's so damn clumsy. Four years ago I got furious with him because he never made love to me except when he was drunk, and I told him that unless he did it when he was sober that I was not going to sleep with him any more. He never has, and so we haven't slept together since. Jesse goes off on weekend parties. I don't know what happens. Once when he came home, he told me he had spent sixty dollars for liquor. He said he never gave me more than half his pay check and that the rest went for liquor. I don't see any way out except divorce or separation. The only reason I haven't done it before is that I don't want to have to go home and live with Mother and Daddy. Also it would upset Daddy's plans. He wants to buy a farm and retire in a few years and run the farm for the members of the religious group they belong to. He wouldn't be able to do that if he had to support me and my kids.

Play Therapy with the Twins

Each boy was seen separately for one hour. The technique employed in the play sessions was very simple. Crude clay figures representing the family constellation were modelled and placed on a low table in front of the boy. He was asked to name the figures. In the first session the therapist suggested certain games to play. During succeeding sessions no suggestions were made. The therapist sat at the table beside the boy and wrote down everything that he did or said. Both boys thought it was fun to have their words written down and occasionally wanted to identify a written word. The room included a variety of other objects—toys, sand, etc.—which the boys occasionally used also.

First Play Session with Samuel. Samuel was eager to go to the therapist's office. He ran ahead and seated himself at the little work table. He asked many questions about the clay figures and was very proud of the therapist because of what he considered the excellence of the figures.

The subject was told that we were going to play a game and that for the game we needed a mother and father, two boys and a girl. The mother was moved forward.

S.° Is she bad?
T. Do you think so?
S. Yes, she is. She's bad and she's supposed to be dressed.
T. Now let's give them all names. What shall we call the mother?
S. Joan.
T. And the two boys who are eight?
S. Joe and Billy.

° S stands for Samuel; T for therapist.

T. And the little girl?
S. Jane.
T. What shall we call the father?
S. Billy.

T. Let's play another game. For this game we need a bed. Let's make one. (S. made a bed out of clay.)
T. Now mother and father are going to bed. (T. puts mother in bed on her back. S. places father beside her. He is lying on his side, facing mother.)
T. Joe comes into the bedroom and sees mother and father in bed. What does he do? Do whatever you think.

S. Joe says I guess I'll go to bed. He goes to lie on mother's chair. Then the mother gets up and sits down. Joe says to father, "What are you doing? Why don't you get up and stop being so sleepy?" Goodbye, I'll go. I guess I'll go to sleep. (He takes father out of bed and places mother and Joe in bed.) The daddy says, "Why do you lie in mother's bed? Want to sleep in my bed? All right." Mother gets up and sits down out of bed. (S. picks her up and sticks a fork in her head and pushes her over. Then he picks her up and pushes her over again and says "Button, button." He then leaves the mother, takes up the father and says, "I'll make a belt for him," and begins doing so.)

First Play Session with Donald. Donald came to the office willingly. He ran ahead and was busily exploring various objects in the room when the therapist arrived. We sat down at the little work table, and he wanted to know who had made the figures and if Samuel had played with them.

He was told that we were going to play a game and that for the game we needed a mother and father, two boys and a girl.

T. What shall we call them?
D. Call the two boys Donnie and Sammy, and the mummy Mary, and the daddy Joseph.
T. What about the little girl?
D. Call her Anne.

T. Now we are going to play another game. For this game we need a bed. Let's make one. (T. and D. make a bed out of clay.) Now father and mother are going to bed. (T. puts mother in bed and D. places father beside her.) Now this is the game. Donnie comes into the bedroom and sees mother and daddy in bed. What does he do? Do whatever you think.
D. Donnie comes in. He runs and tells Sammy that mummy and daddy are sleeping. (He brings the figures of the two boys forward.) Then I make a spear for each one, and they're going to stick it in mummy and daddy, because mummy and daddy never take care of them, never feed them. (Makes a spear for each figure and attaches one to the right hand of each.) Sammy sneaks up and sticks daddy in the nose—or was it the eye?—yeah, it was the eye. (All of this action the subject has the figures carry out.) Donnie goes up to the mummy; she's snoring. He hits her on the head. He boshes her in the face. He takes part of his spear and smothers her. He

puts a patch over her nose and mouth. Daddy wakes up. They hear him and run out. Mummy doesn't wake up, 'cause she's smothered. Finally the Blue Fairy comes and wakes mummy up too. Doesn't daddy have any clothes on? I want him to have clothes on. Mummy and daddy hear someone knocking at the door. Daddy says, "Who is that? Is that Sammy and Donnie?" He thought that they smothered mummy, and they said, "No, we don't know anything about that." Then daddy calls the cops, and the cops say, "We know who did it. Sammy and Donnie, and now they're in trouble."

We've got to have a police station. (Whereupon he makes one out of clay, and places the figure of father in it.) Daddy is in jail now. (Makes bars all around him.) Mummy wonders where daddy is. Daddy is in jail. The little boy sees a sign and thinks it is his daddy and says, "Yeah, yeah!" They have a sign that says daddy so mummy will come and see it and they will get her. So they catch mummy and blind her and bind her up. (Brings the mother in and covers her face with clay and puts large strips of clay around her legs, body and arms.) They handcuffed her legs together. They take daddy's feet and plaster them together with stuff. And look what happened to mummy and daddy; and then they're all dead afterwards.

I'm going to take Sammy and Donnie and put them in a high thing. (He binds the two boys together with clay). I'm going to make a wall around them. They put the whole family in jail. Anne died. Then they're all in jail. Mummy sits on a stone. She feels sorry about daddy. She can't feel sorry 'cause she's all patched up and dead. Daddy's not dead yet. She is though.

Mother's Interviews (*continued*)

Fourth Interview

C. Can you tell me why I don't get mad any more, except maybe once or twice a year? I used to raise hell all the time and I guess it didn't get me anything. But now even when I don't like things, I don't get mad.

T. Would you like to tell me about some of the things you don't like?

C. I don't like the way the children are so messy. They give me a pain. I just don't like them. They have flat faces, and I don't like their fat fannies. They destroy everything they own. The play room is littered with broken toys. A week after Christmas everything was broken. The shades are torn off; the walls and windows are covered with crayon marks. They never pick up anything. Oh, they like to help sometimes, emptying wastebaskets and so on, but they never take care of their own things. And Sammy, I could choke him when he wets the bed and makes it himself without telling me. It smells so stinking. I've read in books that you shouldn't make anything of it and so I don't. I just ask him why he doesn't go to the bathroom and he says he dreams that he is already there and lets go. Well, anybody can do that, so what can you say. I used to lock them in their rooms at night and had a potty there for them, but they wouldn't use it. They'd go any place they happened to think of. For a while they urinated out the front window until there was a long yellow icicle hanging there for all the neighbors to see. And their table manners are atrocious. They eat with their

fingers and slop things all over the table and themselves. They're awful.
Sometimes I get so mad with them that I yell like hell. And boy can I yell!
I used to do it a lot, but it didn't do any good. They still mess around like
a couple of little savages.

Fifth Interview. Mrs. Burke was a half hour late for the appointment.
When she arrived she explained spontaneously, after apologies, that she
had been running an errand for her mother.

C. Do you wish me to continue talking about my feelings toward the children?
T. Anything you like.
C. I just don't like the twins—their fat fannies and messy beds irritate me. I've
never had any positive feelings for them, and it bothers me. I know a
mother is supposed to love her children, but I can't have any such feelings
for them. Even when they were babies, I didn't like them. I've tried to set
aside a time when we could do things together, but it doesn't seem to work
out. I'm just not interested in their silly questions. When five o'clock comes,
I feel like screaming. They just go around calling "mummy, mummy,
mummy" all day long, and asking a thousand questions. They nearly drive
me crazy. I try to think up some game and get them started doing something but they won't stick at it. They just want to hang around me. And
Jesse has no time for them. He doesn't want to do anything with them
except for a few minutes a day. He never wants to see them in the morning, says they upset him, so they have their breakfast separately and he
doesn't see them. When he comes home at night, he doesn't care to play
with them. He wants them out of the way. So they have to stay outdoors
or be upstairs in their own room. In the winter time they have their supper
and are upstairs out of the way before he gets home. He usually has two
or three drinks as soon as he gets home. Then he goes up and sees the
children and says their prayers with them. He thinks kids ought to be left
alone, and all this bother coming over here he says is nonsense. Children
will grow up naturally if you leave them alone. I try to get him to talk over
some of the difficulties I have with them, but he won't. He just sits around
and drinks all evening. I think he's annoyed because I won't drink with
him any more. I haven't had anything to drink for four or five years now,
and I think it's silly, so I won't.

Once I thought it would be nice to have the twins have dinner with us, so
we tried it. But it was miserable. They were so messy and made so much
noise. Jesse didn't like having them there anyway, so we stopped. He gives
me a pain. Who does he think he is, having everybody do things just to
suit him? If he had any guts, he wouldn't let mother push us around the
way she does.
T. (After a pause of several minutes) Would you like to tell me about your
feelings toward your mother?
C. I think I've always hated her. She's so bossy and interfering. She's not
happy when things are going right. She's always got to be thinking up
something new to change. She's ruined my dad with her reforming attitude.
All the things he used to like to do she disapproved of, and so he gradually

gave them up without a fight. She's made him old before his time. He's wonderful and strong, and yet he's weak too. I don't think anybody has ever fought my mother except me. I've wanted to hurt her as she hurt everybody else. I can see now that all my rebellion was an indirect way of getting even with her. Whenever I would do anything she wouldn't like, she would get ulcers and go to bed and stay there until I told her I was sorry and promised to do better. Sometimes I just refused to apologize and she'd stay in bed for days and days, and then when she finally did get up, she'd try to bribe me to be better by buying me things. She still does. She'll call up and tell me to come down to the store and have a new dress or something after we've had a fight. If I refuse, she'll buy things for the twins and send them over. Or she'll come over and get a basket full of darning and do it. Who could refuse to let her do that? I learned to deceive her in order to avoid having a scene. I'd tell her I wasn't doing something, but I kept right on doing what I wanted to, only I didn't let her know it. She's always been the biggest liar. At first I didn't catch on, but finally I did. She'd say do one thing and then do the other herself. I told her once that she was a big liar, but she couldn't see it.

She's always tried to possess me—to make all decisions for me—to run my life. Even her friends in the religious group saw that, and they hopped all over her about it. She wept and said she realized it now and would never interfere again. It lasted about two weeks and then the whole thing started all over again.

Sixth Interview. The interview began with the client discussing the masturbatory activity of the twins. She talked about the sex education which she had imparted to them and how difficult it was to give them a healthy picture since the father was so "squeamish." She described him as having a "Miltonian Complex," and said that he takes great precautions never to undress before her or the children. "You'd think he was deformed, the way he acts." She reiterated his extreme prudishness.

C. Mother was prudish too; she would never even let me in the bathroom when she was in there. She always went in and locked the door as if some great event was going to happen. She used to harp on masturbation all the time. When I was about thirteen, mother and daddy sat me down to tell me all about sex. Daddy wanted to tell me everything—about intercourse and everything—but mother kept saying, "Oh, not that, don't tell that." It was a fiasco. They were much more embarrassed than I was.

T. (After a long pause) Would you like to tell me more about your father?

C. My pop? Oh, he's a great guy. Daddy and I were always supposed to be the best of friends and understand each other, but we seldom talked to one another. Even now when I try to talk to him about Jesse, he won't listen. He doesn't want to admit that there's anything wrong between us. He still thinks of me as his golden-haired little girl and is deeply disappointed in the way my life has turned out—getting pregnant and having to marry and all that. He must resent having to put out money for us. When I was a little girl, I loved to go on camping and hunting trips with daddy.

Mother went along sometimes, but she never ventured into the woods, just daddy and me. He could do anything. He taught me to shoot a bow and arrow and a gun. He taught me to row a boat and swim and everything. Gee, he was wonderful. I adored him. Who wouldn't adore a man who could kill a moose with a bow and arrow? We romped and played like a couple of kids. But mother always disapproved of these trips. She didn't have a good time, and so daddy gradually gave them up. He has given up everything he liked to do because she didn't approve. She had some silly notion about indulging oneself and not living up to one's responsibilities or something. I went into the bathroom twice when daddy was taking a shower. (This occurred between the ages of 7 and 9) He was all covered with red hair, and it scared me. I didn't like his hair. Now I think it's kind of fun. I don't mind it any more. Ever since I was a little girl, daddy has always liked to hold me on his lap and hug and kiss me. And his kisses were always very ardent and masculine, not at all fatherly. He held me close to him and would kiss me for a long time on the lips. When I was about fifteen, I told him I didn't think it was nice, but he kept right on doing it, and still does.

Second Play Session with Samuel

T. I want you to make up a game using the figures.

S. I can break them if I want to.

T. Yes, you may.

S. Did you dress them yet? I'll dress them. I'll put some buttons on the little girl. (He takes the figure of the girl and puts three buttons down the front, one of them covering the genital region. Attaches a piece of clay to the buttocks, then removes it and places it around the neck. Puts the girl down and takes up mother.) I'll make her a skirt. She's going to be an Indian girl with a shield in her hand. (Brings father and the two boys up in a row beside mother. Throws father down on his face.) He's bad so I'd better dress him like an Indian too. (Takes strip of clay and covers abdominal region.) He's going to have a shield too. (Makes shield and attaches it to back of father.) Two Indians dressed up. Now I'm going to make their pack—Indian pack.

T. What do they carry in the packs?

S. Arrows, don't they? (Makes arrow.) You stand it up here and have an elastic and it goes off this way (demonstrating by holding up the clay and pulling the right hand back as one would a sling shot. He then puts the father on his knees, and picking up Billy, puts a piece of clay on his head and another around the genital region.) He's a blind Indian. He's dead though. (Makes a strip of clay one inch long and places it in an erect position coming from the genital region of Billy. Picks up an arrow, points it at therapist, and says, "I'll shoot you." After this action ceases for a while.)

T. Now what are they going to do?

S. Now they're going to fight. Joe has to have a shield so they can't hit him. (By now it is clear that the figure of Joe represents himself. He places a piece of clay over Joe's face.) An Indian wants to hit him, no, a cowboy. I'm going to make a red light so the cowboys won't dare come near. (Takes two strips of clay and places them in front of the two boys. Then places a long strip behind the father.) Father just has this long thing so they can't hit him. (Takes Jane up.) She's going to throw her ball at the cowboys. (Places father and mother behind the other figures.) She's dead (indicating the mother.) Father's dead, too. (Then all the other figures are pushed over except Joe.) They're dead, except Joe, because he had a shield up and they couldn't kill him. (Puts another large strip of clay around Joe.) I'll put this around him so they couldn't kill him. See how he is built up? He couldn't be killed, could he?

Second Play Session with Donald

D. (Takes the mother in his hands) Hey, what good are you? I guess I'll smash you. (Cuts large hole in abdomen with fork, cuts breasts off, cuts face to pieces, breaks legs off and pushes the remains into a corner. Picks father up.) Daddy's bare. (Sticks finger in the father's anus and pokes it around for several seconds. Puts father down and takes mother up again.) I'm going to take you and smash you and throw you in jail. (Throws her around a bit. Pulls father toward him.) You too, father. You're bad, daddy. Daddy won't let them go indoors when they want at night, so they kill him. They stick a fork in his stomach and face, and chop him up. (This he does with great vehemence. He scrapes the fork over father's body; jabs him scores of times; picks him up on the fork and pounds him up and down on the table, saying:) Take that and that and that. (Turns to therapist.) Would you like that done to you?

T. No.

D. Neither do they, only it's done. (For several minutes more he sticks the fork into father, scratches him, jabs him, pokes and punches him, and finally tears him all to shreds.) See what they done after he's dead? They dig his bones out and roll him up in a ball. (This done, he sticks the fork into the pile of clay and pounds the mass on the table for a while.) Who do you like better, Sammy or me?

T. I like you both the same.

D. Sister stands up. (Takes the figure of Anne and holds her.) Sammy comes in and says, "What are you doing?" (Picks up Samuel and takes his legs off.) Take your bones out. And I dig and I dig and I dig and I smash and I smash. (Pounds Samuel to pieces and rolls him into a ball. Inadvertently he has rolled Anne up with Samuel.) Where's sister. (Looks around and discovers he has rolled her up with Samuel.) Did I take her, too? (Pries her battered body from the mass.) I'll take her head and I'll roll her up again. She's put on a statue. (Places her on a piece of clay.) Listen here, you! Listen here, you! I'll smash your head in; I'll stick you and I'll bang you. (Pounds all the broken figures together, sticks fork into the mass and hammers it up and down on the table, with great effort.) That's the end of all you people. I'll take you and break you and hammer you and rip you and break you to pieces. And I'll stick screws into you, and I'll yank you and pull you and pound you and cut you up. I'm going to flatten you out. (Whereupon he takes a stick of wood and beats and pounds the mass until it is flattened.)

(All this time the figure of Donald has been standing to one side. Then he picks up Donald.) Now I'll make a house for myself. (Turns back to flattened figures and says:) I'll smash you and pull you and yank you apart. (Picks up the mass and tears it all to bits.) That's the end. (Donald is left standing alone.)

Mother's Interviews (*continued*)

Seventh Interview.

C. I've been thinking a lot about my daddy since last time. He's my ideal of what a man ought to be. Do you suppose if I found a man like him I'd be able to live with him happily? (Following this there was a pause of several minutes.) Golly, I just thought of something I hadn't thought about for a long time. When I was going to school, there was a very popular boy whom all the girls liked and wanted to date. He had curly red hair. He liked me most and wanted to go with me, but I couldn't stand to be near him and especially to have him touch me. I didn't know why I didn't like him, he was very nice, and the girls all thought I was crazy. Do you suppose it could have been because his hair was exactly like the red hair on my daddy's body? (This was said with that wide-eyed wonderment which accompanies a new insight. After musing over this for a while, she said:) Well, what's a person to do? You can't have him, and you don't want anybody else.

(Mrs. Burke then talked about how she enjoys writing. Recently she has been selling her work to help support the family, because she desires to be financially independent. She does not enjoy writing, however, when she does it for money. Her inspiration seems to leave her when she sits down to a commercial job.)

Eighth Interview.

C. I had a grand weekend. I've been applying something I learned here, and it has worked wonders. It's this business of taking responsibility. I've never wanted to assume any responsibility. I've always done things grudgingly, thinking to myself that somebody else ought to do the dirty work. But these last two days I suddenly saw that I had a job, and I've gone about doing things like cleaning up after the children, and washing their socks and so on, and actually singing while I was doing it. I think it's wonderful how I can do these things now. I told a couple of people of my discovery and my new determination, and they just laughed, but that didn't bother me. My daddy is just like me as far as responsibility goes, and I want to help him. I'm sure he has never thought things through. I think I'll have a talk with the whole family and straighten them out too. Don't you think I ought to try to help them now that I see things so much better? I feel kind of responsible for Jesse too, but I can't see where I can do any more for him than I have already done. I've tried to praise him when he does something halfway nice, and I've tried to get him interested in gardening and things, but all he wants to do is drink. If I show the least little bit of

attention to him, he gets all over me like a tent and wants to have intercourse right then. I haven't felt any love for anybody for so long I don't
know how it would feel.

Ninth Interview.

C. What am I to do about my pop? I can see now that the relationship with
him has been very bad. I've needed him and depended on him, and at the
same time I've hated my mother. Some of the bad qualities I have attributed to her have been colored by my hatred. She probably hasn't interfered with his interests and activities as much as I thought she did. Still,
I'm sure they have never had any satisfactory sexual relations. Would a
man who was satisfied fondle his daughter so much? Why, he used to feel
my breasts when I'd sit in his lap. I felt defiled and all funny inside. He
was an old rat.

I remember when I'd go to a dance how I'd look around the floor and
pick out the man I thought would be the hardest to get and then go after
him. And I usually got him. I wanted to hurt people as I'd been hurt. Do
you suppose all my affairs and running around could have been because
I wanted to hurt somebody? I wanted to break up marriages. That's what
I wanted to do to my mother and daddy. (She remained silent for several
minutes.) Golly, I hadn't thought of this, but when I was fourteen and we
were camping, one day I went out to the waterfall and took a bath in the
nude. I had a beautiful body. I took a long time bathing, splashing about,
jumping up and down and having fun. And all the time my dad was up in
a tree with a camera taking pictures of me. I didn't know it until he showed
the film. He never wasted so much film on anything else. And it's the only
one he ever shows now. He's so coy about it, and makes such a fuss over
it while he's showing it. What am I to do with him? He still wants to feel
me and hold me on his lap. You know, he called me up the other night and
said he heard I was being psychoanalyzed and not to get too excited about
it, it wouldn't last. He said he had been psychoanalyzed three times. But
if he had, don't you think he would have understood what he was doing
to me and stopped? Maybe I ought to explain to him what's been going
on—or would that just hurt him and not do any good? He said he wanted
to tell me something when he called, but then he wouldn't, just teased me.
I think he was afraid I would learn his secret.

(Two appointments were broken because one of the twins had German measles.)

Third Play Session with Samuel

S. (Takes a flat piece of clay and begins to put another long round piece of
clay on it.) Nice little table, nice little table. Now do you know what it's
going to be?

T. A table?

S. Yes, how'd you guess? (Puts all four legs on table. Takes father and bangs
him on table crumpling the legs. Bends father's legs back.) See how father
has to walk? (Pushes him around like a crippled man. Throws father down
and reaches over and strikes mother.) I'll fight you. (Picks her up and

turns her upside down.) What a funny-looking fanny. Want me to make her a good fanny? (Plays with her anus, poking it and pushing his finger into it.) It looks like a cow's fanny. See, now I'll break her leg off. (Throws her down.) Now I'll squash Jane's face. Where's her face? I'll take her ball. (Picks up Billy and takes his head off.) I'll make a ball out of his head. I took the father's off and squashed it. (Rolls all the heads together until they are one big ball. Throws all the figures into the basket except Jane. Then he throws her in and says:) She came down like a bomb, didn't she? (Takes lots of clay and makes several balls and throws them at the figures, saying:) Bombs, bombs, bombs. You'll have them dressed next time, won't you?

T. I'll let you dress them.

S. No, you dress them, will you? (Takes Jane out of the basket and rolls her into a ball.) I'm going to drop a bomb on you. (Puts her down and begins to roll out clay.) What do you think I'm going to make? Is that how you start it? I'm going to make a cave. This cave's going to be all fixed good, better than you can fix it. (Takes several pieces of clay and moulds them together, leaving a hollow inside.) A white bear is in the cave. He's going to come out and bite you. He's going to push a big brown ball at you, all right? He only has two legs. (Takes a large ball of clay and throws it at the cave.) A big bomb came and blew the cave up (laughs) and another bomb came and blew the bear up. And you were safe, you didn't get hurt.

Third Play Session with Donald

Donald ran ahead to playroom. When the therapist arrived he was seated at the table and rolling some clay into a ball. The figures are all in clear view. He took a flat piece of clay and said, "I'm going to make a fence."

D. (Still fingering piece of flat clay.) You don't know what's going to be here . . . Does my mummy talk to you every morning?

T. No, every other morning.

D. What do you talk about? Do you ever talk about fighting? I talk about fighting all the time. Why did you come here and play with us?

T. Because I like you.

D. This is going to be a good fence, isn't it?

T. You bet.

D. What did she talk about today, my mummy? (Looks up at picture on wall.) Who are they? What are they doing, watching a parade? Why do some stand up and some sit down? Do they ever march in the parade?

(By this time, has made a fence. It consists of a base of clay with four sides, supported by small match sticks. He picks up Jane and brings her into foreground. Pushes her over with a stick and then pushes father over also. Mother comes in and says, "Oh, yeah?" and he pushes her over. Then he picks her up and seats her. Takes Jane and punches her. Jane pushes Donald over. He picks Samuel up and brings him in. Samuel says, "Why did you knock my brother over?" to Jane. Samuel knocks Jane in the face, and smashes her head with a stick. Then he says her head is all out of shape and tries to fix it. Makes eyes and mouth for her. Then he turns her over and spanks her. Donald picks up Samuel and says he is going to make a belt for him. Makes several stripes over body and then punches him in the nose. Puts Samuel down and takes a pencil and sticks it up in front of him. Then he takes a fork and stick and places them in front of Donald.)

T. What are they for?

D. They're to hit the mother and father with. (Takes Jane and says:) Little girl's going to be covered because she's been bad. You shall be smothered, sister; you shall be blinded, sister. Then they put her in a cage. You shall be sorry, sister; you shall be sorry, sister. (Repeated several times in a sing-song voice. Covers her and puts her in cage.) She can't get her arms free because she's smothered. (Takes clay off face.) She's not smothered any more. They only smothered her so she can't breathe and smell. (Puts her down. Looks around and says:) Who shall be hurt? (Picks up father. Puts him down. Picks him up and throws him down.) He shall have a pinch shell on him—a pinch shell pinches you when you are in jail. This is only make believe.

T. Sure, I know that.

(Donald rolls clay out for several minutes, all the while humming contentedly to himself. Rolls clay out flat.)

D. It's for somebody sitting down. It's going to be for somebody that's going to be killed. You guess who.

T. Donald?

D. No.

T. Samuel?

D. No.

T. Jane?

D. No.

T. Father?

D. No.

T. Mother?

D. Yes. Why did you guess her last. I said somebody sitting down. It might be father, I don't know. Now you shall be killed, mummy. Now you shall be rolled over. Now you shall be rolled over. (Repeated several times, while he rolls her about on table.) And you shall be beaten and pounded and stuck and killed (with great emphasis) and pounded in the face and stuck with clay and you shall be struck on your own little stool. (All this is acted out. Then he sticks a fork into the mother, saying:) Now look at mummy. (Throws her into the basket.)

(He looks around at all the figures and says:) Who's good? He's good. (And he picks up Donald and puts him to one side.) He's good. (And he takes father and puts him beside Donald.) Is he good? (pointing to Samuel.)

T. What do you think?

D. Yeah. (And he too is placed beside Donald and father.)

T. Is Jane good?

D. No. (Then he throws her into the basket with mother.)

Mother's Interviews (*continued*)

Tenth Interview.

C. I've been going ahead thinking on my own, and I've made some gains. I feel much better and I can see a tremendous change in myself in a month's time. I've begun to show some affection toward the twins, and when I do they just slobber all over me. It's amazing. I wouldn't have believed it could happen. The boys are much happier, and not nearly so destructive. Sammy's had a pack of cards for a week now without tearing them to pieces and scattering them to the four winds. I've always liked Donnie better than Sammy, and it's funny how they know, even though I try to treat them the very same. Donnie knows he's a good guy.

   I'm able to handle everything better now except my relationship with Jesse, and I don't want to work that out. He's so disgusting and repulsive. He used to be so rough when we'd have intercourse. Many times I used to have black and blue marks on my arms afterwards—even my lips hurt after he kissed me. Everything about him annoys me—the ways he blows his nose; he's so sloppy; he doesn't take enough baths; his feet smell, oh, everything.

Eleventh Through the Seventeenth Interviews. Mrs. Burke slowly assimilated and consolidated the insights which she had gained. She made considerable headway in her ability to express affection for the twins and was overjoyed with their response. During this time she decided to divorce her husband and retained a lawyer for that purpose. She announced her intention to her husband and her parents. The husband received the news with complete passivity; he was nonplussed and bewildered. Apparently he had never entertained the possibility of such a move before. Not until four days later did he feebly propose that they go off to another house and start over again. Because he seemed to think that drinking was the major bone of contention, he swore that if he ever took another drink, she could then divorce him. If the husband was passive, the mother was inversely aggressive and irate. The father followed his wife's suit. It was their business in their religious group affiliation to patch up such domestic estrangements, and pride would not permit them to accept defeat in their immediate family. So, in long and not unemotional conferences, they smothered their daughter with such stock and hackneyed words as "sin" and "evil thoughts" and "absolute honesty," "purity," "unselfishness," and "surrender." They entreated her to "listen" to God, with the promise that there would be a "change." What she needed—what any "sinner" needed—was "God-guidance." They reiterated how they had "found God" and how wonderful it was no longer to be "self-indulgent." They knew that "revival would continue in survival"; and so on.

   Through days and days of these tirades Mrs. Burke held steadfastly to her goal without becoming too excited or upset. One thing which annoyed her parents so much was her composure and self-confidence. They recognized a source of strength within her and a certain *joie de vivre* which had been absent for years. Her mother was so curious and suspicious that she asked her if she were not in love with somebody.

The pressure exerted on Mrs. Burke was terrific, and she was not altogether immune to it. Partly out of a desire to cause the father as little pain as possible and partly because she still needed to depend on others, she finally agreed to a separation rather than a divorce. Once the parents had squeezed this concession from her, however, they were not satisfied; they began trying to show her that she was just being "stubborn" and "childish" and that if she would "submit" to God and go on living with her husband, everything would work out splendidly.

Mrs. Burke consulted her lawyer and, with his encouragement, she decided to go ahead with her former plans for immediate divorce. She faced the realistic problem of supporting herself and children if her parents withdrew support and Jesse should fail to support the children. She investigated several jobs, none of which was suitable. She then thought of seeking a loan from a wealthy old friend to tide her over the transition until she could establish herself independently. The friend responded with a most generous proposal. She had the historical source materials concerning her family and asked Mrs. Burke if she would work through them and write a history, or genealogical sketch, for her. She would pay her $80 a week for at least two years, or longer if necessary. When she reported these developments, Mrs. Burke said, "It's too wonderful. I think of something I read recently to the effect that 'If you start a web, you're sure to find the thread.'"

Fourth Play Session with Samuel

Samuel decided to play with the farm animals in the sand box. He put the horse in the corner and said, "Horses like to be alone." Next he placed the baby calves near the cows and said, "Each baby stands near his mother." The three little pigs and the mother sow he put in a small box by themselves. Then he remarked, "They like to play in the mud, and I ain't kidding. They're dirty things!" Over this he giggled and giggled. Two of the pigs were removed, and, using one as an implement, he pushed the other into the sand saying, "You're dead!" When asked why he had killed the pig he replied that he did not like him and the mummy didn't either. Then the mummy pushed the dead pig into the sand, after which she dug him out and said to both of the pigs, "You two are big enough to stay out there." Samuel picked up the two pigs and placed them outside the box, leaving the smaller pig with the mother. Then he made a place in the sand for the pigs to "do their duty," so they would not "dirty up the whole barn yard."

Fourth Play Session with Donald

Donald sat at the table fingering the clay. Without looking up he said, "Do you like babies?" When asked if he did, his reply was, "No." Then he took the baby from the mother's arms. "Now I'll fix the lady," he said; "she's too old to have those feet." He spent some time fixing the feet. "Now the mother's all fixed. Look at the bosoms. Isn't that funny? Guess what she's holding, a can of food. Where are the holes in the bosoms?" Then he punched holes in the breasts and put the baby back in the mother's arms to nurse. He picked up Joe and said, "I'm going to break Joe and flatten his nose." Which he proceeded to do. Next he picked up Billy and broke him to pieces. After this, mother and baby were torn apart. And he was quiet for quite a while.

Finally he picked up the remains of the clay and rolled them into a large ball and said, "This is a cave." He poked around in the cave with his finger for several minutes and continued speaking, "Donald and Samuel are in the cave. They are looking around. It is dark. Winky and Donald and Samuel are inside the cave. I'm going to put him inside. Winky's mother is down inside the cave. His father is working outside, and mother comes out and sees what father is doing. Father was looking at a horse. And mother says, 'What are you doing, Father?' He's looking for his horse. Mother closes the gates so the horse won't get in. Winky chased Donald and Samuel out 'cause he thought that was his cave, but they went back in."

Fifth Play Session with Samuel

Samuel ran willingly to the playroom. A new room was used and he busied himself for a few minutes exploring it, asking questions about various objects in the room. Then he seated himself at the work table.

S. (Picking up father.) I'm going to make father's belt. You always have to make them dressed now, 'cause I'm going to make you. I'm making this now, guess what it is.

T. What is it?

S. Mother's stool. See how quick I get it smoothed; quicker than you can. My mother doesn't believe I know forty-one words. I do. I learned them all today. When do you talk with mummy? When do you talk with me and Donald?

(T. explains that he sees the mother every other day and the boys alternately.)

S. What do you think I'm making now? Two chairs and a stool. Guess what this is? (Holding up mother with a piece of clay around her.) She's tied up. She's a bad girl. Father tied her up. (Samuel hears a noise outside, which sounds vaguely like a siren; actually it is not.) Fire! It went ooh, ooh. Did you hear? I hope the house isn't on fire. I'd jump out the window. You'd jump out the window with me, wouldn't you? Would it hurt us? (Long pause.)

T. Are you afraid of fires?

S. No, I'm not. Once our house caught afire. We jumped out the window. Sunday was a fire—two men got killed. I heard it in the paper, didn't see it. (Pause.)

T. When was the fire at your house?

S. It was at night. We jumped right off the roof. You know why? My father left the fire going. He did it by mistake, though. We were awake and climbed out of the window, Donald and me. You ask Donald if you don't believe me. (Pause.)

Fifth Play Session with Donald

Donald rushed into the new playroom. He looked around quickly and spotted our table. He went over and sat down and began playing with clay, after taking it out of the basket. The figures were left in half-finished condition just as they had been the previous session. This irritated Donald.

D. I'm going to bat your teeth in (addressed to the therapist). (Fingers the clay more.) Oh, gee, whose leg is this? Gee, where's father? (Finds him.) He's lost his head. I'll have to make a head for him. I guess I'll make a green head. (Uses green clay and makes a head.) Why didn't you do what you used to do, put them out? Well, you smashed them all around. Where's father's arm? (Sings.) La, la, la, la, smashing arm, smashing arm. (Lights match and burns a piece of clay.) It melts, doesn't it? Aren't there any more matches? I'd just like to kill you. (Looks around for other figures.) And where's the other little boy? You ruined all the clay. Did Sammy get mad yesterday? What did he say to you? Oh gee, look at that. Look at the way you ruined these things. Why? Were you in a hurry making them? Why? Why couldn't you make some yesterday before you went? This time I'm not going to ruin them all. (Makes large pointed breasts on mother. Gently hammers her legs and belly into shape. Plays with breasts.) Mr. Dalton is too nutty; nutty Dalton. Old dumpy Mr. Dalton. (He pours all the clay out of the basket onto the table.) Get all these big hunks out of here, so I can use something. (He takes small piece of clay and rolls it into shape of arm and puts it on the mother. It is about one and a half times the length of the other arm.) This young lady has an awful long arm. This is so she can spank people. Well, she's not going to have a very long spanker very long; because before she does, she's going to have it sawed off. (Cuts it off in a see-saw fashion with a fork.) She's going to have it sawed off before it grows any longer. (Mumbles to himself. Takes mother and places her face up on a hunk of clay.) She needs to be worked on, to have her legs broken. (He hammers legs flat and breaks them off.) Have her smashed right through. (Pounds her violently with hammer until she is completely destroyed.) Nothing left of you. Now you shall be hammered to death. (So saying, he takes up the two figures of the boys.) I shall take the two twins and smother them. (Forces them together with an angle iron.) Now I shall smash them. (Drives screw into the head on one.) They ruin people, they kill people. Nobody in the family shall be living but the grandmother. (Drives pencil into the head of other figure.) Look what I'm crowning them with. The two of them, too. In the electric chair. Right together, too. Look what I did to them. They're killed for this time. One right after the other is killed.

Sixth Play Session with Samuel

When Samuel came into the playroom, the first thing he said was, "Donald broke the roof of my barn, and I beat the daylights out of him. He cried and cried. He had a black eye, and he had to have medicine for it." He also said that Jane breaks all his toys and steals them. He did not let her see the barn.

He wanted to finger paint. He chose black "because nobody else had used it yet." He began to smear on the black paint. Then with one finger he made marks around and around and up and down. As he did this, he told a story about a little boy starting out for school but being blocked by something in the way which he had to go around. The boy met several obstacles and had to back-track and go around them. With his finger Samuel showed the path taken and the detours.

Sixth Play Session with Donald

Donald announced when he came into the playroom, "I broke Sammy's barn, but he blamed it on Jane, so I wouldn't get into any trouble."

He started playing with the clay figures. "Billy has a gun. Boom! I'm going to shoot Joe." This was said while he made a hole in Joe's face, another in his chest, and a third through his arm. "See, we shot his arm right off, the bullet was so big." Then he took a nail and made many holes in Joe. "Off comes his legs. He's not bleedy yet. Wait 'til his heart goes open. He's shot so much it took a hunk right out of his heart. He's not bleedy yet." He completely mutilated Joe. "Look what he did to his head. You bad, bad, bad. You goggy, old bloody old. Take your arms and legs and stuff 'em in a big hole. I'll smash his face and bloody body."

He turned toward the therapist and said, "I know lots of ways to hurt your body." The therapist acknowledged his desire to hurt him as well as other people. Later Donald said, "I like you, too." He continued playing with the clay and began humming to himself.

Seventh Play Session with Samuel

S. I've got to fix my stand up. Jane needs a stand. (Hammers clay for awhile, then gets up and goes over to desk and turns the lamp on.) See how it shines. (The socket of the lamp came apart.) See what happened? Did it ever happen before? Do people come here in the afternoon?

T. Yes.

S. What time do you go home?

T. Six o'clock.

S. My daddy comes home at six, too. What train do you take? I'm making a stand. You know what I do after I get it made? I cut off the edges and bend it down and then we can make a few more stands out of this. Here she comes in a minute (prying out a piece of clay which he has cut). I have to cut down the other side which is a little thicker. (Works on stand quietly for a few minutes.) What time is it? (T. tells him. S. hammers clay contentedly.) This is for Jane. Does your mother know you come home at six? (Takes Jane and puts her on the stand.) Our uncle was in the navy, but he's in the hospital now. He got the German whooping cough. (After a few minutes he picks up a large piece of clay.) I can make a chair out of this. Want to see me?

T. Yes.

S. I go to another school in the afternoon.

T. What do you do there?

S. I play out doors, after I have lunch. Where do you eat? Do you have to pay money? How much? Do you eat much; I don't. (All this time he has been working on the chair.) See the chair, it's all made. Want mother to sit down in it? (Puts her in.) Want to make it taller. (Removes mother and builds up the back of the chair, then replaces her in it.) Where's father? Did you dress him? Now father's going to sit in it; see him. (Takes mother out and places father in the chair.)

T. That's a wonderful chair, with arms and everything.

S. Yes, and a beer holder where father keeps his beer, and a place for books, and an ash tray.

Seventh Play Session with Donald

D. (Takes father out of basket.) Look, he has a bended leg. I'll fix him. Now they're going to be shot. Not really. (Takes the boys out.) You didn't make a good stand, so I'll show you what I can do. I'll use another stand. Those legs are awful. I can make better legs than those. (Makes new legs for the little girl.) You like me, Oh Bethlehem, Bethlehem is a Bethlehem of yore, tra, la, for me, for me (sings). Somebody's going to have a hit on the head; who do you think? The little girl. (Taps her lightly on the head.) I'm your stand. I'm sorry, get out of the way. (Pushes figure aside and hammers clay.) Sammy's not as good a clay maker as I am, is he? (Works quietly for a while on the stand.) After a while they're going to be shot, all three of them, mummy and daddy and Sammy. No, two of them, mummy and daddy at the end. Have you ever seen the story about Mickey Mouse? He was thirsty. He went up and left the spigot open and pretty soon the whole house was flooded, and he jumped out the window. It was a good movie. You didn't roll on top of your stand, did you? There, I have to make the edges. (Hammers edges of clay and shapes up the ends with a fork.) Where did you get this table? Which room? Upstairs or downstairs? This isn't so good, is it? So I stand it up. (Pats and hammers clay quietly.) I can't make them any good any more, can I? (Continues working on clay. Picks up old stand and works with that a few minutes.) I have to fix this one. This is Monday, isn't it? There are four more days in this week. Did God decide the week, or the people?

T. Who do you think?

D. I guess God. (Continues flattening and rolling clay.) This is where I usually work with clay. (Changes position on table.) Where does Sammy usually work? Here, too? This one is going to be better than before. Do you always want us to work in one place. If you work all over the table it gets the whole table dirty, doesn't it?

Mother's Interviews (*continued*)

Eighteenth Interview. Mrs. Burke related a dream which had occurred the previous night.

C. I dreamed I was going down a very long corridor. A light was shining at the other end. There were endless doors all along the corridor, and people kept coming out of them and talking to me. I was all confused and didn't know what to do. I ran ahead of them, and then I'd stumble, and the people would disappear and come out in front of me from other doors. Finally I began to float on the air; my feet were not touching the floor, and it seemed as if I were being wafted along without the slightest effort. The light became larger and larger, and when I finally reached it, all the people who had been pursuing me were there and they were all smiling.

    What do you think of it? I tried to interpret it and it seemed so obvious. It's just what I've been going through and all those people were my family. In the end I came through all right and everybody was happy.

T. Yes, also the floating on air and arriving at your goal by this passive manner is indicative of your desire to depend on someone and have your problems solved without much effort.

C. Yes, I see that. I've always been told what to do and what not to do and even though I've rebelled against it rather violently at times, it has also been easier to have someone else make decisions for me. The other day when I asked you what you would do about the divorce, I knew I was trying to get you to make up my mind for me. I'm glad now you didn't tell me. I feel so much more confidence in my own decisions and in my ability to make them.

Nineteenth Through the Twenty-Fourth Interviews. During these interviews Mrs. Burke talked more about her plans for the future and reported concrete steps which she was taking to bring them about. Her lawyer was going ahead with the divorce suit. He felt that there would be no real difficulty in securing the divorce. The husband's family, however, became resistive and threatened to fight the action. She felt that this was probably just an attempt on their part to coerce her into dropping the suit, and that when the time came, they would offer no resistance because of their dislike of publicity. She searched the outlying towns for a suitable house and neighborhood for a permanent place of residence.

    Her parents continued to exert tremendous pressure on her to acquiesce in their wishes. Notwithstanding this, she remained firm and determined in her plans. She did not argue with them, but calmly announced her intentions. She felt more pity for the parents than she did hostility, although the latter emotion was not absent. On one occasion she said she would like to slap the father's face because he was so blind and weak and stupid.

Her relationship with the twins remained excellent. And her joy in participating in their activities persisted. An occasional flash of resentment toward them came out. She realized that if she did not have them, her immediate future would be much less entangled. She faced the wish to be rid of them squarely and was convinced that no sacrifice was too great in order to retain them.

Eighth Play Session with Samuel

S. (Plays with chair he had made last time.) This is for books, and this is for ashes, and this is for beer, and this is for cigarettes. (Attaches a piece of clay to the back of the chair.) This is a seat on back for a baby to sit on. This is for the baby to keep a milk bottle on, and she lays down on this. (Makes a support for baby's seat.) She's going to get a new baby and give that one away, 'cause I want a new baby. I'll make big sides, so she won't fall off. She needs a blanket. (He gets up and goes to the window.) What are those boys hollering for? Look at the boys playing ball. (He then returns to table and makes a blanket. Then he takes another piece of clay and starts to roll it.) I'm making a bed for mummy. This is the mattress. Do you think that's long enough? Do you think I should cover it over more? I'll get some and roll a hunk on. I'll hammer this piece. (Picks up clay.) Looks nice, doesn't it? I better cut some of that stuff off and make it short and not so thick. I made it too fat.

Eighth Play Session with Donald

D. What does Sammy do in here? Does he make them break? I'm going to make them play together. Look, they're all broke. (Some of the legs were off the figures.) I'll fix daddy's leg and mummy's. Now I have to fix them all up again. (Takes Donald and Samuel.) Now I guess they'll play baseball. (Makes a ball.) They really are going to play ball. This one is going to have the ball. (Puts the ball in the hand of one of the boys.) Now he's got the ball. (He throws it to Donnie.) Donnie's got to have a bat. (Makes a bat and puts it in Donnie's hands.) Has Sammy ever made them do that? Now I'm going to make a good stand. This is part of a chair. (Holds up a piece of clay.) Now he throws the ball and he hits it. (He has Sammy throw the ball and then makes Donnie swing the bat. He takes the bat out of Donnie's hand and has him run around imaginary bases. Then he returns to starting place and goes through the action again and again. After several times Donnie and Sammy change places, and Sammy runs the bases. He then stops this game and goes back to making the seat.) Have you ever been to a baseball game in the spring?

T. Yes.

D. Who won? What was the number at the end?

T. Who is your favorite team?

D. I like the Yankees. (Turns to the figure of father, which has been standing to one side throughout all the action.) Daddy, how did you like the game? (He then looks at the pencil with which the therapist is writing.) Do you like that pencil? It's not the best kind there is. My daddy has one with a flashlight and everything on it.

Interpretive Summary

One thing is clear; the lives of Katherine Burke, Donald, and Samuel were so interwoven that whatever influenced one influenced all. If we, for the moment, look at them separately it is only to provide background the better to understand their interactions. We will review first what we know about Mrs. Burke, then the boys, and finally the influence of one upon another.

Mrs. Burke

When Mrs. Burke first appeared at the clinic, she exhibited many signs of a person with a very weak ego. She was easily diverted by sudden impulses and distractions; her days were a series of unoriented, wasteful efforts; she was unable to make serious plans and follow them; and she had no dominant purpose, or hierarchy of aims. She gave a history of frequent periods of indecision, anxious vacillation and perplexity, and told of repeated unresolved conflicts of aim. In her daily life she often fell below her own moral standards, and seemed unable successfully to battle inner impulses.

Behind the manifest personality of Katherine Burke stretched years of relationships with people in which she had been treated as a plaything, a pretty doll. She had been manipulated by her mother in various subtle and insidious ways, chief of which was using illness as a means of control. Her father had gone beyond the bounds of paternal affection in fondling her as he did, thus arousing in her unexpressible passionate longings. Neither parent in his dealings with Katherine exercised the kind of restraint necessary to encourage the building of defenses within her against expressions of any dominant impulse. Even the kinds of schools they chose operated on the principle of the free expression of one's impulses. Of course the schools eventually had to draw limits, and Katherine had to go. But Katherine acted as she had been taught to act; she believed it was the schools that were at fault. The parents thought these little escapades were the cute expressions of a high-spirited, willful little girl; they chuckled over them.

As Katherine grew older she continued to act the same way, only now her impulses led to somewhat more serious and public consequences. She became pregnant, and married a man whom she did not love. The parents were bewildered and shocked. Had they not always led very moral lives? Had they not always practiced the best religious principles and taught them to Katherine? What had gone wrong? They failed to see that Katherine was continuing to act as she had always acted—impulsively. And when she settled into an unfortunate marriage, Mr. and Mrs. Martin continued to act toward her as they always had. They bought her affection—or attention would be a better word—by showering her with gifts and money, by robbing her of initiative and responsibility; and thus they maintained their control over her.

Although Mrs. Burke expressed hostile feelings toward her mother, the extent of her hatred and the fantasies accompanying it were not conscious. She felt exceedingly guilty over her relationship with her mother, a guilt expressed both in words and in the usual acquiescence to her mother's demands after a short period of defiance. She could not understand this, nor why she could not talk things over with her mother and straighten out their differences. In one interview when she was talking about her feeling of guilt and her inability to understand it, she was asked if she remembered the story she had told in the TAT about the school teacher who had choked her landlady and what significance it had for her. She immediately interpreted it as a desire to get rid of her mother.

In this instance Mrs. Burke recognized the hostile, aggressive wish directed against her mother. She talked about it, gained considerable understanding of its genesis, and was able gradually to free herself from its oppressive influence. She could now defy the mother without being overcome by guilt as a result of her defiance. She did not need to go begging for forgiveness when she had determined upon a course of action which was contrary to her mother's wishes. Once she felt the power of this new freedom, she was in a position to undertake steps which would further release her from the yoke of domination imposed by the mother. She now felt a security and a sense of the validity of her own values. She could see that the expression of these values was, in the proper perspective, the most important duty and obligation of her life.

The TAT stories were helpful in determining the course and direction of treatment. The stories revealed rejection of her children, contempt for the husband, a father fixation, repudiation of her mother. Knowing these areas of conflict, it was possible to direct Mrs. Burke's attention to them. As is always true in psychotherapy that is more than palliative, clarity with respect to such problems which are largely repressed must precede any attempt at establishing new patterns of behavior. In this case Mrs. Burke was just waiting for an opportunity to express her pent-up feelings toward those most intimately associated with her. Because of the intensity of her hostility, she was unable to appreciate the ambivalent character of her feelings until the negative had been aired. These negative feelings were so great that they were indiscriminately expressed toward anyone who was a source of irritation to her—however minor. Until the pressure of these feelings was reduced, there was little opportunity for any positive feelings to break through the barrier to overt expression.

The other important area of understanding gained from the TAT, and later verified, was Mrs. Burke's manner of reaction to crucial life situations. Her approach to life was emotional rather than rational. There was a strong urge to submit passively to her own unconscious images and strivings; and yet there was clearly demonstrated strength revealed in her counteraction to repetitive difficulties. In addition, there was conflict between her desires for dependence and independence. In order to face her immediate predicament, she had to understand rationally the various means which she characteristically used to meet perplexing situations. Contempt for her husband remained a constant throughout the treatment. Too many times Mrs. Burke had tried to improve their relationship through alteration of her own behavior only to be frustrated.

The ambivalence which Mrs. Burke felt toward her father was one of the most difficult problems which she had to face. She was clearly attached to him. Although he remained in her eyes a wonderful person, he was weak and he could not understand her true feelings. When she decided to divorce her husband, her father opposed such action, not out of consideration of what was best for his daughter but because it would be embarrassing to him in his religious group. Because this reaction infuriated Mrs. Burke, she was able to express her hostility openly and vehemently.

As she gradually realized that she was a person in her own right and began to feel confidence in her right to believe what she did and not what others imposed upon her, Mrs. Burke's self-assurance grew perceptibly. Her independence and initiative in both judgment and conduct increased. She no longer felt the extreme need to depend on others. Beginning to assume responsibility for herself and her children, she initiated a course of action designed to free her from the stultifying atmosphere in which she had lived for so long. Moreover, she resisted unacceptable coercions and forces from without which bore down upon her when she announced her intentions. She said "no" with a calm assurance and meant it. Likewise she resisted and controlled unacceptable impulses and emotions from within herself.

The greatest hurdle for her was the realistic one of practical plans. She talked about the ease with which she could get a job which would meet her economic needs and still require only a few hours of her time each day. She went out in search of such a job. When she failed to find it, she did not give up, but she gradually became more and more objective in her planning and began to look at her life with a longer time perspective. She recognized the possibility that she might have to receive more training before her talents could be put to greatest commercial advantage. Her intention to find herself never weakened; and she began to take steps to provide for the immediate future, so that she could then begin to work out her long-range plans. She learned to look at herself without distorting the facts and to give an accurate appraisal of her abilities.

The Twins

The basic problem of both boys was a deprivation of parental love and support. Both mother and father admitted that they did not love the twins. Even before the birth of a sister they had received little affection; that event only intensified their rejection. It appears quite likely that their aggressiveness, destructiveness, and distractibility may be directly related to the absence of parental love. Compare their reaction in the play situation at the beginning and end of therapy and you will observe the radical change which occurred in their behavior after the mother began to express genuine affection for them. We will return to this hypothesis in a moment.

The interpretations of the TAT were substantially confirmed in the later play situations and in conversations with the mother. The expression of aggression which Samuel gave in the stories led the therapist to feel that he was the more aggressive of the two in overt behavior, but this turned out to be untrue. That he had considerable aggression was verified, but it was strikingly less, both in the play activity and in his relations with the members of his family, than Donald's outbursts. Having always been the less favored of the two boys, he had learned that it was wiser to withhold his hostile feelings than to express them and risk losing the little parental support he had been able to obtain.

Other tests given the boys indicated that their intelligence and hearing were within normal range but that their reading ability and word recognition were quite below normal for their age.

The developmental history of the twins, as reported by the mother, indicated rather severe retardation in the areas of creeping, walking, and talking. It is not certain how reliable was the mother's recollection of the exact time of appearance of these important functions. In general, mothers' recollections of such events cannot be trusted, although usually they err in thinking their children completely normal, if not superior; here it is the opposite. There seems to be no doubt that the twins were retarded; just how much we cannot say. Nor can we specify the reasons for the retardation. It might be said that the boys were constitutionally inferior at birth, although this does not seem very likely in view of the known stock on both sides of the family from which they came, and in view of the easy birth which they had. A more reasonable hypothesis seems to be that the twins received their primary stimulation from each other, and this stimulation was not conducive either to early walking or intelligible talking. The mother, who clearly rejected them, spent as little time as possible with them. Had there been only one child instead of twins, it is entirely conceivable that a schizophrenic condition might have arisen. The boys at least kept each other from lapsing into complete autism. We have seen, in Chapter 4, in the case of Peter and Carol Chisholm, how much interaction is required between a mother and child to establish a mutually satisfying communication system. This kind of interaction was lacking between Mrs. Burke and her boys. As a result, they developed neither as rapidly nor as fully as they might have.

The boys made excellent progress in their reading ability during the three months of attendance at the clinic. They were able to go into second grade the following year and keep up with their classmates without much difficulty.

Another area in which remarkable progress was made by the twins was in their personal relationships, especially within the family.

Interaction Between Mother and Twins

When Mrs. Burke brought her boys to the clinic, she could hardly say anything good about them. They were in a state of almost continuous conflict. She openly admitted, "I don't like the way the children are so messy. They give me a pain. I just don't like them." She had many aggressive, even death wishes directed toward the twins. Another evidence of these negative impulses was the manner in which she spoke about the boys, even outside the clinical relationship. One day when she had to miss an appointment because of bad driving conditions, she telephoned and said to the secretary, jokingly, "I don't want to kill them on St. Patrick's Day; any other day would be all right."

For their part the boys killed the mother in fantasy over and over again. Not only the mother was the target of their aggression, but also the father, the sister, and even each other. Nor was this aggression confined to fantasy. Their destructiveness of property, their quarreling, their extreme distractibility testify to the turmoil which was going on within. Then gradually there was a change.

In such a clinical relationship as this, one cannot possibly control, or even estimate, all the variables operative in the modification of behavior. At best only an approximation of the factors influencing change can be arrived at; only the outstanding elements can be isolated and analyzed. The first element observed here was a renascence of positive feeling on the part of the mother. In one of the last interviews which the writer had with her, she related an incident which speaks for itself. Samuel had been outside playing and had been worsted in the competition. He came into the house with a hangdog expression on his face. He was filthy. He had been defeated, and he came to the mother for consolation. Her first reaction was one of revulsion over his weakness and inability to cope with the situation (the same feeling she had so often with respect to her husband). Although her impulse was to scold him and tell him to go wash himself, at that moment she said, "I had a feeling which came from the pit of my stomach—a feeling of love and protectiveness." She felt that she really loved the boy with all his inadequacies and weaknesses. Instead of chiding him she sat down and listened to his story and comforted him. Both felt immeasurably better afterwards.

It is likely that the change in the mother's need-disposition of affiliation toward the boys was the most effective element in producing a brighter, happier outlook in them. Simultaneously the boys began to act in a more positive manner toward their mother and others.

Certain conditions were met in the play situation which probably had some influence. There was deliberately created a permissive, understanding, protective atmosphere in which the twins could feel free to play out some of their pent-up feelings. Quite unself-consciously and unwittingly, they projected their fears and wishes and past and present anxieties into the objects with which they were playing. Thus they learned to express their true feelings without the anticipation of danger or the loss of support. Equally important with this projection of their conflicts into the play materials was the motor outlet for emotion which the situation provided. They were markedly active during the sessions. Pent-up emotions were released, the cathartic effect of which cannot be overlooked. Throughout, the therapeutic relationship was an educative process, although no verbal interpretations were made. The situation itself was a learning one; and what the boys learned, primarily about their emotions, they utilized in their daily relationships.

Not to be forgotten also is the effect which the twins' improvement in reading had upon the mother. She was delighted with their progress. We have here, of course, a chicken and egg problem. Whether the mother's feelings for and actions toward the boys changed prior to the change observed in them or subsequent to, and perhaps as a result of, that change we cannot say. We can only repeat: whatever influenced one, influenced all.

7

SOCIAL MOTIVATION

Interaction between persons is usually organized and directed. Direction, we have suggested, results from conditions both internal and external to the individual. These internal and external conditions determine the immediate behavior space and thus constitute the antecedents to action. The external conditions in a dyadic relationship we have already discussed in terms of instrumental acts, or cues. In this and Chapters 8 and 10 we will elaborate on what is meant by internal conditions.

An Example of Motivated Behavior

In the second play session with Samuel, reported in the preceding chapter, you may recall that his behavior was very aggressive. During one sequence the following words and action occurred:

. . . They're going to fight. Joe has to have a shield so they can't hit him. (. . . Joe represents himself. He places a piece of clay over Joe's face.) . . . Father just has this long thing so they can't hit him. (Takes Jane up.) She's going to throw her ball at the cowboys. (Places father and mother behind the other figures.) She's dead (indicating the mother). Father's dead, too. (Then all the other figures are pushed over except Joe.) They're dead, except Joe, because he had a shield up and they couldn't kill him. (Puts another large strip of clay around Joe.) I'll put this around him so they couldn't kill him. See how he is built up? He couldn't be killed, could he?

What are the outstanding characteristics of this play sequence? First of all, there is its aggressive character—but it is not aggression expressed at random, willy-nilly. It is controlled and directed; only special persons are killed. Second, one figure stands alone in a central position related to all the others, a figure which represents Samuel himself. Third, this figure which represents himself is carefully protected and defended. But the unnecessary defense and the question at the end suggest uncertainty as to the safety of his position. In order to understand why Samuel acted the way he did in the play situation, we must know more than the stimulating conditions confronting him. Why the extreme aggression? Why the protective self-defense? We will consider only the first question at present.

Some Roots of Aggression

There have been two viewpoints as to the way in which aggression arises: One view says it is because of an inborn drive or instinct; the other view says it is because of an acquired drive resulting from frustrations entailed in the course of experience. Most psychologists today agree with the second hypothesis. However, it is sometimes difficult to account satisfactorily for the different individual behavioral expressions of aggression solely on the basis of frustration. We should recognize that there are different thresholds of frustration; and these thresholds are probably correlated with constitutional variations which are inherent. While we do not have enough evidence to settle this question now, much aggression can be shown to be related to specific antecedent conditions, not only immediate antecedent conditions but long-range ones as well. One attempt to show the relationship between aggression (and also dependency) and some child-rearing antecedents is that of Sears, Whiting, Nowlis, and Sears (1953), which we shall review at some length. The study is noteworthy, even though it is inconclusive, because it recognizes that the response of a child to a given stimulus depends on the learning experiences which he has had throughout his life.

Sears and his colleagues report a pilot study of some child-rearing antecedents of dependent and aggressive behavior in forty children of preschool age, twenty-one boys and nineteen girls, enrolled in the Pre-school Laboratory of the Iowa Child Welfare Research Station during the school year of 1947–1948. The ages of the children ranged from 3.4 to 5.5 years. The families from which the children came were predominantly Protestant, Middlewestern, and upper middle class, with a tendency toward recent upward mobility by means of higher education.

Three types of measurement were used to secure scores on the various aspects of aggression and dependency in the children: Teacher ratings and behavior observations were designed to measure the amount of the different kinds of aggressive and dependent behavior in the school, while doll play was used as a measure of fantasy activity.

The mothers of the forty children were interviewed concerning their child-rearing procedures. The interviews, lasting from two and a half to four hours, were transcribed and then categorized as to subject matter relevant to twelve scales, related to infancy frustration, current frustration and nurturance, and maternal punitiveness and responsiveness.

On the basis of the data, the authors suggested several hypotheses to be tested by a later verification study.

1. Dependency is established during the first year of life. Higher correlations between amount of later dependency and severity of weaning than between dependency and rigidity of scheduling suggest: (a) the crucial period for the development of dependency is between the fourth and twelfth months. A positive relationship between feeding frustration and dependency, and a lack of such relationship in the case of toilet-training frustration, suggest: (b) the dyadic relationship created in connection with the feeding process is the main requisite condition of learning dependency. (c) There is adequate reinforcement to produce a dependency drive in all children in the first year; and (d) the actual drive strength is determined by the amount of frustration experienced in connection with feeding.

2. In the preschool years, the amount of dependency behavior exhibited (toward parents, siblings, teachers, and other children) is a curvilinear function of the amount of frustration and punishment of dependency-instigated behavior. That is, the maximum occurrence of dependency reaction is produced by moderate amounts of frustration and punishment. The low dependency behavior resulting from severe punishment is part of a generalized inhibition that includes inhibited general activity, overt aggression, and independence.

3. Girls identify more strongly with their mothers than do boys, a finding supported by the sex differences in choice of doll-play agents, in rated tendency to emulate teacher, and in choice of dependency objects in school. (a) A given degree of maternal frustration or punitiveness has a stronger effect on girls than on boys. (b) There is a tendency for dependency to be positively correlated with maternal punitiveness in boys and negatively correlated in girls.

4. Object choice for dependency behavior in preschool is a complex function of the strength of dependency toward the mother and the severity of her dependency frustration by punishment. This relationship was demonstrated in the more frequent choice of the teacher than of other children by girls, and the opposite choice by boys. Effects of the girl's higher identification with the mother are: (a) to produce in girls a greater tendency than in boys for dependency to generalize to the teacher. Identification also produces a greater effect by the same amount of maternal punitiveness; hence, (b) girls will show a relatively greater tendency than boys to displace their dependency choices from teacher to children.

5. Mothers behave differently in rearing boys and girls during the second, third, and fourth years of childhood. These differences are most noticeable with respect to (a) the greater demands placed on girls for nondependent behavior, and (b) a greater tendency for girls' mothers to reverse their policies, in terms of severity of frustration, from the infancy years to the later preschool years.

6. The strength of the aggression drive, as measured by aggressive be-

havior in preschool, is unrelated to feeding frustration in infancy, but may be in part a product of severe toilet training.

7. Overt aggressive and dependent behavior are highly correlated with respect to frequency. The sources of dependency and aggressive drives are sufficiently different that the two drives can vary independently in strength.

8. The amount of current frustration in the home contributes a small amount of variance to the measures of aggressive behavior in preschool.

9. Severity of punishment for aggressive behavior, by the mother, has a curvilinear relationship with the amount of aggression displayed in preschool. A moderate amount produces the most, while lesser and greater amounts produce less. Since girls identify more strongly with the mother, they exhibit less overt aggression than boys. Amount of displaced aggression is a positive function of the severity of punishment for overt aggression.

10. There is an unknown factor in the learning conditions that influences differentially the development of dependency and aggression in boys and girls.

Returning for a moment to the case of Samuel whose history shows severe rejection at the hands of both mother and father, no punishment can be worse than this. In addition he was regularly scolded and shouted at, and occasionally whipped. With this amount of information, and using some of Sears' hypotheses, one could predict that Samuel would show: (a) high aggression in fantasy, (b) low aggression in overt relations with adults, and (c) high dependency in relation to adults. This, of course, is what we observed.

Theories of Motivation

Probably no construct in psychology has had a more tortuous history than has "drive"; and it has not come to a resting place of agreement yet. The difficulty is that one cannot see and point to a drive; one can only observe what is assumed to be its effects on behavior. It is because it cannot be seen and measured directly that so much controversy has arisen over the use of this term. Nevertheless, the drive construct, in one form or another, is central to most theories of motivation.

Search for the springs of human action has been the concern of many of the world's great thinkers. Murphy (1954) has reviewed briefly man's attempt to account for motives. The pleasure-pain theory has been espoused in one form or another by most of the philosophers of the West. Pleasure is sought by man, pain eschewed. But it is not always obvious what for a given individual constitutes pleasure or pain; for example, physical delights and comforts may be renounced by the monk, who considers the spiritual life to entail greater happiness. This problem of knowing what produces pleasure and what pain, led to a search for the basic impulses which energize action. Descartes spoke of "passions" and Thomas Hobbes suggested that fear, rage, and sex were the most powerful impulses—fear being the most important. It remained for Darwin to set the stage for modern theories of motivation. Darwin destroyed the lofty illusion of man as a creature set apart from lower animals; animal life was seen as a continuum. Man had evolved because of his ability to adjust to changing environmental conditions. His adjustment implied mainsprings, or motives, to action which made it possible for him to survive. Such a concept demanded that attention be paid to the motives of man and animal. Psychologists were not long in responding.

At the turn of the twentieth century we find Freud maintaining that sex (libido) is the sole driving force in human life. Later, after World War I, he was to add a second drive, aggression. Contemporaneously, McDougall (1908) insisted that there were many springs of action, which he called instincts and which he conceived of as inherited predispositions to perceive, feel, and strive in specific ways. In the instincts he found the source of motivation; but he did not view instincts as relentlessly unfolding patterns of behavior, a notion which has sometimes been attributed to him. The instincts were the energies of men, but full-blown motivations were the resultants of these energies interacting with and being modified by the environment. For a brief period American psychologists were intent upon explaining all behavior in terms of a few or many instincts, drives, or wishes. The terms were not clearly differentiated. Thus W. I. Thomas (1923) listed four wishes motivating action: security, new experience, recognition, and emotional response from others. Whereas Thorndike (1913) had listed almost a hundred springs of action, Woodsworth (1918) was satisfied with a little over fifty.

Today the concept of instinct as an inborn pattern of response in man is thoroughly discredited. For a time Pavlovian conditioning ruled out instincts and all other intervening variables which attempted to account for energy and direction in behavior. But in the 1930's the tide turned back, and now we find terms like *drive* and *need* being used. But we also find a good deal more restraint in the naming of these springs of action than was previously the case; neither one nor an endless listing of needs is satisfactory. Rather, there is assumed to be a limited number of major needs common to men of a given culture which may serve to classify and explain their behavior.

One of the landmarks in dynamic psychology and a model of need theories was the publication by H. A. Murray of *Explorations in Personality* (1938). In this book Murray set forth the major assumptions and postulates of dynamic psychology. He also named and defined at great length the needs which empirical investigation had revealed necessary to explain the behavior of the fifty college men who had been intensively studied.

Some of these needs and their definitions were listed in Chapter 3. Murray's conception of need was one of the chief spurs to research attempting to relate internal states to differential perception of stimuli. Recently Murray (1951) has come to view needs as "dispositions operating in the service of a certain kind of value."

Two Classes of Drives

Most psychologists have found it necessary to divide drives into two classes, the physiological or viscerogenic drives and the psychological or psychogenic drives. The physiological drives are presumed to be rooted in organs or tissues of the body and to be unlearned, whereas the psychological drives are conceived as having no locus outside the nervous system and are learned in social interaction. These distinctions, however, are not always adhered to, and confusion arises immediatedly one tries to account for direction in human behavior on the basis of physiological drives. Only at the animal level can we conceive of drives as automatic regulatory devices. Even with animals it is sometimes very difficult to tell when a response is unlearned. For this reason it seems preferable to use two motivational terms, *drive* and *need-disposition.*

Drive refers only to the unlearned initiating physiological condition; it is the energizer of action. *Need-disposition* refers to a learned tendency to orient and respond to specific objects in specific ways. There is nothing in these definitions to suggest that behavior results from internal states alone. Action, as we have insisted all along, proceeds from a field of forces which includes both internal states and external stimuli. What we wish to emphasize here is not the absence of external stimuli, but the necessity of formulating internal states.

Up to now, most of the work on motivation has been undertaken with animals, in connection with physiological drives of hunger and sex. Skinner's and Tinbergen's work are illustrative of this approach, although they differ significantly in the concepts they employ. Skinner (1953) ruled out the conceptualization of inner states; not because, as he himself said, they do not exist, but because he did not find them relevant in a functional analysis. In his work he uses only dependent and independent variables. The dependent variable is the effect—that is, behavior—for which he seeks a cause. The independent variable is the cause and is sought only in the external conditions. The laws of science can be found, he believes, in the relationship between the two variables. When studying hunger in pigeons, for example, he rules out "hunger" as an internal state, or intervening variable, and measures the "external conditions" in terms of body weight of the animal after so many hours or days without food. In this way he obviously can be more objective.

Tinbergen (1951) is equally objective in his studies, but he does not hesitate to speak of internal states. For Tinbergen the fundamental question is the same as it is for Skinner: Why does the animal behave as it does? However, for Tinbergen there are two broad causal categories: Internal nature and confronting stimuli. He speaks of "spontaneous" and "reactive" behavior. To the extent that behavior is more dependent upon external stimuli it may be called reactive; to the extent that it is more dependent upon internal motivational factors it may be called spontaneous.

Usually both internal and external factors are involved in behavior. The stimulus which is adequate to evoke a response may be assumed to be related to the internal condition of the organism. Tinbergen has demonstrated this relationship in his work on reproduction in both the grouse and stickelback fish. When the male grouse is in "sexual condition," that is sexually aroused, he will mount any grouse (whether it be male or female) that is in the crouched position of the willing female. He will even mount dead or stuffed birds, for he cannot resist the powerful sign stimulus of the crouched position. But it is not the stimulus alone which causes the behavior; it is that in combination with the sexual condition of the bird.

Working with the female three-spined stickelback fish, Tinbergen used dummies with varying markings, or signs, to stimulate live fish. He found that during the autumn and winter the best dummies failed to evoke the mating response. This he accounted for by saying that the *drive of the fish was too low in intensity.* He found further that when the drive was of medium intensity, it took a relatively strong stimulus to get any response at all. When the drive was strong, however, even the slightest stimulus was followed by an explosive reaction. Under the latter conditions the female responded to a dummy which simulated a live fish by only one sign stimulus—it might be movement or color markings or something else. To quote Tinbergen (1951, p. 73):

. . . there is a mutual relationship between internal and external factors in the sense of an additive influence on the motor response. A high intensity of one factor lowers the threshold for the other factors. A high hormone level increases the responsiveness to external stimulation; if the hormone level is low, very intensive external stimulation is required to bring the total causal factors above threshold value.

One other observation of Tinbergen's, in line with the discussion of the interaction process in Chapter 5, is worthy of note. When the male and female stickelbacks were in reproductive behavior, the reactions of each were released only by the preceding reaction of the partner. This observation alone should serve to banish any lingering notion that behavior can be explained simply by reference to a single drive or a single external stimulus. If behavior in the lowly fish is multi-determined, how much more complicated is it in ordinary or extraordinary human endeavor! This thought suggests that interpretation of behavior on the basis of any stimulus, except the most massive, without knowledge, or postulation, of internal states is highly unreliable.

Beach (1951) supports this point of view. In his work on reproductive activity in animals he concluded that a complete analysis of the behavior required examination of internal correlates. Some of the internal variables which influence physiological readiness are: nervous system, ovarian function, hormones, and previous learning. In the human female, ovarian function is influenced by still other factors. Beach points out that menstruation may be appreciably delayed in some women who are suffering from homesickness, fear of pregnancy, or chronic anxiety. Returning to animals, some of the external stimuli which influence sexual behavior are: illumination, temperature, and pressure of other animals. Stimuli afforded by the sexual partner include chemical (olfactory), visual, auditory, and tactual. If the cues which the female normally provides are altered, the result may be attacking behavior rather than copulatory.

A person does not react to all the stimuli which impinge upon his sense organs. Why not? Evidence from two sources is needed to answer this question. First, you must know the condition of the physiological drives of the individual. Second, you must know the history of his learning in relation to the stimulus—which we have conceptualized as need-dispositions. Even with animals it is sometimes necessary to know the latter. In his observation of the cichlid fish, for example, Tinbergen found that they learn to confine their parental activities to the young of their own species during the first time they breed. If it should happen, or be experimentally arranged, that the eggs of another species are given to a young pair in exchange for their own first brood, the young when born are accepted and raised. But from that time on, the pair will never raise young of their own species. If they hatch their own, they will kill them immediately.

Need-dispositions: Their Influence on Behavior

Let us turn now to a consideration of need-dispositions, how they arise and how they direct action. Social psychologists have long sought for an organizational concept in motivation theory. A concept is needed which will account for stability and flexibility in the person-environment interaction, for personal identity or the congruence of personal experience, and for the ordering of drives into functional patterns of behavior. The concept of attitude, which Allport (1935) called "the most distinctive and indispensable concept in American social psychology," has served the function for many. The concept of sentiment, as developed by McDougall (1908, 1933) and as recently employed by Adams (1954), likewise attempts to account for the progressive organization of the propensities in systems. These systems bring consistency, continuity, and order to our life of striving and emotion. Both concepts—attitude and sentiment—are in use in the psychological literature today. Looked upon as nearly synonymous, they have come to mean acquired psychophysical structures referring to specific objects. Thus when a person is placed in a certain situation, the attitudes or sentiments toward the objects present are supposed to determine how he will feel, think, and act in relation to those objects. Still other attempts to formulate organizational concepts have been made by Freud under the terms *cathexis* and *fixation;* by Janet and Murphy using the term *canalization;* and by Parsons and Shils, as we have already pointed out, employing the compound word *need-disposition.* While the latter term will be used here it should be clear that it is not a new concept and that almost any of the other terms could be substituted for it.

Need-disposition is a hypothetical psychophysical structure which derives its energy from the physical organism and its direction from previous commerce with the object. It is the organizational unit of motivation. It can be identified by its reference to an object and by the increase or decrease of tension in the person after commerce with the object. It is distinguished from drive by its higher degree of organization, and by its specifically directing power. Drive is a diffuse tension. When the organism, motivated by drive tension, acts in relation to objects in a way which increases or reduces the tension, a need-disposition is born. Not all need-dispositions are born as a result of drive tension reduction. Need-dispositions may generate other need-dispositions. For example, when the need-disposition for affiliation in the case of Samuel and Donald was frustrated by their mother and father, it led to the creation of a new need-disposition for aggression. The latter persisted and became the basis of interaction between parents and children until circumstances were altered sufficiently so that the need-disposition for affiliation was once again satisfied. It is assumed that the need-disposition for affiliation toward the parents grew out of commerce with them during an earlier period when they were adequately meeting the physiological requirements of the twins.

Characteristics of Need-dispositions

1. *The tension of need-dispositions tends to rise and fall in cycles.* When the tension has recently been reduced, there follows *a refractory period* during which no stimulus will arouse it. After a period of time, which varies considerably both with respect to individual need-dispositions and to persons, there is what may be called *a susceptible period.* During this time the need-disposition may be activated by appropriate stimuli. And finally there is *an active period,* during which the need-disposition is triggered by the slightest stimulus and determines the behavior of the whole organism. The similarity to drive cycles, cited above by Tinbergen, is obvious. How far we may go in drawing an exact parallel waits upon further empirical evidence.

One illustration from everyday experience will suffice to show the plausibility of thinking of need-dispositions in cyclical terms. When a person is living in his usual environment where he has many friends with whom he associates regularly and satisfyingly, he does not think much about affiliation. He certainly does not go out of his way deliberately to make new friends. But if he is taken out of this environment and placed in a strange one, he soon becomes lonesome. He may begin to look around for friends because his need for affiliation is not being satisfied. If he does not find friends to his liking, his need-affiliation grows stronger. Eventually he may strike up a friendship with the first person who happens along, whether they have common interests or not, simply because his discriminative powers have been blunted and his threshold of stimulation lowered by his overpowering need-disposition for affiliation. The story is told of how Bismarck formed a friendship with a woodcutter on his estate after he had fallen from power and had been banished to his lands. Previously he had not even noticed the existence of the same man; his need-affiliation was regularly satisfied through other human contacts.

2. *Need-dispositions function in combination with the self system, the abilities of the individual, and the stimulating conditions to produce overt behavior.* This is what we have termed the immediate behavior space of the person. The need-disposition accounts for the energy and direction of action, but in the human being, especially the mature personality, the final outcome of action depends also upon perception of the socially acceptable demands of the situation, the rational value system and the superego, as well as the abilities of the person in line with the proposed action.

In young children, before they have developed highly organized and stable self-systems, need-dispositions play a proportionally larger part in consummatory behavior. We have seen in the case histories of Peter Chisholm or the Burke twins that when they were thwarted in the satisfaction of a particular need-disposition, the mounting tension caused them to exert even more force in the same direction. If they were still unsatisfied, they tended to explode into aggressive outbursts. The older person or adult, under similar circumstances, will be restrained by other forces within the personality tending to control and hold in check such violence. If the condition of mounting tension persists for a long period, release of tension may be sought through one of the psychodynamic mechanisms, for example displacement, which will be discussed in a later chapter.

3. *A need-disposition refers to a particular object, but the object may be generalized to include other objects which are equivalent to it in one or more of its properties or attributes.* For example, a need-disposition toward the mother tends to be applied under certain circumstances to other women who are like the mother in certain ways. Or again, take a need-disposition developed toward a particular person who happens to be a member of a certain class of persons, say Negroes or Chinese. There is a strong tendency to act in relation to all persons of the same class as one

would toward the particular person. The antidote to this unwarranted generalization, of course, is sufficient commerce with other members of the class to bring about discrimination with respect to the unique individuals within it.

4. *Reduction in tension of need-disposition following a response is reinforcing of that response. When the same, or similar, conditions are repeated, the probability of recurrence of the same response is increased. Conversely, increase in the tension of need-disposition following a response reduces the probability of recurrence of the response under future similar conditions.* Take affiliation, for example. If one feels happier and less lonely after associating with a particular person, one is likely to seek out that person the next time the need for companionship is felt. On the other hand if communication is difficult or impossible with a certain person so that one feels more distant and lonely, one is not likely to seek out such a person as a companion.

5. *Stability and flexibility of need-dispositions are the properties which facilitate their endurance and reorganization.* Need-dispositions may endure throughout a period of fifty years or a lifetime, providing that commerce with the object continues to be intermittently reinforcing. Need-dispositions of a child for his parent, a husband for his wife, are cases in point. A need-disposition toward one's life work provides another good illustration. If the work is satisfying and challenging, the individual remains positively oriented toward it for many years. At the same time need-dispositions may change gradually or abruptly if commerce with the objects proves continuously or increasingly dissatisfying. Mrs. Burke's need-disposition toward her husband is an example of such a change occurring over a period of time. In *The Doll's House* Ibsen provides an excellent illustration of an abruptly changing need-disposition. You may recall that the wife looked upon her husband of several years as a complete stranger with whom she could not spend one more night, after he had failed to defend her financial transaction.

6. *A need-disposition in abscission may remain inflexible, albeit dynamic, for many years despite the quality of the commerce with its object.* This characteristic describes, even if it does not fully account for, the phenomenon of persistent non-adjustive responses. It happens sometimes that persons continue to perform acts in relation to other persons which time after time bring nothing but rebuffs. This is typical of what is called neurotic behavior. For example, a person may seek affection from another, but since the manner in which he attempts to reach his goal repulses the object of attention, he may receive only unkindness or even cruelty. It is assumed that the need-disposition in abscission (outside the awareness of the individual), in this case a deep craving for affection, is shut off from the usual forces of reinforcement and punishment which bring about modifications in its structure.

7. *When two need-dispositions arise simultaneously, whether they are in abscission or not, so that the reduction of tension in one increases the tension in the other, conflict is the result.* Carol Chisholm in her relationship with her parents-in-law provides us a clear example. Whenever she went to their home, she was in severe conflict, the repercussions of which were widespread and lasted beyond the immediate visit. On the one hand, she had a need-disposition for acceptance, based upon generalization from her experience with her own parents, and upon a transfer of her feelings for her husband to his parents. Nor must we forget that the parents had physical possessions to which she was attracted. At the same time she had a need-disposition for aggression toward the in-laws—a feeling which grew out of the treatment she had received at the hands of the father-in-law and the persistent domination of all parties to the family by the mother-in-law.

Need-dispositions and the Direction of Behavior

We have maintained that need-dispositions, in addition to providing energy for action, also help to determine the direction of behavior. We shall now review some of the evidence relating to this hypothesis. When Carol Chisholm came into the presence of her son, Peter, after a few hours absence, her need-dispositions for affiliation and nurturance, which had been highly developed, became very active and dominated her whole behavior. She picked him up and hugged and cuddled him. She sang to him and danced with him. She nursed him. Only after both she and Peter were satiated, did she put him back in his crib and turn her attention to other things. How different was her behavior when she came in the presence of her parents-in-law! Here her need-disposition for aggression was aroused. She wanted to attack and say nasty things. But the direction of this force was opposed by a counter force from her need-disposition for affiliation, in the opposite direction. The need-disposition for affiliation was aroused because of the association of the in-laws with her husband whom she loved. The result was a standstill. The tension generated could go in neither direction. It became displaced by the mechanism of illness.

At this point you may ask, "How do you know that these need-dispositions were aroused in Carol to direct her behavior?" The reply is that, while we do not know for certain, it is the most likely hypothesis available. Carol's responses to these situations were observed time and again; her responses were invariable. Although she was observed many times in the presence of other young babies, and of older men and women of the ages of the parents-in-law, she never once responded to either in the manner described above. The most economic explanation of Carol's behavior is that it resulted from previous commerce with the specific objects, recorded as psychophysical structures in her nervous system—this is what we mean by a need-disposition.

You may say, "All right, something which you call a need-disposition
was aroused in Carol in the presence of these objects, but how do you
know it was the specific need-dispositions which you have named?" We
must admit we do not know; it is an inference. The statement is undoubtedly over-simplified. Many factors enter into every response. But the evidence from other sources tends to support the position taken here. What is
some of that evidence?

Throughout this book it has been maintained that behavior results from
the immediate behavior space of two or more persons in interaction. Immediate behavior space in turn results from all the forces, internal and
external, impinging upon each person during a given moment in time. One
of these forces is the need-disposition. An attempt to isolate the need-
disposition and use it as a variable in experimental research has been attempted. The findings from these efforts are equivocal, probably because
of the failure to recognize the multi-determination of behavior.

One of the earliest attempts to demonstrate the relationship between
perception and internal states was an experiment conducted by Murray
(1933) on the effect of fear upon estimates of the maliciousness of other
personalities. At a weekend house party given by his eleven-year-old
daughter for four girl-friends, Murray planned that they should play a
game called "Murder." In this game, played in complete darkness, one of
the players who has been chosen "murderer" through the drawing of lots
pretends to murder another player. A third player, who draws the role of
detective, then tries to decide who committed the crime. Murray assumed
that the game aroused fear in the girls. The assumption was partially supported by the girls who said they were frightened when playing the game
and by the fact that one of them awoke the same night with a feeling that
burglars were ransacking the house.

Murray measured the effect of fear on the girls in the following way.
He had two series of fifteen photographs, each matched as nearly as possible in terms of general appearance of the faces. The day before the
murder game was played he showed one set of pictures to the girls, and
the day after the game he showed them the other set. He asked the girls
to make judgments of the benevolence or maliciousness of the faces. They
did this by rating each picture on a nine-point scale which ranged from
generous, kind, loving, and tender, as one extreme, to cruel, malicious,
and wicked at the other. Immediately after two games of murder had
been played both series of pictures were rated.

The differences in the judgments of the girls on these occasions clearly
showed a tendency to rate the pictures as more malicious immediately
after the game, when they were afraid, than on either of the other times
which served as control ratings. This experimental evidence is confirmatory of the hypothesis concerning the effect of internal states—in this case
fear—upon the perception and response of persons.

Levine, Chein, and Murphy (1942) have used hunger to demonstrate the influence of internal states on perception. Ten subjects were employed. There was an experimental group of five people and a control group of five people. The experimental subjects were tested after they had been without food for one hour, three hours, six hours, and nine hours. The control subjects were tested on four separate occasions after they had eaten. The testing procedure consisted of having the subjects give one association to each of eighty pictures displayed one at a time behind a ground-glass screen. Because the screen caused the pictures to appear vague and blurred, they were so ambiguous as to be susceptible to a variety of interpretations. The pictures were equally divided between colored, and black and white prints.

The object of the experiment was to see if hunger would affect the number of food associations in response to the pictures. While the experimental group did show an increase in number of food associations, the increase was not consistent with the number of hours of food deprivation. There was a rise in food-related associations for all pictures up to the third hour, after that the responses varied.

Atkinson and McClelland (1948) also used food deprivation to test the effect of hunger on perception. Their subjects were male trainees at a submarine base whom they deprived of food up to sixteen hours. They tested these subjects after one, four, and sixteen hours, using a thematic apperception test. Pictures were chosen which to a greater or less extent suggested the possibility of eating. After the deprivation periods the subjects wrote stories in groups. Analysis of the stories showed that imaginative responses of a food-oriented nature occurred more frequently as the number of hours of deprivation increased.

McClelland and his associates (1953) have worked extensively with the need-disposition for achievement as the internal variable. The incentive for achievement was aroused in a variety of ways. For example, a group of subjects might be given an intelligence test after a build-up about the importance of intelligence to the future welfare of the individuals. Immediately following the test, these subjects would be given a TAT. Another group, acting as controls, would be given the TAT following a period of testing in which the seriousness of the test was deliberately underestimated. Results showed significantly more achievement-oriented responses on the part of the first than of the second group.

There are many other studies which have attempted to demonstrate that responses of various sorts are influenced by need-dispositions. The evidence is not conclusive that motivational conditions directly sensitize perception. Perception is influenced by other factors also. Few would deny, however, that motivational conditions play an important part in orienting perception and hence the immediate behavior space of persons in everyday situations. Murphy (1947, p. 353) comes closest to stating this point of view when he writes:

> Organization is not molded exclusively by the need pattern or by the stimulus pattern. . . . The outer world can never be so completely unstructured as to make perception depend solely upon the perceiver; but it can never be so sharply and clearly organized as to obliterate individual differences among perceivers.

Other Social Motives and Nonmotivated Behavior

Thus far, throughout this book, we have named perhaps two dozen different need-dispositions, including Murray's list. Does this exhaust the motives known to generate the many forms of behavior which are observed in complex social organizations? Will these few need-dispositions explain such diverse behavior as stealing, seeking political power, amassing a fortune, beachcombing, vegetarianism, pacifism, exploration, growing a beard in a beardless society, and self-flagellation? Obviously they won't; those who attempt to reduce all behavior to a few needs fall into the same trap, although not to the absurd degree that Freud did when he tried to derive all behavior from libidinal and aggressive instincts. The zeal to discover a few motives which determine behavior has been dictated by the scientist's ideal of economy and his desire to classify. To admit that there are an infinite number of possible need-dispositions is to court confusion and defy a neat classification system.

At the present time, however, this is exactly what we must do. There are as many need-dispositions as there are objects toward which people form attachments, varying all the way from mother's breast to rare fossil specimens.

There have been many attempts to bring order to human motivation. Some attempt to group motives. Maslow (1954) has done so by listing five basic needs: the physiological needs, the safety needs, the belongingness and love needs, the esteem needs, and the need for self-actualization. Some attempt to enumerate the specific, predominantly determining, central needs in a given culture, for a given age and sex. This was Murray's way (1938). Still others, like Gordon Allport (1937), make any behavior pattern a potential motive in its own right. More recently Allport (1958) has proposed that instead of seeking endless motives from the study of the "average man" we recognize that each individual is unique, and attempt to discover the "individual structural pattern" for individuals.

And so we go around and around; from Freud's libidinal reduction to Allport's pluralistic functional autonomy and back again. The simple fact of the matter is that we do not know what are the most adequate motivational units. This does not mean that we should deny all motivational constructs, as Kelly (1958) does. It does mean, however, that we must be cautious about explaining all behavior in terms of any list of motives. We must stop hiding behind hypothetical constructs which we cannot identify or adequately demonstrate. It means also that perhaps there is a larger area of behavior that is unmotivated than we had heretofore realized; and that conscious intentions, plans, purposes, values, and goals may be powerful motivators which do not fit into the usual motivation categories. These latter will be dealt with in subsequent chapters; for the moment let us look at what is meant by nonmotivated behavior.

Nonmotivated Behavior

Nonmotivated behavior does not mean nondetermined behavior. What it does mean is that the units of motivation which we have used to explain behavior are not the only causes of behavior. Let aggressive behavior again serve as an illustration. If aggression refers to any action, thought, or impulse the aim of which is physical or psychological injury, we can appropriately speak of Samuel and Donald in the play sessions reported in the preceding chapter as aggressive. We can go further and say that this aggression was a motivational disposition. When the stimulating causes of this disposition were modified, we saw a corresponding modification of the behavior. Now suppose we observed the same behavior on the part of Samuel and Donald but knew nothing of the frustrating conditions of their lives, would we be correct in assuming that a need-disposition called aggression was motivating them? Some of the time, yes. And in such extreme aggressive behavior as they displayed, perhaps all of the time. But many times when we observe an act such as knocking something over or being mildly destructive, we cannot make the assumption that the behavior is motivated by aggression. It may simply mean that this is the characteristic style or way of acting of the person in question, without any hostile or destructive intent whatsoever. Some people greet others by slapping them on the back so hard as to almost knock them over; the gesture may be a friendly act even if one's hat is knocked into the mud.

The distinction here is between instrumental acts in the service of motives, and behavior which is stylistic. Maslow (1954) speaks of the former as coping behavior. The latter he calls expressive behavior. Expressive behavior may have nothing to do with motives—for example, certain kinds of play, creativity, singing, sauntering, extemporizing at the piano. Still other kinds of behavior are nonmotivated, like style of handwriting, manner of walking or talking, or head-scratching.

Needs and the Organization of Behavior—a Recapitulation

Two groups of needs are recognized: viscerogenic and psychogenic. Viscerogenic needs are grounded in the physiological systems of the organism. They may be highly specific, as the needs for sleep and breathing, or relatively specific, as the need for food. The object most appropriate for the satisfaction of a drive (and its subsequent cathexis) is seldom absolutely specific. This does not mean, however, that the range of variability is limitless. Bark from a tree regularly fed to a baby can hardly be expected to satisfy his nutritional requirements; on the other hand, he does not absolutely require milk, either from the mother's breast or from a bottle.

In addition to the viserogenic needs, there are what we are calling psychogenic needs. These needs grow out of social relationships—interactions with other personalities. But whether such needs have the same status initially as the viscerogenic needs, or whether they are derivative in their origin (that is, growing out of situations in which drives are satisfied) is not known. At any rate they acquire autonomy as the individual develops. It is generally agreed that most, if not all, of the psychogenic needs are derived through social experience.

Positive-Negative Discrimination

There is one property of needs which plays a large part in the development of the motivational system of need-dispositions, namely positive-negative discrimination. The baby rejects tree-bark and accepts milk or other gratifying food objects. Thus he discriminates most of the time between the need-gratifying and need-depriving aspects of the objects available in his environment. Objects which are need-gratifying tend to become positively cathected, or in Lewin's term, positively valent; conversely, need-depriving objects tend to become negatively cathected. This is especially true in relation to social objects. It is for this reason that the mother generally becomes so positively cathected rather early in the life of the child.

Need-disposition implies that objects in a field have been positively or negatively cathected and that they have been cognitively discriminated from other objects. This is the first step toward ordered behavior. When a sufficient number of cathectic discriminations have been made and organized in relation to one another, they form a motivational system which orients the individual in a given situation.

A by-product of commerce with objects through which cognitive-cathectic orientation has emerged is the expectations and evaluations associated with the objects. If the mother regularly attends to the child's needs, he comes to expect certain actions from her and to evaluate her in terms of the gratifications received from her ministrations. When certain needs are active, then, the child's action is oriented toward the mother, an action which he has learned to be functional in the service of need-gratification. The word "learned" here implies that the child has acquired a new pattern of orientation to the object world.

Interaction and the Complementarity of Expectations

The distinction between objects which interact with a person and objects which do not is important to point out. Analysis of the interaction of two people requires that the focus of attention be shifted constantly from one to the other. Social interaction implies expectations on both sides. One does something and expects a certain response from the other. It is this expectation on both sides which distinguishes social interaction from interaction with a nonsocial object. This fundamental phenomenon Parsons and Shils (1952) have called the *complementarity of expectations*. It does not mean that two people do the same thing, but that each does what he does because of his expectations of the other. Thus motivation cannot be studied adequately by reference to one person alone. Motivation, being a social phenomenon, must be viewed in the context of the person toward whom behavior is directed.

Motivation is conceived as the establishment of a consistent system of need-dispositions which are relatively specific and definite, and which operate as selective reactions to the alternatives which confront the individual or which he seeks out. When a person develops an organized system of interaction with other persons, stability in social behavior is the result.

Suggested Readings

Atkinson, John W. (Ed.). *Motives in Fantasy, Action and Society*. New York: Van Nostrand, 1958.
Forty-six papers dealing with the way motives affect fantasy and behavior.

Bruner, J. S. and Goodman, C. C. "Value and Need as Organizing Factors in Perception." *Journal of Abnormal Social Psychology*, 1947, *42*, 33–42.
This is a good introduction to Bruner's studies on the nature of perception. The major thesis of all his studies is that the precise organization of material in perception is influenced by the needs and values of the person.

Lindzey, G. (Ed.). *Assessment of Human Motives*. New York: Rinehart, 1958.
A series of papers presented in a symposium at Syracuse University. Some interesting and pertinent problems concerning motivation are raised, including the question: "Is the concept of motivation necessary?"

Maslow, A. H. *Motivation and Personality*. New York: Harper, 1954.
A collection of some of the author's more important papers; a refreshing challenge to much contemporary theory on motivation.

McClelland, D. C. (Ed.). *Studies in Motivation*. New York: Appleton-Century-Crofts, 1955.
Fifty papers concerned with all aspects of the problem of motivation. An excellent source book.

Nebraska Symposia on Motivation. Lincoln: University of Nebraska Press.
Beginning in 1953, and yearly thereafter, papers presented in the Nebraska Symposium on Motivation have been published under that title, except the first which was called "Current Theory and Research in Motivation." Taken together, they constitute an excellent treatment of the subject.

8

THE CONSTRUCTS OF SELF AND EGO

The concept of self has been a problem ever since the first curious man tried, for a moment at least, to leave himself and to look at himself from a distance. Many psychologists have offered solutions to the problem, although it is true that there are other psychologists who maintain that there is no place in psychology for a concept of self. Still the fact that the problem has come up again and again over the centuries and that there is a renascence of interest in it among many psychologists at present point up its role as fundamental in the search for the nature of man.

In talking about the self one of the first difficulties encountered is one of terminology. In the psychological literature there is considerable confusion and inconsistency in the use of the two terms *self* and *ego*. The confusion has persisted because of the paradox of being at once perceiver and perceived, or subject and object. Some writers have attempted to bring order out of the confusion by arbitrarily defining the two terms. Symonds, for example, in a little book called *The Ego and the Self* (1951) makes ego correspond roughly with the subjective aspect of the paradox, self with the objective. Specifically, he uses the term *ego* to refer to the functions of personality which determine adjustments to the outside world "in the interest of satisfying inner needs in those situations where choice and decision are involved." Ego becomes the executive aspect of personality in the service of motivating forces. The self, on the other hand, is the object of ego's perception and attention. It refers to "bodily and mental processes as they are observed and reacted to by the individual," that is by the ego. These distinctions are representative of contemporary usage, but they do not solve the problem.

It seems necessary to preserve the two terms at present. Each author must define them as he proposes to use them. Let us agree here that ego and self are no more than constructs convenient for the classification of certain responses of an individual. When we have better ways of classifying these responses, both terms may well be dismissed from psychological terminology. Until such time, *self* will refer to those responses of personality which denote personal conceptions, or how the individual conceives of himself. *Ego* will refer to those responses of personality which have to do with control, regulatory, and time-binding functions. Included are rational, evaluative thinking, and planning, which we refer to as ego functions, and inhibiting forces, which are both ego and superego functions. The capacity to exercise regulatory functions and functions of control varies from time to time, depending upon changing circumstances in the life of the individual. Self-conception is both a determiner of behavior and a reflection of ontogenetic and contemporary interactive conditions of the individual's life.

In the present chapter we will review some of the outstanding historical attempts to grapple with the problems of ego and self. Following this theoretical review, brief consideration will be given to the genesis of ego, to self-esteem as a criterion of adjustment, and to the genesis and functioning of the superego.

Survey of Ego Theories

Recognition of the importance of the effects of ego on the personality was a determining factor in the thinking of men long before the advent of the scientific method. Plato, for example, in his dialogues has Socrates prove the existence of a soul, which had a real life before birth and after death. In this manner such phenomena as self-consciousness, self-awareness, self-seeking, self-fear could be incorporated into his philosophy and account for the apparent difference between the feeling of "I" and the perception of "me." Thus started the tradition of dichotomizing, and even placing in juxtaposition, the mind (or self) and the body. Even such a thoroughgoing materialist as Lucretius found it necessary to draw special distinctions for those "extra smooth, round and delicate atoms" which he said constituted the soul. But from Lucretius came the tradition of dealing with the soul or self in a material way, a tradition which gave force to the later attempts to establish a scientific approach to ego.

Long after the Greek and Roman philosophers, men were still fumbling with the many queer paradoxes resulting from the awareness of something more than the body, and the many attributes of this something. Descartes, recognizing that there were intimate connections between the mind and body, and still feeling it necessary to postulate a soul which was independent of the body (thereby accounting for, among other things, the contradiction of something which simultaneously acts and is aware of its activity) postulated an organic interrelationship between the two substances. According to him, the soul impinges its energy onto the "corpuscles" of the body at the center of the body (the pineal gland for Descartes), thereby accounting for the interaction of the two.

Later philosophers recognized the fallaciousness of these arguments; how could one substance, for example an apple, make an entirely different substance, for example a clock, work? So they became involved in the problem of how these different aspects of an individual (dropping for the moment the original question of the nature of the differences between the aspects) could get knowledge of each other and therefore interact. The question went through several stages: "What is the process by which knowledge is achieved," was the first. This led, of course, into a conflict between the view that all knowledge is contained in the soul and waits to be unfolded (shades of Socrates!), and the view that knowledge is the accumulation of experience upon the originally blank sheet of the mind—the voice of Lucretius, and later of John Locke.

This philosophical conflict has had far-reaching influence on later approaches to the problem of the self in psychology. It became increasingly obvious that behavior is contingent upon the explicit and implicit knowledge available to the individual; and that, further, the meaning and function of the self are a product of the accumulation of such knowledge. The self has come to be defined by the knowledge it has at hand. This knowledge is: information about the self (the paradox), and about the external world and its many relationships. The question of the source of knowledge and the nature of its accumulation by an individual has become the question of the nature of the ego and the process of its development and function.

As psychologists slowly became scientists rather than philosophers, the same general lines of battle were drawn in the new field. On the one side, the theory of instincts suggested that hidden away in the inner caverns of one's living vitals are propensities to action—unlearned and unsolicited.

On the other side, and as a reaction to the somewhat teleological thinking of men like MacDougall, the psychologists comprising the Behavioristic and Structuralistic Schools presented opposed theories. Such men as Wundt, Titchener, and Watson, following in the footsteps of John Locke, posed theories grounded in empiricism; instead of explaining and accounting for ego and self, these men were bent on denying the concepts. In their stead they placed the mechanical operation of the organic substance composing the body, out of which came the apparent habits and emotions composing behavior. Thus these schools represented the philosophic tradition which had claimed that knowledge was developed progressively through contact with the external world. But so interested were they in structuring this machine which reacted with the objective world that they ended up with only a machine—a static entity capable of no more than automatic reactions to stimuli. However, they made the point that it was through contact with the external world that the human organism developed.

For various reasons, many psychologists found themselves ill at ease with the extreme of either position. They could neither accept the simple instinct theory, nor the simple machine theory. Rather, they have attempted to make a complete organism out of the individual and, as Gordon Allport says, have tried to put the "person back into personality." They have viewed personality theory as an ego-directed concept, and have been consistently interested in seeing that the dynamics of human behavior was taken into account.

C. H. Cooley

One of the earliest of the social psychologists who found it necessary to conceive of self and not be forced into a strict instinctual theory was C. H. Cooley. Recognizing the importance of the social milieu from which each individual comes, he postulated a theory of the self with the interpersonal interactions of social situations as the source of the structure and operation of self.

Cooley (1902) conceives of the self as a system of ideas drawn from communicative life that the mind "cherishes as its own." What is important here is that this system of ideas is characterized by the feeling of "mine," everything which elicits the feeling of "I," of self. The material body is the locus of "I" and its feelings, but the "I" does not mean body; it means self feeling. Where and how does this self feeling come about?

It comes originally from some form of generalized instinct, which is assumed to be a feeling of individualization and which is justified throughout life by constant contact with the world, which supplies the content of this feeling of individuality. That is, this generalized instinct for self feeling (not self possessions) becomes associated with sensations, perceptions, conceptions, and ideas, so that every self feeling is associated with something, somebody, some idea. These specific self feelings about something are called, by Cooley, "self sentiments," a collection of which constitutes the adult self. Since these feelings must be conscious (by definition), they are the basis of the recognition by each individual of the unique aspects of his life and personality. Further, since the self is made up of psychological objects derived from the real world, it too must be considered as a function of the real world. Hence Cooley points out that there cannot be an "I," as in pride or shame, without its correlative sense of "he," "you," or "they."

The development of the self has been hinted at above. Starting with a generalized instinct, the self feeling becomes associated with various objects in the psychological field. The selection of the objects is based on two criteria: (1) congeniality—that is, the self feeling attaches itself to things congenial to itself and remains at variance with uncongenial things; and (2) social suggestion, aided by the image of various selected and accepted masters which may serve as an adequate basis for evaluating the suggestions. In a sense these two criteria are the same; they merely make explicit the fact that various objects require varying degrees of pushing onto the individual before he will accept them as his own. Fundamentally, of course, only those objects which are proved to be congenial or consistent with the structure of self sentiments will be attached to self feelings.

It is not necessary to go further into Cooley's theory. We can say that he attempted to formulate a theory which roots an individual in the material world of his existence. In this way Cooley can explain a good deal of social behavior, as well as the nature of values and the genesis of personality integration. But is this enough? In the first place, Cooley starts off with a generalized instinct of whose origin and nature we learn nothing. Next, he does not account for abnormal behavior or for the phenomenon of anxiety. He neither allows for contradictory structures in the personality, nor explains how feelings can become attached to ideas. In addition, he states that the self can judge what is and what is not congenial to itself, implying that a feeling can perceive, think, judge, and act. Obviously Cooley's theories have many deficiencies. Merely to postulate the looking-glass self does not explain how the glass got there, how it reflects, nor how the perceiver acts when not looking at the glass.

George H. Mead

A somewhat more sophisticated view of the self was developed by George H. Mead (1934). Mead, as Cooley, felt it absolutely necessary to root the self in the social conditions relevant to the individual and to derive the content of the self from the interaction between the individual and those conditions. One of the most difficult of all problems relating to the ego is just the problem with which Mead starts off and his answer gives the hint to his general theory. The problem is: *How can an individual get outside himself to become an object to himself?* Mead suggests a simple answer: By becoming an object to himself in the same manner that others are objects to him. This feat involves becoming one with the rest of the world and behaving as if it were the world looking at himself. In other words, the individual experiences himself from the particular standpoint of other individuals in the same social group or from the generalized standpoint of the group as a whole to which he belongs.

Viewing the interaction between individuals in any social setting, it becomes obvious immediately that the most significant aspect of behavior is the communication between the individuals. Interaction is, almost by definition, communication. What is most important is that the symbols used by the participants have the same meaning to all involved; otherwise communication cannot be said to have taken place. When the symbols are the same to all, they elicit the same response from each one. Actually this means that the symbol has been directed to the source of the symbol (the speaker) as well as to the object of it (the listener). This kind of symbol, which Mead calls the "significant symbol," constitutes communication.

The infant does not make use of such symbols—but precisely because he cannot respond in the way he comes to expect the objects of his communication to respond. Hence, we say the infant has no self. As time goes on, however, the child learns the responses to his gestures (which become symbolic as he learns the more complicated forms of gesturing, including speech) from contact with the recipients of his gestures—other individuals. With this learning process comes the development of the self, since, learning how others respond to his gesturing, the child learns to respond to himself in the same way. He is now capable of communicating to himself, which means that there is simultaneously a speaker and a responder (a "me" and an "I"). In effect, having taken the attitudes of specific individuals into himself, he can view himself from a point outside himself corresponding to the position of others.

Later on, he learns the responses of a general society (relevant to the child) and acts toward himself as if he were this generalized organization of other individuals. Required for this new relationship with the generalized other is a more perfect integration of the self into the complex and multiform institutions of the society of which the individual is a part. The customs, mores, traditions then become the "other" to him, since their responses to his approaches are incorporated (via the significant symbols) into a social self which is really a subjective reflection of the social scene. This self, if it is born of a consistent and unified society, is a consistent, unified structure. Presumably, abnormalities arise when inconsistencies in the generalized or specific other occur, or when for some other reason there is incomplete development of meaningful symbols in the individual. That is, if for one reason or another the individual is not able to recognize the meaning of a response, or if he is forced to reject the response, there we find abnormalities.

Admitting for the moment the genesis of the social self in the social set, we have yet to account for what William James called the "pure ego," the fundamental point of emotional reference. We have yet to account for the existence of contradictory demands placed on individuals by themselves, whether consciously or otherwise, and hence we have yet to deal with the nature of the mechanisms of ego defense.

We recognize the extremely valuable contribution of both Cooley and Mead in showing that many of the seeming contradictions in the concept of self were not contradictions at all, but merely an outgrowth of the unjustified separation (on the part of theorists) of man from his society. When we ponder over the problem of a self knowing itself, we must admit that there are areas of an individual which must be rooted in and grow out of something outside of or more inclusive than the "pure ego."

William James

Another attempt to answer the same sort of questions was made by William James (1890) in his classical discussion of the egos, subsumed under the "empirical ego" and the "pure ego." He approached the problem of the self as an object to itself by first describing the object, that is, the empirical ego. "In the widest possible sense, a man's Self is the sum total of all he can call his own." James then proceeded to describe the areas of possession by differentiating the material, social, and spiritual selves, which are all empirical.

The *material self* is the individual's material possessions; namely, his body, clothes, house, family, lawn mower, etc. And James rightly points out that an attack on any of these material objects constitutes an attack on the owner—hence the material self.

The *social self* is a bit more confusing. According to James, there are as many different social selves in one individual as there are human beings perceiving him in different ways. Does this mean that the social self is defined by other individuals? It could not possibly be so, since it is only possible for an individual to act in terms of the perceived situation —perceived, that is, by himself and not by anyone else. The social self must be the self which an individual wishes to think is perceived by others. From this fact it would of course follow that an individual acts in different ways in situations which he perceives as demanding different things from him. He tries to act in one fashion at a party and in another way at a baseball game, depending on his desires to impress those with whom he is involved at the moment. Although James left the question open as to the source of the definition of the social self—the person in question or other individuals—we must assume that he meant the individual in question.

The *spiritual self* is still more vague. It is what James calls the "psychic faculties or dispositions taken concretely." It would seem that James meant by "taken concretely" the conscious recognition of feelings, emotions, and attitudes. Awareness of these inner states, then, becomes the really experienced self.

Of course the above description in no way pretends to explain the rise of any of the selves or the relatedness of one to the other. However, James did attempt to account for some of the peculiarities and contradictions in the self and ego. He dealt too with the problem of the knower's relation to the known and the question of the meaning of personal identity through time, and his answers are provocative.

Starting off with a definition of stream of consciousness as a succession in time of thoughts built on one another, James gives us a hint of his solution. If one thought gives birth to the next and so on, then, concludes James, each thought must incorporate into itself a good portion of the thoughts preceding. Thoughts can be considered only as belonging to something—in particular to a self. It follows therefore that a succession of thoughts—the stream of consciousness—is the medium for the connection between the present self and the past self. What then gives the experience of viewing the self as an object? It must be the present thought connected to the present self, since the present thought must include within itself the past thoughts. Thus the present self is the knower, and since it is in the present sequence of the temporal succession, it cannot be known. The pure ego, then, is the passing thought, the thinker, the rememberer, which by definition cannot be known, but which knows and which is continuous in time (since present thoughts are continuous in time). The various selves related through thoughts and continuous in time, by operating in successive inclusive steps, give rise to the experience of personal identity and the feeling of the self as an object—the pure ego.

There are a number of deficiencies in this theory, ingenious as it may be. It must be obvious that all past thoughts cannot be included or remembered by the passing thought. James does not account for the development of the many selves he describes—selves which were to supply criteria for action. How then are these criteria manifested, and how can they be related to the pure ego, which must of course deal with present behavior? In other words, what is the relationship between remembering and behaving which is so important to the clinical analysis of an individual?

James does not go into these questions. He does suggest, however, the extremely important concept of the temporal and emotional integration of the individual into the organized self of the present. The past as well as the future is psychologically in the present to form a time—and self-bound organism in constant interaction with itself and the social setting around it.

Cooley, Mead, and James gave us provocative, ingenious, and insightful discussions of self and ego. Let us now turn to some of the men who have been engaged in approaching the problems of ego from the vantage point of scientific rather than philosophical psychology.

Sigmund Freud

The most important of the psychologists who have dealt with ego is Sigmund Freud, from whom most other psychologists have taken their cues. According to Freudian theory, the ego is the aspect of personality which is in direct and immediate contact with reality. The mechanisms of perception and rational intellectual activity are parts of the ego, as well as the mechanisms by which the demands of the "id" are postponed to satisfy the demands of reality. Hence, consciousness is also a part of this surface area of the personality and belongs to that group of functions which characterize man as a rational animal.

The question now is, what are the steps by which this ego develops? At birth and through most of infancy, the neonate is little more than a bundle of drives embedded in a flabby, incoherent, incompletely structured neuro-physiological system. The only contact with the outer world comes in the process of drive satisfaction; and the infant finds that process highly efficient. Later on, however, some "bad" stimuli appear and some drives are not immediately satisfied—the inevitable consequence of living in a mortal world populated by finite things. At any rate, an assumption made by the infant at an earlier time no longer holds—that there is no difference between his own drives and the satisfaction of them. That is, the infant was incapable of differentiating himself from the world, since (aside from the lack of perceptual tools designed to separate objects into meaningful units) his demands and the satisfaction of those demands were intimately related to the point of giving the appearance of unity. He was fused with the outer world. This assumption, however, he can no longer hold, since the facts no longer support it. A very vague and amorphous line between the world and himself is set up on which the outer crust of the organism lies. It is the crust which develops into what is called the ego.

The steps that follow are all logical. If in the beginning there was complete identification between drives and their satisfaction, it would follow that nonsatisfying stimuli are not part of the undifferentiated mass, whereas satisfied and satisfying stimuli are part of it. The first act of differentiation has then taken place between the "good" and the "bad." This separation is enhanced by the automatic reaction of accepting or swallowing the good and rejecting or spitting out the bad. As the flow of stimuli becomes more evenly distributed among good and bad factors, however, the selective process is forced to become more operative. That is, all stimuli cannot be taken in, tasted, and then the bad ones spit out. They must be selected carefully and screened before admittance. Perceptual processes are found which can organize the continuous impingement of stimuli, so that the individual will not be flooded with them (such floods being defined as anxiety-producing situations). With this judgment-dynamism comes the further differentiation of the surface of the id, which is the area that receives the stimuli from within and without the individual. The mechanisms, being rooted in the surface of the id, are therefore the content of the structure called the ego. It follows then that the function of the ego is to handle the external world and the impulses from the id to that world. The processes mentioned above are designed for that end.

In dealing with the world, the ego develops more attributes and functions as new problems have to be solved. Required for dealing with these problems is the ability to recognize them as such and to relate them to the needs of the id. This process of objectively perceiving reality in

terms of the inner drives via the sensory mechanisms is defined as consciousness. The higher intellectual processes are also the mechanisms of
that aspect of the personality which deals with a complex and manifold
world and must solve its intricate problems. Attempting to master the
world is more efficient (successful) when the symbolism used in the pre-
logical thinking of an infant becomes related to the objects symbolized
together with words. Symbols in the very beginning were used by the
infant to represent a drive satisfaction which is actually not present; that
is, the infant imagines the drive to be satisfied via some symbolic representation. Slowly this symbolism becomes related to the specific object
for which it serves as a representative. Still later, words take the place of
pictorial representation in conscious thought. Symbolic thinking—speech
—is now used to master and organize the world for the purpose of drive
satisfaction, which is one step beyond the use of symbolism merely to
fantasize about the satisfaction. Fenichel makes the point that a consequence of the use of symbolic thinking is that some of the energy which
ordinarily would be used in immediately satisfying a drive is used in this
behavior, thus slowing down the speed of satisfaction. The realization of
a necessary time interval between awareness of a drive and its satisfaction again leads to a further differentiation of the ego, lending to it the
ability to postpone immediate gratification for future good. Thus the ego
is forced into temporal relationships which make the stimuli of the past,
present, and future psychologically equipotent; and hence the ego becomes time-binding.

Although the problem of the functions of the ego is relatively simple,
the problem of the relation of the ego to the personality is much more
complicated. If we say that the ego must defend itself in dangerous situations, we are justified in asking what it is that is in danger. If the ego is
no more than the crust of the id, whose sole function is to be able to deal
with the world and the other parts of the personality solely for drive reduction, how is this construct related to the drives themselves or even to
the particular drive involved in self-preservation?

Although Freudian theory is not explicit on this point, we can conjec-
ture. First, we can say that a feeling of self does result from the differentiation of the ego; for what does this differentiation mean but that the
objects of the world are separate from the conscious awareness of the
drives of the organism? Next, it is true that the operation of the ego is
fundamental to the existence of the organism—how else can the drives of
the individual be satisfied if they do not come in contact with the external
world? The point of such contact is the very ego in question. Further, since
the onset of anxiety is a function of the ego's ability to organize and
control stimuli (both internal and external), when anxiety is defined as
the flooding and overwhelming of ego by stimuli, it follows that the very
existence of the organism is intimately related to the ego.

Gestalt Theory

The Gestalt concept of ego represents the kind of position taken by many who do not feel satisfied with the Freudian view. It postulates the ego as a segregated object in a psychological field containing many other objects that are dynamically equal to the ego but are structurally different. It is the view put forth by Kurt Koffka (1935).

This postulation of ego as an object in the psychological field of the individual is quite different from anything ever before presented in ego theory. Lewin (1935) developed a theory of ego very similar to Koffka's. For our purposes we shall consider the two theories as almost identical, to the point of saying that what will be presented here is the Gestalt theory of ego rather than either Koffka's or Lewin's, although we shall call on both for help.

Gestalt theory divides the world into two realms: The geographical and the behavioral. The geographical field is the material world; the behavioral field is the world as perceived by the person. Assuming, in the infant, the perception of the world as an undifferentiated mass, we can see how the development of the ego takes place. As soon as an object becomes segregated in the behavioral field of an infant, it stands apart in relation to all other objects. Nearer objects with which there is more commerce soon receive special definition and meaning. In time, one object becomes differentiated as a point of reference for all other objects. It has the characteristic of being separated from the rest of the world on all sides. That is, it is located behind what is in front of the perceiving mechanisms, in front of what is behind the object, to the left of what is right, to the right of what is left. The object is now spatially located and is labelled the ego.

Parts of the individual's body, stemming from this particular point of localization, are therefore part of the ego, as is anything else which also becomes so related. The result is that the limits of the individual vary according to what objects belonging to the ego are being perceived. Thus the ego can extend from the world to which the individual perceives himself as belonging, to the bridge of the individual's nose. The ego acquires the aspect of self, because it is integrated with all the sensory apparatus of the organism which gave rise to the feelings which in turn are considered "mine" because of their special localization.

It must be remembered, however, that the ego is still really an object in the behavioral field and that other objects may exist in this field without necessarily belonging to the ego. Thus it is possible to perceive an object and to have an emotion about the object—and the ego be non-operative at the same time. Koffka gives the example of having a feeling of sadness when listening to a particular piece of music; but the emotion is related to the music and not the ego.

Before going any further, the meaning of an object in the psychological field must be stated. The existence of the field can be nowhere else but in the cortical region of the brain, although it is the personal organization of forces and objects in the world. The objects in the field are, then, percepts or traces of percepts which, if enough physiology were known, might be analyzed and measured objectively. Since we are as yet unable to deal with such percepts *per se,* we must be content with hypotheses concerning their structure and laws of function. We can test our hypotheses, however, since we can make predictions about the operation of our hypothetical constructs, and since the operation of percepts and traces is manifest in behavior. To use other words, we are developing constructs which will allow us to control, measure, and predict psychological behavior. The behavioral field is one such construct; it contains the various traces of the manner in which the world is perceived by the organism. One of the major traces is that of the ego-percept. Although there are many other kinds as well, it is the ego with which we are now concerned.

It must follow from the discussion above on localization of the ego, that there is more to the ego than an object in the field. It is an object made up of traces of various objects; hence Koffka's use of the term "sub-systems" within the ego. The term "system" is significant, since it implies the movement of forces from a less stable to a more stable relationship with each other. An analysis of the nature of the systems was undertaken in experiments by Zeigarnik (1927) and Karsten (1928). The results of those experiments lead to something like the following description of the systems which make up the ego.

When the geographical field is perceived by an individual, the behavioral field becomes organized, and the percepts of the objects in the field become operative. Since these percepts are dynamic systems corresponding to the objects in the field, they are structured according to the forces regulating the objects themselves. The sources of the forces are essentially twofold: they come from the inherent structure of the object and from the manner in which they are perceived (their relationship to other objects in the behavioral field). These forces tend to distribute themselves in the same manner that all forces become distributed, namely, according to the laws of Gestalten. Distribution of forces (as used in this discussion) means a tendency toward an equilibrium or a state of stability. When forces are not distributed in that manner, there is a natural pressure to become so, which continues until the state of equilibrium is reached.

A simple example will illustrate the point. In Zeigarnik's experiment, subjects were asked to perform a task but were interrupted before the tasks were completed. This is the same as saying that a system had been set up which had not fulfilled its potentialities of completion, stability, or equilibrium. There is a tendency to maintain the system of trace (corresponding to the incomplete task which is an object in the field) which manifests itself in motivating the individual to "do something about it." Zeigarnik showed that this tendency or tension in the system does exist and that by and large it does not exist in systems corresponding to completed tasks which have reached a state of equilibrium by discharging the tension. Further experimentation showed that tension in systems can be discharged in various ways, some of which are by having the systems in functional contact with other systems and allowing the tension to be siphoned off, as it were, to these others. Lewin has made a valuable contribution in showing that tension can be discharged by making the boundaries of the systems more permeable and letting the tension "leak off." This process is called day-dreaming, fantasy, or levels of irreality—according to your preference.

The simple example given above represents what has been called a quasi-need or tension. The ego, however, is made up of more permanent tension, systems which correspond to the persistent needs of an individual and which are the source of many of the forces operative in objects perceived in the field. That is to say, needs have a determining effect on perceptions which organize the behavioral field, giving the perceived objects the qualities of tense systems. Lewin, as we saw earlier, called these qualities of objects valences, signifying their relationship to the motivational structure of the individual.

The ego system, then, is made up of many sub-systems having varying degrees of persistence and permanence. These varying degrees are represented operationally by describing the systems as more or less permeable, in more or less communication (functionally related) with each, and in terms of one other variable not yet described. This variable has to do with what Koffka calls the depth of the ego. Deep in the center of the ego system is a solid, permanent core, called the self (Wertheimer calls it the matrix; Lewin calls it the ego). Although not really dealt with in Gestalt writings, we can assume it to be a system corresponding to the biologically based needs for self-preservation and self-realization. It is, no doubt, that to which the "I" is referred; it is the personal aspect of the perceptual ego. This self system is by definition the most permanent, stable, and impermeable of all systems. The degree to which the sub-systems are related to this core is the degree to which the behavior corresponding to the systems is considered as ego-involved.

Perhaps we should return now to the problem of the self as an object to itself, and the Gestalt treatment of that problem. Although it has not been worked out in detail, we can assume that since the ego is an object in the field and does contain various sub-systems which are coordinated in a special localization and integrated with the core system, the various systems can be perceived in relation to each other. This relationship involving that which is the self, in being perceived, gives rise to self-awareness, observation, and consciousness. Incomplete as it is, this is the general direction taken by Koffka and Lewin in the solution of the problem.

From the point of view of building ego theory, there are a number of important factors to be kept in mind which have been suggested by the writers discussed here.

1. The first is that the ego is as much a product of environmental forces as it is of strictly personal, internal forces. This point is conceded by all. It must be agreed, however, that ego operation is also a part of the environmental field and that it perceives itself as such. The paradox of self-awareness can be overcome only when it is fully recognized that ego has social roots and as such owes its consciousness to social interaction. Although the point is most obvious in the work of such men as Cooley and Mead, it can be made explicit in the others as well.

2. The next point is that the ego is not only time-binding but enduring in time, so as to generate the feelings of unity and consistency of self-awareness. Taking into account the philosophical history of the problem, this is obviously an important point.

3. A third point conceives the relatedness of the ego to the drives and need-dispositions of the individual; the result of this relatedness is the development of ego operations designed to be of service to other motivational forces within the person. Such a concept presupposes a developmental sequence of ego which parallels the development, change, and transformation of need-dispositions and their satisfaction or nonsatisfaction. In other words the ego is not static and serves other aspects of the personality.

4. Still another point involves not only the spatial localization of the self and its structural characteristics, but also the relationship between the visual ego bounded by the sensory range (the optic range in particular) and the phenomenal or experienced ego bounded only by the imagination of the individual. The existence of a visual field presupposes, and in a sense defines, the phenomenal field. The ego can take flight over all manner of objects only when it is rooted in the localized integration of need-dispositions, tensions, or forces—whatever one chooses to call them. For example, a fantasy of commerce with a loved one who may actually be many miles away nevertheless tends to reduce loneliness and desire for that person temporarily. This is an ego function. In other words, it is possible for the behavioral field to extend a thousand miles only because it is anchored in the before-the-behind, and behind-the-in-front-of. An object a thousand miles away can be a force in the behavioral field only because the behavioral field can bring that object to the "here and now" via the spatial localization of the ego.

Genesis of the Ego

Other people are an indispensable part of the environment of the human organism. The impulsive animal which emerges at birth is transformed into the self-conscious, rational human being only through a process involving social experience and activity. Out of this experience as a member of a social community the ego develops. As Mead (1934, p. 134) puts it:

The self is something which has a development; it is not initially there at birth but develops in the given individual as a result of his relations to the social process as a whole and to other individuals within that process.

At birth, the human organism is merely a mass of sensory impressions and feelings arising from a body which in no way is felt to belong to him. The infant's actions are determined solely by bodily drives, by responses to stimuli, internal and external—not by any reference to a self. Moreover, the newborn child has no consciousness of his body as something apart and different from the environment.

At six or eight months he has certainly formed no clear-cut notion of himself. He does not even know the boundaries of his own body. Each hand wandering over the bedspread for things which can be brought into the mouth discovers the other hand and each triumphantly lifts the other into his mouth . . . He draws his thumb from his mouth to wave it at a stranger, then cries because his thumb has gone away. He pulls at his toes until they hurt and does not know what is wrong (Shinn, 1924, p. 172).

Slowly the infant learns the boundaries of his own being, makes distinctions between what is part of his body and what is part of something else. Shinn (1924, p. 172) has described two incidents in this process.

The 181st day her hand came into contact with her ear; she became at once very serious, and felt it and pulled it hard; losing it, she felt around her cheek for it, but when her mother put her hand back, she became interested in the cheek and wished to keep on feeling that . . . To the end of the year she would feel over her head, neck, hair, and ears; the hair she discovered in the eighth month, 222nd day, while feeling for her ear, and felt it over and pulled it with great curiosity.

Even after the child has learned to differentiate his body from his environment, however, and to realize that his body is unique and different from the surrounding world, he cannot be said to possess a self. Social factors, over and beyond mere biological maturation, are essential to the existence and development of self-consciousness.

Until the rise of his self-consciousness in the process of social experience, the individual experiences his body—its feelings and sensations—merely as an immediate part of his environment, not as his own, not in terms of self-consciousness. The self and self-consciousness have first to arise, and then these experiences can be identified peculiarly with the self, or appropriated by the self; to enter, so to speak, into this heritage of experience, the self has first to develop within the social process in which this heritage is involved (Mead, 1934, p. 143).

Mere organic sensations of which the individual is aware and which he experiences do not constitute self-consciousness. Deprived of human association, the biologically developing infant could scarcely develop a sense of self. "It is the social process of influencing others in a social act and then taking the attitude of the others aroused by the stimulus, and then reacting in turn to this response, which constitutes a self." (Mead, 1934, p. 142). Until the individual organism acquires self-consciousness through interaction with others, it responds only to parts or aspects of itself; and it regards them, not as parts or aspects of itself at all, but as parts or aspects of a different kind of environment from the one in general. Only through the social process of interaction with others can the self arise.

The first instance of this kind of interaction occurred, in the case of Peter Chisholm, between the fourth and fifth week of his life. Carol recorded that he "smiled at me after feeding. This was a less fleeting and stronger smile than other two times he has smiled." And again at seven weeks the record shows that he "smiled and smiled when I talked to him in a high voice." The significance of the smiling response is its indication that the infant has reached that level of development at which it becomes able to differentiate subject from object. This is the beginning of the ego.

Spitz (1946) has demonstrated that children of less than 20 days do not respond to smiling stimulation. During the first few weeks the perception mechanism is inadequate; attention thus is unfocused and reactions are diffuse and uncoordinated. The average age at which smiling can be evoked by direct stimulation is around three months. After six months, indiscriminate smiling tends to disappear. Now the child begins to distinguish between "known" and "unknown," "friend" and "stranger." With this step the child ceases to relate to "human beings in general" and responds to specific individuals in specific ways.

The advent of self-feelings in childhood is gradual. From its beginning in the smiling response, growth is normally continuous until the child has a fairly definite conception of himself as an independent person who can exert a force counter to those forces impinging upon him. This recognition, and the action following upon it, constitute one of the critical stages in ego development. When a child can say "no"—that is, exert his own force in opposition to other forces—and follow through in vigorous action, he can no longer fail to recognize that there is a difference between himself and others. There appears to be a real sense of pleasure in this recognition, for the child may say "no" to every request of the parent for a time, to the parent's considerable dismay and sometimes consternation. The height of this so-called "negativism" normally occurs during the second year of life. From the point of view of ego development, it is a positive reaction, because without it the controlling and regulating functions of personality would not be strongly developed. The ego, like a muscle, requires exercise to develop strength.

Evidence of Change in Self-Perception from Psychotherapy

Carl Rogers and his students have undertaken to measure the change in self-perception which takes place during psychotherapy. In general, they have found that successful therapy and increasing self-approval tend to be positively correlated. By analyzing the content of the conversations of fourteen patients who had engaged in from two to twenty-one therapeutic interviews, Raimy (1948) confirmed the general proposition. His analysis consisted of counting for each patient the number of positive, negative, ambivalent, and ambiguous self-references from the beginning to the end of therapy. At the beginning of therapy he found a preponderance of negative and ambivalent self-references. By the time therapy ended, self-references had changed in the case of those patients who were judged to be improved, so that the preponderance was positive.

Rogers' students also tested the proposition that as one becomes more accepting of self, one becomes more accepting of others. The same method of content analysis of conversations was employed; only here, in addition to self-references, references to others were counted, using the same categories of negative to positive. Although the evidence is not so clear-cut as in the studies which simply measured changes in self-perception, nevertheless it tends to support the proposition. What this means is that one's opinion of other people fluctuates, depending in part upon the way in which one perceives one's self. The findings are congruent with the interaction theory set forth throughout this book. In short, others are perceived in terms of their responses to us. Their responses to us in turn are in part determined by the cues which we provide them; and the latter are the product in part of the evaluation which we place upon ourselves.

One other method which Rogers' group has used to measure self-perception is an adaptation of Stephenson's (1953) Q-technique. In the method as employed by Rogers, a person is given a number of statements and asked to arrange them in piles or categories ranging from strong agreement to strong disagreement. There are a hundred statements, and a forced distribution is required; that is, a certain number of statements must be put in each category. This is done for statistical purposes in order to insure a normal distribution. The statements all refer to the self—for example, "I am a worthless person," "I am likeable," "I am a submissive person." The subjects sort them into piles before and after therapy, in order to get a measure of change in self-perception. They also sort them in terms of the way they see themselves at present and the way they would like to see themselves. This method gives a measure of the discrepancy, if any, between the self as perceived and the ideal self. In addition to the group of patients, a control group of persons not interested in, or apparently not needing, therapy was also asked to sort the statements.

The results are extremely interesting. The patients had an average correlation of zero between the sortings representing perceived-self and ideal-self before therapy. After therapy the correlation was .34. The control group showed an average correlation between perceived-self and ideal-self of .58. It seems clear from these findings that persons who seek therapy are very dissatisfied with themselves, whereas persons who do not seek therapy tend to be much more accepting of themselves as they are. It is also clear that therapy, when successful, tends to increase self-acceptance. This effect was apparent in Chapter 6 in the case of Katherine Burke and her boys and will be seen later in Chapter 9 in the case of Sally Ferranti and her mother. Because the treatment of Mr. Ferranti was not nearly as successful as the treatment of his wife and daughter, his perception of himself was altered very little.

Genesis and Functioning of Superego

Superego is the name given to those responses which in the history of the individual have been punished by significant others. Whenever the situation tends to evoke one of these responses, the anticipation of punishment evokes guilt or anxiety. These secondary responses may be quite inappropriate in the light of current social demands; nevertheless, they linger as unextinguished response tendencies, sometimes throughout life. The main reason why so many people in our culture experience guilt in relation to the expression of sex or aggression, for example, is that these tendencies have been aborted in childhood by the harsh dealings of parents supporting the cultural taboo. It makes no difference that both sex and aggression have a place in adult life; if the individual has been systematically punished in connection with their expression in childhood, he will continue to experience guilt until such a response has been extinguished.

Only in very early childhood are drives gratified almost as soon as they arise. The infant urinates or defecates as the bladder or colon becomes distended. A sharp cry, stimulated by stomach contractions, brings mother to succor the child. Not long does society permit a continuation of this state of affairs; if it did, the functions of personality which we subsume under the ego concept would never develop. Impositions and restrictions are soon placed upon the child. His reactions vary, depending upon his own unique constitutional endowment and the extent and character of the pressure exerted upon him. He will continue to express his drives, but he will learn that there are certain times when he may expect to satisfy a drive and other times when he may not; for example, he will learn to eat at mealtimes. He will learn that there are special places where he may expect to satisfy a drive; for example, in our culture the toilet for evacuation. And he will learn that certain modes of expression are preferred; for example, while he may not long continue to strike his mother in the face when angry, under certain conditions he is expected to strike another child his own age and sex.

The demands and expectations of parents and cultures the world around are quite different, even though there are also many similarities. The pattern of need-dispositions a person develops, the modes of expression he finds satisfactory, and the defensive processes he acquires, vary with the demands placed upon him from birth to death. The child does not take lightly the restrictions and requirements placed upon him. He reacts, sometimes with violence. Conflict with his parents ensues. A reconciliation between the pressures of the parents and the counter-pressures of the child must be worked out. Out of this conflict the ego is born. The awareness of the opposition of others and the successful mastering of the resultant conflict, in a manner which is an acceptable variant of group practice—this is the seed-bed of the ego system and the sub-system, superego.

Typically in early infancy, strivings are very loosely connected with objects. The neonate is indifferent to the people who bring satisfaction to his drives. Differentiation and fixation upon objects come later, as a result of experiences in which he has been forced to recognize that he is a separate entity. This entity, or object, which he learns to refer to as "I" and "me," is set apart from all other objects. Gradually the individual, as he now is, comes to associate with the "I" and "me" certain functions of the personality. These are mostly control and time-binding functions. They include persistence and perseverance, resistance to unacceptable external forces and internal impulses, initiative and coherence in striving, time perspective and planning and foresight. These we call ego functions. The ego is conceived as the differentiated governing aspect of personality.

Sequence of Events Leading to Superego Formation

The young child has to be controlled and trained before his ability to reason has developed. This fact, plus the almost universal custom of using punishment to effect control, provide the first conditions out of which the superego develops. The sequence of events is somewhat as follows: The child is inhibited in some way by the parent, who at the same time says "No," and perhaps "You are a naughty child," reinforced by a spank or physical separation—that is, removal of the child to his own room or a closet. In either case the child experiences a sudden loss of support, or love, and feels that something is wrong with him. Subsequently when the impulse to act in the forbidden way arises, anticipation of the punishment arouses anxiety, the child himself says "no," thus avoiding unpleasantness and reinforcing at the same time the avoidance behavior.

Punishment before the child is able to understand its rational connection with his own behavior is interpreted by him as a loss or withdrawal of love. Here is the first condition necessary to the development of superego. The second condition is the existence of a prior love relationship. You cannot withdraw something which does not exist. Superego simply does not develop in a child who has no mutually responsive, loving interactions with another person who sometimes acts to restrain him. The two conditions, then, are love and withdrawal of love. Sears, Maccoby, and Levin (1957) in their study of child-rearing patterns found essentially the same forces at work. On the basis of interviews, they rated mothers in terms of *warmth* and *withdrawal of love*. A high score on either of these variables alone was not significantly correlated with development of superego in the child; when the two were put together, however, there was a very clear influence on superego. Mothers who love and accept their children, and who sometimes withdraw that love as a means of punishment, produce children with relatively high superego.

Psychoanalytic Interpretation

Throughout the centuries it has been assumed that the conscience was God-given, that it was the divine guide in man. Denying this claim, Freud tried to explain its origin entirely in naturalistic terms. In *The Ego and the Id* he said that the instinctual forces are controlled through the influence of the external world by an introjection of the parents into the child. The latter takes place as a result of the threats and punishments of the parents, which create anxieties in the child and force conformity as the price of reward, or renewal of love and good will. How such an internalization of the parental dictates occurs is still not known. Learning theorists would explain it largely in terms of reinforcement. The Freudians use a more mystical language, and the keystone to their explanation lies in the Oedipus Complex. Sometime around the fourth year of life, culminating in the fifth, the child is supposed to prefer strongly the parent of the opposite sex. This preference, which has a sexual basis, produces jealousy of the same-sex parent, because of rivalry over the preferred object. Thus for the first time the child becomes involved in an emotional triangular relationship. He realizes that love has to be shared, but he does not wish to share. The emotions of love and hate are involved: love for the preferred object and hate of the rival.

Here is a very complicated emotional situation for the child, and one which is highly anxiety-provoking. If he expresses his hate toward the father, the father may turn on him and, being more powerful, actually kill him, as in fantasy he would like to do to the father. Even the mother, because she loves the father too, perhaps better than she does the child, will be angry if overt aggression is shown. The father will be angry in any event if too much love is showered on mother. This is truly a perplexing dilemma. How is it resolved? By identification with the parent of the same sex, thus aligning oneself on his side and removing the threat. Such a solution means accepting the reality-principle of sharing love, loathsome to the young child, and abiding by parental wishes. Thus the superego is born as an anxiety-reducing mechanism.

It seems evident that this drama does take place with some children, but certainly not with all, nor perhaps with most. It must, therefore, be a situationally produced conflict. Some likely guesses as to why it occurs at all are: (1) that the child, who is completely egocentric in the beginning and for a long time holds the center of the stage, must gradually take his place as just another member of the family; (2) that there is a generally heightened awareness of the world and various relationships at about this time; (3) that there is possible rejection by one or both parents at this time, especially if a younger child is coming along who holds the spotlight.

Melanie Klein (1944) has cast doubt upon the central role of the Oedipus drama in the formation of the superego, for she maintains that she has found an even more rigid superego in children between 2¾ and 4 years of age. This she believes develops from fear—either from imaginary pictures of being devoured by wild and mythological animals, or from real objects which the child views under a fantastic light. Anxiety, however, is still the prerequisite.

Piaget's Theory of Moral Development

To understand Piaget's theory of moral development it is helpful to keep in mind his ideas concerning the psychological state of the young child. Perception in the infant, according to Piaget, is fuzzy and blurred. The infant cannot separate specific objects from their context or differentiate clearly figure and ground. The thinking of the young child is characterized by an inability to see essential relationships; contiguity or juxtaposition, rather than integration, is the rule of association. Enumeration, rather than interpretation, prevails. This kind of thinking Piaget calls "syncretism."

The infant shows the same vague, uncertain differentiation of the self that he shows in relation to other objects. He learns only gradually, for example, to recognize his physical body and his voice, and to connect the two. The inability to recognize the self as a separate entity Piaget calls "egocentrism." As the child grows older, he becomes more and more sharply aware of himself and can make allowances for his own bias in observing; but the very young child is incapable of recognizing that there are points of view differing from his own. The tendency to believe that things must be as they appear to him, Piaget calls "realism." As a result of his realism, the child confuses what he imagines with what actually happens. If he sees something, that makes it real. There is no difference between appearance and reality. Even to think of a thing makes it real, or at least likely to become real. The tendency of the child to project inner thoughts upon the outer world, so that it mirrors his thoughts, Piaget calls "participation." The child also attributes to people, animals, and objects around him the same kind of feeling and thought that he has in his own experience. This is the process of "animism."

In brief, then, the young child has no well-defined ego or self. He does not clearly distinguish between what is internal and what is external, subjective and objective, real and unreal. He is extremely suggestible, completely dominated by adults and older children. His perspective is limited to his own viewpoint, and he assumes that things must be the way they appear to be.

In studying the moral development of the child, Piaget (1932) made it clear that he was interested in the child's verbalization of moral judgment, rather than the practice of morality. His method was simple and direct. He observed and questioned children of various ages. In his investigations he concentrated on three general areas: (1) an analysis of the consciousness of the rules of a social game (marbles) and their application; (2) children's reactions to the moral rules laid down for them by adults; (3) the ideas of justice displayed in the relations of children to each other.

Piaget was aware of the danger in his method, namely, that of causing the child to say what he, the investigator, wanted him to say. He believed, however, that a sufficient safeguard would be provided by the collaboration and checking of other independent investigators.

In infancy the child's behavior is purely motor, limited only by his level of physical development. Rules and laws do not exist as such. He does, however, perceive a certain regularity in things. Day follows night, he eats and sleeps according to some schedule, mother comes and goes more or less regularly, and so on. When he is given a new toy, such as a rattle to play with, his behavior is at first adaptive and exploratory. He discovers what can be done with the new object and proceeds to assimilate it into his existing knowledge and experience. When adaptation and assimilation of the new object are complete, his behavior in regard to this

object becomes relatively fixed or ritualized to conform to his precon-
ceived notions of regularity. Behavior in this early period is motor and
individual, and the rules are motor rules. The child handles objects according to his desires and motor habits. Simple individual regularity prevails. If, by chance, he encounters real rules of a game as played by older
children, these are not considered to be coercive; they are received as
interesting examples to be imitated, rather than as obligatory realities.

With the development of language there comes intervention by adults
and older children. Contact with others brings from outside the example
of codified rules. This external constraint, operating upon the child whose
ego is not yet developed, produces egocentric behavior, which is often
misunderstood as deliberate disobedience. The child imitates others in
play, but interprets the rules of the game in his own fashion—this because he still cannot differentiate what comes from outside from what
originates within himself. Although he may indulge in parallel play, there
is no psychological interaction and no attempt to win over the other child.
Everyone wins according to his own understanding of the game.

The question arises, how does the child feel about rules and regula-
tions at this stage, and to what point has his moral judgment developed?
The child of three or four is saturated with adult rules, explains Piaget.
His universe is dominated by the idea that things are as they ought to
be, that everyone's actions conform to laws which are both physical and
moral. Universal order prevails. Revelation of the "rules" of the game as
played by his seniors is immediately incorporated into his universe; such
rules are felt from the first to be something obligatory and sacred. The
child has no conception of his own ego. External constraint works upon
him, and he distorts its influence in terms of his subjectivity; but he does
not distinguish the part played by his subjectivity from that played by
the environmental pressure. Rules, therefore, seem to him external and of
transcendental origin, although he often fails to put them into practice.

From the moment the child receives from his parents a system of commands, rules and the world order itself seem to him to be morally necessary. This situation is what Piaget refers to as the "morality of duty,"
based on unilateral respect. An important characteristic of the morality
of duty is moral realism. This, according to Piaget, is the tendency of the
child to regard duty and the value attaching to it, as self-subsistent and
independent of the mind, imposing itself regardless of circumstances.
Piaget distinguishes three features of this moral realism in the child:
(1) Duty is heteronomous. Any act which shows obedience to a rule or to
an adult, regardless of what he may command, is good. Any act that
does not conform to rules is bad. A rule is not to be elaborated, judged,
or interpreted; it is given, ready made, and external to the mind. It is
revealed by the adult and imposed by him. The good is rigidly defined by
obedience. (2) The letter, rather than the spirit, of the law is kept.

(3) Moral realism involves an objective conception of responsibility. Since he takes rules literally and thinks of good only in terms of obedience, the child will at first evaluate acts not in accordance with the motive that prompted them, but in terms of their exact conformity with established rules.

It has been pointed out that moral constraint is characterized by unilateral respect. This unilateral respect is the source of moral obligation and the sense of duty, for every command coming from a respected person is the starting point of an obligatory rule. "Speak the truth," "Do not steal" are duties which the child feels very deeply, although they do not emanate from his own mind. Because they are commands coming from the adult, they are accepted by the child. Originally, therefore, this morality of duty is essentially heteronomous. "Right" is to obey the will of the adult. "Wrong" is to have a will of one's own. There is no room in such a system, Piaget points out, for what moralists have called the "good" in contrast to the "right."

In regard to the child's ideas of justice during this period, Piaget found by his questioning that justice is subordinated to adult authority. Notions of just and unjust are apparently not differentiated from those of duty and disobedience. Whatever conforms with adult authority is just. Provided the adult is consistent, every punishment is regarded as perfectly legitimate. The need for punishment is rated above the need for equality, and belief is strong in an automatic justice which emanates from physical nature and inanimate objects.

As the child grows in years and escapes from the tyranny of adults, the nature of his respect for other people changes. Now he tends toward cooperation as the normal form of social equilibrium. In so far as individuals decide questions on an equal footing, the pressure they exercise upon each other becomes collateral. Mutual respect, rather than unilateral respect, is the necessary condition of autonomy, both intellectual and moral. From the intellectual point of view, such mutual respect frees the child from the opinions that have been imposed upon him, while it favors inner consistency and reciprocal control. From the moral point of view, it replaces the norm of authority with the norm of reciprocity and sympathy. As the child grows up, the prestige of older children and adults diminishes; he can discuss matters more and more as an equal, and increasingly has opportunities of freely contrasting his point of view with that of others. With constraint thus replaced by cooperation, the child is able to dissociate his ego from the thought of older people. Henceforward, he will not only discover the boundaries which separate his self from the other person, but he will learn to understand the other person and be understood by him.

The great difference between constraint and cooperation, or between unilateral respect and mutual respect, is that the first imposes rules ready made and to be accepted en masse, while the second only suggests a method, a method of verification and reciprocal control, for elaboration of the rules. From the moment when children really begin to submit to rules and to apply them in a spirit of genuine cooperation, they acquire a new conception of these rules. Now rules are codified and understood by all, something that can be changed, if it is agreed that they should be. The truth of a rule does not now rest on tradition, but on mutual agreement and reciprocity. It is still important, however, that new rules be in conformity with the "spirit of the game."

The relations between parents and children are, fortunately, not entirely those of constraint. There is, Piaget points out, a spontaneous mutual affection which prompts the child to acts of generosity and self-sacrifice which are in no way prescribed. This is the starting point for a morality of "good" which develops alongside the morality of right or duty. The good is a product of cooperation, while moral constraint leads to duty, heteronomy, and moral realism.

Autonomy is attained when the child discovers that truthfulness, for example, is necessary to the relations of sympathy and mutual respect. Autonomy appears with reciprocity, when mutual respect is strong enough to make the individual feel from within the desire to treat others as he himself would wish to be treated.

Piaget stresses that adult authority is not in itself sufficient to create a sense of justice. Such a sense can develop only through progress made through cooperation and mutual respect: Cooperation between children at first, then between child and adult as the child comes to consider himself as the adult's equal. The sense of justice in older children Piaget found to be characterized by a feeling of equity, which he defines as equality tempered by relativity. Equal rights prevail, but in relation to the particular situation in which the individual finds himself. In judging an act, attenuating circumstances are usually taken into consideration.

Here, as in the other cases, Piaget found the same "opposition of two moralities" which is the cornerstone of his theory of moral development. Ideas of authority, duty, and obedience lead, in the domain of justice, to the confusion of what is just with what is established. Ideas of mutual respect, good as opposed to duty, lead, on the other hand, to equality and reciprocity based upon solidarity between equals.

In considering the problem of the relation of social life to the rational consciousness, Piaget finds the same trends. The morality prescribed for the individual by society is not homogeneous, because society is not just one thing. Society is the sum of social relations, and among these relations can be distinguished two extreme types: These are relations of constraint, whose characteristic is to impose upon the individual from outside a system of rules with obligatory content; and the relations of cooperation, whose characteristic is to create within the mind the consciousness of ideal norms fundamental to all rules.

Piaget sees a parallelism between moral and intellectual development. He believes that neither logical nor moral norms are innate. Logic, he points out, bears the same relation to intelligence that morality bears to the affective life. Unilateral respect leads to an egocentric form of logic, or verbal realism, whereas the feeling of equality leads to discussion and criticism. Thanks to the mutual control introduced by criticism, spontaneous conviction and blind faith are suppressed.

It is generally recognized that Piaget considers the child's mind to be qualitatively different from that of an adult. The question may arise—how can this idea be reconciled with the obvious continuity of growth? In answer, Piaget points out that there is an adult in every child, and a child in every adult. There exist in the child certain attitudes and beliefs which intellectual development will more and more tend to eliminate (realism, egocentrism). There are others which will acquire more and more importance (manifested in cooperation with equals). These are not derived from each other; indeed, they are partly antagonistic. Proper growth and development bring simply a change in the relative proportions of these variables.

Stages in Development

Four stages in the practice or application of rules were noted by Piaget by actually playing with children of different ages and observing how they applied the rules.

1. Motor and individual. Up to 5. Child handles marbles according to his desires and motor habits. Simple individual regularity. Adjustment and assimilation. Child does what he is able to do.

2. Egocentric stage. Age 2–5. Child receives from outside the example of codified rules. He imitates others but still plays by himself—psychologically, at least. No attempt is made to win over another; some contact with others is needed.

3. Stages of incipient cooperation. Age 7–8. Child now tries to win. Conditions of mutual control and unification of rules arise. Ideas of rules are vague.

4. Codification of rules. Details fixed. Rules known to all. Age 9–12 approximately.

Three stages in the consciousness of rules were ascertained by questioning.

1. Motor period and first half of egocentric stage. Rules not coercive. Received as interesting examples rather than obligatory realities. Child seems aware of "regularity."

2. Middle of egocentric to middle of cooperating stage. Rules sacred

and untouchable, emanating from adults and lasting forever. Suggested alteration a transgression.

3. Last half of cooperating stage and whole of last stage (codification period). Rule a law due to mutual consent. May be altered by majority approval. New rule must be in conformity with "spirit of the game" or reciprocity. Some interest in rules for their own sake.

Adult Rational Codes

Piaget's studies provide a basis for understanding the adult rational moral code. Not all socialized behavior results from punishment; rather, cooperation and a morality of respect characterize the adult rational moral code. Here we find a diminished prestige of authority. Mutual respect supersedes authority and domination from others. Rules, which are valid only if agreed upon, are maintained only after empirical testing and common consent.

The rational moral code is a function of the ego, not the superego. The superego by definition refers to those responses which have been punished in the history of the individual. Such responses, or even impulses or fantasies of such responses, evoke guilt and anxiety. Because the superego is rooted in experiences which by and large are beyond awareness, it is very difficult to modify. The rational moral code (sometimes called the adult conscience), on the other hand, is a product of conscious plans, intentions, and goals, subject to modification as these latter change. It is not unusual indeed, for the adult moral code and the superego to be at variance, thus producing conflict. Such conflict and the attendant guilt and anxiety have to be tolerated if one's actions are to be freed from the shackles of the superego.

In the next chapter we will present the history of an adolescent girl whose superego was not well-developed enough to sustain her in the face of internal desires and external stimulations. She had not yet come to any firm conclusions about a rational code to guide her conduct either. The result was that her behavior brought extreme distress to herself, as well as to other people.

Suggested Readings

Aichhorn, August. *Wayward Youth*. New York: Viking, 1935.
Two chapters, "The Meaning of the Reality Principle in Social Behavior" and "The Significance of the Ego-Ideal in Social Behavior," discuss the ego of the delinquent child from the point of view of the conditions leading to delinquent behavior. Aspects of treatment are also discussed.

Bettelheim, Bruno. "Individual and Mass Behavior in Extreme Situations." *Journal of Abnormal Social Psychology*, 1943, *38*, 417–452.
Breakdown of the ego and identification with the aggressor are discussed. The setting: conditions of extreme provocation in two Nazi concentration camps.

Erikson, E. H. *Childhood and Society*. New York: Norton, 1950.
   Excellent discussion of ego-identity as well as a reconsideration of the theory of
   infantile sexuality.

Freud, Anna. *The Ego and the Mechanisms of Defense*. New York: International
   Universities Press, 1946.
   A very important contribution. A new direction in the concept of individual re-
   sponsibility for defenses against anxiety is set forth.

Freud, S. *The Ego and the Id*. London: The Hogarth Press, 1927.
   Here Freud discusses the structure of the personality.

Sherif, M. and Cantril, H. *The Psychology of Ego Involvements*. New York, Wiley,
   1947.
   The ego is discussed as an attitude. Very critical of psychoanalytic theory.

Symonds, P. C. *The Ego and the Self*. New York: Appleton-Century-Crofts, 1951.
   A review of contemporary theories of ego and self.

9

A CASE STUDY OF AN ADOLESCENT CRISIS

The low-slung, rebuilt car comes to an abrupt stop at the curb in front of Sally's house. Bill, a nineteen-year-old, recently graduated from high school, leans on the horn and blatantly announces his arrival to the entire neighborhood.

The setting is typical of many middle-class suburbs in American towns across the nation. Lots are neatly laid out in small plots, separated by shrubbery or small picket fences. Lawns are trim. Most of the houses are frame, styled after the architectural pattern of a generation ago, although here and there can be seen trends toward the modern style. There is an air of respectability devoid of primness. Every house bears a television aerial, and in every yard there is a good car, none over ten years old. A good deal of pride is invested in these cars; both men and women can be seen on occasion washing and polishing in front of the garage.

The people who live on the street are people who have found their niches in life and are more or less comfortably settled into them. The families vary from two to five or six; large families, such as many of them had grown up in, tend to be frowned upon as being "lowbrow." Mr. Jones is a bank clerk, Mr. Gingold works for his uncle in a clothing store, Mr. Brown is an electrician, Mr. Peifer teaches in the local high school, Mr. Ferranti, Sally's father, is a bank teller. The wives of about half of these men work full or part time at various jobs outside their homes. Mrs. Ferranti currently is not working, although previously she has been employed in a canning factory and as a waitress in a first-class restaurant. She likes to work, and she misses the extra income; she is eager to take another job as soon as she can.

It is just supper-time. Mr. Peifer is mowing his lawn, wondering why he has not been called in to eat. No one else is in sight as Bill drives up and blows his horn. Mr. Peifer looks up momentarily from his work to see what is going on. In a few seconds the Ferranti screen door bursts open and Sally comes running down the steps. "Hi, Bill," she says, as she comes to rest with her head and shoulders leaning over the door into Bill's car.

Sally is fifteen—dark-skinned, plump, and rather well-proportioned, except that her nose is a trifle large. She is physically mature. Her full, dark, wavy hair is worn loosely, hanging down almost to her shoulders. She is wearing bobby sox, saddle oxfords, plain but not unattractive skirt, and bright red sweater. Her deep brown, mirthless eyes bespeak at once a sad wisdom and alert anticipation of uncertain danger. When she speaks, her voice is soft, almost inaudible, and hesitant. She asks hopefully if they are going roller-skating with the gang or to see a movie.

Bill is brusque and impatient, "Naw! I don't want to mess around here. Let's go out to the ranch," he replies.

"But Bill, you promised we wouldn't do that next time," she says.

"So what! If you want to go with me, we're going to the ranch. Make up your mind."

"Oh, Bill, couldn't we go and get some of the gang and just ride around?"

"Not me, kid. If you don't want to go, say so. I'll go and get Carol."

"But Bill—" she protests, as she opens the door and crawls in beside him.

Bill pushes the gears into second (he has never even turned the motor off) and away they go in a burst of speed. When he shifts into high, his hand slides onto Sally's knee. She pushes it away, saying, "Stop, Bill."

On the edge of town they stop at a filling station for gas. Bill carries on chitchat with the attendant while he is filling the tank. Sally sits quietly in the car covering the lower part of her face with a handkerchief.

Once again they are off. Neither says a word. They go through rolling, brown California hills, climbing gently. The ranch they are headed for is a small sixty-acre farm where Bill's father keeps a few horses. Fairly isolated, it has but one small two-room structure on it, the caretaker's house, in addition to the barn. During the summer there is no caretaker, and Bill is responsible for the horses. He sometimes spends the night on the ranch, but generally he sleeps in town, going out only to do the chores.

When they arrive at the ranch, Bill jumps out of the car and starts toward the cabin. Sally remains in the car. He shouts, "Come on, slowpoke." When she does not move or say a word, Bill retraces his steps, goes around the car, opens the door of the side on which she was seated, and peremptorily says, "Come on out." Still she does not move, and he takes her hand and starts to pull her.

"Oh, Bill, don't—not tonight," she cries.

"What the hell did we come out here for," he spits out, "to sit and watch the moon? Come on and let's get down to it."

"Don't talk like that, Bill," she says, as she allows herself to be pulled from the car.

In the cabin there is a kitchen with a wood stove, a crude sink, and a table and chairs. The other room is a bedroom. There is an iron bed, two straight chairs, and a chest of drawers with a dime store mirror hanging over it. They go into the bedroom, and Bill throws back the covers on the bed and promptly undresses. Sally begins to pull her sweater slowly over her head. She unbuttons her skirt and lets it drop to the floor and stands staring incredulously at Bill.

When they go out to go to the car, she vomits beside the cabin. Neither speaks until they reach the city limits.

Sally says, "Bill, if that's all you want from me, I'm not going out with you any more."

"O. K.," he replies, "if that's the way you feel about it, skip it. There are plenty of other girls around."

"Oh, I hate you. I never want to see you again," she blurts out. Then she begins to cry softly as the car turns into her street. Bill stops the car in front of her house. It is about ten-thirty. Sally opens the door and rushes out, leaving her pocketbook behind on the seat of the car.

This episode, with variations, occurred several times between midsummer and early October, when Sally was brought to a clinic suffering with an acute anxiety neurosis, precipitated largely by the anticipated consequences of her sexual behavior.

In order to approximate an understanding of why Sally permitted herself to be used as a sexual pawn by a completely self-centered, ill-mannered boy, it is necessary to inquire into her motives and the social and cultural conditions surrounding her. Sally did not enjoy these sexual escapades in any physical sense; she had never experienced an orgasm. Morally she was horrified at what she was doing; she was in mortal fear. Socially she was oppressed with terror lest her delinquencies become known and she be institutionalized. Why then did she continue to associate with Bill?

No behavior is isolated, truncated from its motivational roots. At the same time it is not easy to unravel these roots from the nexus of social-psychological forces of the contemporary scene with which they are entwined. Thus we must concentrate on the main themes. Probably the most fruitful source of dynamic influences in a person's life—particularly before that person has separated himself emotionally, economically, and spatially from home—is the family. Therefore we shall explore the personalities of Sally's mother and father, and, to a lesser extent, the other members of her immediate family; in the process we shall hope to see how these persons interact with one another. We shall get a glimpse into the social and cultural patterns of the larger society, the peer group in which Sally moves. And finally, we shall concentrate upon Sally herself in our attempt to explain her behavior.

This approach to the understanding of Sally represents the underlying point of view developed in these pages. Personality is made up of the tendencies and powers, actual and potential, within an individual. Personality during any epoch of one's life is defined by the more or less persistent tendencies toward behavior on the part of a person in relation to other persons. Thus a long view of a person under varying conditions is necessary to spell out his identity. Any judgment, on the basis of a few frames snipped from the whole reel of life, must give at best a partial view, at worst a distorted insight. Our view of Sally covered eight months. We shall concentrate on one main theme, her sexual behavior, and try to explain that.

The Method Used in Securing Data

The data to be presented here were obtained in eighty hours of interviews. Mother, father, and daughter were interviewed at the clinic in consecutive hours, one day a week over a period of eight months. They were seen in the following order: daughter, mother, father. The three, plus a younger brother, aged three, arose at 4:00 A.M. in order to drive the 130 miles between their home and the clinic. They were never late and never missed an appointment, except the last, which the father did not keep. The method used in the interviews was largely analysis of the immediate relationship. Historical material was utilized for interpretive purposes only when it bore directly upon a current problem. The interviews ordinarily were written up during the afternoon of the day on which they took place, although on two occasions they were postponed as much as forty-eight and ninety-six hours. The inadequacy of this method of recording is recognized, as also the fact that in abstracting the interviews for the present purpose a selective bias in favor of the writer's theoretical orientation was operating. Thus we have two critical sources of error in the mere presentation of data. Perhaps the error was reduced somewhat by an ever-vigilant attempt on the writer's part to keep the biasing factors clearly in mind, both in the recording and abstracting.

A Brief History

Sally Ferranti's behavior was described by her mother when she first came to the clinic: "She cries and screams, trembles and shakes, and can't seem to get her breath; she thinks she is going to die and clings to me like a baby. She won't let me out of her sight, not even to do my shopping or gardening."

Sally's whole carriage told of lack of discipline in physical training. When she first came into the therapist's office, she slouched into the chair; her chin was lowered, and she held a handkerchief up to her face—an attitude which the therapist came to recognize as an indication of guilt. Her first words and movements indicated her great anxiety; she clutched her throat, breathed heavily, and asked pleadingly if her parents would put her in an insane asylum as they had threatened to do.

Sally was fifteen. She was born in a small city with a population of 17,000 in California, where she lived together with her mother, father, and four siblings: Annie Louise, 17; Susie, 10; Martha, 7; and Joseph, Jr., 3. Sally had entered the ninth grade in public school in the fall of 1954; although she was apprehensive about entering a new school, she thought it would be exciting to be a freshman. She had many friends, both boys and girls; always sociable and genial, she had enjoyed going to parties, dances, and athletic contests. She had never been particularly interested in school work; with no special encouragement at home or school, she had a spotty and mediocre school record. Her intelligence was in the normal range.

The following facts from her developmental history are of interest. She was a quiet, fat, breast-fed baby. Weaning, walking, talking, and the establishment of toilet habits all occurred at normal times. She sucked her thumb until she was nine. Occasionally she walked in her sleep between the ages of ten and thirteen. Kindergarten did not please her; she ran away several times and went home. Finally her mother took her out of school until time for her to begin the first grade. Just prior to entering first grade, however, she had a tonsillectomy, followed by a hoarseness of voice which lasted several years. On one occasion when she was called on to recite in class, the children had all laughed at her because of her hoarse voice. After that she did not want to recite in school; she became self-conscious, critical of herself, and convinced that everything was wrong with her. Menses began at twelve with no complications.

Mother

When Mrs. Ferranti came to the clinic she appeared thin, nervous, and extremely tense. Dark circles surrounded her deep brown eyes; her face was drawn with care. She sat on the edge of her chair, inexpensively and plainly dressed, almost trembling with emotion. She relaxed little during the hour's conversation. At thirty-six she looked old; yet her black hair, fine features, well-proportioned body, long tapering fingers, and thin ankles bespoke a past physical beauty. Her mouth was sensuous, smeared unevenly with a deep red lipstick.

Mrs. Ferranti was the youngest of her family. Her Italian parents had met and married after migrating to this country. They had died when she was sixteen; she had continued living at home, where now only her older brothers resided. Mrs. Ferranti had been a strong-willed young girl. She did not submit easily to the strict discipline imposed upon her by her older brothers, who attempted to supervise her activities. They were apt to beat her severely if she stayed out too late at night or did anything else which they considered improper or impudent. The adolescent smarted under this treatment. Already eager to get out of this situation, she met Mr. Ferranti while she was hanging around her favorite soda shop with her gang listening to juke box music. After seeing him three times, all on the public street during the daytime, she arranged with him via correspondence for an elopement. She was nineteen, he was twenty-six.

Father

Mr. Ferranti was a small, wiry man, five feet two inches tall and a hundred and ten pounds in weight. His eyes were dark and sharp, like an alert animal. His face was thin, his skin sallow from little exposure to the elements. He had small feet which barely touched the floor when he sat in a full-sized chair; his hands, though stubby, were nervous in their almost constant motion. He was shy. Although he looked you in the eye, it was a defensive, expectant look, not open, and he kept his knees tight together.

Mr. Ferranti was a first-generation American of Italian parents. He had been orphaned at five. The father had grown children by a former marriage. One of the half-brothers, married and living on a ranch, took the young boy and his sister, two years his senior, to live with them. For six years little Joe had lived on the ranch. He was required to get up at 5:00 a.m. to take care of the horses and perform other chores. This he did not like. Neither did he like the long walk to and from school, nor the round of duties awaiting him upon his return home. With no particular fondness for his parent-surrogates, at the age of eleven he ran away from home. For three years he travelled about the country, riding the rails, eking out an existence by doing all sorts of odd jobs wherever he could find work. He was never in one place long. He wrote home but his family did not insist that he return.

When he was fourteen, he came to the town in which he and his family presently lived. He got a job in a grocery store and remained there for fifteen years until the store went out of business. These were depression years. Unable to find another regular job, he worked spasmodically here and there for a year and a half. It was during this time that Sally was born. At the end of eighteen months he secured a position with the local bank as a teller; this position he had held constantly ever since. His present annual income was $4600.

Soon after the war the Ferrantis had built a house in a middle-class suburb. They were currently paying for it at the rate of $76.00 a month. They were also paying monthly for a new Pontiac sedan. The family were members of the Roman Catholic Church, but at present rarely attended services. Mr. and Mrs. Ferranti engaged in no activities together outside the home.

Psychological Tests

Sally was given the MMPI (Minnesota Multiphasic Personality Inventory) and the TAT (Thematic Apperception Test). The former profile was elevated over all with the exception of the Masculinity-Femininity Scale. The most pronounced peaks were on the Schizophrenic and Psychopathic Deviate Scales; both scores were so extremely high as to suggest an exaggerated, situationally reactive condition rather than any genuinely psychotic state. In response to a period of particular stress both schizoid and "acting out" tendencies had been pushed to their respective extremes in an attempt to cope with the situation. This "acting-out" of Sally's conflict had temporarily threatened her sense of inner control and resulted in feelings of unreality, social alienation, and a generalized chaotic subjective experience. If we level off these exaggeratedly high peaks, which appear to be reactive to a transitory state of trauma, the profile suggests that her more stable pattern of adjustment was characterized by psychosomatic and phobic expression of conflict and anxiety, respectively.

The TAT stories were full of a sense of decisions to be made, of hostile and rebellious actions contemplated. Pervading the stories, however, was an anxious indecision over the consequences of such autonomous moves. Her "enemies" appeared for the most part to be vicious, gossiping women; retaliation was left up to a moralistically operating "fate." The recurrent theme was one involving heterosexual relations in which her own role was seen as that of the woman being deserted, left, or subject to the rivalry and plots of other women. Her confidence in her own status as a woman in competition with the rest of the feminine world was undermined.

Questions to Keep in Mind While Reading the Case

As you read the case make notes so that you can answer the questions below. Before you read the author's interpretive summary at the end of the case, write your own answers.

1. What are the principal methods of defense used by Sally and by her mother and father?

2. How do you account for Mrs. Ferranti's feelings toward the therapist?

3. How do you account for Mr. Ferranti's seclusiveness and fear of getting close to people?

4. How do you explain Sally's anxiety attack in the therapist's office on February 9?

5. How would you interpret Mrs. Ferranti's dream as reported on February 16?

6. What factors contributed to Sally's sexual delinquencies?

7. Why was Sally singled out from the other children for special identification with the mother?

8. How did Mrs. Ferranti transmit her covert wishes to Sally?

9. Can you find illustrations of the proposition that a person's actions betray his motives even though his conscious intentions may be otherwise?

Seriatim Account of Interviews with Sally, Her Mother, and Her Father

The words spoken, the silent communications, the suppressed emotions seen only in a sudden tremor or a slight bit of moisture on the forehead, the outpourings of feelings released by cues not always apparent, the technical problems of working with three members of the same family concurrently—these and many other aspects of the hours and months spent with this family are too numerous to record here. In the seriatim account that follows has been abstracted the data pertinent to an explanation of Sally's behavior. The material is presented in the manner chosen in order that the reader may more clearly see (1) how the feelings and actions of each person influence the others, and (2) how the perceptions of individuals vary with respect to the same event or episode.

November 3

Sally. Sally was frightened; her breath came in gasps and sighs. Clutching her throat with one hand, with the other she held a handkerchief to cover her face, except the eyes, which were downcast. She had a very guilty appearance. She said she had had an "attack" while coming to the clinic, about an hour before. She could not recall what had been going on, what she had been thinking about, or any events immediately preceding the attack. Such attacks occurred frequently; she described them as coming on suddenly, without warning. They consisted of extreme apprehension—a feeling that something dreadful was imminent—accompanied by uncontrollable crying, shaking, and screaming.

Sally's talk for the remainder of the hour revolved around Bill and her family. Bill, nineteen, a recent high-school graduate, was a "big wheel" in her eyes. Four or five months ago he and a friend of his had taken Sally out driving. On a back road they had stopped the car and demanded, on threat of using force, that she have sexual relations with them. She had submitted to Bill, but when the other boy approached her, she had jumped out of the car and run away crying. Subsequently she had had many dates with Bill. On each occasion they parked or went out to his ranch, to neck and usually to have sexual intercourse. Sally protested against Bill's behavior, although feebly, because she felt that if she did not submit to his wishes, "he won't take me out any more."

Sally said she hated her father and could not bear to be with him. Indeed, everybody in the family hated him. Her mother had told her and Annie Louise, her older sister, that she herself had never loved their father; she had married him only to get away from her own home. She had regretted it ever since.

Sally described Annie Louise as being extremely aggressive and querulous, herself as more or less passive. Recently her father had ripped to pieces a dress which Annie Louise had received from a boy friend. He said it was immoral for her to take clothes from a boy; whereupon Annie Louise, in a fury, had set upon him, slashing out and cursing. She had clawed his face with her fingernails until the blood came.

Her father had threatened to put Sally in an "institution," saying she was crazy. "Do you really think they will?" she asked.

Mother. Mrs. Ferranti talked only briefly about Sally. She said that Sally clung to her like a baby, would not let her out of sight; she could not even go shopping without taking Sally. At night Sally insisted on having the light on in her room, and the door open. Frequently the mother had to get up from her bed, because Sally was crying or openly calling her.

Most of the hour, however, Mrs. Ferranti talked about herself. She described how she had eloped at nineteen to escape an intolerable home situation. Her brothers had been unspeakably cruel to her. She did not love "him," referring to her husband, when she married him. She had seen him only three times, and then on the public street, before they were married. "That man won't do a thing around the house. When he comes home, he just goes to sleep until supper." She described him as having a violent temper. "When he gets mad, he just throws vases or chairs or anything he can get his hands on." The only thing about which she had no complaint was that he had always been a good provider. But he did nothing else to please her. They never went anywhere together, not even across the street to visit neighbors. "And I have never got any satisfaction from him. He says it's because I'm cold. Well, how can I get excited when I know I won't be satisfied?" Rarely now did they have sexual relations, and then only because she wanted to prevent him from going out with other women.

Father. Mr. Ferranti was very reticent. He furnished no information during almost the entire hour without a direct question. Asked about Sally's condition, he described how she clung to her mother and how she had attacks which puzzled him. He did not know what to make of them. That morning, for instance, she had had an attack coming to the clinic, but he had no idea what had started it. Just as they came into the city, they had decided to stop at a restaurant. He had remarked, "This don't look too good to me. It looks like skid row." When he got out of the car, Sally refused to go and would not let her mother leave her. Mr. Ferranti and little Joe went into the restaurant alone. Then, having told this episode, he lapsed into silence.

When asked how he felt about coming to the clinic, he replied, "Oh, I don't know. It's all right. I don't know what else to do. I guess you fellows know what you're up to." Then another silence.

About three-quarters of the way through the hour the therapist pointed out to him that he had said very little, and especially had avoided talking about himself. "Well, you're the doctor," he replied. "You ask the questions, and I'll answer them." Then he began to talk about his daily routine: how he went to the bank, got out his money, opened up his window, the number of people he served. When he finished his work, he would go home and lie down to sleep. "But I won't if you think I shouldn't," he added.

November 10

Sally. Sally talked about a fight she had had with Annie Louise during the week. The fight arose over a sweater she had "borrowed" from Annie Louise's closet without asking her. "She has all the clothes in the world. She's so selfish; she won't let me use a thing she has. I hate her."

Her mother and father had also been fighting, and that made her unhappy, for she did not like to see them fighting. She felt so sorry for her mother. "I wish I could get well for her sake. I don't know how she can stand being so tied down. I don't wonder she's mad at me. Even my aunt and cousin were mad with me this week. And they're the ones I can usually count on."

There was more talk about Bill. Sally said that she was responsible for the continuing sexual relations with Bill, but she did not know what else to do, "Because if I don't, he won't take me out." She said that a few hours with him were worth the guilt she felt afterward. Then she asked if her affair with Bill could make her feel the way she did. However, she denied that it could, because, "I have felt like this for years."

Mother. Mrs. Ferranti reported that Sally was feeling better. She had not had to get up with her during the night all week, and she had even gone shopping once during the day, although she rushed right home afterward. One night they had wanted to go to a movie, but when Sally threw a scene, they stayed home.

She had had two fights with "that man," and had felt terrible and cried all week. She had not wanted to fight with her husband; she wanted to be able to tell me that she had controlled her temper. He had yelled at her and said, "You're just as crazy as Sally." She had never loved him.

She told him she ought to go off and leave him; whereupon he said go ahead and get a divorce, he didn't care. But how could she get a divorce with all those small children; and besides, "I wouldn't have as much money as I do now."

She berated Mr. Ferranti during the remainder of the hour for his cruelty, his inconsiderateness, his lying.

Father. Mr. Ferranti said he thought that much of their trouble was over money. They had gotten into a big fight this week, and he had told his wife to go ahead and get a divorce if she wanted to; it wouldn't make any difference to him. He never seemed to have enough money for all the things they wanted. "I only make $4600 a year, and that don't go far once we've paid on the mortgage and the installment for the car," he said. He recalled that during the war for a period of about two years, when he was carrying two extra jobs, he had been making around $7000. Then he bought toys and everything for the kids. It made him feel good. But now he could not afford these things. "And they just keep after me!"

He said he hated arguments, which he tried to avoid in any way he could. He used to go to sleep. "But I don't do that anymore," he added quickly, with a note of pride in his voice. Now he just left the house; he just went away.

November 17

Sally. Sally looked better. Her head was held erect; she smiled; and she said she felt better. She was not going to school, however, for she was afraid she might get a bad feeling. Also she was embarrassed by the questions of her friends regarding her illness.

She had gone out with Bill again. She said,"I just couldn't help it, even though you didn't want me to." Indeed, she had not wanted to come to the clinic today, but her father was very stern with her and made her come. There was a long talk about why she clung to her mother; she felt safer in her mother's presence.

Mother. Mrs. Ferranti smiled; she looked happier and neater. The dark rings around her eyes were gone. Her make-up was put on carefully and moderately, in contrast to her previous appearances. For the first time she called her husband "Joe" instead of "that man" or "him." She spent most of the hour talking about why Sally clung to her and would not let her go off alone. Although she loved Sally, she also wanted time alone. She tried to sneak out of the house to go to Mass, but Sally heard her going and complained. So she stayed home.

Father. Mr. Ferranti came in smiling. He said he felt better. He felt isolated and sad, he said, when his wife was angry with him. What he had said last week about not caring if she got a divorce was not true. He needed her and the family very much. He talked about the loneliness of his childhood, when he had never felt loved by anyone. Most of the hour was spent recounting the facts already mentioned concerning his early life. He had wanted so much to have a home and someone who cared for him.

November 24

Sally. Sally said everything had gone well all week until last night, when she suddenly had felt funny in her stomach and her heart began to beat fast. She had cried and screamed. Try as she might, she could think of nothing which might have precipitated the attack. Her mother had had a cold and it was awfully hard on her, having to get up in the middle of the night. She felt sorry for her mother. She had not wanted to cry out, but she could not help it. "I feel so funny. My chest hurts. My heart is beating so fast and I'm all out of breath. Maybe I'm not normal. I have an aunt who is not quite right. Maybe I inherited it from her."

Mother. Everything was better, she said. She had gone to the store alone and the store clerk had remarked how gay she was. She and Joe had talked about sex without arguing. Although they still did not enjoy sex, neither blamed the other for the whole difficulty. She felt he was more to blame, but she admitted she was cold and unresponsive.

She and the therapist talked about her indecisiveness in leaving Sally alone and what it might mean. For instance, she announces that she is going out; she makes preparations; Sally fusses; her mother stays home. Why the ambivalence? Why does she need to keep Sally clinging to her?

Father. Mr. Ferranti said everything was fine. He even wondered if the moon had affected Sally. Maybe she needed some drugs, hormones, or something. He talked about his need for independence: nothing ever scared him; he could take care of himself. As he talked, he seemed very small. Any expression of tenderness, he said, or any need for affection on his part or on the part of others frightened him. He trusted no one. Once when he was "on the road" (meaning the time between the ages of eleven and fourteen when he roamed the country), for a short period he had a "room-mate," a companion who travelled with him. He liked this fellow, who was older. One morning he awoke to discover that his companion had fled with all of his belongings.

December 1

Sally. Sally had had an attack while coming to the clinic. She had wanted to go back home, but her father would not let her.

After a long pause, during which she squirmed, held her handkerchief over her face and looked very uncomfortable, she said she had been out with Bill again. He had taken her to his family's ranch, where he had a shack. She had gone to bed with him. She said repeatedly that she knew it was wrong and she should not have done it, but she couldn't help it. She had to have Bill, even if he just wanted her for that, no matter what happened to her. She had a date, in fact, to go back to the ranch tomorrow night. She was afraid she might be sent to the home for delinquents, as a friend of hers had been recently.

She talked about not going to school. She knew she would fail, which she did not want. She said too that she was losing all her friends, because she was not going out any more. In addition, she was depriving her mother of her freedom. She was rejecting everybody and every activity except going out with Bill.

Crying, she asked whether she should keep her date with Bill tomorrow. She thought maybe she would not, but her voice revealed no conviction.

Mother. Sally had had an attack coming to the clinic that morning. But generally, things were better. The family had gone for a ride Sunday night. Sally wouldn't go, said she felt bad; instead, she went out with her boy friend after they had gone, and left a note. This irritated her mother, that Sally had gotten over her attack so soon when Bill called. She said she did not know what Sally and that boy might be up to. She had quarreled with Joe later that evening, but realized afterward that she had been angry with Sally.

She said that Sally and Annie Louise fought like cats and dogs and that Annie Louise hit Sally. The Mother took Sally's part, but was frightened of Annie Louise, for the latter hits her mother also. Mrs. Ferranti had gone to Mass alone, and also shopping. Once when she handled a situation with Sally well, she said to herself: "This is what the doctor would want me to do." She had sneaked out to go downtown, but while there she had fantasies of something happening to Sally. She expected to see an ambulance in front of the house when she returned.

Father. Mr. Ferranti reported that everything had gone better during the week, but Sally still had attacks. What do they mean? He talked about the fact that she was not going to school, and said he thought she ought to go back.

December 8

Sally. Sally had asked her cousin what the church said about what she was doing. Her cousin had replied that she would never be forgiven. This possibility worried Sally very much. Indeed, she had told her mother what she had been doing; her mother became very angry, slapped her, and called her cheap. Sally asked pleadingly if she could ever be forgiven.

She had told Bill on the 'phone she would not go out with him if that was all he was taking her for. He had said "O. K." and hung up. Later in the week he had called again, but she had refused to go out with him. He had given her his telephone number in case she changed her mind. Although she had felt like telling him off, she did not, for fear he would not come back on a different basis. She said she would never have sexual relations with him again. He was just using her and she hated him—but there was little conviction in her voice.

When the therapist asked how Bill came to be so important to her, she said. "Well, he was older and a wheel. I remember the first date I had with him. When I came home later, I woke Annie Louise and told her I had been out with one of her friends, but she didn't seem interested." As she talked on, it came out that she felt very lonely; it seemed to her that no one loved her, and she tried to imagine that Bill did. Also, her home was unhappy; her mother and father were always quarreling. Once she started having sexual relations with Bill, she had experienced a new sense of power and excitement which urged her to continue. Even though she knew Bill did not care for her, at such moments she was in control and felt good.

She said she was angry with the therapist because he was going away for two weeks at Christmas and leave her. She said she was also angry with her mother; her mother had seemed to turn against her. Her cousins and her girl friends were likewise very impatient with her, and laughed at her because she was frightened to go downtown without mother. She would have nothing to do with them. She was certain that there would be a huge explosion and the world come to an end on January 1.

Mother. Mrs. Ferranti reported that she had gone to Mass fifteen minutes late because of Sally's objections. She had expected something terrible to happen to Sally while she was away. She felt very angry toward Sally. When she had come home, Sally was crying; she had cried all day. In the afternoon, she had told mother about her affair with Bill. Mother said, "I didn't say anything for two or three minutes—just walked up and down the floor trying to decide what my reaction should be." Meanwhile Sally was asking if she would be forgiven, by God. Mrs. Ferranti said she didn't know, maybe if she went to church and confessed she would be. As she recounted all this, Mrs. Ferranti smiled and occasionally laughed. When the father came home, she had told him; he had been angry. They had talked to Sally, who said she had told her cousin about it. At this they both became very angry indeed and slapped her and told her how stupid she was; she should have told no one outside of the family. Still Mrs. Ferranti was smiling as she related this.

The therapist told her that he had the feeling she was enjoying Sally's escapades. He asked her what she was thinking and feeling as she heard the confession. She said, of course, she felt ashamed and sorry; she had warned the girls about such things, pointing out how a cousin had gotten in trouble and had had to marry.

The therapist repeated: "But why do you smile and laugh? Do you enjoy it because you have thoughts of sexual relations with men other than your husband?"

Looking very much embarrassed, she blurted out: "Of course I daydream. How can I help it? But I never told Sally. Yes, I have thought that I could enjoy myself with another man." Then she hastily added: "You won't tell Joe I have such thoughts, will you?"

Father. Mr. Ferranti said he was very confused. He could not decide whether Sally was sick, putting on, or "loony." If he knew, he would know how to deal with her. He emphasized her screaming, her habit of throwing things, and the consequent destruction. Then he talked about his own tendency to throw things when he got angry. He identified with Sally and took her side in arguments. He was afraid she would hurt someone or herself when she got in a rage. Recently when the family had started out of the driveway in the car without Sally (she had refused to go with them), she had come running out of the house with a carving knife. Very much frightened, they had not gone for the ride.

December 15

Sally. Everything was better. Sally said she had gone to school all week for the first time since October. She had gone only mornings, because math came in the afternoon, and she was not good in math. The girls had been very friendly, which pleased her.

Bill had called several times to ask her out. At last she had agreed to sit in the car in front of the house with him. While she told these things, she held her handkerchief in front of her face, an old habit when guilty. Asked if she realized that she did it, she said, "no." When asked what she was feeling guilty about, she explained that when she went to school the boys teased her, said dirty things to her, caught her in the hallway, and felt her and kissed her. She pushed them away, but gently. She said she did not know why they acted that way. Then she asked if the therapist thought she was leading them on. The talk then centered on how she led the boys on by the way she tossed her head, smiled at them, sidled up to them, and refused to be firm with them. She recognized these techniques clearly, and said she led Bill on too, even on the telephone, by teasing him and leaving him in doubt as to her intention.

Mother. Mrs. Ferranti was depressed and berated herself. Sally blamed her for her illness; she was to blame for everything. Nearly the whole hour was spent in her asking how she could be responsible for Sally's difficulty. Then she talked about the therapist's leaving on vacation, and she said she didn't know how they would get along without him. Finally she said, "That boy called on Sally again." She had not known what to do. Not wanting to deny Sally company, she had let her sit in the car in front of the house with him.

Father. Mr. Ferranti said that he did not get angry any more. The children's noise did not bother him so much. He got angry sometimes, but he could put up with anything.

Two regular appointments were cancelled while the therapist was away on vacation.

January 5

Sally. Sally was dressed in a new sweater; she said her mother had bought one, and that she was jealous. She had asked for a sweater; her mother had said there was no money. Whereupon she had screamed and cried and told her mother she did not love her, until her mother had bought the sweater. Sally seemed very guilty over the method she had used, but said it was the only way.

She had dated Bill during the holidays; in fact, she had gone with him and a "college man" to Bill's ranch. When Bill had made advances, she had said "no" and begun to cry. A carload of drunken boys had driven up, and Bill's friend had said, "I'm going to take you home before those boys rape you." When his car wouldn't start, Bill had agreed to take her. He had driven down the road, stopped, and made further advances. She had kicked him, and he had driven back to the ranch, which was now deserted. When he had dragged her from the car, she had fallen to the ground, but he had picked her up and taken her in and put her on the bed. Pretending to be badly hurt, she had cried and begged to be taken home. Finally he had complied. She was furious with Bill. When she got home she found she had left her wallet in his car.

Mother. Mrs. Ferranti complained that everything accomplished at the clinic had been undone. Joe had ruined both Christmas and New Year by not coming to dinner; she wished she could be free of him. The real trouble was that he was mad because she wouldn't have sexual relations with him. But he was a good man; he gave her money for Christmas. Then she berated herself. Everybody said she was to blame, and she guessed she was. Everything she was doing was wrong.

Father. Mr. Ferranti had a faraway look in his eyes and was unusually reticent. He wanted to know how long they were going to have to continue coming to the clinic. He thought Sally was a lot better; her mother could go shopping without her. When asked if he would rather stop coming, he replied, "Oh, no, I think everything's coming along better. I'll come a year if necessary, only I don't quite see how my talking's going to help Sally." He did very little talking throughout the hour.

January 12

Sally. Sally spent the hour talking about her jealousy toward Annie Louise. She had everything—looks, clothes, boy friends, blue eyes, and light hair—"not at all Italian." Annie Louise often got angry with Sally and teased her about her big nose. Sally said she had started going with Bill and his gang in order to make Annie Louise jealous. Bill had brought her wallet back and had accused her of leaving it deliberately, which she denied.

Mother. Mrs. Ferranti wondered what she was going to do when she stopped coming to see the therapist. Would she have to go to someone else? Everything was a jigsaw puzzle, and she couldn't figure it out.

Joe was a good man, did the best he could. She did what she thought best as wife and mother, but she could not get close to Joe—he had a wall around him. Usually when she slept with him, she had fantasies of being with another man.

Father. Mr. Ferranti began by saying, "It's no use my telling you what Sally and her mother have already told you about." After a brief pause he asked, "They did tell you, didn't they?" After the therapist had reiterated his policy of not telling one what the others had talked about, he told of refusing to let Sally have the light on at night. She had been furious. During the night he had heard a noise, had gone into the kitchen and found Sally there with the gas oven turned on. He had slapped her and accused her of trying to kill her family. Then he had put the light bulb back in her room.

He talked about his feeling of isolation. He could not get close to people. If things got tense, he went to sleep. When he was too strict with the children, and they turned against him, he felt miserable.

January 19

Sally. Sally said she was feeling better. She was going to school regularly in the mornings and she was no longer worried about her mother's going out without her.

She had asked for new shoes, and when her mother had refused, she had put on a scene and got them.

She expressed confusion over her mother's attitude toward cigarettes. Annie Louise had asked if she could smoke in the house. Although her mother said no, later she had said it was all right. Mother had told Sally not to smoke, but she felt her mother didn't really care, so she and Annie Louise smoked in her room. This indecisiveness and ambivalence on her mother's part troubled her. She did not know what to make of it. That was the way she generally perceived her mother.

Mother. Mrs. Ferranti expressed very positive feelings toward the therapist. She related a dream: Joe and Sally had gone to the clinic without her. She took Joe, Jr., and went to the park; the therapist came and opened up a book to show her interesting things; the dream ended. Her feelings toward the therapist and her jealousy of the attention Joe and Sally were getting were discussed. She said she looked forward to coming to see the therapist.

Father. Mr. Ferranti asked, "How long will it take for Sally to get well?" The therapist wondered if he was concerned about his own progress and perhaps angry because of what he had revealed about himself. He denied anger. He said he thought the therapist was wonderful—he and Mrs. Ferranti had talked about it. Two things had helped him especially: Thinking about the effect of his quarrels with Mrs. Ferranti on the family; and the knowledge of his own seclusiveness, which he had not realized before.

January 26

Sally. Sally had a cold and looked very unhappy. She said she had had two attacks during the week; she still could not go downtown with her friends. She thought her girl friends must think she was awfully queer.

Mother. At the beginning of the hour Mrs. Ferranti was giggly and coy, squirming and twisting in her chair. She looked slyly at the therapist and then quickly away. She was like a high-school girl confronting the boy with whom she was having her first love affair. The therapist told her how she appeared, to which she replied, "Can I help it if I feel the way I do about you? You're the only person in the world I have any confidence in." Then she poured out her love for the therapist for almost an hour. She was glad she had not got some cranky "fuddy-duddy" for a therapist; he was just right, etc. The therapist acknowledged her feeling and said it was natural; that it was not just the therapist who caused her to feel as she did. "Oh, that's what you think, is it?"

Father. Mr. Ferranti wondered what caused "those feelings" to come over Sally. Last week they had gone downtown in Los Angeles to window-shop. Sally had asked him to stay in the car, so that in case she felt funny, she could come back to the car. He thought that she was ashamed of him and did not want to be seen on the street with him. He said, "It's a fine thing when you raise up kids and have 'em turn against you." The therapist acknowledged his feeling of aloneness.

February 2

Sally. The conversation centered around her jealousy toward Annie Louise. She started by saying her mother liked Annie Louise better. This morning, getting out of the car, mother had asked Sally how her hair looked. Sally had replied, "Oh, I don't know. All right, I guess." Her mother had retorted, "That's why I don't like you as well as Annie Louise. You never talk to me."

Mother. Mrs. Ferranti was fidgety and uncomfortable, saying she couldn't help feeling as she did toward the therapist. She could not look him in the eye. Finally she stopped talking and blurted out, "Oh, I might just as well tell you—you probably know it anyway. How else would you know that my life with Joe wasn't right?" She then told of an extramarital affair she had had when she was twenty-one and had already had one child. The experience had been very satisfying. She felt quite guilty and said, "You won't tell Joe?" When asked if she was reminded of this affair because of her feelings toward the therapist, she said, yes, if she had not felt that way toward him, she could not have told him.

Father. Mr. Ferranti continued talking about how isolated he felt. He said he thought Sally ought to go out more, so she would have things to talk about, like Annie Louise. He could not talk to Sally. She just snarled at him and answered him uncivilly. He in turn snarled back. He felt estranged from her, but would like to get closer.

February 9

Sally. Sally, anxious and disturbed, had had two attacks during the week. The first had occurred Saturday night after she had learned that a little girl whom she knew had died, and after she had heard much talk about the recent atomic bomb explosions. She had felt that she was going to die. The second attack had occurred when her mother was getting ready to take Annie Louise to see her boy friend at a nearby army camp. While talking she felt as if she were "tightening up" inside, and she clutched her body in the region of the solar plexus.

Her associations during the hour were as follows: She recalled that the therapist had once said she did not love Bill but went with him only because he was a member of Annie Louise's set and in her eyes a "big wheel." She hated Annie Louise and her mother. Last week her mother had said she liked Annie Louise better. Moreover, last week the therapist had twice called her Annie Louise (these were slips of tongue which actually occurred), and it made her angry. Mother had treated her pretty badly recently and she blamed the therapist for it, because she thought he had told her mother not to baby her by staying with her all the time.

In connection with death, she recalled an incident when she was eleven. Annie Louise and another girl had been talking about death and had frightened her. She had gone to her room and cried. When she was younger, she had thought that when people died they just left you, went away, and you never saw them again. She thought she was going to die. She didn't know what would happen to her. She was frightened.

Bill had come up in a new car—"real snappy." She really liked him, even though she did not love him. She was knitting some socks for him, but little Joe, her brother, took out all the needles. She had been furious with the youngster and started beating him and slapping his face. Although he did not cry, she had burst into tears. Another boy ("he's awfully cute") had called on her and she had gone out with him, but she was uneasy and unhappy with him. She did not like him as well as she did Bill.

She asked what caused her attacks. When asked if she saw any relation between what she had been talking about and her attacks, she said she did not.

The therapist then interpreted. He reminded her that death meant separation from people, being isolated and alone. She had felt unloved by her mother, Annie Louise, and Bill. She had reacted to this by being very angry and wanting to hurt, even kill those whose love she wanted. This reaction, however, removed her further from the objects of her affection and also made her feel very guilty. Psychic separation was like death to her, and death meant unknown terrors.

She accepted this interpretation as valid and said that sometimes she felt completely withdrawn into herself. At such times she could not even hear people talk.

Suddenly she clutched her stomach with her right hand and held her head in her left. She turned pale, looked frightened and breathed hard. She squirmed and moaned. She reported terrific pain in her head and a feeling of nausea.

Mother. Mrs. Ferranti said, "I get so mad with Sally when she has one of those attacks and accuses me of being to blame for it." During the week she had wanted to take Annie Louise to a nearby town to see her boy friend, but Sally had screamed and yelled so hard in protest that she could not go. Mrs. Ferranti had just sat down and wept. When Joe told her that she was just as crazy as Sally, she had been furious and had got in the car and gone off alone for two hours. "Maybe I am crazy to live with him," she said. "The only reason I do is because of the children." Joe made her angry also because of the way he spoiled Sally by giving her money. Then she added, "I don't have money like that to give her."

She said that she could not bear to be alone; she had to have people around to talk to. When she was alone, her thoughts bothered her, for she kept thinking about having an affair with some man. In order to prevent these fantasies she kept herself busy doing things, anything, like polishing the car even though it did not need it.

Father. Mr. Ferranti, worried about Sally's attacks during the week, thought maybe she ought to have some pills. He also felt she ought to be sent away for a month or two to her aunt's to separate her from her mother. She was too dependent on her mother, and her mother gave in to her too easily. Mother had blamed him during the week for one of Sally's attacks because he had given in to her. When Sally had asked him for twenty-five cents, he had given her fifty cents. Mrs. Ferranti had felt that this spoiled Sally and only made her demand more. He said he just felt confused. He and Mrs. Ferranti had had an argument and she had left home for several hours. But he would not ask her where she had gone. She was angry for two days, so he just did not come home after work. Why did she have to stay mad? He got over things like that quickly. Their personalities were just different—like fire and water. He tried to do the best he could, but everything got all mixed up.

February 16

Sally. Sally blocked a good deal in her speech; she would start to say something and then stop. The therapist told her he felt she did not trust him as she had previously. She stammered out that she wondered what he had told her mother. It seemed to her as if her mother knew everything she told him. They discussed this at great length and she said she knew she really could trust him, that she herself told her mother practically everything, and that was how she knew. Still, she could not help feeling jealous of her mother.

She then talked about going to visit her married cousin, and how she had got sick when the cousin talked about the intimacies of married life— so sick she had had to leave. She had been both curious and repelled by the conversation, though she didn't think other girls would feel that way.

Mother. Mrs. Ferranti's first comment upon entering the office was: "It would have to be this office today." The office being used was not the usual one but the one used on two previous occasions. When asked what she meant by that statement, she replied that she had had a dream last night involving this particular office. "I was sitting in this chair," she said, "and you were sitting there with your hands folded, looking rather sad.

I was sad too. I looked on the desk and there were papers with writing on them—paragraphs. You had written down all that I had told you. Suddenly the door opened and a nurse came in with a hypodermic needle on a tray. She said, 'Here is what you wanted.' Then I jumped up and ran out and hid in a closet with lots of clothes." At this point she had wakened, feeling very frightened.

She said the hypodermic needle in the dream meant nothing to her— "A hypodermic needle is for sticking people, and you certainly wouldn't do that to me." To the closet and the clothes she associated the need for more clothes and the need for a trip, a rest. She stammered and blocked frequently. She said she did not care if the therapist did write down what she told him; she could still trust him. She spoke again of how her thoughts bothered her when she was alone; in order not to have time to think, she engaged in furious activity.

The therapist asked her if her daydreams included sexual fantasies directed toward him. She shrugged her shoulders and said: "Daydreams are no good—a waste of time."

Father. Mr. Ferranti said that Sally was much better. "Only she doesn't go out of the house, except to go to school." Her mother babied her too much, he thought.

He wondered what the therapist did with Sally. Did he let her just talk as he did, or did he give her advice? When asked if he was curious about what went on between Mrs. Ferranti and Sally and the therapist, he said, "Yes, but I didn't ask 'em." Did he think they were getting something he wasn't? "It didn't matter, if it was good for Sally."

February 23

Sally. Sally talked more about death, and why she thought she was going to die. Her associations were as follows: Someone had told her the world was coming to an end. She hated Annie Louise and was jealous of her; she was so much cuter. Her home was so unhappy; she wanted to escape from it. She had thought of running away. She had thought Bill might provide an escape, but her experience with him had only made her feel guilty. She had been afraid to start high school, but wanted to now, because she thought freshman year would be fun. Mother had urged her to stay home so she could work, but she had refused. It made her mad for her mother to suggest such a thing. She was very angry with her mother and wanted to pay her back. Mother hated her—she had always hated her. Only this week Mother had said, "I guess I'll never get rid of you. You'll never marry." Mother was very unhappy, and Sally felt responsible somehow for her unhappiness. But not really; it was really her father's fault. They did not love each other. She had wondered to herself whether, if she were out of the way—if she should die—her mother would be happier. She wished she could be prettier, so people would like her better. She had thought when she was younger that her mother might like her better if she were pretty. Now she thought boys might like her better if she were pretty like Annie Louise.

Mother. Mrs. Ferranti reported that Sally was much better. She herself had had an argument with Joe and refused to sleep with him. He had said she was crazy. Next night he had had his way, but she did not cry as previously she had on such occasions.

She and Joe had talked about divorce again, and he had told her to go ahead and get one. She really wanted to be rid of him, but didn't see how it could be done.

Father. Mr. Ferranti discussed his belief in fatalism. Maybe the moon affects people, he thought. But the moon was full now, and Sally had not had an attack in several weeks. He said that a man can't do anything for himself; he just has to take what comes. Talking does no good. When his feeling of dissatisfaction with what he had received at the clinic was discussed, he grinned and said, "Oh, I think you're doing O. K. Sally is getting better. At least it's as good as giving pills. I know a lady's been taking pills for ten years, and she ain't well yet."

March 2

Sally. Sally said that her mother and father had been quarreling again and she felt badly about it. Once, some time ago, after they had been fighting, her father told her that her mother had been sexually loose before marriage and that she was no good. Sally would not believe it and hated her father for saying it. Subsequently, when her mother had opposed her in something, she had threatened to tell Annie Louise. Afterwards she had hated herself for having made this threat. She didn't really believe it, anyway.

Sally said she had been out in the woods with Bill during the week, and he kept saying, "Let's get down to it." She hated him for saying such things and herself for letting him. She just couldn't help it. She had bawled him out and made him take her home. Bill was going into the Army soon, and he wanted her to go to the ranch with him once more. Then she talked about how excited she got when Bill held her in his arms. When asked if she felt more inclined to have sexual relations with Bill after her parents had been quarreling, she said she did.

She and the therapist talked about her feeling of isolation and sadness when her parents quarreled; this, plus her sexual impulse, constituted two factors which contributed to her attempts to convince herself that it would be all right to go to the ranch with Bill once more.

Mother. Mrs. Ferranti reported that she had had another dream about the therapist in which she was dancing with a tall man. She said she couldn't help it if she dreamed of the therapist, but for him not to get conceited; he wasn't the only man she dreamed about—this was said in a teasing way. She said that dreams don't mean anything, anyway.

She said that the real trouble was Joe was so short—she always said she would not marry a short man. How could she get excited about a little guy like Joe? He was like a little rabbit; when she slept with him she felt as if she were going to bed with her little brother.

Father. Mr. Ferranti reported Sally was doing pretty well—no outbursts for several weeks. Still, she didn't go out; just sat in her room and listened to the radio. Moreover, she had to have a light on at night still. She slept alone. Annie Louise and Susie (the ten-year-old) slept together; the two youngest children slept in the parents' room.

March 9

Sally. Sally reported that she had "felt funny" twice during the week, "like something was going to happen." On one occasion she had been at school, sitting alone with her friends in an adjacent room. She had been just thinking, but did not remember what. Her friends, coming in laughing and giggling, had told her to go look at another girl friend. She had gone out and seen the girl with her dress pulled up onto an ironing board, drying a wet spot. Sally did not understand why everybody giggled so, but she remembered that they had been teasing this girl about what would happen if a boy should come in. On another occasion all the girls had gone into the "Home Ec" room and pulled up their dresses in order to pull their sweaters down; they had discovered a boy sitting there watching them.

The other time she had "felt funny" was at home, when she was alone thinking. Asked what she was thinking about, she said, "I don't know." The therapist smiled and said he had a feeling she remembered more than she was saying. Whereupon she replied, "You don't believe me." Then she spent a long time talking about how she deceived the dean of girls at school and how she got around her mother and other people to accomplish her ends.

Mother. Mrs. Ferranti spoke of her concern about lying to Sally when she went out. She told Sally she would be back in half an hour, when she knew well that she would not. But if she did not lie, Sally would not let her go; if she stayed home, Joe would nag her. She thought Sally was deceiving her about getting out of school early, for she never brought home an excuse slip. She herself was feeling much better, and Sally too was better. It was a good home, except for Joe.

She felt that maybe the therapist was more interested in Sally than in her, but that was all right—Sally was the patient.

Father. Mr. Ferranti wondered why Sally would not go to the movies and church any more, and why she would not let her mother go. He thought maybe she was punishing her mother, although he did not know why.

March 16

Sally. Sally discussed being frightened when her mother had gone out one evening during the week. Mother had told her she would be gone only half an hour, but Sally knew she was lying. She could not understand why she should be so afraid, nor why she was also afraid to go to parties. She used to love them. When questioned about what went on at parties, she said they danced and kidded. Then she told about "stealing" the boy friend of one of her friends once at a party. She had no difficulty attracting him, but she had felt sorry for the girl, "because she liked him so much."

As she talked, it became evident that boys flocked to her; and so the therapist asked if she were afraid of what might happen. She replied, "Yes, I'm afraid of what I might do." She then spoke of how ever since she had been in the seventh grade boys had been making passes at her, feeling her in the hallways and talking dirty to her. In school now the boys always talked dirty. Although she liked it and encouraged them, she felt very guilty for doing so. She thought this was the only way she could attract boys. She did not go to parties now for fear of what she might do.

When asked why she was afraid to stay at home without mother, she replied, "Well, the boys could come here, and anything could happen."

Mother. Mrs. Ferranti sat down with a sigh and said, "Well, at least I have a comfortable chair to sit in!" When asked if she was feeling discouraged over what had been accomplished in coming to the clinic, she agreed that she was disappointed. Maybe Sally was better, but *she* wasn't. After continuing in this vein for some time, she then began enumerating all the things that had been accomplished. All her friends thought she looked better. She had gained weight. Joe told her a hundred times a day how pretty she was. He suggested she must be in love—was she seeing another man?

She wondered whether she and Joe should go and see a doctor about their sex difficulties. She didn't think this talking was going to help. She didn't know whether that would help either. She was looking for something magical, but she agreed the therapist was right when he told her he had no magic.

Father. Mr. Ferranti said he was discouraged at the slow progress Sally had shown. His hopes had been high soon after they started when the crying and screaming stopped. Now her staying home and clinging to her mother were taking longer to get rid of. How much longer would it take? He would come as long as necessary.

He thought there must be a motive behind Sally's behavior. "There's always a motive." But what? He did not know. She must be scared, but of what? When he got scared, he got over it, but she doesn't.

March 23

Sally. Sally reported that she had had a date with Jim. They had walked down the street to where school buses were parked and had sat in one. When they had necked, she had begun to feel sick and shake. After a while the feeling had passed and they had necked some more and gone home. She said, "You think necking is wrong, don't you? Annie Louise says you gotta do it or else you won't have any dates. I don't see anything wrong with it." She and the therapist discussed her sexual impulses and her desire, and her fear of going too far. She wanted to know why she got those "funny feelings" at home in the daytime sometimes. The therapist suggested that maybe she daydreams. She said she dreamt over and over of having a house of her own and a couple of kids. She added, "Sex is all right when you are married."

Mother. Mrs. Ferranti was apologetic over her criticism last week. Her life was different because of the therapist and she didn't care who knew it. Even the grocer noticed how much better she looked. She didn't know how she would get along without the therapist, etc., etc.

She said that Joe had been mad and had said, "What are you looking for, a man to sleep with?" He was jealous of a neighbor.

Father. Mr. Ferranti said that on Sunday Sally had hidden the car keys so they couldn't go to the movies. He had tried to get them by lying to her, saying they wouldn't go. He and the therapist discussed lying as a way of dealing with people, and he said he thought all people lied in order to get along. When the fact that lying leads to uncertainty in all one's relations was brought up, he said he had told Mrs. Ferranti not to lie to Sally about going out.

He thought Sally must either have something against her mother and want to hurt her, or else be so attached to her that she did not want to be separated.

March 30

Appointments cancelled because of illness of the therapist.

April 6

Sally. Sally said that, although she had been apprehensive about going, she had gone to a dance during the week. She had met Jim there and had had a wonderful time. Also she had gone downtown one day with girl friends, though still afraid she would have an attack.

She talked mostly about the way boys treated her at school. They were always talking about sex and what they were going to do to her. She said she was to blame for their conduct; she led them on both by her physical attitude and by replying to their remarks in a seductive manner. She realized she enjoyed their attention, but hated herself for the way in which she had to get it. At the same time, she believed it was the only way open to her.

She said her mother had teased her about how red her face was when she left the office. Her mother had said, "He must really give you a working-over."

Mother. Mrs. Ferranti said that Sally had gone out to a dance, but first had made her promise to stay home in case she needed to leave.

Mrs. Ferranti wanted to get back to work. She hoped Sally would stay home from school next year and care for Joseph; it would be better for Sally. She asked the therapist what he thought. He asked her what her motives were. As she examined herself, she saw chiefly her own desires motivating her and not Sally's interests. She could employ someone to stay with Joseph, she finally decided.

Father. Mr. Ferranti reported that Sally had gone out a couple of times, and he was pleased. Maybe Sally's trouble was with her nerves. Would a nerve tonic be good for her? The doctor had given her some before she came here, but it hadn't done any good.

April 13

Sally. Sally started by saying she had not been out all week, except to go to school. There was no place to go save Selkirk, and that was too far away. (Selkirk was four or five miles distant from her home town.)

She had had that "funny feeling" once during the week, but not so severe as previously. She had been in an English class, where the teacher was talking about Shakespeare. She could not remember what she had been thinking about until asked if she had thought of the therapist during the week. She then recalled thinking about how smart he was while the teacher was talking about Shakespeare, and she wondered how she could get along without him when he left the clinic. This led to a long discussion of her feelings concerning termination of therapy. Alternately she maintained that she felt much better and that she was in no way improved.

The tenor of her talk was: How could the therapist possibly desert her? Would there be time in the remaining hours to do all that had to be done? After all, she still had the same feelings: she was still frightened to be alone or to go out. At home and at the clinic were the only places where she was not afraid. What was she going to do? She had learned a lot about herself, enough to know that her own impulses caused her to be frightened in certain circumstances, but the knowledge did not help her to be free from the fear. Well, it helped her not to be really so frightened, but the most important thing was her fear of death and the therapist had not helped her with that at all.

The therapist then asked her whose death she feared.

"Mine, of course," she replied.

"Anybody else?" he pressed.

"No."

"No one?" he asked again.

"Well, sometimes I'm scared Mother will die."

Her associations following this were that she would go to Hell because of what she had done with Bill. Her friend had told her so, her mother had confirmed it. She did not want to go to her priest for fear he, too, would confirm it.

When asked what she thought about when she thought of death, at first she said, "Nothing, nothing." Then she said, "I wonder what everybody will say and do." She imagined her family and friends being sorry for her and feeling how badly they had neglected her and wronged her. Chiefly her mother and sister figured in these fantasies.

Mother. Susie had had the flu, and Annie Louise had had to stay home from school that day to take care of her so they could come to the clinic. "Don't be surprised if I have to stay home next week to take care of sick kids. But it doesn't matter what happens to me. Sally is the important one. We must get Sally well, and everything else will be all right. I don't expect anything for myself; I can get along." Her talk continued in this vein. Everything was the same between her and Joe; nothing had really changed; even Sally was still frightened and didn't get out of the house. All this as if to say: "How can you possibly go off and leave me when I am so helpless and you haven't done anything to help me?"

When the therapist verbalized the feeling which she was expressing, she began to talk freely about her feelings toward him and how helpless and dependent she felt. During her talk she said: "I'll be here next week, all right."

During the week she had had two fights with Mr. Ferranti. She had not had sexual relations with him for two weeks.

Father. Mr. Ferranti declared he was not worried about the future, but Mrs. Farranti was. She worried all the time. When the therapist had been sick, she kept worrying about him and talking about him. After the therapist had called, she said to him, "See how thoughtful he is of his wife? If you'd been sick, I'd of had to get out of bed and call for you." The therapist said it must not make him feel very good to have her talk that way. Mr. Ferranti said, "Oh, I don't mind. You've done a wonderful job, and I appreciate it."

Then he talked about Sally's going to school next year. He thought she should decide for herself. Schooling was a good thing for one who wants to make a success.

April 20

Sally. Sally had had "funny feelings" again this week, but she really felt a lot better. With considerable satisfaction she said she had slept all week with the light off.

She had gone out with Bill on Sunday night, and they had parked in the woods. He had been drinking and offered her beer, which she refused and threw out of the car. After a while complaining of feeling sick, he had got out of the car and gone into the woods. An hour, or an hour and a half, had passed without his return. Sally had got frightened, and when she heard a noise, she had screamed for Bill. No answer. She had jumped out of the car and run up the hill and toward home. Furious with Bill, she had hoped he would die in the woods. Then she was afraid he really might die, and her fear had mounted. She started back to the woods, got half way, but been too frightened to go farther. A street light providing a measure of safety, she had cringed near it for another half hour until she heard the car start and assumed that it was Bill. She had run all the way home.

Bill had not called since. She hated him and did not ever want to see him again. At the same time she liked him and hoped he would call. Bill carried a gun in the car. Although she had been too scared to use it when she heard the noise in the woods, she was afraid she might use it on Bill sometime; but really knew she would not. She got so mad with him sometimes that she felt like killing him, but then she felt very guilty. She felt as if she were going to die, as if she had all kinds of ailments—heart trouble, shortness of breath, all kinds of diseases.

She had felt angry toward the therapist during the week, because he was going to go away and leave her. But she didn't really feel that way toward him because he had done so much for her. He accepted her and trusted her. How could she get along without him? When she thought about his going, she didn't know how she could carry on alone. She felt sick and like going out and doing as she pleased (meaning engaging in sexual relations).

Throughout the hour she looked the therapist in the eye and spoke with a firmness which she had rarely exhibited before.

The therapist acknowledged her ambivalent feelings toward him. He asked her if she felt angry with anyone else. She replied, "You mean Annie Louise?" He said that he did not mean anyone in particular, but that frequently we hate the people whom we also love. She said, "Well, I certainly don't love Annie Louise." A little later she said, "I've always wanted to be like Annie Louise, to have what she has."

"Why do you hate Annie Louise?" the therapist asked.

"Because she has all the boys she wants and plenty of clothes," she replied. (Annie Louise earned money as an usher in a movie theater and bought her own clothes.)

"Did you not hate her before you were interested in boys?"

"Yes."

"Why?"

"I don't know."

"Do you hate anyone else?"

"Well, my mother and father."

"Why?"

"Because they never loved me as well as they did Annie Louise."

She then spoke quite emotionally of how she hated her mother especially and hoped she would die. She asked if she would be able to let her mother go to work after the therapist left, and then recognized that she had been punishing her mother by demanding that she stay at home with her. At this point she broke down and sobbed. She had suddenly realized that she loved her mother very much.

Mother. Mrs. Ferranti reported that Sally had slept all week without a light in her room. "That's the important thing—for Sally to get well." When asked if she was angry with the therapist for terminating the interviews at the end of May, she poured out her mixed feelings of love for him and anger over his leaving. She hated herself for dreaming about him, but she could not help it. If she were only satisfied by her husband, she would not have to dream of other men. She asked how she could forget about the dreams and still retain the good feeling about herself that she had gained. She thought the therapist had more confidence in her than she had in herself.

She then talked about how she planned to go to work as soon as her children's school was over and how pleased she would be to have a job again—to be with people and earn money.

Father. Mr. Ferranti said, "Sally is better. She didn't have the light on all week." He had been telling Sally that she was all well and that the only reason they were coming to the clinic now was just to polish off things during the last week or so. He wondered if the therapist would tell her the same thing and that then maybe she would believe it. Practically the whole hour was spent in discussing his fear of the future, his feeling that Sally did not fully accept him, and his desire to gain support through the therapist.

Toward the end of the hour, he expressed the feeling that he was much more confident than he had been when he first came to the clinic. Then he had thought he should have to put Sally in a hospital. Now he did not believe that was necessary; he would stand by her, no matter what happened, and not desert her.

April 27

Sally. Sally had been downtown with her friends during the week and had had a good time, although she had been afraid before she went. She still could not go to Selkirk because of fear, but she wanted to very much. When asked what she was afraid of, the only reason she could think of was that it was too far. When asked, "What do you think about when you think of Selkirk?"

She answered promptly, "Don."

She said that Don was the nicest boy she knew; she used to go out with him. They had gone to parties together and to the movies, and they had done a little necking. Don was rich. She would like very much for him to like her. She had been out with him the night before she got sick.

"How do you think you can make Don like you?" the therapist asked.

She paused, looked away, shifted in her chair, clasped and unclasped her hands. Upon further questioning, she replied hesitantly: "Like I did with Bill."

She and the therapist discussed at length her feeling that the only way she could attract boys was by submitting to them sexually.

After a while she volunteered: "Do you suppose the reason why I'm scared to go to Selkirk is because of what I might do?"

Mother. "Sally is feeling much better," Mrs. Ferranti said. "She went out twice during the week alone and several times with me and the family. Sally does not hold back now, but is one of the first to be ready to go. She does not require the light on at night any more, and sleeps right through the night. If she is asked to stay home and take care of the younger children, she does not complain. I feel very happy about Sally." She could invite Sally with more warmth to go places with her now. "It's only natural," she said, "when someone treats you better, to be happier with them."

With some embarrassment Mrs. Ferranti told about her "phobia" of high places. On Sunday she, Joe, and Sally had been riding over a mountainous road. She had been frightened when the car came too close to a cliff, and had called out to Joe: "Don't get so close to the edge, for God's sake. What're you trying to do, kill us?"

Joe had told her to mind her own business, that he was driving. He had added: "Are you crazy?"

Sally had spoken crossly to her father and had comforted her mother. This pleased her mother very much.

Recently Joe had been "bribing" Sally with money whenever she asked for it, "to get close to him." Her mother did not think this right: "I don't have money to give her whenever she wants it."

Joe was very jealous, and talked about any man Mrs. Ferranti saw, even was jealous of Annie Louise's boy friend. She said, "I don't know why he should be so jealous."

Father. Mr. Ferranti was much pleased with Sally's progress, and said he felt much closer to her. He said he had been very confused at the beginning of her illness. Not knowing what to do, he had taken her to a doctor, who had said she was all right physically; so he thought she ought to be able to control herself, and he had put pressure on her to "cut out the foolishness." When she did not respond as he thought she should, he had put on more pressure and threatened to "put her away" if she did not stop. This step, however, had made him feel "awful bad." He had not wanted to do that. Now he felt a lot better able to deal with her when a touchy situation arose.

He and Mrs. Ferranti had not believed in "just talking" when they had started coming to the clinic. They had wanted something else. Now they didn't know what had happened, but something had taken place. "Maybe you have some magic after all," he added. Mrs. Ferranti listened to programs about psychiatry on the radio, and read all she could in the newspapers. He did too.

Mrs. Ferranti was frightened of high places. Sunday when they had gone out for a ride, she had been frightened and Sally had comforted her mother, which he thought was good.

May 4

Sally. Sally had been downtown with girl friends during the week and had had a good time. She had planned to go to the May Carnival, but at the last minute her girl friend could not go—all the other girls had already gone—and she did not want to go alone. She badly wanted to go to Selkirk.

Suddenly she stopped talking. When asked why, she replied: "You were looking at me like you hated me." The therapist told her he did not feel that way. There was discussion on how she felt toward herself. She said she didn't like herself very well. She added, "But I feel much better about me than I did. I don't know how I could have been so filthy."

Although she wanted to go back to church, she did not feel she could. Ashamed, she did not think she would be forgiven.

The only way she would be able to get a man was "to trap one." "Nobody will ever love me for myself." She had even wished that she might become pregnant to trap Bill. However, she had been deathly afraid that she was pregnant, even though she knew she really wasn't. She thought it was terrible to try to trap Bill that way.

Mother. "Sally is much better," she said, "but she still doesn't want the family to go to the movies at night and leave her at home alone."

Mrs. Ferranti said she did not want to complain this week. She asked what she should talk about. She twisted in her seat.

After a long pause, she began to complain about Joe. He got very cross with her because she would not have sexual intercourse with him as often as he would like. She said she knew she was hurting Joe, and that she did not want to hurt him. He had told her that it made him feel bad not to be able to satisfy her sexually as she wanted; she believed him. The therapist suggested that his outbursts of anger might spring as much from the depreciation of himself which followed his failure to satisfy her as from his own sexual frustration.

She then began to talk about the extra-marital affair which had taken place during the early years of her marriage. This affair had taken place during the summer before Sally was conceived, and it had lasted three weeks. It was the only time she had ever "enjoyed myself" during sexual intercourse. She had taken awful chances, meeting him at all hours of the day; although constantly afraid she might be discovered, it had been worth all the worry. He was a "dream man" and she had had fantasies of lying with him long afterward whenever she had intercourse with Joe. She felt badly about cheating Joe in this way. She felt guilty about marrying him the way she did without loving him. She had just used him to get away from her brothers.

None of the children was really planned, but she had always wanted children. For Sally she had always had a special place in her heart; somehow she felt closer to Sally than she did to the others. She wondered why. "Sally," she said, "is much easier to get along with than Annie Louise. Annie Louise always fights so much."

Father. Mr. Ferranti said he felt that things were much better at home and that they would be able to get along all right after they stopped coming to the clinic. He was pleased that Sally was going out more. He had given her two dollars to go to the May Carnival and was disappointed when she did not go. He had told her she ought to make more friends, so that if one let her down, she would have another to fall back on.

He spent a good deal of time talking about how hard he had worked during the war. He hardly ever saw the children for five years. During this time he worked seven days a week, without ever taking a day off. Sometimes he would only stop after working ten or eleven hours. Usually, however, he worked from 5:30 A.M. to 11:00 or 12:00 at night. Once he worked the clock around.

May 11

Sally. Sally told of an "attack" the previous Saturday. Mother and Annie Louise had moved Susie's bed into her room. When her mother had told her she was going to do it, Sally had objected. Annie Louise had pitched in and helped eagerly. This had infuriated Sally. She had begun to cry and scream, but her mother had insisted on going ahead. When her father had come home, he gave her two dollars to quiet her down. He had asked her to leave the bed in her room, promising to take it out after a week if she could not get along with Susie. Mother had accused her father of "bribing" Sally and had been very angry with him. Asked how she felt about taking bribes from her father, Sally replied, "Not very good, but it's the only way I can get money."

She objected to having Susie in her room, because often she wanted to be alone, and Susie brought in her friends. Also Susie made such a mess, whereas Sally liked to keep her room neat. When they had moved to the new house, she and Annie Louise had planned to room together, but finally Annie Louise would not. It made her feel badly to be turned down like that. When asked if she had thought how Susie would feel about her own objections to rooming with her, Sally said she had never thought of that. The therapist asked, "Couldn't it be that you want special privileges for yourself?"

"Well, no," she replied and gave a knowing smile.

She wanted to know why she screamed so at home when she had an "attack." Without any comment on the therapist's part, she continued: "They expect me to act like that. Even Susie told me I was crazy."

The therapist pointed out that she was living up to her family's expectations of her and that she had never screamed at the clinic, even though she had at times felt ill. At this point she had an acute anxiety attack. She breathed heavily and laboriously, and said she felt dizzy and sick all over. She cried and clutched her stomach. She wanted to go home with mother. However, she sat quietly for about fifteen minutes.

Mother. Mrs. Ferranti's hour was fifteen minutes late in beginning because Sally had run over her time. The therapist apologized for the delay, explaining that Sally had had one of her "attacks" and that he had thought it well to keep her overtime. Mrs. Ferranti wanted to know what caused the attack, but the therapist reminded her that he could not tell her what he and Sally had been talking about. At that she became angry and asked how she could be expected to deal with Sally if she did not know what was wrong with her. She blurted out: "Oh, it's easy enough when you don't have to live with her. Joe's always telling me I should be calm when she gets that way. It burns me up." The therapist acknowledged her hostility toward him and her feeling of helplessness.

Then she told about moving Susie's bed into Sally's room, and that Sally had thrown a tantrum. She had been furious with Sally and would not take the bed out. She had told Sally to go into the front room and scream all she wanted. And Sally did. When Joe came home, he had bribed Sally with two dollars to get her to shut up. She herself didn't have two dollars to give Sally to quiet her every time she got excited. Indeed, she thought that was no way to treat her; and she got very mad with Joe. This led to the expression of her feelings about Joe in general.

Father. The session was fifteen minutes late in beginning, because Mrs. Ferranti had been kept her full time. The therapist explained that Sally had had an attack and that he had kept her overtime. Mr. Ferranti relaxed visibly when he learned that it was Sally who had had extra time and not Mrs. Ferranti. He wanted to know how Sally had acted and said he had told Mrs. Ferranti not to get excited when Sally had an attack. His method was "to just talk her out of it."

He told about the bed-moving episode. When he came home, Sally had been screaming and crying. He had wanted to know what all the fuss was about. When he learned, he had said, "Well, why not move the bed out if she doesn't want it?" Mrs. Ferranti and Annie Louise were adamant, however, and insisted that the bed stay. Mrs. Ferranti told him not to dare to move it. So he went in and talked to Sally. He gave her two dollars to quiet her, which it did. He thought this tactic would please Sally and at the same time satisfy her mother, since the bed could stay where it was. It looked like a real compromise. But when Mrs. Ferranti learned what he had done, "She was hopping mad and accused me of bribing Sally." He had told Sally that he would move the bed out of her room in a week, if she couldn't get along with Susie. He hoped she would forget it by that time; if she didn't, he would be in a real pickle.

May 18

Sally. Sally reported that she had been out several times during the week with both boy and girl friends, and on double dates. One night she had gone to Selkirk. She had not felt particularly anxious except once when they had parked in lovers' lane, and the feeling had passed quickly.

She said she had been angry with the therapist during the week. She hated to see him go and did not know how she would get along without him. She did not know whether she would continue doing so well after he had gone. The therapist reiterated how her illness had seemed to get her certain concessions. Although some of her behavior was involuntary, driven by unconscious motives, some of her actions were quite voluntary, such as the scene she had put on last week over the bed. She recognized both types of behavior clearly, and added: "The bed's okay now. I was afraid Susie would interfere with me and tell on me when I smoked. She came in Monday and caught me smoking, but she didn't tell. Susie and I are going to be pals."

She said she felt much more self-assured and confident, capable of handling most situations. She wondered, though, what would happen if she needed help again; she was not sure her parents would put up with coming to the clinic any more.

She asked if dizziness and pain in the heart and stomach had anything to do with being frightened. The therapist assured her that they did and discussed briefly physiological changes under emotional stress.

Suddenly she changed the subject completely and asked what would happen to her if she "got stewed." She wanted to see what it was like. Annie Louise had told her it was a lot of fun, but she was worried about what she might do if she really got drunk.

Mother. Mrs. Ferranti began by talking about the weather, about taking a walk with Joseph, and several other equally unconnected topics. There followed a long pause. When asked what she was thinking about, she replied that she was angry with the therapist. She was angry over his leaving. Then she said: "I might as well tell you—you know it anyway—I lied when I said I didn't dream of you any more. I think about you all the time and don't know how I'm going to get along without you. I don't know what I'll do. The only reason I do as well as I do is because I know it will please you."

The therapist acknowledged her feelings and said that she had come to like him because she could reveal herself in his office and still be liked and accepted. She thought this was true, and added that he had made her feel so much better, she would never forget it. Everybody told her how much better she looked, and she felt much more confident. Not all of her problems were solved, certainly, but she could manage everything better.

Father. Mr. Ferranti expressed pleasure over Sally's activities during the week. When asked how he felt about his own experiences at the clinic, he said in the beginning he was confused; he didn't know how talking alone would help. He thought Sally should be given medicine: "All the bottles of drugs in the store must be good for something." When Sally began to get better, he thought the therapist must have something, maybe some magic. He didn't understand how his own talking could help Sally, but then he began to see that what happened to him affected the whole family. The way he behaved was partly responsible for the way they acted. A while back, Susie was beginning to yell and scream, just like Sally, to get what she wanted. When he was able to tell her what she could and what she could not do, with firmness and the feeling that he was right, she had stopped screaming; and she didn't scream any more. Even Annie Louise was not so aggressive now and got along better with the whole family.

May 25

Appointments for this, which was to have been the last week, were cancelled because of an emergency which took the therapist out of town. Ten days later the Ferrantis were written to and an appointment set for June 8.

June 8

Sally. On Sunday night Sally had gone out with Jim and had engaged in sexual relations. She was very much embarrassed, saying she had thought she would never see the therapist again. She did not know what she would do without him; she cried and wondered if she would ever be better.

Mother. Mrs. Ferranti said that Joe had been very nasty and demanding since their last visit. She felt that he had just waited until their visits to the clinic ceased before he began acting like his old self. On Sunday they had had an argument, and Joe had kicked her out of bed. Although she did not feel that he would ever change, or that she would ever be happy with him, she felt much more capable of managing her life, much more grown-up. She enjoyed the children now. This summer she planned to take a job.

Father. Mr. Ferranti did not keep his appointment. He sent a message by his wife that he had a business appointment. She said he did not come in because he had thought they were all through.

Follow-Up

It has been over four years now since the treatment ceased. Several letters were received from Mrs. Ferranti, excerpts from which follow.

Letter from Mrs. Ferranti, dated July 12, of the same year:

A few nights ago Sally was in an automobile accident. She was out with some friends, and their car was forced off the road by another car. She received a few bumps but nothing to speak of. I understand she got pretty upset and was crying. They took her by ambulance to the hospital.

She was in a good mood when she arrived home.

That night she wanted her light on. She called me once. She has been all right since.

Letter from Mrs. Ferranti, dated September 10, of the same year:

I want you to know Sally is going to school. She is going all day. I don't know if you remember she used to go only half day.

She don't stay home very much anymore. She has a girl friend that lives in the next town [Selkirk], and she goes out with her all the time. She takes the bus to go to her house. Sometimes we take her with the car. Most of the time they both come back into town and different places.

She still won't walk very far alone. A few times I didn't have the car and she wouldn't walk to the bus from the house. If someone walks with her, she is all right. She walks to school every morning. We are not very far from the High School.

Once in a while she will come to me before she goes out and say: "Will I be all right?" I just tell her "yes," and she goes out.

Later in September of that year, Mrs. Ferranti took a job in a "high class" restaurant. She was very happy to be back at work. Everything continued well with Sally. No mention was made of Mr. Ferranti in any of her letters.

One year later, in September, Sally was married to a young man who had just been inducted into the army. Mrs. Ferranti reported that they were all very happy over the event. Mrs. Ferranti had continued working right along.

Letter from Mrs. Ferranti, dated August 4, over two years after treatment ceased:

I hope you are well. We are all well here. I am a very proud grandmother now. (Sally had had a baby girl, weighing 6 pounds, 9 ounces, on June 20th.)

Annie Louise is married now. She has been married since April of this year. Her husband is overseas. He will be out in December. She is staying with me now.

Joseph is in the first grade now. I am still working in the same place. It will be two years in Sept. that I have been there.

Interpretive Summary

Sally had learned that what you want must be purchased; however, her only coin was her sex appeal. In an attempt to gain affection and status, and to be rid of an unpleasant home situation, Sally seduced a boy with her mother's implicit approval, if not encouragement. The increased burden which the strain of this relationship, with its shame, guilt, and fear, placed upon a poorly integrated ego system was sufficient to precipitate in defense an acute anxiety neurosis. The therapeutic problem was clear; to modify the immediate situation so as to remove or alleviate the precipitating factors; to help the participants gain increased understanding of themselves in relation to the principal persons in their lives. The scientific problem was to explore the intricacies of dynamic interactions within a family.

The course of therapy can be summarized briefly. During the first phase Sally was concerned chiefly with her guilt over sexual relations. Almost every time she went out with Bill, she had sexual relations with him. She was extremely phobic. She would not go to school; she would not go downtown alone or get out of her mother's sight. She thought she was in imminent danger and that the very world would end.

During this period the mother talked almost exclusively about her unhappy relationship with her husband. She had never loved him, had never received sexual satisfaction with him, and did not feel that they could ever make a happy adjustment together. She also expressed a feeling of responsibility and guilt over Sally's illness, wondering how she had contributed to it.

Mr. Ferranti, at this time, talked mostly about money matters and the relationship between money and their problems. Having explored the meaning of his more overt behavior in terms of its effect upon family interactions, he modified some of his behavior, notably his habit of going to sleep in the afternoon and of breaking furniture when he got angry.

The second phase of therapy began when Sally told her parents about her sexual escapades. Concurrently she returned to school. She ceased having sexual relations with Bill and began to scrutinize her motives in all social relations.

The mother recognized her own desires for extramarital sexual experience and concerned herself with her problem of attempted gratification through fantasy. She developed a strong positive transference toward the therapist and expressed her feelings fairly freely.

The father, during this second phase, was confused and jealous. Perceiving changes in his wife, he accused her of being in love with someone. He felt alone and isolated and talked about similar feelings which he had had throughout his life. He began to do little things to curry favor from Sally. He complimented his wife, but also expressed hostility toward her.

The last phase of therapy was marked by a gradual lessening of most of the symptoms which Sally had complained of originally. She continued going to school. She ceased clinging to her mother. She was able to go downtown and go out with friends of both sexes. She had no sexual relations with Bill. After she thought the visits to the clinic were ended, she had sexual intercourse with another boy once. Her anxiety attacks were greatly diminished in number and severity. During this time she came to see clearly the seductive manner she used with boys and some of the reasons underlying it. She delved into her feelings of rage and love for her mother. She appreciated the father more, but continued to behave so that he would bribe her with money.

The chief therapeutic problem with Mrs. Ferranti during the last phase was analysis of the transference relationship. She came to appreciate, in the main, why her affections were transferred to the therapist. Her attitude toward her husband was modified to the extent that she did not blame him for all their difficulties, but she was sorely disappointed that she had not worked out a satisfactory sexual relationship with him. Her positive feelings for Sally came to the fore. She continued to puzzle over the feeling that somehow she was responsible for Sally's illness.

Mr. Ferranti became more confident of his ability to weather the family storms. He recognized his loneliness and need for affection, but he did not know how to gain the love he desired without buying it.

Dynamics of Family Interaction

Our concern here is to try to unravel whatever we have learned about the dynamics of interaction within this family that will help to explain the behavior of the mother, father, and daughter. We shall not attempt a complete analysis. Relatively little will be said, for instance, about the commerce between the parents. We shall rather concentrate upon the sexual behavior of Sally. In so doing we shall bring other members of the family, as well as the larger society, into the picture. We choose to focus upon Sally because the central problem is clear, and, since we have more information about her, we can stay closer to our data in making interpretations.

It is not uncommon to think and speak of the family as a unity of interacting personalities. It seems more likely, however, that there is a plurality of interacting systems within the family rather than a unitary system.* No two pairs of individuals relate to each other in exactly the same way. Empirically we know that no two systems are the same, whether they be comprised of two, three, or more individuals. It follows that the psychological climate of systems varies and that hence each individual within the family partakes of a somewhat different social and psychological environment. If to this we add individual differences in constitution, and the variable social contacts of each member, the stage is set for the emergence of very different personalities from the same family. Surely the Ferranti family illustrates the argument. Sally and Annie Louise were as different as night and day, and neither resembled any other member of the family. Sally's relationship with her parents was different from that which obtained between the parents and any other child.

* See Henry and Warson, *Journal of Orthopsychiatry*, Jan., 1951.

Sally's behavior consequently was different. We must ask ourselves exactly how was Sally's relationship different, and what effect did the difference have on her behavior?

Sally was different because she, of all the children, was singled out for special identification with her mother. This is a fact which was stated by the mother when she was sufficiently secure and confident in her relations with the therapist to admit it—or, perhaps, to recognize it. Sally was different because it was she to whom the mother transmitted her own covert sexual desires, desires which Sally acted out while the mother kept in restraint her own impulses. This use of a child as a vehicle for the expression of covert wishes on the part of a parent is a phenomenon well known to clinicians. It remains, however, an hypothesis. Discussion of the hypothesis will continue in Chapter 11. However, it seems reasonable to suppose that the experience of Sally and her mother constitutes evidence in support of the general hypothesis that a child may act out the covert wishes of a parent.

There remain three questions: Why was Sally singled out from all the children for special identification with the mother? How did the mother transmit her covert wishes to Sally? What other factors contributed to Sally's sexual delinquency?

Why Was Sally Singled Out for Special Identification with Her Mother?

The child's ego develops slowly, imperceptibly, out of the interchange with the personalities about him. Certainly as a young child he perceives himself largely in terms of the responses of those closest to him. He gravitates toward those who satisfy his needs and wishes; he avoids or rejects those who frustrate him. Now this interchange between the child and his parents, out of which the beginnings of the young ego occur, is not entirely the resultant of conscious attempts on the part of parents to teach the child. Were this so, there would be far fewer casualties of the learning process, for the intentions of the vast majority of parents toward their children are altruistic, if not noble. Even admitting ignorance of proper teaching techniques, we still could not account for the many failures in child-rearing unless we credited incidental—or if you please accidental—learning which is concomitant with the conscious plans of parents. "Incidental" and "accidental" refer only to the fact that the parents did not mean for such learnings to take place. But the child does not respond alone to what the parent intends; he responds to the total matrix of forces surrounding him which tend to reinforce one or another of his actions. It is of no consequence what the parent's intentions are. Thus if a thirteen-month-old baby cries out as soon as his mother has settled him for the night and turned off the light, his mother may protest a thousand times, "No, no, you mustn't cry; you must go to sleep," while she picks him up and cuddles him. He will respond to the cuddling, however, not to the "no, no"; and persist in the crying whenever the light is turned off. So, if we would discover the reinforcements at work, we must look at the whole behavior of the parent-child interact, not just at the mother's intentions with respect to her behavior.

Sally responded to the totality of forces in her environment. She repeated those actions which were followed by gratifications. We have Sally's word for it that she preferred her mother above all others in her family. In addition to her word, we have her action in turning to her mother for comfort and protection as confirmation of her preference. We also have Mrs. Ferranti's word that she preferred Sally above all the children, plus the vigilant care and attention which she showered upon Sally. That each was angry with the other on occasion does not detract from the fact that they had a strong common bond. How do we account for this? Sally responded to what was presented to her, as any other child would. She took joyously the attention, the loving and special comforting. The real question is, why did Mrs. Ferranti lavish her gifts especially on Sally?

The answer lies in the special meaning which Sally had for her mother. You will recall that three weeks prior to Sally's conception Mrs. Ferranti had a brief but romantically exciting extra-marital love affair. This by her admission was the only satisfactory sexual experience of her life. For a long time after the affair had ended as abruptly as it had started, Mrs. Ferranti kept it vibrantly alive in her fantasy. When she went to bed with her husband, it was not in his arms that she lay but in those of her lover. Under such circumstances was Sally conceived. She was the symbolic offspring of a love affair which had ceased, save in the mind of one of the partners.

This fact alone, of course, is not sufficient to account for the mutual identification. It only sets the stage. Had Sally been unresponsive to her mother's special attentions, undoubtedly Mrs. Ferranti's overtures would have been extinguished. But Sally was a healthy, responsive baby. She thrived on the attention she received, learned to demand it, and in payment returned all of her little favors to her mother. Such a mutually reinforcing situation tends to be perpetuated. Now this is only speculation, since we do not have the direct evidence pertaining to the early childhood of Sally. But extrapolating from all the current data we do have and the recollections of both Sally and her mother of former times, it is not unreasonable to assume that something like the picture drawn must have occurred.

Let us briefly review some of the evidence on which such a conclusion is based. Sally was a "quiet, fat, breast-fed" baby. She did all the right things at the right time. That is, she walked, talked, and developed sphincter controls on schedule—all activities sure to delight the heart of a lower-middle-class mother. And when the time came and kindergarten did not please her, she ran home to her mother, who opened her arms and refused to send her back.

How Did Mrs. Ferranti Transmit Her Covert Wish to Sally?

It is not enough to point out that Sally's behavior coincided with her mother's secret desire. Nor is it enough to point to the mutual identification which existed between the two. Once the child is selected through whom the parent will act vicariously, it remains for the behavior appropriate to the parent's needs to be engendered. We must demonstrate how the mother's wish was mediated to the child. By what cues did the mother give direction to Sally's behavior, and by what reinforcements did she establish the behavior once engendered?

As a background, and before pointing out specific cues, let us remember that Sally was especially attuned to her mother through long, mutual identification. Her mother had encouraged a dependent relationship on the part of Sally. Sally had responded by remaining close to her mother and, at the slightest indication of external danger, running and clinging to her. Through long, close association Sally had come to be able to understand the slightest physical evidences of change of mood or desire on mother's part. She had come to perceive cues so minimal that the casual observer would not detect them, and to act on the basis of her perceptions in response to her mother's demands.

Now what cues did her mother give which were indicative of freedom, if not command, for Sally to engage in sexual play? To begin with, Sally perceived her mother as indecisive and ambivalent in many of the things she did and said. Not infrequently her mother reversed a decision or permitted an activity which she had just forbidden, looking the other way, as it were. On one occasion, for example, you recall that Sally expressed confusion over her mother's attitude toward smoking. Annie Louise had asked if she could smoke in the house; her mother had said "no" and then changed her mind. Sally had asked if she could smoke; Mother had said "no." When Sally had gone ahead and smoked anyway with Annie Louise, her mother never reprimanded her or said anything about it. This behavior puzzled Sally. She thought that sometimes her mother meant the opposite of what she said. Ambivalence and indecisiveness on the part of a parent open the door to forbidden activity by the child, because he perceives two images of himself in the parent's mind. And sometimes he senses that the stronger image is the one connected with the activity proscribed.

Mrs. Ferranti said that she had warned both girls concerning the danger of pre-marital sexual relations. She had pointed out as an example how a cousin of theirs had had to marry because she became pregnant. With what excitement or secret satisfaction she had related this to the girls, we do not know. We do know, however, that by telling them of her own experience, she had already established in their minds the thought that one way to escape an unpleasant home was through marriage, and that love was not a necessary antecedent. Now she made another connection—namely, that through sexual experience and pregnancy one may force a marriage. That these connections were made by Sally there can be no doubt. In discussing her relations with Bill she admitted that she had looked upon him as an escape from her own unpleasant, bickering home and that she had sought to "trap Bill into marriage" by becoming pregnant. The message of the mother had been received. The possibility of action along the lines which Sally took had been suggested by an ambivalent mother. And the mother was worried. She admitted concern over Sally's possible sexual involvement before she knew of her affair with Bill. Could it be that she had perceived some subtle cue in Sally which warned her, or was her own wish projected at that point onto Sally?

If Sally needed any further stimulus to her sexual exploits from her mother, let us look at the reaction she met when she anxiously, guiltily revealed her relationship with Bill. In Mrs. Ferranti's own words, "I didn't say anything for two or three minutes; just walked up and down the floor trying to decide what my reaction should be." Is this the reaction of one taken off guard, or surprised or horrified by the intelligence delivered? Does it not say to Sally, "Well, I'm not sure what to think about your behavior?" There was no disapproval. "If she went to Church and confessed," maybe she would be forgiven. The mother thoroughly enjoyed telling me about the interview with Sally. The only wrath expressed in connection with the whole episode was over Sally's indiscretion in talking about it outside the immediate family.

Even if these affirmative cues had been missed by Sally, which is conceivable, she could not have failed to perceive permission for her behavior when, a week later, Bill called and her mother had allowed her to go out and sit in the car with him. Mother's rationalization on this occasion, as expressed to me, was, "I didn't want to deny Sally company." The next time Bill called, she was permitted to go with him to his ranch, completely reinforcing Sally's perception that her mother approved her behavior all along. But by now the conflictive forces were so arrayed that Sally herself rebuffed Bill.

What were these forces? She had her mother's open approval—which horrified her and caused her to blame her mother for everything that had happened to her, including her illness. She had a strong desire to continue receiving Bill's attention and even to marry him. She enjoyed the game of keeping him coming to her or calling and guessing what her intentions were, even though at the same time she felt extremely guilty and frightened. She was guilty because her superego told her that she was doing wrong and because her therapist had reinforced the dictates of her superego. She was frightened lest she be detected in her delinquencies and committed to an institution. And she realized that to Bill she was nothing more than a sexual plaything to be discarded when he was through with her. Thus the forces arrayed against continuation of the affair were, for the moment, stronger than her mother's message.

What Other Factors Contributed to Sally's Sexual Delinquency?

The covert wish of her mother was an important, probably necessary, determinant of Sally's behavior, but alone insufficient to tell the whole story. There were other contributing factors; behavior is always multiply determined. Certainly Bill played an important role, but by no means the most important; there are always "Bills" available for a girl driven like Sally. Before we discuss Bill, however, and other social group influences emanating from Sally's larger society, let us look at some of the other factors operating within the home which, compounded, spurred Sally along the path on which we found her.

Further Influences Within the Home

We begin with a tense or anxious atmosphere, where fighting and bickering subtended the unhappiness written upon the faces of all participants. Here was a situation which provided a veritable breeding ground for the development of protective defenses. And each member of the family contrived his own special way to ward off the imminent threat to his self-security. Mr. Ferranti alternately slept and went on rampages—swearing, throwing any handy object, breaking furniture. Mrs. Ferranti used her tongue and the eternal feminine prerogative, crying. Annie Louise was a fighter, using both verbal weapons and her sharp fingernails. Sally alone withdrew into herself and harbored her conflictful feelings without immediate expression. Only the terror in her eyes revealed the depth of her passion and the sorrow in her heart; for Sally loved her mother, and she was hurt by the vortex of bitterness surrounding her and into which she was inevitably drawn. The younger members of the family remained in the wings off-stage in the main. Occasionally one was seen in the spotlight for a brief moment, but he did not appear to affect Sally in any calculable fashion. Only the mother and father and the older sister, Annie Louise, could make Sally's heart race or stop in response to their profferings.

Mr. Ferranti was a little man who felt weak, inadequate, and isolated. Long experience had taught him to be alert, on guard, and to trust no one. Although he desperately wanted to be close to someone, he did not know how to accomplish his end. He could not tolerate the slightest rebuff; it called forth two mechanisms of defense—attack and rejection. The first, attack, was a primitive reaction such as any animal in the jungle would use when taken by surprise or cornered. The second, rejection, he had learned from hard lessons; the way to avoid being hurt is to avoid attachments. He was a little man not only in physical stature but in the stunting of his psychological growth. He could not be an adequate husband and father because he wanted to be a little boy mothered like the other children. But when he did not get the mothering, he became hostile and rejecting. He alternately fawned over his wife, seeking her favors, and abused her. He suspected her of infidelity and told his daughters that she had been "sexually loose" before marriage. He vied with his wife for the affection of his children, using money as bait, but without much success. The money was accepted, but the payment of love deferred.

Sally perceived her father as weak, inadequate, and hostile. No pride stirred her heart when she contemplated him.

Mrs. Ferranti was a fiery woman with flashing black eyes and a sharp tongue. In her youth she had been a beauty; frustration and hostility had altered her aspect so that now she looked angry most of the time. For her husband she had nothing but contempt. She quarreled and precipitated fights without immediate provocation, since she bore an immense reservoir of bubbling, unexpressed aggression. She did not hesitate to berate and belittle her husband in the presence of his children, an act scarcely designed to elevate him in their esteem. Knowing the power of sexuality, she felt all the more bitter because of her lack of opportunity for its expression. Her fantasies were filled with erotic exploits. She loved her children fiercely, possessively; equally fiercely did she turn her wrath upon them when she was crossed, or when her mounting hostility found no other accessible target. She commanded the children by force, love, deceit, and tears.

Sally perceived her mother as the strong one. She aligned herself with her mother. She wanted to be like her, to have what she had, to do what she did.

Annie Louise was beautiful, calculating, hostile, and cold. She neither cared for Sally nor disliked her; she ignored her. This attitude made Sally furious. To Sally, Annie Louise was a paragon of all she wanted to be. Annie Louise was self-reliant, tall, blonde. She had a job which enabled her to be independent and to buy the clothes she wanted; she had a closet full of pretty things. Boys sought her out and vied for her attention. She took them or left them as her mood dictated, bestowing upon them no other favors than an occasional kiss or a bit of innocent necking. She told her parents what she was going to do; she did not ask. Nor did she need to, because they were both afraid of her. Annie Louise was even a good student.

Sally was jealous of Annie Louise. She hated her for her condescending manner. Beside her Sally felt ugly, dependent, and powerless. She would show her!

Compounded in Sally were elements of all three. She knew her father's isolation, her mother's deceit and secret sexual desire, her sister's pride. She had been dependent on her mother for so long that she had not grown strong and self-reliant. Still she wished to be free of the conflict which reigned in her home. Although she had had instilled in her the middle-class virtues, in her superego structure there was a weak spot. Her mother's ambivalent feelings toward sexual expression had been taken over almost whole cloth. She was not yet personally aware of the meaning of sex, except in its transmuted forms—but she was ready to learn. And she found ready teachers.

Influences from the Larger Social Group

The adolescent culture of which Sally was a part was not different from similar groups found in small cities across America today. The center of activity is the high school. There boys and girls come from all over the city, some because they want to learn, some because their parents say they have to, some because the law insists. They come by foot, by school bus, by private car. They represent the highest and lowest of the social strata. Some are very good students, some very poor, the majority are able to keep up without too great effort because the standard requirement is adjusted to fit their output. There are clubs and societies, admission to which is controlled by a few powerful ones amongst the students. The aspiring, upward-mobile boys and girls take the cues for their conduct from this ruling clique. They manage not only school affairs, but also extracurricular dances and parties. They are mostly from the upper-middle-class stratum of the town.

There is another group, less well defined, composed of boys and girls from lower-middle-class and lower-class families who are not accepted in the former society. There are also a few rebels from their own kind, like Bill, who move from one group to the other according to fancy. The activities of this second group are carried on for the most part outside of school. They have parties and dances of their own, unchaperoned in public places, or occasionally in the homes of one of the members when the parents are away. Organized parties and dances, however, are less important to them than the unplanned encounters on the street corner. Their activities range from just "shooting the breeze" to playing pool, smoking, drinking, going to movies or watching TV, doing a bit of necking or perhaps engaging in more serious sexual play. Occasionally someone will suggest a "drag race" and a group will split off, steal a couple of cars and seek out an appropriate hill.

Sally did not properly belong with either of these groups. She admired and envied from a distance those whom she considered "big wheels," but she did not think that she could become one of them. Bill was such a one in her eyes, and when he singled her out for attention, she was flattered. She was ripe for the taking, and Bill took her. Her manner with Bill, as well as her approach to other boys, was very seductive. She brushed by them in the hallways, barely touching them with her hips as she wove her way through a group. She wore tight-fitting sweaters displaying her well-formed breasts. When she heard a remark or a whistle, she turned and acknowledged it with a sly smile and a twitch of her hips. When inevitably some of the boys began to get in her path as she came down the hall, and when their hands sought to explore her anatomy, she made only half-hearted protests. Whether Bill first noticed Sally in these situations we do not know. But it is likely he did, for it is recorded that on the first time he took her out, along with a companion, he forced her to have sexual intercourse with him, dispensing with any preliminary pretense at love-making.

Sally had friends at school who were doing as she did. And, although they were frightened, and occasionally one of them was removed from the group by the authorities when her behavior became too flagrant, they continued in the same way. Not only at school did Sally find tutors and reinforcers of her sexual activity once begun, but within her own family her cousin had done likewise and openly discussed her exploits with Sally, minimizing the wrongness of premarital affairs.

All of these forces together were responsible for Sally's behavior. If she had not also had instilled in her middle-class religious values, she would not have come to the clinic with an anxiety neurosis; because then she would have had no conflict resulting from a sense of guilt over what she did. We might have met her in an institution for juvenile delinquents, among the growing number, without conscience, for whom treatment is very difficult and whom we vaguely label "psychopaths."

10

ANXIETY AND MECHANISMS OF DEFENCE

In Chapter 9 we have seen that when Sally Ferranti's control system broke down, she felt threatened. There followed a severe anxiety attack, which she attempted to alleviate by a number of strategems. Sally did not have the ego strength to control her responses. As a consequence, she felt weak and helpless, unable to cope with the situations of social interaction in which she found herself. She felt herself being swept along by uncontrollable forces which eventually would bring about her destruction, or her isolation through incarceration in some sort of public institution. Only vaguely did she apprehend what was happening to her. But she knew that she felt badly and that she was in danger. She reacted by avoiding the situations in which she was unable to control her responses, chiefly at school and with her age-mates in other situations; and by turning back the controls to her mother, insisting that the mother be with her at all times and make all her decisions. Her anxiety arose because of a diffuse apprehension of danger. Some of the strategems which she employed to deal with the anxiety actually reduced it; thus they were reinforced and became a part of her repertory of responses in those situations which were anxiety-provoking.

Let us turn now to the general problem of anxiety and methods of dealing with it.

Nature of Anxiety

Anxiety is the experience that goes with disorganized behavior in response to threat to existence. When a situation arises that contains threat, it may be met by adequate responses of defensive escape or positive attack. In such a case there is no anxiety. But if the person is helpless to make adequate responses and the threat increases, his behavior becomes disorganized, even catastrophic on occasion, and his experience is that of panic. The usual reaction of an adult, experienced person to threat is relatively controlled and ordered. It is accompanied by only transient moments of anxiety or fear. People of unusual ego-strength—that is, who are able to sustain control under extreme conditions—can sometimes prevent disordered behavior even in the face of imminent death. Examples of such ego-strength are seen in those men who remain outwardly calm facing a firing squad and in martyrs who go to their deaths singing or praising their torturers.

The usual response of a person to a threatening situation with which he is helpless to deal, however, is disordered behavior accompanied by anxiety. The critical variable is helplessness or lack of control. A situation that produces a feeling of helplessness in one person may not do so for another person. Goldstein (1940) has shown that brain-injured patients become anxious, rather than merely tense, when they fail in simple tests. They are helpless to deal with the situation.

When a source of danger is not recognized by an individual, adaptive responses are rendered impossible. On these occasions catastrophic behavior is most likely to occur. Most neurotic anxiety is of this variety. Generally there is a history of threatening situations during infancy and early childhood when the person was literally helpless to do anything about them. Although these experiences are forgotten, probably through the mechanism of repression, the emotion accompanying them may be activated by cues in the current situation which are associated with the original experiences. The emotion is experienced as anxiety, but the cues are not recognized, so the individual frequently can do nothing rational to reduce the anxiety.

A fully developed anxiety attack is a horrible experience. The word "panic" gives the right connotation. When Sally Ferranti clutched her stomach and said she thought she was going to die, she was not lying. She was reporting accurately how she felt. Anxiety is thus the effect one wants most to avoid. No wonder that so many behavior patterns are devised to control it.

Anyone who has experienced an anxiety attack knows that it is a primitive, irresistible impulse which may leave its mark forever on a place or epoch in one's life. The word "anxiety" has become a household one in recent years. Cartoonists employ it to depict ludicrous situations. Popular magazines treat of it with authority. Friends advise one another how to deal with it or try to "laugh it off" when it interferes with social relations. The professional literature of those who deal with emotionally disturbed people recognizes anxiety as the central psychological phenomenon of our time. It is the chief symptom of the majority of those who seek psychotherapy. And yet how little we know about it. Progress in its measurement has been slow; even agreement as to its definition is still controversial. Only the experience remains ineradicable. In our treatment of anxiety we will first try to make clearer what we mean by the term. Then we shall ask and try to answer two questions in relation to anxiety: Where does it come from? What are its effects on personality development and functioning? Unfortunately neither question can be precisely answered at the present time.

Clarification of the Concept of Anxiety

Psychopathologists generally agree that anxiety is a diffuse apprehension. That is to say that the object or cue which is antecedent to the experience of anxiety is not clearly differentiated. Most writers make a distinction between normal and neurotic anxiety, and it is clear that only in the latter case is the definition truly applicable.

Normal anxiety is the apprehensive response to threat to the existence of the self about which the individual cannot immediately do anything effective to protect or defend himself. Thus he feels a loss of personal control and is helpless. His response, however, is proportionate to the threat as perceived by himself and consensually validated by others. For example, persons may experience extreme anxiety leading to reactions of panic when they are confined in an unfamiliar building with others and someone shouts "Fire!" The cue in this instance is quite clear, and yet the response is certainly one of anxiety, but proportionate to the threat.

Neurotic anxiety is also the apprehensive response to threat to the existence of self. Only in this case the response is disproportionate to the threat, and the cue is not clearly perceived. "Disproportionate to the threat" here simply means that there is no consensual validation of the threat. It is not implied that the threat does not exist for the individual, nor that his reaction is not proportionate to the threat as he "perceives" it. Use of the word "perceives" is not entirely accurate, because if you ask a neurotically anxious person why he is anxious, frequently he cannot identify the source of his anxiety. The object or event which he identifies as threatening is not seen in that light by others. Yet no one can deny that his reaction signifies the severe threat which he has verbalized. The discrepancy between his reaction, and sometimes his verbalization of the accompanying experience, and the presumed objective threatening cue as seen by competent observers, is the index of neurotic anxiety.

Fear and *anxiety* are used interchangeably by some writers, especially by experimental learning theorists who employ lower animals as subjects. Generally, however, the term "fear" is reserved for those antecedent conditions which are specific and which do not threaten the existence of the self of the individual. As we said earlier, the situation may contain threat, but it may also be met by adequate defensive escape or positive attack responses. When the individual has an adequate response to the threat, we call it fear. When he does not have an adequate response—in other words, when he experiences a lack of self-control—

anxiety is the result. Mowrer (1950) maintains that even in rats the variable of control is the critical one in determining whether fear or anxiety will be aroused by physical pain. He presents experimental evidence to show that fear is greater in rats that cannot terminate an electric shock than it is in rats that can do so. He concludes that fear is the basis of anxiety, or that we come to fear not only physical pain but also fear itself.

Hilgard (1949) has argued for separation of the terms for much the same reasons. He reasons that in man anxiety becomes intermingled with guilt-feelings, and that this is not the case with animals. Human anxiety as seen in the clinic often carries with it the feeling that the individual has done something wrong for which he must be punished. This guilt-feeling always has a personal self reference. The person has done something (to be sure he may not know what) for which he is responsible and for which he must be punished. It is the quality of self-reference, a threat to the self, which distinguishes anxiety from fear.

Where Does Anxiety Come From?

The genesis of anxiety has been inquired into by philosophers and by both clinical and experimental psychologists. Four of the outstanding theories will be reviewed. They may be summarized briefly as: (1) the conversion theory, (2) the premonitory theory, (3) the drive theory, and (4) the isolation theory.

The Conversion Theory. Freud (1920) originally accounted for anxiety by assuming that the repressed sexual impulse (libido) was converted either directly into anxiety or into symptoms of one sort or another. He saw the sexual impulse as charged with energy. This energy had to be discharged in biologically adequate channels, or, by a process analogous to the First Law of Thermodynamics, be converted. According to this theory, if a person could always express his libido in sexual activity, he would not suffer anxiety. Since this, of course, is impossible in the social world as we know it, everyone from time to time suffers some anxiety from repressed libido.

It must be remembered that Freud's observations were made on adult neurotics in Victorian Vienna. Most of Freud's patients were sexually frustrated, and most of them were extremely anxious. He described what he saw. But he went further than describing a relationship. Later on (1936, pp. 51–52) he was to say:

But I confess I thought I was giving more than a mere description; I supposed that I had recognized the metaphysical process of a direct transformation of libido into anxiety; this I can no longer maintain today. I was unable, besides, to give any account at that earlier time of how such a transformation was accomplished.

Whence did I derive at all the idea of this transformation? At a time when we were still a long way from distinguishing between processes in the ego and processes in the id, from a study of the "actual" neuroses. I found that certain sexual practices, such as coitus interruptus, frustrated excitement, enforced abstinence, give rise to outbreaks of anxiety and a general predisposition to anxiety—which may be induced whenever, therefore, sexual excitation is inhibited, frustrated, or diverted in the course of its discharge in gratification. Since sexual excitement is the expression of libidinal instinctual impulses, it did not seem rash to suppose that through the influence of such disturbances the libido became converted into anxiety.

The conversion theory of anxiety, although it is no longer credited today, caught the popular imagination and had important effects on theory and behavior for a number of years. The so-called moral rebellion of the twenties was based on the notion that frustration of the sexual impulse was psychologically unhealthy. The concept of frustration was generalized to include other impulses as well, and found ardent champions in some "progressive educationalists" and many "liberal" parents who argued for rampant expressionism in children.

The Premonitory Theory. The process of growing up and becoming a socialized human being involves learning to get along with other people. It is to other people that we turn for satisfaction of our basic drives and need-dispositions. Early in life we learn that satisfactions do not come automatically. To get what we want, we have to wait upon and please others; we have to hold in check our impulses until the other is ready to respond favorably. This process of interaction entails many delays and frustrations. In our culture the learning of social mores also involves pain, for the method most frequently used to control impulsive childish behavior is punishment. The punishment may be physical or psychological, or both. As a result, many children in our culture come to anticipate pain in a new learning situation. The anticipation of pain arouses anxiety. Anxiety appears then to be a regular concomitant of the socialization process. It serves the purpose of warning the individual that danger is imminent. It is, therefore, premonitory.

Freud discarded the conversion theory when he discovered that anxiety preceded repression of impulse rather than the other way around. Now the ego perceived the danger, anxiety resulted, and measures to defend the personality were necessary. One of these measures of defense was repression. This insight was the first step in the process of discovering the variety of ways in which mechanisms develop in defense of the ego. The danger which the ego perceived was pain which had become associated through experience with one or another impulse to act. Now when the impulse arose, anxiety was a concomitant.

In one form or another the premonitory theory is held by all students of anxiety today. The other theories are mere elaborations, extensions, or applications of it. Take Horney's view, for example. She believes that an important source of anxiety is found in the hostile impulse. If hostility is expressed toward a person on whom one is simultaneously dependent for various gratifications, retaliation on the part of that person is the natural consequence. Such retaliation, however, brings about a worsening of the interactive relationship with the valued person. The result is that the individual is punished in one way or another. When on another occasion the hostile impulse is aroused, anxiety accompanies it as a danger signal, and the impulse has to be diverted from direct expression in one way or another.

Both Horney (1937) and Kubie (1941) see this process as the repetitive core of neurosis in those situations where it becomes the chronic mode of interaction between parent and child. The basic hypothesis which they advance is that when parents lack affectionate warmth for a child, they tend to frustrate him chronically by withholding love, by outright rejection, or by some other form of punishment. Since the feeling of not being loved is especially painful to the child, he in turn reacts with resentment and hostility. This impulse soon has to be repressed, however, since it only makes matters worse. A situation of helplessness for the child results. The original desire to be loved and the hostile impulse both go unsatisfied. There is no solution. Horney calls the state that develops "basic anxiety." "It means emotional isolation, all the harder to bear as it concurs with a feeling of intrinsic weakness of the self. It means a weakening of the very foundation of self-confidence" (1937, p. 96).

Why does "basic anxiety" tend to develop a neurosis? The answer is that legitimate strivings come to be associated with a feeling of danger. Now, instead of striving for satisfaction of impulse, it is necessary to seek safety and security first. Satisfaction of impulse can come only after safety is guaranteed. Avoidance of danger thus comes to play too large a part in the dynamics of personality. When a person is chronically frustrated and a recurrent need-disposition for aggression comes to be bound into this cycle, a repetitive process results that never terminates in relief of tension. It may be diagrammed like this:

Frustration → need-disposition for aggression → anxiety
→ repression → unrelieved tension.

The situation is one in which there is a tendency toward indirect expression of the tension. A number of possibilities exist; one of them is a neurotic symptom. Satisfactory substitute paths for expression cannot be found if anxiety is conditioned to the need-disposition itself and not to particular modes of expression. Thus the child comes to feel that it is bad ever to feel angry. Such generalized conditioning results when parents are shocked or irritated by any aggressive outburst on the part of the child. These may be an attempt to check all the child's most active, energetic, boisterous, and spontaneous tendencies.

Sullivan, likewise, sees anxiety aroused as a result of real or imagined threats to one's security. According to Sullivan, everyone attempts to fulfill two classes of needs: Needs for satisfaction and needs for security. Satisfactions are desired for bodily needs like hunger, thirst, and sleep, whereas security depends upon successful interpersonal relationships. When the significant other person disappears or dislikes the child, the child's security is threatened and anxiety results. Even if the significant other, say the mother, is not disapproving but feels anxious herself in the presence of the child, the latter is also likely to experience anxiety. This is what Sullivan calls empathy, although he admits he does not know how the process takes place. We have seen an example of the effects of anxiety in a mother on her child, in the case of Carol and Peter Chisholm. It is reasonable to assume that Peter experienced anxiety and that the mediating mechanisms were the changes in voice and manner of handling which took place in Carol under the stress of anxiety.

The Drive Theory. The drive theory is the experimentalists' attempt to bring order into the confusion which surrounds the anxiety concept. The basic hypothesis is no different from that of the premonitory theory; anxiety is still seen as a reaction to threat, only now the formulation is cast in a learning frame of reference and is stated in such a way that testable hypotheses may be derived from it. Essentially the formulation states that anxiety, through learning, comes to be associated with many kinds of stimuli which prior to learning did not elicit anxiety. The contention is made, and is widely held on good evidence, that anxiety has the characteristics of a drive. What this means is that anxiety energizes or intensifies an existing reaction tendency and that reduction of tension is held to increase the probability of recurrence of behavior that immediately preceded it when the stimulus situation is repeated on a future occasion. This is a restatement of reinforcement learning theory, only now anxiety is given the status of a drive equal to hunger, sex, or other drives. The proposition was first stated by Mowrer (1939). Since then a great deal of experimental work has been done to demonstrate the effect of anxiety on behavior in animals. We shall review some of the experiments, in most of which physiological pain has been used as the source of anxiety. The theory is not, however, regarded as confined to anxiety derived from physical pain. Extrapolations to the human situation have been made, and Dollard and Miller (1950) have set forth plausible explanations of learned reactions to psychological threats.

Mowrer (1950) conceived of anxiety as a "learned response, occurring to signals (CS) that are premonitory of situations of injury or pain

(US)." The anticipatory nature of anxiety has biological usefulness, in that it motivates the subject to deal with traumatic events adaptively in advance of their actual occurrence, thereby diminishing their harmful effects. As an example Mowrer cited the reduction in anxiety a mother experiences after her child has been vaccinated against a dreaded disease. The CS is an originally indifferent stimulus. When it is presented a number of times in close temporal contiguity with a painful stimulus (US), it will also arouse the state called anxiety or fear, which is the conditioned form of pain reaction. Mowrer (1939, p. 557) then argued that the anxiety so aroused could "motivate innumerable random acts, from which will be selected and fixated . . . the behavior that most effectively reduces the anxiety."

Subsequently Miller (1948) demonstrated that anxiety can become attached to previously neutral stimuli, and that the anxiety can motivate the substitution of a second and even third response for the original one. In his experiments, rats were shocked through an electric grid in a white box, and were allowed to escape the shock by running through a door into an adjoining black box. Prior to training, the rats had exhibited no preference for one or the other compartment. The animals received ten training trials by being placed in the white box where shock was administered. The door was opened between the two compartments, and the animals ran into the black box.

On subsequent trials, when no shock was administered, the rats continued to run from the white into the black compartment. It was Miller's assumption that the cues present in the white box were sufficient to arouse anxiety of sufficient strength to motivate the running response. Now if anxiety were an acquired drive, Miller reasoned, it should be able to stimulate new behavior responses. So he closed the door between the two compartments. Now the only way the door could be opened was by manipulating and rotating a little wheel above the door. The rats, put in the white box without shock, gradually learned to escape by turning the wheel. Since the new response of turning the wheel was reinforced by escape, it was reasoned that anxiety, acting as a drive state, had been reduced. Later, still in the absence of shock the rats learned to substitute a bar-pressing response for the wheel-rotating response in reaction to the anxiety aroused by the cues present in the white box.

Brown and Jacobs (1949) criticized the interpretation of Miller's experiment. They argued that the response-substitution might actually have been motivated by frustration aroused by the presence of the now closed door. The frustration they thought might result from the blocking of a previously established running response. In order to test this hypothesis, they trained rats in either of two identical compartments, pairing a light and buzzer with shock. During the shock trials the door between the compartments could not be opened. In subsequent trials without shock, the door was replaced by a low barrier. Animals were placed in one half of the apparatus; now the tone and light (CS) were turned on and kept on until the rats had crossed into the other compartment by crossing the barrier, at which moment the tone and light were turned off. The rats quickly learned the crossing response under these conditions. Since the running response had not been frustrated, Brown and Jacobs concluded that Miller had correctly identified the drive involved in his study as anxiety and that the learned responses in both studies could be attributed to the reduction of anxiety.

In addition to demonstrating that anxiety acts as a drive, the experimental work of Miller and of Brown and Jacobs also validates one of Freud's assumptions, to the effect that there may be an infinite variety of reactions to anxiety wholly unlike the response to the original traumatic situation. Turning the wheel, pressing the bar, jumping the barrier—in the studies just cited—were all response substitutions learned in effecting anxiety-reduction. "Thus," as Farber (1954, p. 11) has pointed out, "the responses of rats, like the symptoms of clinical patients, may represent modes of resolution of current anxieties; they are not necessarily copies of the responses elicited at the time the anxieties were acquired."

Studies of anxiety in human experimental work have not been so clear-cut and conclusive as the animal studies, since the techniques found successful in evoking anxiety in animals cannot be employed with human subjects. One experimental study was concerned with secondary stimulus generalization, but it illustrates the part anxiety may play. It might be well before discussing the study to review what is meant by primary and secondary generalization.

Generalization may occur with either stimuli or responses. Primary generalization has been extensively studied. Primary stimulus generalization occurs when the subject fails to distinguish between stimuli which are in some way objectively similar. The stimuli usually impinge on one sense modality; often they lie more or less near each other on a continuum of a physical characteristic, such as frequency, intensity, amplitude, temperature, or shape.

Secondary stimulus generalization, on the other hand, occurs between stimuli which have no discernible objective similarity. Here generalization is presumed to occur because each of the stimuli has separately and independently been associated, through learning, with the same response. The response serves as mediator for the generalization from one stimulus to another. Hull (1942) described the process by which secondary generalization is effected. A subject learns a response, A, to Stimulus 1; then he learns to make the same response, A, to Stimulus 2. Now suppose that he learns a different response, B, to Stimulus 1. Subsequently the presentation of Stimulus 2 will tend to elicit response B.

An experiment designed to demonstrate secondary stimulus generalization was performed by Shipley (1935) and repeated by Lumsdaine, as reported in Hilgard and Marquis (1950). These experimenters conditioned the eye-blink response in human subjects by combining a bright light and a puff of air directed at the eye. Then they paired electric shock administered to the fingers with the puff of air until the shock elicited both eye-blink and finger retraction. On subsequent trials when the light alone was presented, finger retraction was evoked. The eye-blink response is assumed to have mediated the stimulus generalization from electric shock to the light. It is not unreasonable to assume that anxiety intervened between the presentation of the light and the retraction of the fingers, in which case it may be said that anxiety mediated the response.

Although the hypothesis that anxiety mediates secondary stimulus or response generalization requires much more experimental proof, we may speculate for a moment as to how it works in life situations. When anxiety is aroused in a situation where there is no clearly appropriate response, another response which has been successful in reducing anxiety in another situation may be evoked. For illustration let us recall the experience of Katherine Burke in the case history in Chapter 6. When she got what she called a "jangled feeling" (anxiety), she resorted to masturbation. The act of masturbation temporarily brought relief, but did not basically change the situation, since it was an inappropriate response.

The Isolation Theory. Isolation is a painful experience. Children use it to bring other children in line—"I'm not going to play with you any more." Adults put children in their rooms or otherwise separate them from company as a control measure. Adults ostracize one another. Probably the worst form of punishment that man has devised against man is isolation. Prisoners dread nothing more than solitary confinement. You may recall the moving story of Philip Nolan, the famed "man without a country," who was separated from his country forever. There can be no doubt that isolation is a condition which most people wish to avoid. Why is it so anxiety-provoking? There are two theories, one psychological, one philosophical.

According to the psychological theory, the conditions of childhood provide the antecedents of all future anxiety. The child, especially the very young child, is dependent on the adult to satisfy nearly all his needs; his very life depends upon someone else taking care of him. When he is hungry, when he is in pain, when the blanket gets wound too tightly around his head, or when he slips into a pond, tension mounts; failure to get adult help can lead to acute anxiety. Aloneness in these cases is associated with helplessness. Helplessness, or loss of control, is the prime condition of anxiety. Because every child knows helplessness at some time, we are all historically conditioned to experience anxiety. How strong that tendency may be—to react to situations of threat with anxiety—varies with the peculiar learning of each individual.

Freud, Rank, and others have argued that separation from the mother at birth was the original trauma. Any subsequent situation which simulates this first separation has the power to renew the anxiety experienced in the birth trauma. The theory is not subject to proof. Freud also maintained that fear of castration, separation from a prized object, was the origin of anxiety. At first he held this to be fear of literal castration, which many of his patients reported. There is no doubt that such a fear exists in some persons. We saw in the case of Sammy that he had reason to be anxious over the possible loss of his penis. But even Freud recognized that it was going too far to make fear of literal castration the basis of all anxiety. He came to look upon this fear as symbolic of separation, separation from any cathected object. And so again it is the separation, or isolation, which provides the antecedent to anxiety.

It seems reasonable to say that there are enough occasions of isolation and helplessness in the life of everyone to account for the tendency toward anxiety in all people. But there are philosophers and theologians who maintain that, quite aside from individual experiences, the nature of man's relation to the universe is such that inevitably he will feel isolated and lonely, and hence anxious. Although we cannot review the arguments of these writers here, suffice it to say that what they write about is rooted in reality and cannot be dismissed lightly. Many of the critical experiences of life have to be faced absolutely alone, even though there are people on all sides, and at such times man feels his aloneness in the universe.

Defensive Processes Against Anxiety

When anxiety is present, and the individual has no adequate, direct way of dealing with it, a variety of strategems will be activated to be rid of it. These strategems have been labeled defense mechanisms by psychopathologists who see them in connection with very severe anxieties where emergency reactions are employed. We preserve the term, even though we recognize that the strategems constitute only a part of the learned repertory of responses of the person and that some of them are innocuous and even constructive in social relations. There are a great many ways of coping with threats. In the final chapter we shall deal with some of the more positive, creative of these ways. At present we are concerned with the defensive processes which are employed to the detriment of free, adaptable living. Rigidity characterizes the person who employs many defense mechanisms in interaction. Defense mechanisms cannot be readily altered, because they gradually get built into the personality as habit patterns. As any clinician knows, if a mechanism of defense is forcibly overcome or too readily interpreted, anxiety immediately follows. We saw an instance of this in the last chapter when Sally Ferranti was given an interpretation by the therapist as to what caused her attacks.

We shall list and describe some of the defenses commonly found in psychopathological persons and, to a lesser extent, in all of us.

Denial

In word, act, or fantasy one may deny the existence of an anxiety-provoking situation. This is a primitive mechanism, used by children and psychotics, and is characterized by loss of touch with reality. In schizophrenics denial of reality is the prime symptom. Young children can deny certain situations without sacrificing other reality-testing perceptions, for in the child the worlds of reality and fantasy are not clearly discriminated. When such discrimination has been made through learning, denial ceases to be available as a satisfactory mechanism. One may pretend, as in a game, that a situation does not exist. But the pretense is always recognized as a game and does not relieve the tension produced by the anxiety.

Repression

The threatening situation may be eliminated from consciousness by forgetting. One can no longer deny that a threat exists if he is conscious of it; but if it is excluded from consciousness, the same end is achieved: one does not have to deal with it. Both stimuli and responses may be repressed. One of the clearest illustrations of repression is found in post-hypnotic amnesia. Here a subject on command of the hypnotist may forget an event or epoch in his life, he may not recognize his closest friend, or he may be unable to perform a simple manual task to which he is thoroughly accustomed. That these things are only temporarily forgotten is demonstrated when under further hypnosis the subject is told that he will remember them when he wakes up. Invariably he does.

The clinical literature is filled with instances of two types of situations which are repressed. One is the isolated traumatic event. Here the person forgets a crucial anxiety-provoking experience. The other is the chronic anxiety-provoking conflict between two incompatible impulses—for example, the desire for sexual expression opposed by the superego.

Avoidance

The mechanism of avoidance consists of staying away from situations which provoke anxiety. One avoids the anxiety, but at the same time sacrifices whatever positive values may inhere in the situation. If there are many situations which arouse anxiety and the use of the avoidance mechanism, an extremely restricted life may result. It is at this point that we may properly speak of avoidance as pathological. Ordinarily we all employ this mechanism of dealing with anxiety, and to good advantage. If one cannot deal with an anxiety-provoking situation by facing it—dealing with it realistically and thereby extinguishing the anxiety or at least reducing it to manageable proportions—the better part of wisdom dictates that one should stay away from it. The real question one must put to himself here is by what criterion shall he determine to avoid rather than face and work through an anxiety-provoking situation.

Reaction-Formation

Under the category of reaction-formation we find behavior and conscious attitudes that are the antithesis of persisting unconscious impulses. Certain kinds of intense, rigidly-held behavior, despite the character of the external circumstances, are properly placed in this category. The writer once knew a scholarly Christian gentleman from China who illustrated this mechanism. He was pursuing advanced studies in a school of theology in the United States when the Communists overran China. At home were all his family, including his wife, children, and parents. For a while some news got through to him; it was all bad. His family was suspect because he was in America. Manuscripts which had been in his family for centuries were confiscated. One of his children was ill and not getting adequate medical attention. Then no letters came. Months passed and his anxiety mounted. During all this time he continued to preach in various churches. The central theme of all his sermons was "Love your enemies." No one ever heard him utter a harsh word against the Communists in public or private. He wore a continual smile; he always had a friendly and even a joking word. After about a year and a half of such strain, he was rushed to the hospital one night with perforated stomach ulcers.

The question may be raised as to how one may distinguish between behavior which is a genuine expression of an impulse and that which is a reaction formation. For instance, many people preach "Love your enemies," and certainly it is not all reactive. The answer probably lies in the criteria listed above—intensity and rigidity, plus compulsivity. When behavior is marked by these characteristics in the face of circumstances which impartial observers judge should produce the opposite reaction, you may be reasonably sure that it is a reaction-formation.

Projection

Anxiety arising from an internal source, either from an unacceptable impulse to act or from guilt feelings, may be attributed to some external object; such a substitution of an external source of danger for an internal threat is called projection. According to Freud (1936, p. 81), "Such a process has the advantage that from an external danger protection may be gained through flight and the avoidance of the perception of it, whereas against a danger from within, flight is of no avail."

Studies of projection—defined by Sears (1936) as the attribution of traits—revealed that persons assign to other people in exaggerated measure their own undesirable traits of which they wish to remain unaware. Likewise Frenkel-Brunswik (1948) has shown that in certain cases hostility which takes the form of anti-semitism has nothing to do with any direct experience with Jews, but rather is a disguise for hostilities and insecurities arising from a person's own early childhood experiences. Such projections relieve anxiety by allowing the individual to express his impulses under the guise of defending himself against his enemies.

Fixation and Regression

As one masters each new phase in the course of development from infancy to old age, there is a tendency to wish to remain at that particular stage. Such a desire is understandable in the light of reinforcement theory. A series of related acts which have been reinforced will, other things being equal, tend to be repeated. New acts have to be performed before they can be reinforced. Thus the old modes persist until they are extinguished or until more satisfactory modes supplant them. When a person clings to an especially satisfying group of responses, it is called fixation. By this procedure the anxiety entailed in facing the unknown is avoided.

Closely related to this mechanism of defense is that of regression. When in the process of growing up the demands for new learning are too anxiety-provoking, there is a tendency to revert to older, established patterns of behavior. This is regression. The term regression has the unfortunate connotation of turning back the clock, as if one could somehow go back in time. No such meaning is intended. The older patterns are present in the repertory of responses. They have not been extinguished, else they could not be re-evoked. They have simply been temporarily supplanted by other responses, which, being now aversive, are given up in favor of the former. Ordinarily regressions are temporary and last only until new modes of responses integrated with advanced stages of socialization are established. But if the demands of the current situation are too great—that is, too anxiety-provoking—regressive behavior may persist for long periods. And in extreme psychopathological cases, the individuals may resort to earlier and earlier modes of responses until they become virtual babies again. Most of us retain some unextinguished infantile modes of behavior in our repertory of responses which, under stress, may be temporarily called forth. Or sometimes they may be elicited even without great stress. The experience which many adults have of reverting to some kinds of childish behavior when re-visiting their childhood home is a case in point.

All of these mechanisms of defense, and we have mentioned only the principal ones, have two common characteristics: (1) they falsify or distort reality, and (2) the individual has no control over them since they operate unconsciously.

Suggested Readings

Freud, Anna. (See readings at the end of Chapter 8.)

Freud, S. *The Problem of Anxiety*. New York: Norton, 1936.
   Freud revises his earlier conversion theory and sets forth the dynamic theory of anxiety as the determinant of the mechanisms.

May, Rollo. *The Meaning of Anxiety*. New York: Ronald. 1950.
   A review of theories of anxiety taken from philosophical, biological, and psychological literature.

Miller, N. E. "Learnable Drives and Rewards." Chapter 13 in Stevens, S. S. (Ed.), *Handbook of Experimental Psychology*. New York: Wiley, 1951.
   Experimental attempts to demonstrate that anxiety is a driving force in behavior.

11

SOME DETERMINANTS OF PERSONALITY:
A RECAPITULATION AND EXTENSION

*He is at once a person seeking his own
proper ends and the member of a
community in whose texture the
ends of others are incorporated.**

Behavior is multidetermined. Any attempt to explain a complex social phenomenon by a simple proposition of cause-effect relationship is futile. What does it mean to say that "every child who feels rejected is a potential delinquent?" Or what does it signify to point out that 98 per cent of a group of five hundred delinquent children played with other delinquent children, whereas in a group of matched nondelinquent children the percentage of those playing with delinquents was only 7 per cent? Or again, with what confidence can one say that "children who are problems in school and community come from families in which parents lack genuine affection for the child and tend toward extremes of rejection, punitiveness, or overindulgence?"

There is certainly truth in all these statements. But the truth here is only partial. In the case history in Chapter 9, could you explain Sally Ferranti's behavior by any of these statements? She felt rejected. She played with other boys and girls who engaged in acts which are labelled delinquent. On the surface her parents seemed to lack genuine affection for her. If Sally were a subject in a particular research in which these variables were being studied, she would lend statistical weight to such statements as those made above. And quite rightly so. But could we make any generalizations from these statistics about the actual causes of Sally's behavior? It seems doubtful. Sally is much too complicated a person to be reduced to such a simple formula. And even the statistics would be only partially correct. There were times when Sally felt strongly

---

* W. Macneile Dixon. *Tragedy*. London: Edward Arnold & Co., 1938, p. 104.

rejected, but in fact she was not rejected. Her mother and father did not lack genuine affection for her, although at times, when they were very angry with her, they acted as if they did. Of course she did play with boys and girls whose acts might be called delinquent, even though legally they were not delinquent since they had not been so declared by a juvenile court, except in one instance. How many responsible citizens do you know who did not at one time or another themselves engage in acts, or play with other boys and girls who engaged in acts, which had they been detected and dealt with harshly, could have been branded delinquent?

The fact is that all such statements, although they contain a measure of truth, are inadequate to explain a complicated social act. A great deal of harm has been done by over-generalization of partially true statements. For example, if a child gets into trouble and comes to the attention of public authorities, there is a tendency to look immediately for neglectful parents as the probable source of the difficulty. Unfortunately this tendency is found in professional as well as nonprofessional people. If some evidence of neglect is uncovered, the cause is presumed to have been found and the search ceases. How easy! And how misleading. What an injustice to parents and to our own scientific ideal. Genuinely loving parents, using the best methods at their command, sometimes have children who become problems to the school or other authorities. Boys and girls respond to other influences than those emanating from the home. And yet if one sets out to find evidence of neglect on the part of even the most loving parent, one can probably find it if one searches long enough and if one is satisfied with isolated acts as evidence.

Each of the personalities we have presented in this book was markedly different from every other personality. Even the twins were dissimilar, despite the fact that they had much in common. No longer can one subscribe to a banal theory which states that at a given time children brought up in the same home are subject to the same environmental influences. Nor can one accept as explanation the vague or meaningless type of theory such as "empathy," or the statement, "interparental frictions may exert an adverse influence on children's adjustments." What does it add to our understanding of Peter Chisholm to say that he empathized with his mother? And can we explain Sally's jealousy of Annie Louise by generalization from the common statement, "jealousy springs from having to share the mother's love when a new baby arrives?" No, we cannot.

Each personality studied was unique. Yet each responded to general laws. Each developed internal systems and patterns of response which were characteristic of him and more or less stable. Each changed during the short time we studied him. The greatest changes, of course, occurred in Peter, because fewer systems of response had been impressed upon his nervous tissue. As impressions were made, he began to resist influences counter to what he had learned. Under the gentle persuasion of a loving mother, however, he made the changes necessary to fit into the living pattern of the Chisholm family. In the normal process of social development the child gains the ability both to assert and to yield without surrendering his integrity. It is the positive affirmation of impulse, with the mother's support, that enables the child to satisfy his needs, and in this way he grows dependent upon the mother. At the same time while he is learning satisfactory modes of response, he resists change; in this way he asserts his independence and grows strong, again with the mother's support. Through this process of interchange—the mother giving and withholding, the child accepting and resisting—the world is defined for the child. He becomes aware that he is a separate entity, at the same time enmeshed with others. If there were no limitations or bounds set for him, if there were no impositions which he could resist, he would not develop a strong ego.

The process of becoming a human being is synonymous with the interaction process which takes place between the child and the significant persons in his world. Personality cannot be isolated from this complex interaction process. Personality is a product of, but not simply a reflection of, the personalities with which an individual comes in intimate contact. Whatever these personalities are like in their total impression, conscious and unconscious, the child receives and integrates into his own growing, separate personality. Parents reflect what they *are*, not just what they *want* to reflect. But each child receives and integrates differently because he brings a different potential for response to the interaction situation; thus his immediate behavior space is always different from that of everyone else. If the parent is chiefly hostile, the child is likely to be hostile. If the parent is oriented toward certain goals, these come to have positive valence (value) for the child. If the parent is outgoing and boisterous, the child tends to follow suit. It must always be remembered, however, that the development of a characteristic is not a matter of simple transmission from parent to child. We cannot always trace the learning process through which the characteristic is born, but we may be sure that it is learned. And it is learned out of the total experience of the child, not from an isolated act.

Socialization

The way in which a child learns values is called socialization. Socialization refers to the manner in which a person becomes a participating member of the family group, the society, the culture to which he belongs. Study of socialization, therefore, entails investigation of the process whereby the individual through *interaction with others* receives and *integrates into his developing personality the habits, attitudes, and values of the group.* Certain assumptions which should be made clear are implicit here. These assumptions concern the terms *interaction* and *integration.*

Interaction with Others

Socialization of a child is a function of the relationships of which he is a part. Early interpersonal relationships in the family are particularly significant for the development of personality.

The family is the primary agent for interpreting the culture to the child. It selects certain cultural habits and standards for emphasis, and de-emphasizes or ignores others. The family members provide the models which the child imitates in the acquisition of his social behavior. The family members are active guiding agents who set up goals, means of achieving these goals, and provide the instigations to the child. By rewards and punishments they reinforce appropriate behavior, and extinguish the inappropriate. The family setting provides the laboratory in which the child tries out his first social responses and in which he learns to discriminate between behavior which leads to gratification and that which does not.

As the child grows older, interpersonal relationships in groups other than the family become increasingly significant for his socialization. He acquires membership in other social groups whose goals and sanctioned instrumental acts may complement or even conflict with those he has learned in the family. An hypothesis which needs further investigation is that this period of transition from membership in the family group to membership in other groups is a crucial one for socialization. The degree of discrepancy between the goals of these groups, and the ease or difficulty with which a child is able to reconcile them, are highly significant for determining his later social adjustments.

Integration of Group Habits, Attitudes, and Values

The way in which the child takes over group habits, attitudes, and values, and the degree to which he accepts or rejects them depend upon the reinforcements of specific acts on his part as well as the accidental contiguous relationships which he experiences. That children have the same psychological environment merely because they came from the same family is an unwarranted assumption. The immediate behavior space of two children is never identical. Some of the outstanding factors which help to create a different environment around different children are the following:

1. A unique constitution. Since behavior results from interaction, what the child does to stimulate another is important, e.g., whether he is pretty or ugly, sluggish or active, sickly or well.

2. Sex differences. If the parents want a child of one sex and get the other, this fact influences their reactions to the child.

3. Differences due to birth order. The only child has no sibling with whom to share or compete. The second child is preceded by one, the third by two siblings. The position of each in the family is unique.

4. Changes in parents occurring between the births of successive children. The child who is born when the parents are twenty years of age experiences very different parents from the child who is born when the parents are thirty. Not only are the parents physically different, but they are also psychologically changed.

5. Changes in socio-economic status that may have occurred between the births of successive children.

6. The symbolic meaning which each child has for each parent. A first boy has special significance for many parents, or a child born to parents of advanced age. Sometimes a child symbolizes an episode or epoch in the life of a parent or of both parents.

There is a vast literature reflecting studies of socialization undertaken chiefly by students of child development and social anthropology. The bulk of socialization studies have been, and continue to be, concerned with isolating and measuring single variables, either as antecedents or consequents of the interactive process. The resulting evidence is impressive. But when one attempts to apply it to a given case or in the rearing of his own children, he is disappointed. The child acts as a whole, and the relation of variable to variable has little meaning when applied to the individual. The problems of multivariate analysis are so complicated, however, that there is little wonder most workers are discouraged from the attempt.

Our concern in this book is mostly with the influence of the family in the socialization process. The family is conceived as a multivariate system antecedent to the development and functioning of personality. But we have not been able to treat the whole family at once because, despite the notion widely held in some quarters, the family is not a unity of interacting personalities. We have suggested above some reasons why each member lives in a different environment. It seems more reasonable, therefore, to think of the family as a plurality of interacting systems, within the framework of the larger social and cultural systems. Each of these systems must be understood as it influences the socialization process.

In this book we have concentrated upon certain interactional systems plucked from the total number of systems operating within the families we studied. From concentration upon these few systems, we have tried to extrapolate principles of interaction which may be applied to other systems. How much injustice has been done to the whole complicated process of socialization, we cannot tell. We know at least that we have seen only part of the picture. The systems focused upon were viewed as fields of forces within the family field. The family in turn is a part of the larger fields of society and culture. Our view has presented only parts of the whole. Although we did this so that the details of the process could be seen more sharply, we must not confuse the details with the whole. The social and cultural systems continue to operate with gradual changes despite the individual variations and individual fluctuations within them. Before we go on to the family as a system and to some important aspects of the family in the socialization process, let us look briefly at some examples of the influence of social and cultural variations on the family.

Cultural and Social Variations

Our first illustration will deal with the differences between the socialization of Navajo and American children. In the American culture a child has only one mother. In the Navajo culture every woman of a certain generation is called "mother," and in turn calls a boy "son." This custom makes a great difference in the rewards and punishments that the "mothers" use. After being punished by "mother number one," the Navajo boy can run to "mother number two" for comfort. The shock at the death of a "mother" is much cushioned, because there is no disruption of the linguistic habits of the child. He does not have a stepmother as an American might; he merely has another mother.

In the Navajo culture, there is no sharp dichotomy between age-group and parental standards. The parents are always with the children. The children do not spend much time together by themselves.

Another significant difference is that the Navajo parents do not shoulder the sanctions as do American parents. The formula is not, "You do this because I know what is right," but rather, "You do this or people will laugh at you." The Navajo parents thus displace the responsibility for punishment of the child's acts; indeed, very often supernatural agencies are appealed to. The formula is, "Such-and-such a being will do so-and-so to you," rather than, "I will spank you."

Nor does the Navajo experience moral choice when he makes decisions. He learns that acts have consequences, and that his parents have no control over them. He finds that his parents are not omnipotent, that the mother herself is scared in the face of the supernatural. Thus, the Navajo child is disabused as to the amount of protection he can expect from his parents. Not only is he brought face to face with reality earlier than American children, but the Navajo child has unrealistic anxieties communicated to him. This situation contrasts with the American culture, where the parents are considered to be omnipotent. They conceal their anxieties and fears from the child—or think they do.

In the adult society of the two cultures there appear to be clear differences which stem from these variations in the socialization process. Navajos do not show the competitive interest of American adults. Furthermore, although they feel shame, they do not experience guilt; there is no internalization of moral choice. Also, there is less segmentation of culture along age-grade lines.

In contrast, let us look at a segment of the American culture. Although this is not represented as a typical segment—it seems doubtful to expect such a thing—the illustration shows the complex interrelationships of influences from the cultural, the social class, and the individual family on the developing personality.

In *Children of Bondage*, Davis and Dollard attempt to analyze the personalities of several Negro children who were studied in their local setting in the Deep South. The study begins with the assumption that all people are similar in their physical and psychic equipment, and that the difference between persons lies in their cultural characteristics. It follows that to understand an individual, one must know what the characteristics of the particular culture are and the methods (teaching techniques) employed in transmitting that culture. Davis and Dollard insist too that one must pay attention to the first learnings, since "they are the most critical for socialization." Furthermore, one must not concentrate entirely on the conscious habit tendencies of a person, for they do not constitute the whole personality: "The punished and aborted habits of childhood often have to be taken into account if human behavior is to be intelligible."

Now, since behavior is looked upon primarily as a complex of acquired habits, it becomes necessary to discover the source of those habits. Here learning theory comes to the aid of the authors, and allows them to posit that "each of these (i.e., habits) has been learned in a dilemma where society has punished the individual's attempts to follow other courses of action, and has rewarded his learning the prescribed method of attaining the goal response." Rewards and punishment thus become the most important methods by which society stamps in desired habits or extinguishes undesired habits. Where reward follows a course of action, we can assume that no conflict is aroused, and the individual is relatively pleased. But in the case of punishment (whether physical or the more insidious psychological), conflict is aroused. If such a situation occurs often, the individual will come to anticipate punishment when pursuing the direction indicated to satisfy a given drive or need-disposition. If the anticipated punishment is strong enough, it may cause severe anxiety; and when such is the case, the individual's actions may be in response to anxiety rather than to a more basic need or creative urge.

Before we see how these theories are applied in the analysis of an individual history, we need to look briefly at the cultural structure in which the study by Davis and Dollard was made. A system of social privilege is defined by these authors as the condition under which persons have access to fundamental biological and social goals. The systems of privilege found in the South depend upon two factors: (1) social class, and (2) caste. A social class may be thought of as "the largest group of people whose members have intimate social access to one another." The social class system allows mobility between the various groups under certain conditions. The caste system, on the other hand, is more rigid and allows no movement at all out of one's birth group—or practically none.

These are the conditions of socialization of the Negro in the South. To Davis and Dollard, however, personality is not necessarily class-typed, as some social anthropologists have maintained, holding that personality, in more homogeneous primitive societies, is culturally patterned. Rather, they believe that socialization results from the interplay of reinforcements from class and caste with the general controls of family, age, and sex. Thus the history of an individual's experiences must still be sought if the origin of his personal-social character is to be revealed.

The story of the "frightened Amazon," Julia Wilson, is one of Davis and Dollard's best illustrative cases. Here is a girl born into a family composed of a lower-class father and lower-middle-class mother who tries to train her daughter for the same position into which she herself had been born. A rapid survey of some of the highlights of Julia's life must suffice to give us the most pertinent facts. She was weaned at one month. She suffered from colic for the first year of her life. She was severely punished for masturbation and also for mistakes during toilet training. Her mother obviously favored her brother, two years younger; Julia hated him. At eight years of age she was traumatically cured of sucking a pacifier. She hated her mother and older sister. Her lower-class father fought, drank, and indulged in frequent illicit sexual affairs. He never denied Julia anything and occasionally rewarded her by taking her on buying sprees. As she grew older, she appeared to be very sadistic. She loved to fight, and she lured men on with her sexual charms, getting gifts from them, but then refused to have intercourse with them. She had great fear of exposing herself and of illness. In school she found few satisfactions; her chief rewards came from the lower-class people with which she associated and who approved her aggressive behavior.

Davis and Dollard sum up the case thus: "Coming out of her early family training with basic frustrations and violent aggressiveness issuing from a deep sense of rejection, Julia found in the life of her lower-class gangs and cliques not simply approval of habitual aggression, but a demand for it." The chief reason, then, for the relative lack of self-restraint of lower-class Negro children, as viewed from middle-class perspective, lies in the fact that there are scarcely any available rewards to reinforce socialized behavior. The renunciation of direct impulse gratification, which provides its own reinforcement, in favor of more complex habits and skills, therefore does not occur.

The Family: A Field of Forces

Contributions to the interactional point of view as a basis for understanding family life and the foundations of personality structure have been made by persons with markedly dissimilar professional backgrounds. Basically, however, they agree that individuals relate to one another through behavioral acts emotionally toned, and that out of this matrix of mutual responses within the family develops the idiomatic character of the primary group, as well as the peculiar stamp of each individual of which it is composed. The family is conceived as a field of forces in which the interrelations of variables form a constellation, which alters the manner in which each of the single variables is related to any particular phenomenon being observed.

Such a view calls for psychodynamic understanding of the total configuration, as well as the cross-currents of interpersonal relationships within the sub-systems of the family. In other words, the actions of each person in the family, through relating to others, produce modifications in the total psychological field. The stimulus bringing about action, or change, on the part of one member of the relating group may arise either from (1) one of the interacting members, or (2) some other source. An example of the first sort is the resistance of a child to a request of the parent, thus calling for some kind of further action on the part of the parent. The manner in which the parent reacts to the child's resistance will determine the extent to which the field of forces will be altered and hence the character of the immediately ensuing interaction. An illustration of the second type—of change in the field due to some external source— might be the result of the father's loss of his job. The resentment, personal doubts, and recriminations, the anxiety which he would experience, would be reflected openly or subtly in his dealing with all members of the family, and produce a rearrangement, temporary or permanent, of interactive patterns.

Thus our problem becomes a study of the specific kinds of relatedness within the family of one individual to another and of each to the total group. When a family is just being started, assuming that the relationship between husband and wife is a reasonably good one, we may represent it graphically thus:

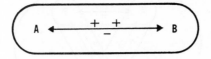

They constitute a field. Let A stand for husband and B for wife. The arrows indicate direction of action and the plus and minus signs positive and negative valences. No quantitative score is assigned to the valences, but it is assumed that at this stage the positive outnumber the negative. Such an arrangement of forces within the field would produce relative harmony within the dyad. The next step in understanding this family would be to determine what the valences represented and what kinds of specific actions and reactions they produced on the part of each person.

Now let us assume this relationship to be fairly stabilized. At this point a child, the first, is born. What happens to the field of forces? Something like this when we may use the data from the Chisholm family:

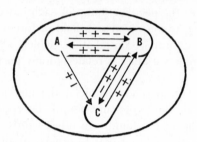

C represents the child. Now that we have two sub-systems within the field of the family, the arrangement of forces is altered considerably. The wife's valences toward the husband remain stable; his toward her increase on the negative side. It is probably not correct to say that his positive and negative valences toward her are equal, but he is certainly more ambivalent toward her than he was previously. Why? Two reasons are apparent. She is giving practically all of her time and attention to the baby, and she is frustrating him in both his affectional and sexual needs. Mother and child, on the other hand, have a predominance of positive valences in their sub-field. As yet the child has no negative valences toward her because he has met no frustrations at her hand. She has experienced discomforts and anxieties in relation to him which have caused slightly negative feelings to arise. The father is ambivalent toward the child; as yet he has not entered the life space of the child. They do not interact; hence, they do not constitute a sub-field.

If all goes well, as it did in the Chisholm family, in time we see a still further rearrangement of the forces within the field. This is a happy family:

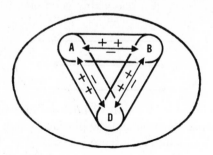

When a second child is born the diagram shows how complicated become the interactional forces, although in this case this is pure speculation, since our data do not carry us this far.

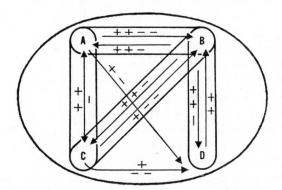

D represents the new baby, the second child. Only one word of explanation is needed. C has more negative than positive valences toward the mother and the new baby because his tolerance for frustration is low. He has been abandoned and neglected temporarily by his mother, toward whom his need-disposition and expectations have become highly differentiated. He reacts with rage and anger when his usual pattern of interaction is interrupted. When he observes his mother in intimate interaction with the new baby, he transfers some of his hostility from the mother to him. Jealousy is what we call this kind of reaction when it occurs. Evidence of it in human affairs is as old as recorded history—witness Jacob and Esau. Jealousy among the Burkes and Ferrantis was apparent for other reasons. The consequences of jealousy are sometimes tragic, as when overt action leads to physical injury or death. Covert action, fantasy, finds us all dealing harshly with those who interfere with our established gratifying patterns of interaction.

So we see in the family, while the child is still very young, the conditions necessary to elicit expressions of the highest sort—mutual love—as well as inclinations toward the basest acts—total destruction. The potentialities for both kinds of action are present in the child; the social forces in which he participates call forth one or the other, usually both. We have seen in this book how some of these forces operated in the lives of our subjects.

Let us now review three knotty problems which the student of personality must face in his attempt to assess the influence of family relationships on the developing child. These problems are: The significance of affiliation in early childhood, the effects of parents' personalities on their growing children, and the push toward conformity.

The Significance of Affiliation in Early Childhood

We have seen above how reactions may be brought about in all members of a family when the forces are rearranged with the birth of a second child. We explained the reaction of the first child as resulting from the temporary separation from his mother, toward whom he had developed need-disposition and expectations. The expectations refer to all the ministrations performed by the mother in the service of his needs, or even whims. Many of these can be taken over by someone else in the mother's absence. The need-disposition refers primarily to affiliation with the mother. The mother has come to represent for the child food, comfort, warmth, tactual stimulation, safety—in short, the secure basis of equilibrated life. Out of interaction with her under such favorable conditions has developed a strong positive need-disposition which incorporates all of her separate acts. This is called affiliation. It is not just a summation of all that mother has done for him. Were that so, someone else could take over for her and execute her duties. The mother herself has now become a necessary condition for the harmonious well-being of the child. For the time being he is dependent on her, and any prolonged separation produces a violent negative reaction in him. Later, this tie will have to be broken if he is to grow into independence.

Allport (1955, p. 32), in speaking of the importance of early affiliation, says: ". . . early affiliative needs (dependence, succorance, and attachment) are the ground of becoming, even in their presocialized stages. They demand a basic rapport with the world before growth proper can start. Aggression and hatred, by contrast, are reactive protests, aroused only when affiliative tendencies are thwarted." For the child who is deprived of the satisfaction of early affiliative needs, the process of development is arrested in early life. "But for the child who enjoys a normal affiliative groundwork, and who successfully enters the more advanced stages of socialization, the situation is different. In his case the foundations of character were established by the age of three or five, only in the sense that he is now *free to become;* he is not retarded; he is well launched on the course of continuous and unimpeded growth."

What is the evidence in support of such an hypothesis? In anticipation of our answers let us say immediately that the evidence is only partial and that some of the conclusions based upon the evidence are open to serious criticism. We shall not review here all of the evidence. Bowlby (1951) has done an excellent job of bringing together the more important studies. Let us be content to summarize the conclusions presented by Bowlby.

The general assumption underlying Bowlby's study is that "it is essential to mental health that the infant and young child should experience a warm, intimate, and continuous relationship with his mother (or perma-

nent mother substitute) in which both find satisfaction and enjoyment."
Where this relationship exists: (1) the emotions of anxiety and guilt
which, when excessive, constitute a threat to mental health, will be mini-
mized; and (2) the contradictory tendencies of the child to demand un-
limited love from his parents and revenge upon them when he feels this
love is not given, will be controllable.

When the child does not have this emotionally satisfying relationship
with his mother, a condition exists which is called "maternal deprivation."
This general concept covers the following situations: (1) A child suffers
from maternal deprivation, even though living at home, if his mother or
mother substitute is unable to give him the loving care small children
need. (2) A child is deprived if for any reason he is removed from his
mother's care. (3) The impersonal care given children in most institutions
may result in situations of almost complete maternal deprivation. With
reference to the effect of maternal deprivation on the development of the
child, the standpoint taken by Bowlby is similar to that taken with respect
to physical injury. Just as physical damage to the organism is especially
important when it occurs early in the child's development, so also are emotional disturbances of a far-reaching character when they occur in infancy
or early childhood.

In his summary of the evidence concerning the effects of maternal deprivation, Bowlby makes the following points:

1. Maternal deprivation can have adverse effects on the development
of children (a) during the period of separation; (b) during the period
immediately after restoration to maternal care; (c) permanently.

2. The evidence suggests that three somewhat different experiences can
each produce the affectionless psychopathic character: (a) lack of *any*
opportunity for forming an attachment to a mother-figure during the first
three years; (b) deprivation for a limited period—at least three months and
probably more than six—during the first three or four years; (c) changes
from one mother-figure to another during the same period.

In the light of the consistent picture presented by various types of evidence, Bowlby concludes that the basic hypothesis investigated has been
established; that is, "that the prolonged deprivation of the young child of
maternal care may have grave and far-reaching effects on his character
and so for the whole of his future life." On certain points, however, knowledge of the details concerning the effect of maternal deprivation is as yet
far from complete. First, it has not yet been determined how much deprivation children of different ages can withstand. Second, the assumption
that all young children have similar experiences in institutions needs examination. Future research must carefully examine not only the ages and
periods of deprivation but also the *quality* of the child's relationship to his
mother before deprivation, his experiences with mother-substitutes during
separation, and the reception he gets from his mother or foster mother

following the period of deprivation. Third, though it is generally agreed that the first year of life is of vital importance, there is lack of agreement as to the age at which deprivation has the most damaging effects. Bowlby, Anna Freud, and others consider that deprivation in the first six months is not so serious as that during the second half of the first year. Fourth, further research is needed to determine the age limit at which a satisfactory maternal relationship can repair damage done by earlier deprivation. The success of babies adopted between six and nine months after having been deprived for the first half-year of life is a strong indication that the effects of deprivation can be overcome if caught in time.

The Implications for Personality Theory

What are the implications of maternal deprivation for the theory of personality development? The development of personality is essentially a process by means of which the individual is gradually emancipated from over-dependence upon his environment. The mature person is one who, among other attributes, is capable of pursuing long-range goals and who can, to a great extent, seek out his own proper environment. That part of the person which assesses reality, strives to harmonize conflicting needs and to attain their satisfaction in a realistic manner, has been called the ego. That part of the person which makes him aware of the rights of others is called superego. During infancy the child is dependent upon his mother for the performance of the functions of both the ego and superego. Later, the child gradually learns these for himself. Thus both the ego and the superego are inextricably bound up with his early family relationships.

Bowlby distinguishes the following phases in the child's capacity to develop human relationships; failure at one stage disrupts or impedes progress to each successive stage. The first phase is one in which the infant establishes a relation to the first clearly identified person in his environment—his mother. This is usually achieved in five or six months. The second phase is one during which he needs his mother as a constant companion, a period lasting to about the third year. The third phase is marked by the child's becoming able to maintain a relationship with his mother "in absentia." In favorable circumstances this can be attained during the fourth or fifth year.

It is during these phases that the child develops his ego and superego in accordance with the pattern set for him by his parents. Failure to complete the first phase of establishing a relation with a mother figure makes it extremely difficult to do so later. Each phase has its normal point of completion if development is not to be distorted. It is because these phases are disrupted by maternal deprivation that the deprived child is at the mercy of his whims, is unable to establish other than superficial human relations, and under extreme conditions does not learn from experience.

Effects of Parents' Personalities on Their Children

Personality is formed by the specific ways in which an individual relates to the world around him. As we have seen, action in relation to the world on the part of any actor depends upon the total properties of the field in which he moves, including his own potentialities for action at any given time. It is universally agreed that the mother person exerts a tremendous influence on the infant and young child. There are cultural variations, to be sure, but in the American scene the mother continues to play a large part in shaping the personalities of her children up to and often through adolescence. The father's role in child training varies considerably from family to family. He has been studied much less than the mother; therefore, the part he plays in influencing the course of personality development is less clear. We have had a look at one father first hand, although not a typical one, in the case history of the Ferranti family. The role of the father as supporter, emotional as well as physical, of his wife were seen, in another case history, through Carol Chisholm's eyes, and later in an interview with both Bill and Carol.

The total family constellation provides the conditions of growth for the child. Even before a child can communicate verbally, the evidence indicates that he may be conditioned and that he responds to the feelings and moods and other actions of the person who is in closest association with him, usually the mother. How this process of communication takes place is not entirely known, but we have seen in the case of Peter and Carol that the mother's moods were perceived and reacted to by the child. We suggested that changes in the usual manner of dealing with Peter by Carol— such as talking and handling as well as other more minimal cues—were the effective mediators of her changed internal state.

Escalona (1952), after studying the relationship between choice of tomato or orange juice on the part of infants and the preferences for the same juices on the part of the persons feeding them, concluded, " When infants and young children are brought into contact with an adult, they perceive the emotional state of the adult and respond to it in a consistent manner." The exact mechanism for the transmission of likes and dislikes, directed behavior and emotional states is unknown. It is probable, however, that all the sense receptors of the infant or young child are keenly attuned to all stimuli and cues originating in the significant person, since so much of his welfare depends upon her. It is also probable that the appropriate response on his part is regularly or intermittently reinforced by her. Despite the fact that the mediation process itself remains a mystery, there is general agreement that transmission from the mother to child does occur.

In general it may be said that persons tend to seek in others the types of responses to which they have been habituated through long experience. There is no reason to doubt that parents in their relations with their children act in the manner to which they have long been accustomed, and that they expect and reinforce those responses of their children which are in tune with their own habituated patterns. What else can they do, in fact? Unless they develop some new philosophy of child rearing, as sometimes happens with middle-class parents, they act naturally. And acting naturally means in their habitual ways. It follows, then, that what the parent transmits to the child is what he has learned through his own history of previous interpersonal relations. This he does in two ways: By conscious educational techniques involving reinforcement and punishment and by the unconscious reinforcement of acts performed by the child, or if you please by tacit or implicit approval. Let us look now at these two categories of parent-child interaction and see some effects of parents' personalities on their developing children.

Conscious Educational Techniques

Ours is a competitive society. We place a high premium upon individuality and success in vocational endeavor. Parents want their children to excel, to be better than their neighbors' children, to win the highest prizes available in their social group. For the most part parents are perfectly conscious of these ambitious strivings. And they set about quite early to bring to fruition in their children the goals which they set for them.

Take weaning, for example. In our culture it is the practice to wean children from the breast after a relatively short period of time. Why this is so is not known. One suggestion is that, because women think that sucking tends to elongate the breast and thus misshape it, they do not want to run the risk of devaluing that part of their anatomy which has such high merchandizing value. The breast is a symbol of feminine and sexual charm. Be that as it may, weaning occurs early in Western society in contrast to other cultural groups. Carol Chisholm's mother was a true culture carrier when she tried to persuade Carol to wean Peter before he was four months old.

Weaning, however, does not occur in isolation, but rather in the total context of mother-child relationship. From birth the child has regularly received a series of satisfactions associated with the ingestion of milk. A disruption of these satisfactions with their attendant expectations produces a negative reaction on the part of the child, sometimes violent. Associated with weaning are concomitant factors important in socialization. The mother frequently feels guilty about depriving her child, but she has the whole weight of cultural tradition to support "her decision." Thus she is ambivalent. If the child, as is usually the case, becomes resistent to change and aggressive in expressing his desires, the mother is likely to become repressive in enforcing her demands in order to cover her own uncertainties and doubts. There ensues the first real struggle between mother and child.

It is from the struggle and the outcome of it that changes in interactive relations between mother and child occur which have important implications for the subsequent relationship between them and which provide significant antecedent conditions to relatively enduring systems of reaction in the personality of the child. Changes in interactive patterns resulting from weaning have not been adequately studied. Most research to date in connection with weaning practices around the world has been concerned with a hypothetical oral drive suggested by Freud. Thus attention has been concentrated upon the time and manner of weaning as a possible frustration of the oral drive, which is supposed to be antecedent to various kinds of oral activity manifest in later life. Most of the studies not only prove little, but seem to focus attention in the wrong place. Instead of looking at the variable of weaning time or what not, it would be more profitable to observe the multivariate relations which take place between mother and child around the time of weaning—before, during, and after. For example, the personality of the mother, studied through her reactions at the time, and the effect of these reactions upon the child, would be most revealing.

The mother has other conscious goals for her child, besides weaning, which are culturally sanctioned. We shall mention only some of them here: Adequate and timely sphincter control, repression of behavioral acts connected with the sexual organs, the appropriate culmination of time, place, and manner in aggressive expression, the proper ratio of dependence-independence, and level of achievement in line with the age, sex and social status of the child. Learning in connection with all of these goals is important in shaping personality development. Again it seems, however, that the specific variables are of less significance than are the interactive relations between parents and child associated with the specific learning. These learned patterns of interaction persist as antecedents to subsequent interactions related to the expressions of sex, aggression, dependence, and the rest.

The technique used by parents in their conscious efforts toward socialization we have said is that of rewards and punishments. Again the direct evidence is meager. What kinds of methods are used? We shall follow Child (1954) in reporting the literature in this connection. He says that there is only one study using the technique of reward as the antecedent variable, that of Winterbottom (1953). Winterbottom was interested in the type of reward mothers used when their children fulfilled their demands for independent behavior as well as when the children accepted restrictions on independent behavior. The rewards on which she collected information were: (1) a kiss or a hug to show how pleased the parent was;

(2) verbalization of the parent's approval—praise; (3) the granting of a special treat or privilege. These rewards were correlated with the variable of achievement in matters of independence, which Winterbottom was studying. The third type of reward did not differentiate between the subjects with high and low achievement scores; the first type was associated with high achievement scores; and the second was not usefully analyzed because of incomplete data.

In studying techniques of punishment Winterbottom's study is less reliable. Again, she investigated three types: Scolding or spanking, expression of disappointment, and deprivation of treat or privilege. There was no evidence of relationship between any of the methods and the consequent variable of achievement tendency. An early study of MacKinnon's (1938) was reported in which cheating in a problem-solving situation, using college students as subjects, was correlated with psychological punishment from their fathers in childhood. The cheaters reported less punishment, but the difference was not statistically significant. In another study, Hollenburg (1953) and Faigin (1953) interviewed mothers in two cultural groups, Pueblo Indian and rural white, respectively, concerning their child-training practices. Guilt in the children of the mothers was measured through use of projective tests. The purpose of these studies was to determine if there was any relationship between guilt feelings and the relative predominance of love-oriented techniques of punishment; the findings showed a striking positive relationship between the two. Still another study, one by the Gluecks (1950) of delinquents and nondelinquents, showed clearly that parents of the former used physical punishment as a corrective measure far more often than did parents of the latter.

Sears, Maccoby, and Levin (1957), in a noteworthy study of child-rearing practices, began by asking three questions of themselves: (1) How do mothers rear their children? (2) What effects do these practices have on the children's personalities? (3) What leads a mother to use one method rather than another? Actually, as the authors freely admit, they dealt primarily with questions one and three. Number two, which is the critical pay-off question for an understanding of the genesis of personality, is a much more complex and difficult one to answer. The method employed in this study was the semi-structured interview. The authors wanted to avoid what they considered the pitfalls of both the unstandardized "depth" interview and the completely structured schedule with its long list of multiple-choice items. The schedule used consisted of a list of open-ended questions. The mothers were all asked the same questions, but each was encouraged to answer in her own words.

The chief contribution of this study by Sears, Maccoby, and Levin lies in its excellent description of what mothers say they do in rearing their children. Up to this time there had been much speculation and relatively little evidence on this score. For example, many people will give an undocumented opinion on the differential treatment children receive due to their sex and ordinal position in the family, but in this study the authors investigated these variables in relation to different dimensions of behavior. One illustration in connection with the expression of aggression will have to suffice. Mothers in this sample were found to be more tolerant of their sons than they were of their daughters in the matter of showing aggression toward neighborhood children. In those families where there were two children, the older child was permitted to express physically more aggression toward other children than was the younger child.

Mothers employed a variety of rewards and punishments in controlling the behavior of their children. Sears, Maccoby and Levin categorized these control measures into "love-oriented"—including, for example, praise as reward, isolation as punishment, withdrawal of love as punishment—and "object-oriented" techniques—including, among others, tangible rewards, deprivation of privileges as punishment, and physical punishment.

Few though they are and partial, these studies are encouraging, because they concentrate upon the interactive process between parents and children. As children grow older, the numbers of conscious goals which their parents set for them increases—scholastic achievement, social grace, thriftiness, honesty, good sportsmanship, to name but a few. And the methods employed to encourage the attainment of these goals, depending upon the personalities of the parents, vary all the way from the use of extrinsic rewards, like money or special favors, to whippings, tearful pleadings, and sometimes chronic nagging and hostile threats.

Unconscious Reinforcements

Few would doubt today that human beings act in part on the basis of motives of which they are unaware. Yet the evidence to document such a statement is hard to come by. Clinical research and the insights of literary artists are the best sources. The case history of the Ferranti family provided us with one graphic illustration. How do unconscious motives of parents influence the developing personalities of children? We shall try to answer this question as best we can with the data at hand.

If a parent has an unresolved conflict which he has retained for many years (or few, as the case may be), behavioral expression in relation to the area of conflict may or may not be consciously recognized. It is in cases where it is not consciously recognized that we are for the moment concerned. When the parent acts in relation to his child in the conflictful area, his feelings and attitudes are conveyed by verbal and physical cues. When in turn the child shows behavior in the area of the parent's conflict, the parent's response acts as a confirmatory reinforcement or, through one form or another of punishment, tends to arrest the behavior. In time, sometimes after much struggle, if the dyadic relationship is to remain more or less stabilized, behavior on the part of each in relation to the area of conflict will become mutually acceptable. For example, if a mother has an unconscious aversion to odors associated with anal evacuation, the treatment of feces by the child in the presence of the mother will be worked out differently from what it would if the mother had no such aversion. The same may be said with respect to other aspects of the socialization process through which the child goes.

History is replete with instances in which parents attempt to realize their ambitions through their children. The Mozart family illustrates the point. Leopold, the father, prodded Wolfgang, the son, who fortunately was a prodigy. Although not all such promptings are unconscious on the part of the parents, they generally proceed from two sources and may be unconscious. In the first instance, parents who are proud of their own achievements are unwilling to accept any let-down in the family record, and in addition want for their children the good things which they themselves have experienced. Mr. and Mrs. Chisholm fall into this category; they directed Bill into mechanical engineering, though they were unaware that they had made his vocational choice for him. The second instance is the case of parents who, thwarted in their own ambitions, eagerly desire their children to succeed where they have failed. They plan far-reaching, glorious careers for their children, careers which frequently are far above the level of attainment of the children.

Parental timidities are communicated to children through simple example. For example, socially shy parents usually have socially shy children. During the second World War in London studies showed that those children who were most afraid of air raids came from families where the parents were also most afraid. Not all of the parents, certainly, wanted to communicate their fears.

These are everyday, normal instances of the effects of parents' personalities on their children. Another source of evidence, which we shall concentrate on primarily, derives from studies of neurotic patients. Since Freud first posited the theory of unconscious processes, clinicians have considered its operation an important factor in the development of neurotic difficulties. Freud's classic case of Little Hans demonstrated the fact that the workings of unconscious processes effect neurotic behavior in children as well as in adults. New light has been cast on the understanding of neuroses and psychosomatic disorders in children by therapists who have been able to treat both the child and his mother in analysis. These analysts have found that the overt symptomology of the child stems from his unconscious and exaggerated reactions to the unconscious wishes of the mother, wishes which often have their roots in unresolved conflicts carried over from her own childhood. One observation leading to this explanation was the manner in which the child's symptom, which may have appeared originally with amazing speed, disappeared for no apparent reason when the mother brought her old conflicts to consciousness and worked them through in the course of analysis. In all cases, both the mother and the child seemed unaware of the relationship between the neurotic behavior of the child and the unconscious conflicts of the mother.

From a study of twenty children with various psychosomatic disorders, Sperling (1949, 1950) reported the case of a young asthmatic boy, John. John's mother, who had a symptom of chronic depression with somatic equivalents, had difficulty in handling her two children. She had not wanted her second child, John, so soon, but had hoped when she found herself pregnant that it would at least be a girl. She suffered from fatigue and migraine. John was a feeding problem and clung excessively to his mother. To the mother, John represented her own younger brother, born when she was two and a half years old. There had been radical changes in her behavior after he was born and she had become moody and sick. The mother carried over this unresolved relationship with her brother to John; she unconsciously needed him to be dependent on her. Toward the end of her first year in analysis, her relationship with the child improved to the point that John could talk about himself to his mother. He said he suffered his asthmatic attacks when she punished him or shouted at him. The mother then began to understand the role she played in John's illness. The reason for John's inability to function physically and intellectually as a boy was his mother's inability to accept him as a boy. She felt that her own mother had rejected her because she was a girl, and consequently she was considered dull and inferior. It was difficult for her to tolerate aggressive behavior on the child's part; she had gone so far as to teach him how to knit.

Sperling points out that the mother, in all the cases studied, showed as a result of her own emotional arrest, an exaggerated desire to keep the child in a state of dependency. Moreover, the closeness of the relationship between the mother and the child, not usually seen after infancy, contributed to a perpetuation of the pre-verbal type of communication found in early infancy. There the wish of the mother is transmitted to the child by cues in the mother's demeanor—visible, audible, tactual—to which the child shows great sensitivity. An infant is aware of changes in the facial expression or tone of voice in the mother, and responds to these. In the cases of the mothers and children treated, this sensitivity, or sense of rapport, is maintained by the child in his interactions with the mother beyond infancy. The wishes of the mother must be carried out, because the child has not been allowed to sever its ties of dependency in normal growth. The specific relationship of mutual dependence and control existing between mother and child is an important factor in the development of a psychosomatic disorder in the child. The child reacts to the unconscious intent, rather than to the manifest content, of the mother's verbalizations, even when the latter seem appropriate to the reality situation.

The child is a creature of sensation and intuition. Through sensation, he comes in contact with the world of objects; through intuition, he becomes aware of the emotional forces at work in himself and others. The younger the child, the less we have to deal with the unconscious elements within himself that give rise to his fears, and the more we deal with the unconscious processes of the adults important in his life; for the child perceives from a person's behavior his unconscious motivation, and responds to this as well as to the spoken word. When working with very young neurotic children, it is necessary to examine the unconscious motives of the parents; when their difficulties are brought to consciousness and worked out, the symptoms of the child vanish almost immediately. In the case history of the Ferrantis, for example, Sally was reacting to the unresolved conflicts of her mother. These conflicts caused disturbances in the psychic life of the child, which, worked out as asocial acts, resulted in a neurotic condition. Projection is repeatedly used in cases where the parents have resentments against each other. One child, who may in some physical aspect or mental characteristic resemble the hated parent, becomes the scapegoat, while the other children are not similarly affected. Sometimes parental projections may arise from anxiety or fears which have their roots in the early life of the parent. The parent's unconscious impulses may also represent needs which cannot be met currently in the adult world.

Hilgard (1951) has concentrated specifically on the repetition of patterns of sibling rivalry which are transmitted from one generation to another, a pattern which she calls social heredity. The vehicle of transmission is the psychogenic influence of the parent on the child. A woman who as a child has not been able to vent her feeling against her siblings, will in all probability set the stage for a reliving of the conflict when she becomes a mother. As a mother, she can carry on the old battle from an authoritarian position. To do this, she will identify both herself and her siblings with her children; then, when as a mother she provokes in her child behavior similar to that of a hated sibling, she has a chance for retaliation. The mother reacts to the child as if he were her own hated sibling; she can give vent to the feelings she had repressed as a child. Hilgard cites several cases where the mother identified one child with a hated sibling, unconsciously provoking in that child the behavior which the mother had hated in her own sibling. It was only in therapy that the mothers were able to understand the part they played in the behavior disorders of their children. The cases were much the same as those reported by Sperling, with the exception that in all cases a sibling pattern of the previous generation was repeated in the current one.

Hilgard repudiates physical heredity as the vehicle of transmission for the personality factors found in two generations; she cites as evidence the case of an adopted child who developed characteristics similar to the mother's hated sibling. Nor does the repetition of personality factors and sibling rivalries necessarily hold to age and sex lines; that is, a younger son may represent to the mother her hated older sister. The mother's unconscious needs or impulses are represented in her unexpressed feelings toward her own troublesome sibling. Hilgard offers a genetic explanation for this repetition of symptoms of the parent's sibling in her child. When the child displays anger or hostility, reminding the mother of her sibling, the mother overreacts to the child. Her overreaction in turn causes an overreaction in the child, of excessive withdrawal or defiance. Thus the mother has unconsciously produced in her child the discordant behavior similar to that of the hated sibling.

Moreover, the mother, if she was herself a younger child, will have great difficulties in setting limits on her own older child who represents the hated sibling. By not setting limits, the mother would seem to increase or aggravate the errant behavior of her child. There are three reasons why the mother has difficulty in setting limits for the older child. First, the child is acting out the aggressiveness of the mother, which she had repressed or suppressed; she gains vicariously through her child's acting out. Second, the mother's parent had been unable to set limits to the sibling's power; the mother had identified with her parent in this respect. Third, the mother experiences guilt over her hostility to the child who acts out the impulses of her sibling. All of these factors seem to perpetuate the discordant behavior of the child, to which the mother must react with aggressiveness or hostility. The mother finds further gratification in the exclusive relationship which develops; she alone will put up with the child's behavior. This is an indirect expression of the mother's own wishes to be cared for on an early, dependent level. A possessive relationship seldom seen after infancy is perpetuated; the mother does not have to share the child with anyone.

Szurek (1942) and Johnson (1942, 1949, 1950) maintain that the unconscious impulses of the parents play an important role in the development of defects in conscience, or "super-ego lacunae"—a lack of restraint in certain aspects of behavior. Szurek defines the conscience as the part of the self which is attained by positive, secure identifications with parents; a person with a defect in conscience is a "psychopathic personality" who seeks immediate gratification for his impulses and is unable to acquire satisfaction in a socially acceptable way. According to Szurek, children are subjected from birth to disciplines which are either directive and permissive or limiting and prohibitive. As far as the results of interaction are concerned, it is not important whether these disciplines are applied consciously or unconsciously. It does make quite a difference, however, whether the disciplinarian does or does not regard the errant behavior of his or her offspring with pained surprise or feelings of injured innocence. If behavior of interpersonal significance and involved with satisfying a need is integrated with the conscious approval of the parent, the child will not suffer guilt or show a lack of integration in this activity.

If the behavior is reacted to by the parent with unconscious or guilty permissiveness, the child, though unable to inhibit the activity, may feel anxiety or guilt right after the act.

Clinical experience with children showing a behavioral problem, and concurrent therapy with the parents offer an explanation of the genesis of some of the characteristics of the " psychopathic personality." In such cases, the more important parent, usually the mother, is seen to encourage unconsciously the amoral or antisocial behavior of the child. The neurotic needs (dependent, erotic, etc.) of the parent are vicariously gratified by the behavior of the child, or in relation to the child. Such needs may exist because of some current inability to satisfy them in the world of adults, or because of some stunting experience in the parent's childhood, or both. The parent's attempt to gain satisfaction for his urgent unconscious needs through the activity of the child leads to distortions in the child's self-regard, expressed in psychopathology of childhood. Thus the parent encourages the amoral behavior of the child by unconscious permissiveness or by inconsistency with regard to the specific behavior, and gains vicarious gratification of his own poorly integrated impulses through the " acting out " of the child.

Johnson points out that one child is singled out as a scapegoat to act out the parents forbidden impulses; often the acting out of the child both serves as a channel for the hostile impulses the parent feels toward the child, and allows the parent vicarious gratification. The child who develops "super-ego lacunae" does so partly because of the constant checking of the parent and the repeated warning not to do something. Such action on the part of the mother suggests that there is an alternative to the mother's order and an alternative image of the child in his mother's mind. Identification with the parent includes a sharing of the parent's conscious and unconscious concept of the child as honest or dishonest, loved or unloved. In addition, because the super-ego is quite rigid in adolescence, the child is disturbed when adults show doubt about it; the lack of good faith suggests an alternative mode which frightens him. Neither Szurek nor Johnson suggests any process of mediation of the unconscious impulses of the parent to the child beyond the statement that the permissiveness, usually unconscious, of the parent with regard to the specific behavior in question encourages the child in that behavior.

Clinicians citing cases of children who interpret and react to the unconscious impulses of their parents suggest some explanation for the process of transmission from parent to child. However, some of the explanations, such as Wickes' "intuits" and Hilgard's "social heredity" seem unnecessarily vague. It is advisable to avoid such terms which offer no clear understanding of the problem, and to seek a more concise, less mysterious explanation.

The process of transmission of the parent's unconscious wishes to the child seems to have two phases. First, the child perceives and reacts to concrete signs given by the parent through ordinary sensory perception —audible, visual, tactual. It does not seem necessary to assume the perpetuation of the close, dependent relationship of infancy and of the pre-verbal type of communication to explain the child's ability to perceive and react to these cues. In interpersonal contacts, even adults can sense deeper meanings than those offered in manifest verbal content, through the tone of voice and facial expressions of the speaker. It is not difficult to understand that the child too can sense these "unconscious" meanings of the parent; it even seems probable that the child, having come from the pre-verbal level of communication more recently, would be better attuned to these unspoken cues.

In this connection it is also desirable to clear up the somewhat occult and mysterious connotation that the child is participating in the unconscious of the mother. What essentially is meant here is that the mother is simply not aware of the cues she is giving the child; therefore she cannot understand that he is able to interpret and react to her unconscious wishes. Since consciously she does not recognize the existence of these wishes or impulses which have been repressed, she probably does not realize that she is communicating anything other than the actual content of her verbalizations. A case cited by Sperling (1950) will serve to point up this fact. The mother of a five-year-old girl, Laura, unconsciously identified herself with the child, using her for vicarious satisfaction of her inhibited, sadistic impulses. Laura had a difficult time with children in the kindergarten because of her provocative behavior. Although she actually liked the children, she antagonized them upon unconscious instigation by her mother, who had herself been a "model child." One day Laura behaved badly to her maternal grandmother and the mother's only sister, saying hateful things to them. This was unusual, as Laura was the grandmother's favorite and always treated her with affection. The mother, in analysis, was beginning to become conscious of her hatred for her mother and sister, and felt that Laura was reading her mind. When she reproved Laura for her behavior, Laura said, "But you hate them, and really wanted me to tell them this." When the mother asked her why she said that, Laura answered, "I heard you talk to them on the telephone, Mummy, and I could hear you hated them."

The second phase of the transmission of unconscious wishes of the parent to the child is the reinforcement of the child's reaction to these wishes. Many people, both children and adults, can understand these unconscious cues without reacting to them with the psychosomatic and neurotic disorders which the children in the reported case studies display. The fact is that one child is picked from the others as the scapegoat to represent the hated parent or sibling and to act out forbidden and repressed impulses. The intensely dependent relationship of infancy is perpetuated with this child, probably making him even more aware of the cues of the mother than another child would be. The child is forced to carry out his mother's wishes because he has never been allowed to sever the ties of dependency in normal growth. When such a child reacts to the cues given by the parent, his behavior is reinforced. The parent reinforces the child's behavior by conscious or unconscious permissiveness and inconsistency toward the child with regard to this behavior.

It is evident that in some cases the parent is permissive because he gains vicarious gratification of his repressed impulses through the acting out of the child. Szurek cites the case of a young boy who repeatedly ran away from home. The boy's running away began at the time his father was transferred from a job requiring a good deal of travel, which he enjoyed considerably, to a job not allowing such travel. When the boy returned from one of his truancies, the father would make him describe his adventures in minute detail, listening intently and interestedly. Shortly before the boy finished his story, the father would become angry and whip the boy severely. It was obvious, however, that the boy's behavior had been reinforced by the father's permissive interest. The running away of the boy was a vicarious gratification of the father's own desire to travel. The continuous running away of the boy might be explained in terms of one of Whiting's theories. Whiting states that actions which are both reinforced and punished, as the running away of this child was, acquire secondary drive status—the conflict between the expectation of reinforcement and punishment providing the drive energy.

In summary, the transmission process may be explained by two easily understandable events. First, the child understands and reacts to cues given by the parent. The parent is unaware that he is giving the cues or that the child is interpreting them, because they represent impulses which have been repressed. Secondly, the parent reinforces the child's behavior in many ways, most clearly by his permissiveness toward that behavior.

From the writings of creative artists one could choose many instances; one sample will suffice. Sherwood Anderson, in a short story titled "Respectability," relates how Wash Williams was affected by the impulses of his mother-in-law. Wash had not been married two years before his wife had acquired three other lovers who came regularly to his house when he was away. Finally Wash discovered what was going on behind his back and his wife went home to her mother. He said nothing because he loved his wife and he sorely missed her. So, after awhile, he was receptive to the call when—

"Her mother sent for me . . .

"I sat in the parlor of that house two hours. Her mother took me in there and left me. Their house was stylish. They were what is called respectable people. There were plush chairs and a couch in the room. I was trembling all over. I was sick of living alone and wanted her back. The longer I waited the more raw and tender I became. I thought that if she came in and just touched me with her hand I would perhaps faint away. I ached to forgive and forget . . .

"She came into the room naked," he went on. "Her mother did that. While I sat there she was taking the girl's clothes off, perhaps coaxing her to do it. First I heard voices at the door that led into a little hallway and then it opened softly. The girl was ashamed and stood perfectly still staring at the floor. The mother didn't come into the room. When she had pushed the girl in through the door she stood in the hallway waiting, hoping we would—well, you see—waiting." [*]

The Push Toward Conformity

Growing up in a community, especially if that community is culturally homogeneous, each individual takes on characteristics which are similar to those of everyone else in the group. He speaks the same language, eats the same food, learns the same rituals relative to the expression of his fears, his hopes, and his several needs. In short, as Macneile Dixon says, "The differences among men, enormous, vital, dwindle to a cipher when set over against their resemblances and their common destiny." [**]

Thus the anthropologist, studying the habits of an individual, can place him in cultural context readily; or if he studies the group, he can make certain highly accurate predictions about the actions of any individual member. This is not to say that any two individuals are alike or experience the same psychological world in its entirety. We have just seen what markedly different relationships exist between people, leading to distinct personalities. Indeed, the more thoroughly one becomes acquainted with any human being, the more difficulty one has in placing him in a category. Nevertheless, the differences between people are largely quantitative. The potentialities for action which constitute his personality in the main grow out of the numbers and kinds of reinforcements which he has received within his social group. Whether these reinforcements proceeded from conscious intention or not makes no difference in the effect which they have on future probable behavior. Many of the things which parents do in relation to their children are performed without rational consideration. They do them simply because that was the way they learned and the way everybody else in the culture does the same things.

The result is that there is a tremendous pressure on the child from birth to conform to the ways and customs of his group. Without this push toward conformity cultures would not exist and societies would disintegrate. It is paradoxical that this very cement of the group, conformity, should at the same time be the greatest deterrent to the progress of so-

[*] From Sherwood Anderson: *Winesburg, Ohio.* New York: The Viking Press, Inc. Copyright 1919 by B. W. Huebsch, 1947 by Eleanor Copenhaver Anderson.
[**] From W. Macneile Dixon: *Tragedy.* London: Edward Arnold & Company, 1938, p. 101.

ciety. Fortunately, however, not everyone conforms in all respects, and so there are here and there innovations; we will return to this phenomenon after we have examined some of the conditions which lead to the more usual pattern of conformity.

Search for an Explanatory Principle

Explanation of the fact of social conformity has been a task which social psychologists have always set for themselves. It is the keystone to understanding not only social organization, but also the development of personality. The history of the attempt to explain conformity in terms of unitary principles has been reviewed by Allport (1954), who points out that the three principles most commonly employed have been sympathy, imitation, and suggestion. These concepts have dominated much of systematic social psychology. The choice of one as against the other has reflected largely, as Allport notes, " the preference of authors for emphasizing the functions of affection, conation or cognition, respectively." More recently identification as a concept has been employed to account for conformity. It includes some of the principles subsumed under the other terms.

Identification. Freud used the concept *identification* to explain how a child comes to develop moral ideas similar to his parents'. Though the term has come to have many different meanings, nearly all of them emphasize the disposition of one person to resemble another person or group taken as a model. Identification may be said to cover at least the following concepts:

1. *Categorical identification.* The recognition of classes and their members. For example: "I am a boy (Democrat, plumber, or what not); boys do these things and do not do these other things"; "This is a cop; toward cops one does these things and does not do these other things."

2. *Imitation.* Matched-dependent behavior in the presence of a model. For example, "Teacher holds the pencil thus; I do too."

3.   a. *Identification with love-object.* One acts as if one were, in fact, a different person to prevent the loss of desired things in the absence of the other person. b. *Identification with aggressor.* One acts as if one were, in fact, a different person to prevent receiving unpleasant things the other person could administer.

4. *Stimulus-generalization.* One acts toward another person or group as though it were, in fact, a different person or group. For example: "This is a man; I react to him as though he were my father."

Categorical identification and *imitation* are said by social psychologists, sociologists, and anthropologists to occur primarily as cognitive behavior. They are simply efficient ways of problem-solving. Categorical identification is said to simplify and order, to satisfy the need for closure. Imitation is said to furnish vicarious trials and errors. One learns a thing more quickly when he sees how an expert does it. For example, one has an easier time as a member of a group if one does as the group expects.

Identification with the love-object and with the aggressor are said, mostly by psychoanalysts and other dynamic psychologists, to occur primarily as defenses against possible psychological harm. Identification with the love-object occurs in order that the individual may free himself from dependence on others for the satisfaction of positive needs. For example, "If mother likes me, then I learn to like me, so that somebody likes me even when mother is gone." Or, "I want mother to keep on liking me. If I adopt as mine the things (ideas, behavior-expectations, values) that are hers, then she will keep on liking me." Identification with the aggressor occurs so that one can control the extent of aggression coming from without in response to one's "bad behavior." For example, " If I do something wrong and punish myself, nobody else will have to punish me."

Stimulus-generalization is said to occur for two reasons: (1) The inability of the individual to discriminate cognitively between cues that are almost equivalent; (2) emotional processes somehow interfere with the cognitive processes involved in stimulus-differentiation and discrimination.

In general, group-oriented workers emphasize the role of reward and punishment extended by the group to its members. Conformity is rewarded; deviation is punished. A social group functions in the same way as the mother (or father): Belonging to a group, a person has many of his needs satisfied; belonging to no group, he is lonely and subject to attacks of anxiety. Therefore, he wants to relate himself, to be accepted; and this desire impels him to conform to the standards set by the group. Kluckhohn and Murray (1953) are representative of the thinkers who argue thus: Man is seen as a "carrier of culture"; the values of the group are so great (and the rewards so many), that the individual strives to maintain them in himself and others. Festinger, Schacter, and Back (1950) find cohesiveness, or the desire to belong to a group, a primary motive underlying identification. Individuals may wish to belong to a group for several reasons. They may like the other members. They may find being in a group attractive in itself. Or they may wish to belong because the group mediates goals which are important for the members.

Typically, dynamic psychologists emphasize the defensive nature of identification. It assures the continuation of the supply of wanted things, and the cessation or avoidance of things unpleasant and not wanted. A. Freud (1937), S. Freud (1938), and Mowrer (1950) maintain that the identification process reduces anxiety.

The Origin of Identification. Almost everyone agrees that the process of identification is a learned one, that the individual learns through trial and error to identify with certain aspects of the behavior of other persons important to him. There is much disagreement, however, as to the nature of the process and the rewards and punishments involved. Holt (1931) thought it was largely an instinctive process, the items that were imitated being selected on the basis of contiguity. Miller and Dollard (1941) explained it on the basis of reinforcement, as do most social psychologists. The rewards and punishments which they conceive to mediate the process come from outside the person. Dynamic psychologists generally conceive the rewards and punishments to be effective in relation to threats felt within the individual himself. The sociologically oriented tend to view the process as imposed on the individual by the group, often deliberately.

The maturing individual learns through reinforcement that those of his needs which can be satisfied only through other people will, in fact, be satisfied only when he conforms reasonably accurately to the behavior-expectations which the others have toward him. Behavior which is not relevant to these behavior-expectations is neither rewarded nor punished by the group; other sources of reinforcement determine whether the individual learns such behavior.

The Results of Identification. All agree that, as a result of the process (however defined), the individual comes to include as part of his behavior the acceptance of, and reaction in accordance with, the attitudes and ideologies of others. In the view of sociologists, the individual accepts the roles he assumes or to which he has been assigned by social conditions. These roles inevitably include beliefs and ideologies. If acceptance as a member of the group is important, then the individual accepts the conditions for membership prescribed by the group. The adult members of the family are by all odds the most important members of groups which are attractive to the individual. He identifies most strongly, then, with the parents' interpretations of the conditions for membership in the groups. The sociologists tend to stress the rewarding and positive results of identification.

The individual psychologists maintain that identification serves the double purpose of maintaining positive attractions *and* of preventing the occurrence of unpleasantness. That both these motives can mediate identification with the same group seems clear. Hitler's youth movements utilized both kinds of pressures on their members.

The acceptance of sexual roles is one result of identification, but how it comes about is disputed. Freud says the boy and the girl first form a primary attachment to the mother as a love object. Later the boy identifies with the father. The girl also identifies with the father, but for unclear reasons. Mowrer says that boys and girls identify with the mother as an undifferentiated source of love, and later identify with the same-sexed parent because this second identification is differentially re-warded in our culture. As one aspect of this second identification, the boy comes to regard females as acceptable love objects.

This process can, and does, go awry. When one's several roles de-mand incompatible behavior patterns, one can avoid conflict by com-partmentalizing his behavior—"Don't let your right hand know what your left hand is doing." It is claimed that identification with the opposite-sexed parent produces perversion (Mowrer, Sears, and others), while in-ability to identify with either parent produces neurosis. An interesting cycle is set up in certain persons: too complete an identification leads to insecurity and lack of self-confidence; this personal discomfort leads to still greater identification, and so on. Because values may be attached both to goals and to the means of reaching those goals, several possibili-ties for maladjustment through faulty identification exist. When both goals and means are laden with punishment-threats for their violation, the individual become overly conformist. When goals, but not acceptable means thereto, are identified with, antisocial behavior often results. When neither is sufficiently identified with, "retreatism"—into nomadism, romantic escapism—may occur. Because subgroups often subscribe to ideologies that are in conflict with the ideologies of other or larger groups of which the individual is concurrently a member, the individual may find himself in severe conflict.

Nonconformity or Innovation

To become socialized by natural progression a boy must first develop affectionate socialized attitudes toward his parents, and then later (and this is equally important) become independent of them. He does the latter by developing self-reliance and confidence in his ability to take care of himself, and by transferring some of the cathexis enjoyed by the mother and father to other objects. When a boy goes to school, for in-stance, he must begin to identify with the group of boys. The demands placed upon him there may conflict with, and cause a weakening of, his primary identifications. If his affiliative relations with his family have been consistent and nonneurotic, however—that is, not over-demanding—he should be able to make the adjustment without difficulty. Always, of course, this is assuming that the demands made upon him are not too great. Conformity to the group standards takes the place of conformity to family standards because the rewards to be derived from the former at this time in life are greater.

But not everyone conforms. How do we explain that? Since we can-not begin to go into the whole problem of social deviation, we shall have to be content with only two suggestions bearing on identification. First, when a person identifies with another person or group whose behavior deviates from the social norms, he takes over their ways and thus finds himself at odds with the larger social group. Children of asocial or anti-social parents fit the category. No new learning principle is required: identification and reinforcement are adequate. The same is true when the individual is a member of an antisocial group. The second way in which nonconformity occurs is through identification with the goal (which may be a cultural goal), but lack of identification with the means to the goal. If a football team, for example, is interested only in winning the game, as is sometimes the case, the traditional rules of fair play are rejected. Slugging the players on the other side, arguing with the coaches unneces-sarily, and even sometimes kidnapping the opponents' coach are all sanctioned when emphasis is merely upon the goal to be attained. When the end justifies any means, innovation occurs. To some extent this is true in the American culture today, as it has been frequently in other cultures in the past. Our boldest men, both good and bad, set aside cultural con-ventions in the interest of ambition.

Determinants and Determinism

Behavior is determined. Social behavior has many determinants. In early childhood the organism responds in an orderly, systematic fashion to determinants before it can speak. With the coming of language and the development of ego functions, the child is able to formulate simple cause-effect relationships. In this he is abetted by parents who attempt to assign to the child's "will" causal properties. In time the child accepts the propo-sition that he is able to do certain things or not do other things, by "exer-cise of his will" or simply "making up his mind." Now he is supposed to accept responsibility for what he does. If what he does is in line with social mores, and particularly if it brings credit to the family, he is praised and labeled a good boy. If, on the other hand, his actions do not conform to social mores and bring discredit to his family, he is criticized, punished and labeled a bad boy. He is told that if he had tried harder, he could have done better.

There is a modicum of truth in this. A person can under certain cir-cumstances decide upon a course of action and follow it. The strong per-son can follow a rationally predetermined course more readily than can the weak. But by and large most of us act most of the time in re-sponse to determinants of which we are either unaware or unable to control. Usually we cannot change the course of our lives simply by mak-ing a resolution to do so. Can you doubt that Sally Ferranti wanted des-perately to be rid of her crippling anxieties? Can you believe that Carol Chisholm wanted to sneeze and become irritable whenever she entered the presence of her father-in-law? Or can you accept the proposition that the Burke twins could voluntarily turn off the destructive character of their fantasies? If not, where does this leave us in terms of a person's ability to control his own behavior and lead a rationally directed life? Does the recognition of determinants rule out voluntary control?

It is not enough to say that the weak and distressed, the neurotic and psychotic, the amoral and the criminal lack the necessary will, and that when we show lapses from our typical behavior it reveals a flaw in our control system. To be sure, the peculiar and difficult circumstances under which some lives are lived can hardly be conducive to the development of strong ego systems. But even the best circumstances leave a man subject to influences and passions throughout his life which are largely beyond his control. In the next chapter we will examine some of the conditions under which a person may be said to lead a self-directed life.

Suggested Readings

Bowlby, John. *Maternal Care and Mental Health*. Geneva: World Health Organization, 1951.
A review and critical analysis of studies on maternal deprivation and the results stemming therefrom.

Centers, Richard. *The Psychology of Social Classes*. Princeton: Princeton University Press, 1949.
A discussion of the subjective aspect of class status, with emphasis on the feelings of common interest and belongingness.

Kluckhohn, Clyde, Murray, H. A., and Schneider, D. M. (Eds.). *Personality in Nature, Society, and Culture*. New York: Knopf, 1954.
An excellent summary of Murray's position in the first two chapters. A discussion of the determinants of personality from the points of view of constitution, group-membership, role, and situation.

Linton, Ralph. *The Cultural Background of Personality*. New York: Appleton-Century, 1945.
An attempt to bridge the gap between the study of the individual and the study of society.

Newcomb, T. M. *Social Psychology*. New York: Dryden, 1950.
An analysis of the developmental effects of social interaction and group memberships.

12

THE PROBLEM OF CONTROL AND FREEDOM

> ". . . to guide a man on his way means to give him
> guidance for an existence which is within his
> ken, and it always implies exclusion of all
> that which is not the way for him." *

If a man *feels* that he is not free, that he is driven by forces beyond his control, he is on the verge of a neurosis or psychosis. If he *thinks* he is not free, he is a normal college student. In the history of human thought there have been few voices raised in defense of individual freedom of action. Men of science have insisted upon unqualified determinism. In classical physics, as well as in other branches of science, indeterminism has been a taboo word. The concept of the importance of man as a free agent, or a determining force, has been gradually whittled down by such men as Copernicus, Darwin, and Freud. Copernicus showed the world to be a tiny speck in the universe. Darwin made clear the evolutionary connection between man and the lower animals. Freud's conception of personality left the ego, the controlling force in man, a tiny speck on the iceberg of unconscious forces.

In America there has always been a conflict between theory and practice over determinism. Theological and scientific thought have been largely deterministic, but popular thought and legal practice have placed responsibility for action squarely on the shoulders of the individual.

Early American theology recognized the paradox of holding simultaneously to the doctrine of determinism and the notion of individual responsibility. The solution offered was in line with deterministic thinking. What a man did was not within his control, but was simply evidence of whether he had been "saved" or not. The "damned" naturally engaged in evil ways, a circumstance which justified punitive restraint when a man's action was deemed contrary to the public interest.

Modern psychology was founded on classical physics and the main

* Buber, Martin. *Hasidism.* New York: Philosophical Library, 1948, p. 9.

tradition in experimental psychology has been mechanistic. Few experimentalists ever talk about freedom. Those who do speak of it can find no place for it in science. B. F. Skinner, who is representative, maintains (1953) that the hypothesis of determinism is "essential to the application of scientific method to the study of human behavior." That there is a free inner man who may be held responsible for behavior he believes to be nothing but a "prescientific substitute for the kinds of causes which are discovered in the course of a scientific analysis." The causes of man's behavior are found *outside* the individual. The biological substratum, the nonsocial environment, and the culture determine how the individual shall behave, and for them man has no responsibility. Praise or blame of the individual in relation to them has no meaning.

"It does not matter," Skinner says (1953, p. 448), "that the individual may take it upon himself to control the variables of which his own behavior is a function or, in a broader sense, to engage in the design of his own culture. He does this only because he is the product of a culture which generates self-control or cultural design as a mode of behavior. The environment determines the individual even when he alters the environment." Men flatter themselves that they possess freedom and control, but science must not fall into this trap, even though its analysis is distasteful to proponents of democratic philosophies. Science has always had the unenviable task of dispossessing men of cherished beliefs regarding their place in the universe.

Although some men who work in clinics, rather than in laboratories, disagree with this point of view, there are many who do not. The greatest clinician of them all, Freud, was a strict adherent to the deterministic hypothesis. The opposing point of view is represented by Carl Rogers (1946, pp. 421–422) who writes:

As we examine and try to evaluate our clinical experience with the client-centered therapy, the phenomenon of the reorganization of attitudes and the redirection of behavior by the individual assumes greater and greater importance. This phenomenon seems to find inadequate explanation in terms of the determinism which is the predominant philosophical background of most psychological work. The capacity of the individual to reorganize his attitudes and behavior in ways not determined by external factors nor by previous elements in his own experience, but determined by his own insight into those factors, is an impressive capacity. It involves a basic spontaneity which we have been loathe to admit into our scientific thinking.

The clinical experience could be summarized by saying that the behavior of the human organism may be determined by the influences to which it has been exposed, *but it may also be determined by the creative and integrative insight of the organism itself.* [Author's italics]

Rogers finds support for his point of view in the theory of Lecky (1945). Lecky is optimistic about man and believes that he has the capacity to create a unified personality in terms of purpose. We must stop assuming that man is a machine, moved by forces, whose behavior in the future is strictly predictable from the records of his past behavior. Man is a "unit in himself" and all his actions are referable to his attempts to maintain his unity, his self-consistency. Lecky calls upon the new physics in his attempt to destroy determinism. He points out that the deterministic concept does not hold for the single atom, studied individually. Extrapolating from this fact, he concludes that a study of individual systems takes us into new territory where the old mechanistic, deterministic ways of thinking no longer apply. Insight and understanding are the goals, not mathematical certainty.

Study of the individual personality, like the atom, certainly leaves much to be desired when predictability of individual behavior is the goal. But can we so easily dismiss the deterministic frame of reference in psychology? Even the physicist has difficulty readjusting to an indeterminate world; he has invented wave mechanics, which Schrödinger calls an "emergency exist," to resolve the dilemma. Schrödinger (1951, pp. 40–41) says:

> There is no gap in this picture of wave mechanics, also no gap as regards *causation*. The wave picture conforms with the classical demand for complete determinism, the mathematical method used is that of field-equations, though sometimes they are a highly generalized type of field-equation.
>
> But what is the use of such a description, which, as I said, is not believed to describe observable facts on what nature is really like? Well, it is believed to give us *information* about observed facts and their mutual dependence. There is an optimistic view, viz. that it gives us *all* the information obtainable about observable facts and their interdependence. But this view—which may or may not be correct—is *optimistic* only inasmuch as it may flatter our pride to possess in principle all obtainable information. It is pessimistic in another respect, we might say epistemologically pessimistic. *For the information we get as regards the causal dependence of observable facts is incomplete. (The cloven hoof must show up somewhere!)* [author's italics]

No one who looks at the facts can doubt that man's behavior is determined by conditions outside himself, as Skinner maintains. But this is only part of the story. Behavior is also determined by the condition of internal systems; and by interaction of the internal and external conditions. Let us look for a moment at some of these activators of behavior, and then return to the question of determinism.

External Activators

The most obvious external activators are observed in the physical effects obtained from decreasing the necessary supply of food or oxygen, or by lowering or elevating the temperature beyond normal limits, or by introducing into the body noxious stimuli. Physical homeostasis is so important that nature has provided diverse mechanisms to insure that internal steady states are maintained. When the balance is upset for whatever cause, emergency reactions follow automatically—the individual is driven compulsively; there is no question of freedom of action. One can readily understand why Claude Bernard said, "La fixité du milieu interieur est la condition de la vie libre."

Dempsey (1951, pp. 210–211) has summarized the evidence concerning homeostatic controls:

When stability is threatened even mildly, delicate indicators give the alarm and activate the appropriate corrective agencies, so that oscillations to either side of the homeostatic norm are slight. The effector organs react as if they were directed toward nullifying a disturbing condition. The second factor concerns the emergency nature of many of the adaptive changes. When bodily security or survival is seriously threatened, the internal fluid matrix is altered. If noxious stimuli occur, such as bacteria, toxic drugs, or physical damage, the organism responds by altering the proportions of the protective white blood corpuscles, by augmenting the protective antibodies, and by elevating the body temperature. If perceptible foes arouse fear or rage, a number of internal readjustments unify and integrate the activities of the body for its maximal physical effort—flight or combat; blood sugar is increased, the circulation to special regions is greatly augmented, respiration is accelerated, extra red blood cells are mobilized to carry the extra oxygen, and adrenalin is produced to reinforce the adaptive nerve impulses. These reactions profoundly disturb the internal environment, but they disturb it in such a way as to render the organism temporarily more effective in a contest that may end in life or death. The ultimate total stability of the organism is therefore defended even at the cost of temporary disturbance to the welfare of its component parts.

Although the endocrine and nervous systems undoubtedly play some part in maintaining the homeostatic norm, their functions are most strikingly revealed in emergency situations. The nervous reflexes which accelerate the heart and constrict the vascular bed operate more forcefully during strong emotional states than in placid situations. The hormones which increase the metabolic rate and facilitate the utilization of sugar are secreted in larger quantity upon exposure to cold. The deficiency resulting from impairment or destruction of these systems is more pronounced in some situations than in others.

By changing external activation, also, individuals can be made to engage in behavior quite unlike that to which they are accustomed. For example, evidence from Nazi concentration camps in World War II indicates that, under certain circumstances, mothers and fathers may steal bread from their own children. Laboratory experimentation is also clear, as far as it has gone, in indicating that what men "see" and "think," as well as the way they act, can to a large extent be externally controlled. Experiments cited earlier concerning the effects of majority group opinions on individual responses indicate the way in which certain subjects tend not only to follow the lead of others under the circumstances, but also to perceive what they think the others perceive.

Behavior can be changed externally also, as Bexton, Heron, and Scott (1954) have shown, by decreased variation in the sensory environment. They studied functioning during prolonged perceptual isolation with male college students whom they had lie on a comfortable bed in a lighted cubicle for twenty-four hours a day. The students were given time out only for eating and going to the toilet. They wore translucent goggles, which transmitted diffuse light but prevented pattern vision, and gloves and cardboard cuffs, extending from below the elbow to beyond the finger tips, which permitted free movement, but limited tactual perception. The experimenters communicated with subjects by a speaker system, but communication was kept at a minimum. The subjects' heads were placed in a U-shaped foam-rubber pillow. The room was practically sound-proof, but there was also a continuous humming of fans, air-conditioners, and an amplifier which served to produce masking noise.

As one would expect, the subjects reacted differently to these conditions. There was, however, a more or less typical pattern. At first they were elated; this was followed by marked irritability. In the beginning they slept a lot; later, sleep became less frequent. They became bored and appeared eager for stimulation. They sang, whistled, talked to themselves, tapped their cuffs together, or explored the cubicle. There was almost constant restless, random movement. Even though the subjects were being paid more than double what they could normally earn, it was very difficult to keep them more than two or three days. When they came out of the cubicle, they were dazed. Visual perception was disturbed for a minute or two. Objects appeared fuzzy, and there was difficulty in focusing. Colors appeared more saturated than usual, and the environment seemed two-dimensional. The subjects reported confusion, headaches, mild nausea, and fatigue, which persisted in some cases for twenty-four hours after the experiment.

Effects on the cognitive processes were marked. Unable to concentrate on any topic for long, the subjects lapsed into day-dreaming and abandoned attempts at organized thinking. There were times, "blank periods," when they were unable to think at all. They were given simple arithmetic tests before, during, and after the experiment; control subjects were given the same tests. During isolation their performance was inferior to the controls on all tests. Some of the subjects reported hallucinations—"having a dream while awake." Auditory, kinesthetic, and somesthetic hallucinations were reported, and control over the context of thought was markedly reduced. There was great difficulty in trying to visualize objects. One subject, for example, when trying to visualize a pen, first saw an inkblot, then a pencil, a green horse, and finally a pen. The subjects reported feelings of "otherness" and bodily "strangeness"; one even felt that his head was detached from his body.

Internal Activators

The absurdity of dichotomizing activators into internal and external must be apparent by now. But let us persist in spite of the language difficulty and point out a few other activators of behavior which presumably spring from impressions made, or traces left imbedded, on the nervous system. Once they were external; now they are internal. The location is of little moment and should not be allowed to confuse the issue.

In the case history in Chapter 4, when Peter Chisholm had developed a number of need-dispositions in relation to his mother, she became the person of central importance in his life. As long as she behaved toward him in the manner to which he had been conditioned to expect, life was stable and serene. When, on the other hand, she changed radically in her behavior, his reactions were prompt and turbulent. He had not yet developed another system of restraint, the self-system, which might hold in check his impulses. Thus his almost instantaneous response occurred to changes in external stimuli, but only after he had developed need-dispositions toward Carol.

In the case history in Chapter 9, Sally Ferranti had developed a self-system. She was accustomed to moving about with relative ease on the assumption that she was more or less in control of her actions. But when she found that under the impact of certain stimuli she was powerless to control her behavior, the result was an emergency reaction in the form of an acute anxiety attack. We say her self-system was not strong enough to withstand the external pressures. What we mean is this. Her ego ideal was confused. Her friends, relatives, and parents set conflicting standards of conduct for her. Her superego in relation to avoidance of sexual activity had not been reinforced, because of her mother's ambivalence concerning sexual expression. She readily perceived the danger (an ego function, we say) of being declared a legal delinquent if she did not check her impulses; but how weak was this recognition in the absence of supporting controls from superego and ego ideal!

This is the first time we have used the term *ego ideal*. To what does it refer? One might say that it is the obverse of superego, if that term stands for the punished and aborted responses. Ego ideal refers to responses which have been approved and rewarded or reinforced. Guilt and anxiety accompany behavior contrary to the superego; pride and joy accompany behavior in line with the ego ideal. Ego ideal, then, refers to the kind of behavior which the individual would like to engage in. It reflects his ideal picture of himself. The context of the ego ideal varies with the experiences of the individual. It may or may not coincide with the mores of the larger society. For a person who seeks to pattern his life after a notorious gangster, such a quest is as surely an ego ideal as the desire on the part of another to become a poet or a man of science. Sally Ferranti's ego ideal concerning sexual conduct was confused and ineffective as a control, because she had had no consistently reinforced behavior in relation to sex. Her friend Bill broke all the same laws which she did, and yet he felt no guilt or anxiety. He was proud of himself.

No man knows all of the punished and reinforced bits of behavior which have been recorded in his nervous system and stand ready to be reactivated by the appropriate stimulus. What is available to consciousness is only a fraction of the total number of such recordings. Most of the time we act without knowing why, and frequently it is impossible to find out why. Penfield (1955) has provided us with experimental evidence to show that even apparently inconsequential learning is recorded in nervous tissue and never lost "as long as man may live and keep his wits." By electrically stimulating the temporal cortex Penfield has been able to reactivate experiences with a vivid freshness which were completely beyond the voluntary control of his subjects to remember. Penfield says (1955, p. 67):

> The evidence suggests that nothing is lost, that the record of each man's experience is complete. . . . Probably no man can, by voluntary effort, completely reactivate any portion of the record of the stream of thought. Except for a few seconds or minutes after the event, he seems to have no voluntary mechanism that rivals the electrode. Memory, as ordinarily conceived, is quite a different phenomenon. It seems likely, however, that the original record continues to be available in some sort of way for the purposes of the comparison and interpretation of each new experience.

As evidence available to everyone Penfield cites the common experience of meeting a friend after many years absence. One is able under these conditions to detect little changes in the friend in a way that proves one "had not lost the detail of original experiences."

Is There Any Freedom in Human Affairs?

We return now to the question of determinism. Is there, or can there be, any freedom in human affairs? The answer depends upon what one implies by the question. If by freedom one means lawlessness, the answer is "no." If freedom means arbitrary escape from antecedent experiences, the answer is "no." But if by freedom one implies a measure of control over his own destiny in this life, the answer is "yes." We are not talking about freedom now in any metaphysical sense, but about freedom in the sense of practical, everyday control of one's behavior and even one's perception of self. To be sure, no one can by taking thought add one cubit to his stature. But he can, by modification of his physical aspect in other ways and especially by changing his approach to and his manner of interaction with others, bring about vastly different responses from people. In time these changed responses will alter his self-perception.

In this we disagree with Skinner, who says that it does not matter whether the individual is controlling the variables of which his own behavior is a function. To the individual concerned it makes all the difference between feeling strong and capable, and self-confident, as against feeling weak, helpless, and defeated. Such feelings have a great deal to do with determining one's destiny in life. Freedom as it is here defined is precisely the ability to control the variables of which one's own behavior is a function. Even so there is very little freedom in the world. But that little is worth any amount of effort and study to understand.

What, then, are the conditions of human freedom? We shall discuss briefly three. They are the minimum conditions that are found necessary for a person to experience freedom of action, and then of course only in limited spheres.

Conditions of Human Freedom

Freedom varies with the control which one has over the immediate situation. It is not an all-or-none proposition; there are degrees of freedom. There is no implication that one is free from, or able to get outside of, natural law. Freedom and reality are correlated one to one.

Certain single, and all complex, stimuli and cues are embedded in a context unique to the individual, leading to perceptions on a continuum from clear to hazy. For example, a remark like "I love you" or "I hate you" may be taken at face value or may mean the opposite, depending on the context and manner in which it was said. Action in response to either pronouncement calls for judgment on the part of the responder. That is to say, the responder must make an hypothesis in line with the interaction theory set forth earlier concerning the meaning behind the statement. Action depends upon the meaning he perceives. The meaning perceived, hypothesis, in turn depends upon the state of the internal systems and the character of the external cues.

Let us pursue for a moment the statement, "I love you," by way of illustration. The situation may be a big party, a very convivial party. Everyone has had a few too many drinks. Now let our perceiver be a rather shy boy who goes out little and who has had no close association with girls for a considerable period of time. We may assume that his need-disposition for affiliation is strong. The girl he is with is one whom he has admired for a long time and secretly wished that some day he might successfully court. She, on the other hand, has no particular feeling for him, but is very popular with boys and dates frequently. In the present situation when, in response to proferred love, she replies "I love you," she is making what she considers to be the appropriate social reply. And almost anyone overhearing it would agree that the statement was meaningless. But not so her partner. Overjoyed, he takes her words as a fulfillment of his hopes, and on the morrow when she scarcely notices him, he can hardly understand how he was so deceived.

The perceptions of our swain were determined more by his internal systems than by external cues. He was perplexed because he did not know the source of his delusion. From this simple, albeit not uncommon, situation we can derive two propositions. (1) The more unaware a person is of the processes and forces present in any given field, the more likely is he to have perceptions and to engage in behavior at variance with the perceptions and behavior of others in the same situations. (2) The more aware a person is of the processes and forces present in any given field, the more likely is he to have perceptions and to engage in behavior in line with the perceptions and behavior of others in the same situation.

Awareness is the first condition of the free or controlled life. It means discovering the internal and external realities of one's life situation. Internal realities include not only the need-dispositions and self-system, but also the abilities—physical, mental, and emotional—of the person. Another way of putting this is to say "knowledge of one's potentialities and liabilities in all spheres." This is the basis on which most psychotherapy is founded. Awareness of external realities implies knowledge of the surrounding world, both immediate and remote. Such awareness calls for an assessment of the motives, intentions, and abilities of those with whom we interact. Among the external realities are the collective beliefs, aspirations, prejudices of one's group. Also, there is the physical richness or poverty of the situation, and one's position in relation to this wealth.

The self-conscious person, aware of his own conditioning and potentialities as well as of the confronting possibilities—and providing he is not driven by some overpowering passion or directed by some intense recurrent anxiety—is in a position to control certain variables in his environment in line with his interests. Two other conditions are necessary, however, for control to occur. One of these is intelligence, the other action. Without intelligence, the multivariate factors cannot be assessed. Without action, old patterns cannot be extinguished, nor new ones established.

Thus the second condition necessary for a measure of freedom in controlling human affairs is *intelligence*—intelligence sufficient to see the possibilities of new combinations and restructurings. Other things being equal, the more intelligence a person has, the more relationships he can perceive. New relationships are new forms, creations, and indicate new ways of moving. Leta Hollingworth (1942), in a study of children above

180 IQ, shows how their perceptions are different from those of children of lower intelligence. For example, they want to organize play in very complicated patterns. Even among children within the upper 1 per cent of intelligence in the population, there is great differentiation of ability to see relationships, from the lowest to the top. The child who is most able in the upper 1 per cent surpasses the child who is least able by as much as the average child surpasses the moron. There is no escape from the necessity of being able to perceive abstract relationships as a condition for seeing the possibility of restructuring one's world.

Self-consciousness, consciousness of the possibilities in one's world, and intelligence sufficient to reorder these variables are not enough to bring about control. *Action* must be taken on the basis of understanding before change will occur. Action is thus the third condition necessary for control, or freedom. Many people have ample knowledge of themselves and the world around them; they may even see the possibilities of changing the stimuli impinging upon them in line with their interests. But they do not act. Hence they feel bound and are in fact not free. In the early days of psychoanalysis it was Freud's hope that insight into the source of neurotic symptoms would be sufficient to banish them. This has not proved to be the case. Insight may be the first step, though even this is not always necessary; but without action, or better, interaction, designed to extinguish the inappropriate response, the neurotic process continues.

Awareness of one's reaction tendencies alone does not modify them. It may even introduce competing tendencies and produce conflict which did not previously exist. However, awareness as a basis for reinforcing competing tendencies and extinguishing the original pattern of behavior does bring about new modes of action. In this sense consciousness, intelligent restructuring, and planned action put control into a man's hands. However, the probability of actually utilizing this control is reduced because action designed to extinguish old patterns usually involves anxiety. If this anxiety is above the threshold of toleration, retreat to the old pattern follows—and constitutes another reinforcement of the old way. Always into the breach between the certainty of the old, even though it be distasteful, and the uncertainty of the new, comes anxiety. In face of this anxiety, and in view of the automatic anxiety-reduction mechanisms, it is not surprising that one finds so little actual freedom in human behavior. Not only anxiety, but also lack of ability, and the peculiar and difficult circumstances of the lives of many preclude the possibility of freedom.

But some men do achieve freedom of action. They are able to arrange their worlds so that their responses are consonant with their interests and with a rational system of values. There is no implication that they rid themselves completely of conflict and anxiety. That is impossible. But, in spite of these restraints, they do act in a creative way.

BIBLIOGRAPHY

Adams, D. K. *The Anatomy of Personality*. New York: Doubleday Papers in Psychology, 1954.
Allport, F. H. *Theories of Perception and the Concept of Structure*. New York: Wiley, 1955.
Allport, G. W. "Attitudes." In Murchison, C. A. (Ed.), *Handbook of Social Psychology*. Worcester, Mass.: Clark University Press, 1935.
————. *Personality*. New York: Holt, 1937.
————. *The Use of Personal Documents in Psychological Science*. New York: Social Science Research Council, Bulletin 49, 1942.
————. "The Historical Background of Modern Social Psychology." In Lindzey, G. (Ed.), *Handbook of Social Psychology*. Cambridge: Addison-Wesley, 1954.
————. *Becoming: Basic Considerations for a Psychology of Personality*. New Haven: Yale University Press, 1955.
————. "What Units Shall We Employ?" In Lindzey, G. (Ed.), *Assessment of Human Motives*. New York: Rinehart, 1958.
Angyal, Andras. *Foundations for a Science of Personality*. New York: The Commonwealth Fund, 1941.
Asch, S. *Social Psychology*. New York: Prentice-Hall, 1952.
Atkinson, J. W., and McClelland, D. C. "The Projective Expression of Needs. II. The Effect of Different Intensities of the Hunger Drive on Thematic Apperception." *Journal of Experimental Psychology*, 1948, 38, 643–658.

Bales, R. F. *Interaction Process Analysis*. Cambridge: Addison-Wesley, 1950.
Baldwin, A. L., Kalhorn, J., and Breese, F. H. "Patterns of Parent Behavior." *Psychological Monographs*, 1959, 58, No. 3 (whole number 268).
Balint, Alice. "Identification." In Lorand, S. (Ed.), *Yearbook of Psychoanalysis*, Vol. 1, 1945.
Beach, Frank A. "Instinctive Behavior: Reproductive Activities." In Stevens, S. S. (Ed.), *Handbook of Experimental Psychology*. New York: Wiley, 1951.
Benedek, Therese. "The Psychosomatic Implications of the Primary Unit: Mother-Child." *American Journal of Psychiatry*, 1949, 19, 642–654.
Berenda, R. W. *The Influence of the Group on the Judgments of Children*. New York: King's Crown Press, 1950.
Bexton, W. H., Heron, W., and Scott, T. H. "Effects of Decreased Variation in the Sensory Environment." *Canadian Journal of Psychology*, 1954, 8, 70–76.
Birdwhistell, Ray L. "Background to Kinesics." *Etc.: A Review of General Semantics*, 1955, 13, 10–18.
Blake, R. R., and Ramsey, G. V. (Eds.). *Perception: An Approach to Personality*. New York: Ronald, 1951.
Bowlby, J. *Maternal Care and Mental Health*. Geneva: World Health Organization, Monograph 2, 1951.
Brown, J. S., and Jacobs, A. "The Role of Fear in the Motivation and Acquisition of Responses." *Journal of Experimental Psychology*, 1949, 39, 747–749.

Brownfield, E. D. "An Investigation of the Activity and Sensory Responses of Healthy Newborn Infants." Ph.D. thesis, Cornell University Library, 1956.

Bruner, J. S., and Krech, D. (Eds.). *Perception and Personality*. Durham: Duke University Press, 1950.

———, and Taiguri R. "The Perception of People." In Lindzey, G. (Ed.), *Handbook of Social Psychology*. Cambridge: Addison-Wesley, 1954. Vol. II, 634–654.

Child, I. L. "Socialization." In Lindzey, G. (Ed.), *Handbook of Social Psychology*. Cambridge: Addison-Wesley, 1954.

Cohen, M. R., and Nagel, E. *An Introduction to Logic and Scientific Method*. New York: Harcourt, Brace, 1934.

Cooley, C. H. *Human Nature and the Social Order*. New York: Scribners, 1902.

Crutchfield, R. S. "Conformity and Character." *American Psychologist*, 1955, *10*, 191–198.

Davis, A., and Dollard, J. *Children of Bondage*. New York: American Council on Education, 1940.

Dempsey, Edward W. "Homeostasis." In Stevens, S. S. (Ed.), *Handbook of Experimental Psychology*. New York: Wiley, 1951.

Dollard, J., and Miller, N. E. *Personality and Psychotherapy: an Analysis in Terms of Learning, Thinking and Culture*. New York: McGraw-Hill, 1950.

Einstein, A., and Infeld, L. *The Evolution of Physics*. New York: Simon and Schuster, 1938.

Erikson, E. H. *Childhood and Society*. New York: Norton, 1950.

Escalona, S. In Swanson, G. E., and Others (Eds.), *Readings in Social Psychology*. New York: Holt, 1952.

Faigin, H. "Childrearing in the Rimrock Community with Special Reference to the Development of Guilt." Unpublished doctoral dissertation. Radcliffe College, 1953.

Farber, I. E. "Anxiety as a Drive State." In Jones, M. R. (Ed.), *Nebraska Symposium on Motivation*. Lincoln: University of Nebraska Press, 1954.

Feigl, Herbert. "Philosophical Embarrassments of Psychology." *American Psychologist*, 1959, *14*, 115–128.

Festinger, Leon, and Others. *Social Pressures in Informal Groups*. New York: Harper, 1950.

———, and ———. *Theory and Experiment in Social Communication*. Ann Arbor: Research Center for Group Dynamics, University of Michigan, 1950.

Frank, L. K. "Cultural Control and Physiological Autonomy." *American Journal of Orthopsychiatry*, 1938, 8, 622–26.

Frenkel-Brunswik, Else. "A Study of Prejudice in Children." *Human Relations*, 1948, *1*, 295–306.

Freud, Anna. *The Ego and the Mechanism of Defense*. London: Hogarth Press, 1937.

Freud, S. *The Interpretation of Dreams*, 1900. In *The Basic Writings of Sigmund Freud*. New York: Modern Library, 1938.

———. *A General Introduction to Psychoanalysis*. New York: Boni and Liveright, 1920.

———. *The Ego and the Id*. London: Hogarth Press, 1927.

———. *New Introductory Lectures in Psychoanalysis*. New York: Norton, 1933.

———. *The Problem of Anxiety*. New York: Norton, 1936.

———. "Three Contributions to the Theory of Sex." In *Basic Writings*. New York: Modern Library, 1938.

Freud, S. "On Narcissism: An Introduction." In *Collected Papers*, Vol. IV. London: Hogarth Press, 1925. First published in German in 1914.
———. "The Unconscious." In *Collected Papers*, Vol. IV. London: Hogarth Press, 1925.
———. *An Outline of Psychoanalysis*. New York: Norton, 1949.
———. *The Standard Edition*, Volume XIV. London: Hogarth Press, 1957.

Glueck, S., and Glueck, E. *Unraveling Juvenile Delinquency*. Cambridge: Harvard University Press, 1950.
Goldstein, Kurt. *Human Nature in the Light of Psychopathology*. Cambridge: Harvard University Press, 1940.
Guthrie, E. R. *The Psychology of Learning*, Revised Edition. New York: Harper, 1952.

Hall, C. S., and Lindzey, G. *Theories of Personality*. New York: Wiley, 1957.
Hartmann, George W. "The Field Theory of Learning and Its Educational Consequences." *Forty-First Yearbook*, Part II. National Society for the Study of Education, 1942.
Hilgard, E. R. *Theories of Learning*. New York: Appleton-Century-Crofts, 1948.
———. "Human Motives and the Concept of Self." *The American Psychologist*, 1949, 4, 374–382.
———, and Marquis, D. G. *Conditioning and Learning*. New York: Appleton-Century-Crofts, 1950.
Hilgard, Josephine. "Sibling Rivalry and Social Heredity." *Psychiatry*, 1951, *14*, 375–385.
Hollenburg, E. "Child Training Among the Zeepi with Special Reference to the Internalization of Moral Values." Unpublished doctoral dissertation, Radcliffe College, 1953.
Hollingworth, Leta. *Children Above 180 IQ, Stanford-Binet*. New York: World Book, 1942.
Holt, E. B. *Animal Drive and the Learning Process*. New York: Holt, 1931.
Horney, K. *The Neurotic Personality of Our Time*. New York: Norton, 1937.
Hugo, G. "Conforming Behavior in Two Groups of Adolescent Children and Its Relation to Certain Parental Attitudes and Personality Characteristics." Ph.D. thesis, Cornell University Library, 1956.
Hull, C. L. "Conditioning: Outline of a Systematic Theory of Learning." *Forty-First Yearbook*, Part II. National Society for the Study of Education, 1942.
———. *Principles of Behavior*. New York: Appleton-Century-Crofts, 1943.

James, William. *Principles of Psychology*. New York: Holt, 1890.
Johnson, Adelaide. "A Contribution to Treatment of Superego Defect." *Social Casework*. 1950, 135–138.
———. "Sanctions for Superego Lacunae of Adolescents." In Eissler, Kr. R. *Searchlight on Delinquency*. New York: International University Press, 1949, 225–245.
———, Szurek, S. A., and Falstein, M. "Collaborative Psychiatric Treatment in Parent-Child Problems. *American Journal Orthopsychiatry*, 1942, 8, 511.
Jung, C. G. *The Integration of Personality*. New York: Farrar and Rinehart, 1939.

Karsten, Anitra. "Psychische Sättigung." *Psychol. Forsch.*, 1928, *10*, 142–154.
Kelley, George A. "Man's Construction of His Alternatives." In Lindzey, G. (Ed.), *Assessment of Human Motives*. New York: Rinehart, 1958.

Klein, Melanie. *The Psychoanalysis of Children*. London: Hogarth Press, 1944.

Kluckhohn, C., and Murray, H. A. (Eds.). *Personality in Nature, Society, and Culture*, Second Edition. New York: Knopf, 1953.

Koffka, K. *Principles of Gestalt Psychology*. New York: Harcourt, Brace, 1935.

Kubie, L. S. "The Repetitive Core of Neurosis." *Psychoanalysis Quarterly*, 1941, *10*, 23–63.

Lambert, William. "Stimulus-Response Contiguity and Reinforcement Theory in Social Psychology." In Lindzey, G. (Ed.), *Handbook of Social Psychology*. Cambridge: Addison Wesley, 1954.

Lasko, J. K. "Parent Behavior toward First and Second Children." *Genetic Psychology Monograph*, 1954, *49*, 97–137.

Lecky, P. *Self-Consistency*. New York: Island Press, 1945.

Levine, R., Chein, E., and Murphy, G. "The Relation of the Intensity of a Need to the Amount of Perceptual Distortion, a Preliminary Report. *Journal of Psychology*, 1942, *13*, 283–293.

Levy, David M. "Experiments on the Sucking Reflex and Social Behavior of Dogs." *American Journal of Orthopsychiatry*, 1934, *4*, 203–224.

Lewin, K. *A Dynamic Theory of Personality*. New York: McGraw-Hill, 1935.

Lorand, S. *Psychoanalysis Today*. New York: International University Press, 1944.

MacClelland, D. C. *Personality*. New York: Dryden, 1954.

———, Atkinson, J. W., Clark, R. A., and Lowell, E. L. *The Achievement Motive*. New York: Appleton-Century-Crofts, 1953.

McDougall, William. *Introduction to Social Psychology*. London: Methuen, 1908.

———. *The Energies of Men*. New York: Scribner, 1933.

MacKinnon, D. W. "Violation of Prohibitions." In Murray, H. A., *Explorations in Personality*. New York and London: Oxford University Press, 1938.

———. "The Structure of Personality." In Hunt, J. M., *Personality and the Behavior Disorders*, Vol. I, 3–49. New York: Ronald, 1944.

Maslow, A. H. *Motivation and Personality*. New York: Harper, 1954.

May, Rollo. *The Meaning of Anxiety*. New York: Ronald, 1950.

Mead, G. H. *Mind, Self, and Society*. (Posthumous: Morris, C. M., Ed.) Chicago: University of Chicago Press, 1934.

Mead, Margaret. *Male and Female*. New York: Morrow, 1949.

Miller, N. E. "Studies of Fear as an Acquirable Drive: 1. Fear as Motivation and Fear Reduction as Reinforcement in the Learning of New Responses." *Journal of Experimental Psychology*, 1948, *39*, 89–101.

———, and Dollard, J. *Social Learning and Imitation*. New Haven: Yale University Press, 1941.

Mowrer, O. H. "A Stimulus-Response Analysis of Anxiety and Its Role as a Reinforcing Agent." *Psychology Review*, 1939, *46*, 553–566.

———. "On the Dual Nature of Learning—a Reinterpretation of 'Conditioning' and 'Problem-Solving.'" *Harvard Educational Review*, 1947, *17*, 102–48.

———. *Learning Theory and Personality Dynamics*. New York: Ronald, 1950.

———, and Kluckhohn, C. "Dynamic Theory of Personality." In Hunt, J. McV. (Ed.), *Personality and the Behavior Disorders*. Vol. I. New York: Ronald, 1944.

Murphy, G. *Personality: A Bisocial Approach to Origins and Structure*. New York: Harper, 1947.

———. "Social Motivation." Chapter 16 in Lindzey, G. (Ed.), *Handbook of Social Psychology*. Cambridge: Addison-Wesley, 1954.

Murray, H. A. "The Effect of Fear upon Estimates of the Maliciousness of Other Personalities." *Journal of Social Psychology*, 1933, *4*, 310–329.

Murray, H. A. *Explorations in Personality*. New York and London: Oxford University Press, 1938.

———. "Toward a Classification of Interaction." In Parsons and Shils, *Toward a General Theory of Action*. Cambridge: Harvard University Press, 1951.

———. "Outline of a Conception of Personality." In Kluckhohn, C., and Murray, H. A. (Eds.), *Personality in Nature, Society, and Culture*. New York: Knopf, 1948.

Parsons, T., and Shils, E. *Toward a General Theory of Action*. Cambridge: Harvard University Press, 1951.

Penfield, W. "The Permanent Record of the Stream of Consciousness." *Acta Psychologica*, 1955, *11*, 47–69.

Piaget, J. *The Moral Judgment of the Child*, Translated. London: Paul, Trench, Truber, 1932.

Postman, L. J. "The Experimental Analysis of Motivational Factors in Perception." In *Current Theory and Research in Motivation*. Lincoln: University of Nebraska Press, 1953.

Raimy, V. C. "Self-Reference in Counseling Interviews." *Journal of Consulting Psychology*, 1948, *12*, 153–163.

Rogers, Carl R. "Significant Aspects of Client-Centered Therapy." *The American Psychologist*, 1946, *1*, 415–422.

Sanford, R. N., and Others. *Physique, Personality and Scholarship*. Monographs of the Society for Research in Child Development, 1943, *8*, No. 1.

Sarnoff, Irving. "Identification with the Aggressor." *Journal of Personality*, Vol. 20, 1951.

Schlosberg, H. "The Relationship Between Success and the Laws of Conditioning." *Psychological Review*, 1937, *44*, 379–394.

Schrödinger, Erwin. *Science and Humanism*. New York: Cambridge University Press, 1951.

Sears, R. R. "Experimental Studies of Projection: 1. Attribution of Traits." *Journal of Social Psychology*, 1936, *7*, 151–163.

———. *Survey of Objective Studies of Psychoanalytic Concepts*. New York: Social Science Research Council, 1943.

———, Whiting, J. M. W., Nowlis, V., and Sears, P. S. "Some Child-Rearing Antecedents of Aggression and Dependency in Young Children." *Genetic Psychology Monographs*, 1953, *47*, 135–234.

———, Maccoby, Eleanor, and Levin, Harry. *Patterns of Child Rearing*. New York: Row, Peterson, 1957.

Shaffer, Laurence F., *The Psychology of Adjustment*. Boston: Houghton Mifflin, 1936.

Sherif, M., and Cantril, H. *The Psychology of Ego-Involvement*. New York: Wiley, 1947.

Shinn, M. W. "Notes on the Development of a Child." University of California Publications, 1924, *I*, 1–178; 179–424.

Shipley, W. C. "Indirect Conditioning." *Journal of Genetic Psychology*, 1935, *12*, 337–357.

Simmel, Georg. *The Sociology of Georg Simmel*. Translated and Edited by K. H. Wolff. Glencoe, Illinois: Free Press, 1950.

Skinner, B. F. *The Behavior of Organisms*. New York: Appleton-Century-Crofts, 1938.

———. *Science and Human Behavior*. New York: Macmillan Co., 1953.

Sperling, Melitta. "The Neurotic Child and His Mother." *American Journal of Ortho-psychiatry*, 1951, *21*, 351–362.

———. "Children's Interpretation and Reaction to the Unconscious of Their Mother." *International Journal of Psychoanalysis*, 1950, *31*, 36–41.

———. "The Role of the Mother in Psychosomatic Disorders in Children." *Psychosomatic Medicine*, 1949, *11*, 377–385.

Spitz, R. A., and Wolf, K. M. "The Smiling Response: A Contribution to the Ontogenesis of Social Relations." *Genetic Psychology Monographs*, 1946, *34*, 57–125.

Stephenson, W. *The Study of Behavior*. Chicago: University of Chicago Press, 1953.

Sullivan, H. S. *Conceptions of Modern Psychiatry*. Washington, D. C.: William Alanson White Psychiatric Foundation, 1947.

Symonds, P. C. *Dynamics of Human Adjustment*. New York: Appleton-Century-Crofts, 1946.

———. *The Ego and the Self*. New York: Appleton-Century-Crofts, 1951.

Szurek, S. A. "Notes on the Genesis of Psychopathic Personality Trends." *Psychiatry*, 1942, *5*, 1–6.

Thomas, W. I. *The Unadjusted Girl*. Boston: Little, Brown, 1923.

Thorndike, E. L. *Human Learning*. New York: Century, 1931.

———. *Man and His Works*. Cambridge: Harvard University Press, 1943.

———. *Educational Psychology*. Vol. 2. "The Original Nature of Man." New York: Teachers College, Columbia University, 1913.

Tinbergen, N. *The Study of Instinct*. Oxford: Clarendon Press, 1951.

Van Teslaar, J. S. *An Outline of Psychoanalysis*. New York: Modern Library, 1924.

Venable, Vernon. *Human Nature: The Marxian View*. London: Dennis Dobson, 1945.

Winterbottom, Marian R. "The Relation of Childhood Training in Independence to Achievement Motivation." Unpublished Doctoral Dissertation, University of Michigan, 1953.

Woodworth, R. S. *Dynamic Psychology*. New York: Columbia University Press, 1918.

Wright, H. W. "The Three Contexts of Human Behavior." *Psychological Review*, 1943, *50*, 351–369.

Zeigarnik, Bluma. "Uber das Behalten von erledigten und unerledigten Handlungen." *Psychol. Forsch.*, 1927, *9*, 1–85.

INDEX